THE SIGNIFICANCE OF FREE WILL

The Significance of Free Will

ROBERT KANE

OXFORD UNIVERSITY PRESS
New York   Oxford

Oxford University Press

Oxford   New York
Athens   Auckland   Bangkok   Bogotá   Bombay
Buenos Aires   Calcutta   Cape Town   Dar es Salaam
Delhi   Florence   Hong Kong   Istanbul   Karachi
Kuala Lumpur   Madras   Madrid   Melbourne
Mexico City   Nairobi   Paris   Singapore
Taipei   Tokyo   Toronto   Warsaw

and associated companies in
Berlin   Ibadan

Copyright © 1998 by Robert Kane

First published in 1996 by Oxford University Press, Inc.
198 Madison Avenue, New York, New York 10016

First issued as an Oxford University Press paperback, 1998

Oxford is a registered trademark of Oxford University Press, Inc.

Library of Congress Cataloging-in-Publication Data
Kane, Robert, 1938–
The significance of free will / Robert Kane.
p. cm.
Includes bibliographical references and index.
ISBN 0–19–510550-8
ISBN 0–19–512656-4 (pbk)
1. Free will and determinism. 2. Responsibility. I. Title.
BJ1461.K38 1996
123'.5—dc20   95-49769

1 3 5 7 9 8 6 4 2

Printed in the United States of America
on acid-free paper

For My Sons
Nathan Robert Kane
Russell Hilary Kane, *in memoriam*

Acknowledgments

Research for this book was supported by the University Research Institute and by a Roy A. Vaughn Centennial Research Fellowship at the University of Texas at Austin. All or parts of the manuscript were read by Robert Audi, Mark Bernstein, Michael Bratman, Randolph Clarke, Charles Dicken, Richard Double, John Martin Fischer, George Graham, Alfred Mele, Timothy O'Connor, Teed Rockwell, Saul Smilansky, Galen Strawson, and Bruce Waller. In addition, I have received valuable feedback on previous work that has had an impact on this one from Peter van Inwagen, William Rowe, Hugh McCann, David Blumenfeld, Nicholas Nathan, Daniel Dennett, Gary Watson, William Hasker, Robert Nozick, John Post, John Heil, Stewart Goetz, Don Sievert, Bernard Katz, Jeffrey Tlumak, Max Hocutt, Bernard Gendron, Fred Kronz, Cory Juhl, Robert Bishop, Thomas Talbott, Pete Gunter, Don Viney, Mark Balaguer, George Scott, John Compton, Noah Lemos, Michael White, David Armstrong, and (over a long period of time when I first began to think about free will issues) Wilfrid Sellars.

During the writing of this book, I also benefited from reading some unpublished work by Bernard Berofsky, John Martin Fischer and Mark Ravizza, Alfred Mele, Richard Double, Kevin Magill, Galen Strawson, Stewart Goetz, David Widerker, James Garson, Matthew Posth, and Gordon Globus. I am especially grateful to Mark Bernstein, Richard Double, Alfred Mele, George Graham, Randolph Clarke, Timothy O' Connor, Galen Strawson, and Bruce Waller for their continuing critical feedback on my views, and to Claudette Kane, whose relentless criticisms of every aspect of my thinking about free will have left a mark on every chapter of this book. The remainder of my debts are many and are made explicit in the text, footnotes, and bibliography. There has been a tremendous amount of good work done on free will issues in the past quarter century without which this work could not have been written. Special thanks, finally, to Cynthia Read of Oxford University Press, whose efforts on behalf of this manuscript were invaluable, and to Robert Dilworth and the production staff at Oxford whose editorial assistance was first rate.

Contents

THE SIGNIFICANCE OF FREE WILL

1

Introduction

There is a disputation [that will continue] till mankind are raised from the dead
between the Necessitarians and the partisans of Free Will.
                                   —Jalalu'ddin Rumi, twelfth-century Persian poet

1. The Free Will Issue in Name Only?

When faced with the great problems of philosophy, we often feel "like owls squinting at the sun," to use the image of Nicholas of Cusa. This is certainly the case with
the multifaceted issue of free will, which is "arguably the most difficult . . . in philosophy," as Susan Wolf has said, and "perhaps the most voluminously debated of
all philosophical problems," according to a recent history of philosophy.[1] But even
though we are squinting at the sun, our understanding of the great issues can mod-
estly progress; and this is so with free will. Since 1970, in particular, there has been
a resurgence of interest in traditional problems about the freedom of the will and
many noteworthy advances in understanding them. One of the aims of this book is
to describe features of this resurgence and to make sense of them in terms of broader
intellectual currents of the twentieth century.

   Another aim is to describe my own responses to current debates about free will.
I have been working on them for twenty-five years, a period coterminous with the
resurgence of interest since 1970, and have defended a view that I further develop in
this book.[2] This view, according to the current idiom, is *incompatibilist* or *libertarian* because it insists upon the incompatibility of free will and determinism; but it is
unlike any historical or contemporary view that goes by these names. I prefer to call
it a *free willist* view for reasons that will become clear in this chapter.

   One such reason is that I take the traditional idea of the will very seriously. For
many modern thinkers (including many libertarians), *free will* is a title used in defer-
ence to the philosophical tradition.[3] The current preference is to talk about free action
rather than free will (or freedom and determinism rather than free will and determinism) even while giving lip service to "the free will issue," or "the problem of free
will."[4]

   There are historical reasons for this change from free will to free action. Worthy
thinkers like Ludwig Wittgenstein and Gilbert Ryle convinced many philosophers

3

that the will and *acts of will* were suspect and should go the way of witches and phlogiston. This trend has been reversed to a degree since 1970, with a salutary revival of interest in notions of will and willing.[5] But the deeper connections between the will and long-standing questions about freedom and determinism are still not well understood, to my mind, even by those who are familiar with current debates. Thus, one of my themes will be that we cannot understand the true dimensions of traditional issues about free will until we understand why they are about the will—why they are *free will* issues in more than name only.

2. The Traditional Idea: Ultimacy, Responsibility, Purpose

Free will, in the traditional sense I want to retrieve (and the sense in which the term will be used throughout this book), is <u>the power of agents to be the ultimate creators (or originators) and sustainers of their own ends or purposes.</u> This notion should be distinguished from free action, and not simply because free will is a power. To act freely is to be unhindered in the pursuit of your purposes (which are usually expressed by intentions); <u>to will freely, in this traditional sense, is to be the ultimate creator</u> (prime mover, so to speak) <u>of your own purposes.</u> Such a notion of *ultimate* creation of purposes is obscure, to be sure—many would say it is unintelligible—but there is little doubt that it has fueled intuitions about free will from the beginning. Its meaning can be captured initially by an image: when we trace the causal or explanatory chains of action back to their sources in the purposes of free agents, these causal chains must come to an end or terminate in the willings (choices, decisions, or efforts) of the agents, which cause or bring about their purposes. If these willings were in turn caused by something else, so that the explanatory chains could be traced back further to heredity or environment, to God, or fate, then the ultimacy would not lie with the agents but with something else.

It is owing to such an image that free will has traditionally been associated with moral responsibility in a deep sense that entails, as Galen Strawson has put it, that we are "truly deserving of praise and blame" because it is "truly up to us" what we do, in the sense that we are the "ultimate, buck-stopping originator[s]" of our actions (1986: 26). The idea is that the ultimate responsibility lies where the ultimate cause is—where the buck stops. This is the traditional image of free will (which Strawson, along with many others, finds problematic). Such an image also accounts for the association of free will with human dignity, expressed in the religious traditions by saying that humans are made in the image of God—being creators *ab initio* of at least some things in the universe, their own purposes and the actions issuing from those purposes—and by Kant (1959) when he inferred that humans are to be treated as "ends in themselves" because they are the originators *of their own ends* or purposes.

Around this lofty conception revolve many of what Ted Honderich (1988, vol. 2: 14) has aptly called "life-hopes"—including dispositions to view ourselves as ultimately responsible for our own characters and achievements rather than as pawns of nature, fate, or the whims of others, including God. Of such hopes, Sophocles said, "we know not whence they come, but they die not" (1962: 29). We might add that these hopes also give rise to many of the deepest of philosophical puzzles.

The conception of free will defined at the beginning of this section as ultimate creation of purposes has been under attack since the seventeenth century for being obscure and unintelligible, and has been dismissed by many twentieth-century philosophers and scientists because of its supposed lack of fit with the modern image of human beings in the natural and social sciences. But I think there is much more to say than is generally realized about the intelligibility of the ancient idea of free will and about its relations to twentieth-century developments in the sciences and in social and humanistic studies.

We have often heard in this century that the free will issue is a "dead issue," that all the passages in the labyrinth have been traveled and retraveled. Logical positivists regarded free will as a pseudo-problem.[6] Similarly, dismissive attitudes came later in the century from social and natural scientists, ordinary language philosophers, and more recently postmodernists.[7] In opposition to these dismissive attitudes, my own view is that there are whole passages in the labyrinth of free will as yet unexplored, important new connections to be looked into and questions to be asked. Some of the old debates have in fact reached a dead end. But there are other as yet untrammeled paths worth exploring. We must continue to explore them in the spirit of Thomas Nagel's apt remark that "nothing approaching the truth has yet been said on this subject" (1986: 137).

[margin handwritten notes: Kane's take on the pseudo-problem problem]

3. Determinisms in History:
Fate, Science, Psychology, Religion, Logic

What is often called the free will issue or the problem of free will, when viewed in historical perspective, is really a cluster of problems or questions revolving around the conception of human freedom described in the previous section: the power of agents to be the ultimate creators and sustainers of their own ends or purposes. These questions concern what such a freedom could be, and if it could be, why it is important, what it implies of our place in the universe, whether we in fact have it, how we are to conceive it, if it is intelligible at all, and how it is related to other important topics such as morality, dignity, responsibility, rationality, creativity, autonomy, desert, and others. These questions in turn reach out to most other areas of human inquiry, from metaphysics and ethics to political theory, religion, and science.

While issues about free will are multifaceted in this way, the problem of free will has often been conceived more narrowly as a problem of free will versus determinism (or necessity) because the earliest and prevailing threats to free will came from doctrines asserting that all of our purposes and actions are determined or necessitated by factors beyond the control of our wills. It turns out that this narrowing of the problem to one of free will versus determinism is ultimately misleading because determinist or necessitarian threats represent only one facet of debates about free will. But the challenges of various doctrines of determinism did initiate the historical debates, and any attempt to understand free will issues must start with these determinist challenges.

The earliest of determinist or necessitarian doctrines that posed a threat to free will involved fate, conceived either as an impersonal cosmic force, or, in the words of Empedocles, as "an oracle of Necessity, an ancient decree of the gods, eternal, sealed fast with oaths."[8] In addition to the concern about fate in general, ancient think-ers were concerned about whether the decrees of particular gods could override human choices or purposes, or whether prophecy left any room for human free choice.[9] In all such cases—fate, divine intervention, prophecy—there was the same pattern of concern that is at the heart of historical debates about free will: humans would not be the ultimate creators of their own destinies if their purposes and ac-tions resulted from forces beyond the control of their wills.

A more sophisticated threat to free will came from the natural philosophers who conceived the idea that all things were determined by the physical motions of the atoms. Such an idea was implicit in the ancient atomist Democritus, but initially came to fruition in the West with the Stoics, who first clearly conceived the idea of universal (causal) laws of nature—the mainstay of all subsequent doctrines of *physi-cal* or *scientific* determinism.[10] It was in response to such doctines of invariable natural law that the Epicurean philosophers invented their notion of the chance "swerve" of the atoms[11] to allay, in Cicero's words, their "fear lest, if the atoms were always car-ried along by . . . natural and necessary force[s] . . . we should have no freedom what-ever, since the movement of the mind was controlled by the movement of the at-oms" (1960: 219).

The freedom whose loss the Epicureans feared fits our pattern: it requires that the ultimate control over action be in "the movement of the mind" of the agent (later to be associated with the agent's will) and not in something else (the movement of the atoms) beyond the control of the agent's mind. Of course, the Epicurean doc-trine caused more problems than it solved because chance or indeterminism gives rise to as many difficulties for free will as do determinism or necessity. In what sense can we be ultimate creators of our own purposes or actions, if they are the products of chance? This question, posed to the Epicurean philosophers by their ancient crit-ics, is still central to debates about free will, and it will be considered in later chapters.

Another traditional threat to free will came from doctrines of *psychological de-terminism*, the idea that choices and actions are determined by prior motives and character, which in turn are the ultimate products of birth and upbringing. A special version of psychological determinism debated by the ancients was related to the Socratic doctrine that we can never freely act against what we believe to be our good.[12] The lengthy debates about *akrasia*, or weakness of will, spawned by this Socratic doctrine are intimately related to free-will issues, as we shall see, though weakness of will and free will are often (mistakenly, I think) treated as separable problems by philosophers.[13]

The more general version of psychological determinism is the view held by Hobbes (1962), Schopenhauer (1960), Mill (1962), and many others, that we are always determined to act by the strongest motives or desires, which are in turn the inevitable products of birth and upbringing. Such a doctrine is often nowadays com-bined with Freudian or psychoanalytic themes, which emphasize that many of the determining psychological causes of choices and actions are unknown to us because they are unconscious, from which it is often inferred that our immediate experiences of being ultimately free and responsible are illusory.[14] These issues about motiva-tion, rationality, and the psychological *springs of action* will also engage our interest in subsequent chapters.

Yet another perennial concern about free will was theological determinism. The religious implications of free will have been a central preoccupation of Western intellectual history at least since the rise of Christianity, and especially since St. Augustine's seminal work *De Libero Arbitrio Voluntatis (On the Free Choice of the Will)*. Indeed, a preoccupation with free will has been a feature to some degree of all the world's theistic traditions, including Judaism and Islam. When Muslim scholars (about a century after Mohammed's death) first asked the Caliphs if they could look at the ancient scrolls of the Western philosophers hidden in the libraries of the Middle East, their main concern was to see if they could get some insight from the pagan philosophers into the vexing question of predestination and free will, which the *Qur'an* did not resolve.[15] In this manner, concerns about free will helped to stimulate the medieval Arab retrieval of ancient Greek philosophical texts, which had such an important influence upon the subsequent development of Western civilization.

In *Paradise Lost*, John Milton has the angels themselves debating about predestination and free will—wondering how they could have freely chosen to serve or reject God, given that God had made them what they were and had foreknowledge of what they would do. The angels who debated this issue, Milton tells us, were in "Endless Mazes lost" (not a comforting thought for us mortals).[16] The theological problem of free will is certainly a difficult one and Milton is not the only great literary figure to feel its power. (Dostoyevsky is another very different writer who was obsessed by the problem.) More than a few Western theologians, including Luther, Calvin, Jonathan Edwards, and perhaps even Augustine, believed that God's power, omniscience, and providence would be unacceptably compromised if one attributed to humans an ultimate control over their choices and actions such as the notion of free will required.[17] And yet theologians on the other side, including the Arminians, argued with equal force that if humans did not have such ultimate control, it was hard to see how they could be responsible for their actions in a manner that would justify divine rewards and punishments. The buck-stopping responsibility, including responsibility for evil, would devolve to God—an unacceptable consequence for traditional theists.

The free will debate took different forms in nontheistic Eastern religions, but it has been a part of them as well. For example, the doctrine of Karma, which is present in a variety of Indian religions—in Hinduism, Buddhism, Jainism, and Sikhism—raises questions about free will and responsibility that engaged Eastern thinkers of different traditions.[18] *Karma* (the Sanskrit term literally means deed or action) represents both the general law of cause and effect in the universe and a moral law according to which punishment and rewards are distributed through successive rebirths. The actions of past lives, according to the doctrine, influence the conditions of subsequent lives in such things as social status, disease, and prosperity, but especially in spiritual condition. Good deeds produce good Karma and lead to progress toward liberation; bad deeds do the opposite.

Questions about human initiative and free will naturally arise for such a doctrine and are mentioned in the various Indian traditions. "Man's will," says the Hindu *Bhagavad-Gita*, "is the only friend of the Atman [the divine self]. His will is also the Atman's only enemy."[19] "Choice is everything," adds a Jain text, "our glory and our agony."[20] Sometimes in these Eastern traditions the burden of deeds in numberless past lives could seem to weigh so heavily on the present that there was nothing one could do to attain liberation. But fatalistic or predestinationist conclusions tended to undermine initiative and were therefore resisted by many of the sages. (The Buddha, for example, attacked a contemporary teacher for holding a fatalistic predestinationism.[21]) The disputed question was whether, at any point in their lives, individuals were free to accept or attempt to change the chain of cosmic events—to "rise above" the effects of past Karma upon character, motives, and conditions in a way that was not completely determined by the past. This is an Eastern version of the problem of free will and it gives rise to many of the same paradoxes and puzzles as the Western versions.

A final determinist threat to free will came from logic. Early in the development of Western philosophy some thinkers of the so-called Megarian and (later) the Stoic schools suggested that the laws of logic alone imply that human wills are fettered and not free.[22] If every proposition must be true or false (as the logical principle of bivalence requires), and if this is the case for propositions about the future as well ("a sea fight will occur tomorrow"), then it seems that every future event would be fated either to occur or not to occur. For if "a sea fight will occur tomorrow" is true, then a sea fight cannot but occur tomorrow. If the proposition is false, then a sea fight cannot occur. Either way, the outcome would be necessitated by the past, together with the requirement that every proposition be true or false. This esoteric argument has exercised thinkers for centuries and continues to be discussed in recent philosophy.[23] Most philosophers, beginning with Aristotle, believed there were ways to avoid its conclusion, but there is no general agreement about the best way to avoid it.

4. Determinism and Free Will

There is a core notion of determinism running through all of these historical doctrines that shows why every kind of determinism—fatalistic, physical, psychological, theological, and logical—has been thought to be a threat to free will. Any event (including a choice or action) is determined, according to this core notion, just in case there are conditions (such as the decrees of fate, antecedent physical causes plus laws of nature, or foreordaining acts of God) whose joint occurrence is (logically) sufficient for the occurrence of the event. In other words, it *must* be the case that, *if* these determining conditions obtain (e.g., physical causes and laws of nature), *then* the determined event occurs.[24] Determination is thus a kind of conditional necessity that can be described in a number of ways. In the language of the modal logicians, the determined event will occur in every logically possible world in which the determining conditions (e.g. laws and antecedent circumstances) also obtain. In more familiar terms, the occurrence of the determined event is *inevitable* (it could not but happen), given the determining conditions.

Historical doctrines of determinism refer to different kinds of determining conditions, but each implies that every event is determined in this general sense. One can therefore easily understand the widespead intuitions that such doctrines pose a threat to free will. If one or another form of determinism were true, there would appear to be conditions necessitating all of an agent's purposes and actions that were beyond the agent's own control and for which the agent was not responsible. But untutored intuitions are only the first word on a subject as elusive as this one. Many philosophers have argued that, despite intuitions to the contrary, determinism poses no threat to free will, or at least to any free will "worth wanting," as Daniel Dennett (1984) has put it. Arguments are therefore needed to support intuitions we might have that free will is somehow incompatible with determinism, and we shall be looking into the most important recent arguments of this kind in chapters 3 and 4.

Some people wonder why worries about determinism persist at all in modern debates about free will, when universal determinism is no longer accepted even in the physical sciences, once the stronghold of determinist thinking. Quantum theory has reintroduced indeterminism into modern physics, giving us a more sophisticated version of the Epicurean swerve of the atoms than the ancients could ever have conceived. We are now told that much of the behavior of elementary particles, from quantum jumps in atoms to radioactive decay, is not precisely predictable and can be explained only by statistical, not deterministic, laws. Moreover, the uncertainty and indeterminacy of the quantum world, according to the prevailing view, is not due to our limitations as knowers but to the nature of physical systems themselves.[25]

One might think these indeterministic developments of twentieth-century science would have given new life to traditional libertarian doctrines of free will that reject determinism. Yet it is an interesting fact about the intellectual history of this century that, while universal determinism has been in retreat in the physical sciences, indeterminist theories of free will have not been thriving. To the contrary, skepticism abounds about views of free will that require indeterminism, and deterministic thinking *about human behavior* has been on the rise in this century at the same time that determinism has been on the decline in physics.

There are several reasons for these apparently paradoxical trends. First, twentieth-century developments in sciences other than physics — in biological, behavioral, and social sciences — have convinced many persons that more of our behavior is determined by causes unknown to us and beyond our control than people of the past had believed. These scientific developments are many, but they surely include a growing knowledge of genetics and heredity and of biochemical influences on the brain and behavior; the advent of psychoanalysis and other theories of unconscious motivation; developments in cognitive sciences involving artificial or machine intelligence; comparative studies of animal and human behavior; theories of psychological conditioning and behavior modification; and deepening evidence of the influences of language, culture, and upbringing on human thinking.[26]

A second reason indeterminism in physics has not undermined determinist thinking about human behavior has to do with quantum physics itself. Contemporary determinists on free will such as Ted Honderich (1988) — perhaps the most well-known defender of determinism in current free will debates — and Roy Weatherford (1991) are willing to concede that if quantum physics is correct, the behavior of elementary particles in nature is not always determined.[27] Yet they insist that this provides little comfort to traditional free willists. For, while quantum indeterminacy is significant for elementary particles, its effects are usually negligible to the point of insignificance in larger physical systems such as the human brain and body. We can therefore continue to regard human choices and actions as determined for all practical purposes, they argue, and this is the determinist claim that matters most in free will debates.

Moreover, one often hears the argument that if undetermined quantum events such as quantum jumps in the brain or nervous system did occasionally have large-scale effects on behavior, this would be no help to defenders of free will. For such events would be unpredictable and uncontrollable by the agent's themselves, like the unanticipated emergence of a thought or the uncontrolled jerking of an arm — quite the opposite of what we think free actions would be like. This point has been made in response to some noted twentieth-century scientists who suggested that quantum indeterminacy might be invoked in support of free will. For example, physicist A. H. Compton (1935) and neurophysiologist Sir John Eccles (1970), both Nobel prize winners in their respective fields, suggested independently that room might be found for free will in nature if undetermined quantum events in the brain were amplified to have non-negligible effects on human choice or action. Unfortunately, this modern version of the Epicurean "swerve" seems vulnerable to the same criticisms as its ancient counterpart. Critics argue that undetermined events in the brain or body would occur spontaneously and would be more of a nuisance — or perhaps a curse, like epilepsy — than an enhancement of the agent's freedom.

5. The Modern Era

But there is a third and even more important reason the advent of indeterminacy in modern science has not given new life to traditional libertarian or nondeterminist doctrines of free will — a reason that focuses not on scientific developments, but on the deficiencies of libertarian doctrines themselves. There are a host of unresolved problems about the intelligibility of a libertarian free will conceived as the power of ultimate creation of ends or purposes. Many thinkers have come to believe that such a power is incoherent and has no place in enlightened contemporary views of human behavior.[28] Challenges to the coherence of free will in the traditional sense I have defined have been a prominent feature of the modern Western philosophy since the seventeenth century. The first important modern figure to mount such a challenge (as I have elsewhere argued) was Thomas Hobbes, whose pivotal role in the history of debates about free will deserves greater recognition. In a celebrated debate with Bishop John Bramhall in the middle of the seventeenth century, Hobbes (1962) developed a line of argument against traditional accounts of free will that has become standard in the modern era.[29]

First, Hobbes argued that the freedoms we recognize and desire in ordinary life — freedoms from physical restraint, coercion, compulsion, and oppression — are all compatible with determinism (1962: 35). Persons are free, for Hobbes, when they are *self determining*, and they are self determining when nothing prevents them from doing *what they will* (or intend or desire) to do (pp. 51–2). And persons may be free in this sense, he continues — free to do what they intend or desire to do — though their intentions or desires are determined or necessitated by antecedent circumstances or causes. "The Actions which men voluntarily do . . . because they proceed from their will, proceed from liberty; and yet because every act of man's will, and every desire and inclination proceedeth from some cause, and that from another cause in a continual chaine . . . proceed from necessity" (1958: 71–2).

This was one half of Hobbes's "modernist" case against free will: the everyday freedoms we commonly recognize and desire are compatible with determinism. But the other half of the case was equally, if not more, decisive for the modern era. Hobbes went on to argue that the kind of freedom which *is* allegedly incompatible with determinism—traditionally called "free will"—is no intelligible freedom at all. The opponent in Hobbes's debate, Bramhall, had argued in defense of a traditional nondeterminist free will, that Hobbes's freedom to do what you will (though the will be determined) is but a "brutish liberty . . . such as a bird has to fly when its wings are clipped" (1962: 29). According to Bramhall, while a person may have the power to do what he or she wills, if the will in turn "has no power over itself, the agent is no more free than a staff in a man's hand" (p. 30). "True freedom," for Bramhall, required that the self not only determine its action according to its will, but also that the will be able to "determine itself," or have "power" or "dominion over itself" (p. 151). It required not only the power to act in accordance with one's purposes, but the power to determine in some ultimate way one's own purposes.

Bramhall was giving clear expression in these words to the traditional idea of free will inherited from ancient and medieval predecessors (the idea defined in section 2). Hobbes, by contrast, would have none of this ancient idea, which he believed to be outdated. Hobbes took direct aim at the expressions Bramhall used to define "true freedom" or free will—expressions such as "the will having power over itself" or "dominion over itself," or the "self determining itself." These expressions made no sense to Hobbes. He referred to them tellingly as "confused and empty words" (p. 35). Nor was Hobbes impressed by Bramhall's attempts to make sense of these expressions by speaking of the Will as a special kind of cause or suggesting that the self was capable of unique kind of agency by virtue of which it could "rise above" the influences of past character and motives (pp. 42–4; 151). To Hobbes, these were more "confused and empty words."

Hobbes saw a dilemma here that was to plague libertarian or nondeterminist theories of free will such as Bramhall's throughout the modern era. In order for the will to have ultimate "power or control over itself," some of its acts must be undetermined. But indeterminism alone does not amount to freedom. Whatever is *merely* undetermined is not controlled by anything, including the agent. It is therefore a confusion to simply identify freedom with indeterminism. But when libertarians like Bramhall went beyond mere indeterminism to account for "self-determination," they invariably posited obscure forms of agency or causation to explain how the self could "determine itself" without being determined by other causes. Libertarians have invoked transempirical power centers, nonmaterial egos, noumenal selves, nonoccurrent causes, and a litany of other special agencies whose operations were not clearly explained.[30] The libertarian dilemma, as Hobbes put it, was one of "confusion or emptiness"—the "confusion" of identifying freedom with indeterminism or the "emptiness" of unexplained accounts of the self's "determining itself" (p. 35).

These arguments of Hobbes against Bramhall anticipated all subsequent attacks on the intelligibility of libertarian free will in the modern era. As Bramhall looked back to an older conception of free will, Hobbes foreshadowed the modern challenges to that older conception. The Hobbesian challenge, which became standard in the modern era, insisted that the freedoms we recognize and desire in ordinary life are all compatible with determinism, while the freedom (of the will) that is allegedly incompatible with determinism is no intelligible freedom at all. If these points are correct, the ancient quarrels about freedom and determinism would be solved—or better, "dissolved," for we would find that there is no real conflict between determinism and any freedom we can have.

Such a "dissolutionist" stategy on free will was not entirely new—it had ancient origins in the Stoics. But it took on new form in the modern era beginning with Hobbes, and had a noble lineage thereafter through Locke, Spinoza, Edwards, Hume, Schopenhauer, Mill, and others—down to the twentieth century, when dissolutionism has become the majority view among philosophers. In its prevalent "modernist" form, as in that of Hobbes and his successors, dissolutionism amounts to "compatibilism"— the view that freedom in every significant sense, including free will, is compatible with determinism. Compatibilism has surely become the dominant view among philosophers today (though many ordinary persons continue to regard compatibilism as the "wretched subterfuge" or "quagmire of evasion" that Immanuel Kant and William James thought it to be).

But there has also arisen in recent decades a new form of dissolutionism that might be called "postmodernist." Thinkers in this mold are skeptical about the adequacy of *both* incompatibilist and compatibilist accounts of freedom and responsibility. These thinkers are less sanguine than traditional compatibilists such as Hobbes about whether compatibilist accounts of freedom capture all of our relevant intuitions about free will and responsibility. Yet they share Hobbes's belief that incompatibilist accounts of free will cannot be made intelligible. Thus, Galen Strawson (1986) insists that compatibilist accounts of freedom do not capture our intuitions about "true responsibility-entailing freedom" (which are indeed incompatibilist[31]), but he also rejects incompatibilist accounts of freedom as unintelligible. Richard Double (1991) argues that our intuitions about freedom and responsibility are an amalgam of notions (to do what you will, to do otherwise, to be ultimate creators of purposes) that are inconsistent with one another. Compatibilists capture some of these intuitions and incompatibilists capture others, but neither gets the whole package because it is not a coherent package. While such views are skeptical about both compatibilist and incompatibilist accounts of free will, they share with compatibilists the "dissolutionist" conviction that the ancient quarrels about freedom and determinism can finally be put to rest by recognizing that there is no real conflict between determinism and any intelligible freedom we could possess.

6. Four Questions

The effect of modern compatibilist and dissolutionist attacks on free will initiated by Hobbes was to bring four questions to the center of attention in subsequent debates. As I see it, these four questions remain at the center of free will debates to this day, and therefore, they will be the focus of attention throughout this book.

The Compatibility Question: Is free will compatible with determinism?

The Significance Question: Why do we, or should we, want to possess a free will that is incompatible with determinism? Is it a kind of freedom "worth wanting" (to use Dennett's useful phrase) and, if so,why?

The Intelligibility Question: Can we make sense of a freedom or free will that is incompatible with determinism? Is such a freedom coherent or intelligible? Or is it, as many critics claim, essentially mysterious and terminally obscure?

The Existence Question: Does such a freedom actually exist in the natural order, and if so, where?

The four questions are intimately related; answers to any one depend on answers to the others. But they can also be fruitfully viewed in pairs. The Compatibility and Significance questions should be treated together, for reasons to be explained in a moment. And the Intelligibility and Existence questions obviously go together. If we cannot say what free will is without obscurity, we don't know what we are looking for when we look for it in the real world.

Imagine that the task for defenders of a traditional incompatibilist or libertarian free will is to climb to the top of a mountain and get down the other side. The ascent of this mountain involves answering the first pair of questions—Compatibility and Significance—in an incompatibilist way. The descent involves answering the second pair of questions—Intelligibility and Existence—for incompatibilist freedom. To get to the top of the mountain, in other words, is to show that there is a significant freedom worth wanting that is incompatible with determinism. In the 1970s and 1980s, considerable debate has centered on new arguments for such incompatibility put forward by libertarians like Carl Ginet (1966), David Wiggins (1973), Peter van Inwagen (1975), James Lamb (1977), and others. Such arguments (which will be considered in chapter 4) have been controversial—partly because they turn on the interpretation of notoriously difficult terms and expressions like *can, power, ability,* and *could have done otherwise.*

But these new arguments, like all arguments for incompatibilism, are controversial for another reason. Even if successful, they would only get us to the top of the mountain. To get down the other side, one has to show how incompatibilist accounts of freedom can be made intelligible (why they are not essentially incoherent, mysterious, or obscure) and how they fit into the natural order. One must, in other words, also address the Intelligibility and Existence questions. Most modern skeptics about libertarian free will believe that it *is* incoherent or unintelligible and has no place in the natural order. So they are inclined to believe that abstract arguments for incompatibilism, like those of Ginet, Wiggins, van Inwagen, and others, *must* be wrong in some way or another; it's just a question of locating the logical or other error in such arguments.

This shows how answers to the "ascent" problem—the Compatibility and Significance questions—depend upon answers to the "descent" problem—the Intelligibility and Existence questions. Abstract arguments for incompatibilism that seem to get us to the top of the mountain are not good enough if we can't get down the other side by making intelligible the incompatibilist freedom these arguments require. The air is cold and thin up there on Incompatibilist Mountain, and if one stays up there for any length of time without getting down the other side, one's mind becomes clouded in mist and is visited by visions of noumenal selves, nonoccurrent causes, transempirical egos, and other fantasies.

For such reasons, when I first began to consider free will issues in 1970, my attention was drawn to the descent problem, and in particular, to the pivotal Intelligibility Question. It seemed to me that the only way to move beyond current stalemates on free will was to take a new, hard look at the Intelligibility Question, using it as a springboard for rethinking the other questions, including the Existence Question. This set me on a different path than most other philosophers during the period of the 1970s and 1980s when the Compatibility Question (and the ascent problem generally) was at the center of philosophical attention, as it has been throughout the modern era. The result of this shift in focus for me, as it turned out, was not only a different approach to the Intelligibility Question, but different approaches to the other three questions about free will as well—all of which are reflected in this book.

7. The Ascent Problem: Compatibility and Significance

Part I of the book deals with the Compatibility and Significance questions—that is, with the problem of ascent. After a preliminary discussion of the will in chapter 2, I turn to current debates about the Compatibility Question in chapters 3 and 4. My own (incompatibilist) answer to this question emerges in chapter 5, and then the Significance Question is addressed in chapter 6. Part II then takes on the problem of descent, treating the Intelligibility and Existence questions together. In the remainder of this chapter, I explain further how the four questions are related and how they will be dealt with in subsequent chapters.

One thing made clear by the initial focus on the Intelligibility Question was that *freedom* is a term of many meanings, some of which may designate kinds of freedom that are compatible with determinism, others that are not.[32] This assumption is crucial, I have come to believe, for any coherent approach to all four questions about free will, including the Compatibility Question. Nothing but confusion can arise from assuming that we all have a single conception of freedom and then asking whether freedom according to *that* single conception is or is not compatible with determinism (though one often sees the matter put this way in writings on free will). As Tomis Kapitan (1994: 93) and Nicholas Nathan (1992: 22) aptly note, there is no good reason to assume "that only a single free/ unfree contrast will suffice" to explicate our diverse references to freedom in ordinary discourse.[33]

It follows that the usual textbook formulation of the Compatibility Question— "Is freedom compatible with determinism?"—is too simple. If there are different kinds of freedom, the question should be: "Is freedom *in every significant sense worth wanting* compatible with determinism?" This richer question shows in turn how the Compatibility and Significance questions are intertwined. To answer the expanded question in the negative, incompatibilists do not have to claim that every significant kind of freedom of action or will is incompatible with determinism. Incompatibilists can (and should, I think) concede that there are significant everyday notions of freedom — for example, freedom from coercion or compulsion or political oppression — that can be analysed without supposing determinism to be false. Gary Watson is correct, it seems to me, when he says that "incompatibilists . . . are wrong to dismiss" notions of freedom picked out by compatibilists "as mere contrivance[s] in the service of a compatibilist program" (1987: 161). For these compatibilist notions of freedom, as Watson says, are also notions we have and use. I, for one, am willing to concede this point to Watson and other compatibilists, and I think other incompatibilists should do so likewise. To concede the point is to allow that, *even if we lived in a determined world*, we could meaningfully distinguish persons who are free from such things as physical restraint, addiction or neurosis, coercion or political oppression, from persons not free from these things, and we could allow that these freedoms would be worth preferring to their opposites even in a determined world.

What incompatibilists should claim (and what they have often historically claimed) is that there is *at least one* kind of freedom that is incompatible with determinism, and it is a *significant kind of freedom worth wanting*. They should not quarrel with compatibilists about whether there are freedoms worth wanting that are compatible with determinism, but rather concede the point and go on to argue that compatibilist freedoms are not the only significant ones. On my view, the additional freedom worth caring about that is not compatible with determinism is what was traditionally called "free will"; and it is the power to be an ultimate creator and sustainer of one's own ends or purposes. Those who defend such a freedom ("free willists," as I call them) believe that free will in this sense is something worth wanting *over and above* compatibilist freedoms, such as freedom from coercion or compulsion or political oppression. This is not to deny the importance of these compatibilist freedoms, but only to suggest that human longings transcend them.[34]

In this manner, the Significance Question (why we should want free will) takes on a greater importance in relation to the Compatibility Question. This greater importance for the Significance Question is related to another noteworthy trend of free-will debates since 1970 — the realization by a growing number of writers that different views on free will reflect not only differences about factual and conceptual issues, but differences about *values* as well, about what is or is not important. This realization cuts across ideological lines. On the compatibilist side, Watson expresses it by saying that "our view of what free will is depends upon our view of what matters" (1982: 2). But similar sentiments have been emphasized in recent writings by an impressive array of philosophers who take varying positions on free will, including (among those already mentioned) Dennett, Nagel, Honderich, Wiggins, Double, Galen Strawson, and Susan Wolf, and also including Bernard Williams, P. F. Strawson, Harry Frankfurt, Anthony Kenny, Bernard Berofsky, John Martin Fischer, Nicholas Nathan, Robert Nozick, Michael Slote, Martha Klein, W. S. Anglin, Bruce Waller, Paul Benson, Tomis Kapitan, Richard Warner, and others.[35]

Yet while the importance of the Significance Question is more widely recognized, discussion of it still leaves much to be desired. Traditionally, the argument has been that free will is significant and worth wanting because it is a prerequisite for other goods that humans highly value. Candidates for these other goods allegedly requiring free will have included genuine creativity, autonomy, moral responsibility, desert, dignity, individuality, being the object of "reactive attitudes" such as admiration and gratitude, and so forth. But debate has usually stalemated over the meanings of these goods and whether they really require an incompatibilist free will. Indeed, some the best philosophical work by compatibilists since 1970 has been devoted to giving analyses of autonomy, moral responsibility, creativity and related notions without appealing to an incompatibilist free will.[36] Compatibilists further argue that incompatibilists are begging the question when they insist that "genuine" or "true" autonomy, responsibility, and creativity require indeterminism.

This is one of those places where free will debates so often end in stalemate. And I think that here, as elsewhere, the only way forward is to dig more deeply into the conflicting intuitions that lie behind the disagreements. I try to do this with regard to the Significance Question in chapter 6 by reference to what I call the "dialectic of selfhood" and a notion of "objective worth." Likewise, I think further progress on the Compatibility Question depends upon looking more deeply into the sources of conflicting intuitions between compatibilists and incompatibilists, and this I try to do in chapters 3, 4, and 5.

8. The Descent Problem: Intelligibility and Existence

Not only must one address the Significance Question in order to satisfactorily answer the Compatibility Question; one must also address the Intelligibility Question. In my experience, most people start out as natural incompatibilists. They think there is some sort of conflict between free will and determinism, and they have to be talked out of this belief by clever arguments—which philosophers are only too happy to supply (in the spirit of their mentor Socrates). What do the philosophers do to undermine the natural belief in the incompatibility of free will and determinism? First, they argue that what we ordinarily mean by freedom is the ability to have and do whatever we desire or choose—in other words, an absence of coercion, compulsion, and other forms of constraint on our behavior. Then they argue, in the manner of Hobbes, that these everyday freedoms are compatible with determinism.

But this line of thought by itself does not usually dispose of incompatibilist instincts. For people persist in thinking that, even if most everyday freedoms are compatible with determinism, there might nonetheless be a freedom of a deeper kind worth having that *is* incompatible with determinism. Thus, to complete the argument, the philosophers also have to show that no further significant incompatibilist freedom can be made intelligible. And they usually do this by pointing out that *indeterminism* is no help in giving us any kind of freedom we should want because indeterminism would undermine the responsibility and control required by genuine free action. This is the argument that usually puts the final nail in the coffin of incompatibilist instincts. It is not enough for one to be shown that many ordinary freedoms are compatible with determinism. One must also be shown that there are no *intelligible libertarian alternatives* to everyday compatibilist freedoms. In this manner, compatibilist answers to the Compatibility Question are only completed by a negative answer to the Intelligibility Question.

We might add that this imagined dialogue in which the philosopher talks ordinary persons out of their incompatibilist beliefs is an exact replica of Hobbes's case against Bramhall's traditional view of free will, which first shows that ordinary freedoms are compatible with determinism and then shows that incompatibilist free will provides no intelligible alternative. When professors go through this little dialogue with students in the modern classroom they are rehearsing the standard case against traditional views of free will, which is one of the defining characteristics of what has come to be called modernity. (Hobbes, of course, is one of the first true modernists on this issue, as on many others—such as the subjectivity of value and the contractual nature of political obligation.) Incompatibilist free will is thereby consigned to the dustbin of history along with other premodern illusions (disembodied spirits, final causes, absolute values) that our enlightened, scientifically oriented age is challenged to outgrow.

As indicated earlier, I think the only way to fruitfully continue the debate beyond this point at present is to take a new, hard look at the Intelligibility Question, as I try to do in part II. Belief is more widespread than ever today that an old-fashioned incompatibilist free will is essentially mysterious and has no place in the modern picture of human beings emerging in the natural, social, and cognitive sciences. Deeply troubled by this situation, I set out in 1970 to try some new approach to the Intelligibility Question that would put the incompatibilist view of freedom into more meaningful dialogue with modern science—with physics, as well as biology and the cognitive and social sciences. Nothing less seemed required to drag the age-old free will debate fully into the twentieth century. The idea was to put aside traditional libertarian appeals to special forms of agency or causation that in the past have evoked charges of mystery or obscurity and seem to have no place in the natural order in which we must exercise our free will. Perhaps we cannot get everything libertarians have wanted this way, but it does not hurt to try something new. At "the price of mystery," as Erwin Schrodinger once said, "you can have anything"—but, he added, too easily, and without honest toil.

My answer to the Intelligibility Question is presented in chapters 8 through 10 of part II after a preliminary discussion of the issues in chapter 7. The Existence Question is also discussed in these chapters, along with Intelligibility. It is worth adding, however, that I do not believe the Existence Question can be fully answered by armchair speculation alone. I reject the view (amply refuted by John Stuart Mill and others) that we can know we have free will by introspection or by a priori reasoning alone. There are empirical aspects of the free will issue that mere philosophical speculation cannot co-opt. If free will of a nondeterminist kind should exist in nature, then the atoms must somewhere "swerve" to make room for it, and they must swerve in places where it matters—in the brain, for example. But neither can philosophical speculation be indifferent to the empirical questions. Thus, in part II, as part of the task of making sense of free will, I suggest some physical modeling in the brain with references to neural network theory, nonlinear thermodynamics, chaos theory, and quantum physics. This approach is in line with the general goal of putting the free will issue into greater dialogue with developments in the sciences and other disciplines. I also think it is a necessary task if we are to move beyond present stalemates on free will and open up some of those uncharted passages in the labyrinth of which I spoke at the beginning of the chapter.

I

THE ASCENT PROBLEM: COMPATIBILITY AND SIGNIFICANCE

2

Will

1. Intellect and Will: Theoretical and Practical Reasoning

"The freedom of the agent," Bramhall said, "is from the freedom of the will" (1844: 30). This claim, which I have elsewhere called "Bramhall's thesis," is definitive of the free willist view I want to defend. As we begin to address the four core questions about free will, the first step is to say something about the traditional notion of the *will* and a host of related notions that play crucial roles in subsequent arguments: self, person, practical reasoning, choice, decision, intention, action, normative judgment, reasons, motives, and others.[1]

Traditional free willists assumed, like Bramhall, that only a *self*, or *person*, or *rational agent* could have free will. (These three italicized terms will be used interchangeably hereafter.) To be a self or person or rational agent was to have Reason, or the capacity to reason, and this was essential, as they viewed it, for the exercise of anything we could call free will. But they also recognized that the capacity to reason was of two kinds, corresponding to a distinction, going back to Aristotle, between two kinds of reasoning—*theoretical* and *practical*. The former was reasoning about "what is the case," the latter about "what is to be done." The capacity for theoretical reasoning may be called in the language of the medieval period *intellect* (*intellectus*) and the capacity for practical reasoning *will* (*voluntas*).[2] In these terms, selfhood or personhood or rational agency, defined as the capacity to reason and to act rationally, would mean having both an intellect and a will.

This is the meaning of *will* in the first of three traditional senses to be considered in this chapter, each of which has a role to play in understanding free will. Will in this first sense, which may be called *rational will*, is a set of powers defined in terms of a family of concepts whose focal member is practical reasoning or deliberation. Practical reasoning is, generally speaking, reasoning about what is to be done. But the expression "what is to be done" is ambiguous. It can signify what I (or someone) "should" or "ought" to do; or it can signify what I "will" (i.e., "choose" or "decide") to do. Thus practical reasoning can issue in two kinds of judgment—*practical* (*or normative*) *judgments*, on the one hand, about what ought to be done (or about what the best thing is to do), and *choices* or *decisions*, on the other hand, which announce that the agent "will" do such and such, now or in the future.

21

Thus, "the will" (as "rational will," in the sense we are considering) is a *set of conceptually interrelated powers or capacities*, including the powers to deliberate, or to reason practically, to choose or decide, to make practical judgments, to form intentions or purposes, to critically evaluate reasons for action, and so forth. These are distinguishable powers, but each is related to, and definable by reference to, the focal notion of practical reasoning. *Intellect*, in turn, is in this context a set of conceptually interrelated powers similarly associated with theoretical reasoning (the powers to infer, conclude, surmise, judge, and so forth). Both the will and intellect—understood in this manner as powers relating to practical and theoretical reasoning respectively—were frequently called "faculties" of mind. The term *faculty* has been out of fashion for some time, but it has a clear and useful meaning in the present context. A faculty is nothing more or less than a set of conceptually interrelated powers or capacities—all related, in the case of rational will, to the exercise of reason in its practical mode.

Some medieval thinkers, such as St. Thomas Aquinas (following Aristotle), defined the "will" as "rational appetite," which makes it appear to be something like a disposition rather than a set of powers.[3] But "rational" appetite, for such thinkers, as opposed to merely sensuous appetite, presupposed powers to form and act upon rational desires—those that were filtered through reasoning; and this meant powers to deliberate and choose and to make practical judgments, as well as other powers that were required for rational will. So, while rational appetites were dispositional, the general capacity to have them involved the powers or capacities characteristic of rational will.

2. Libera Arbitria Voluntatis: Acts of Will and Actions

Of special interest for free will are the judgments that terminate practical reasoning—that is, practical judgments ("X ought to be done"), on the one hand, and choices or decisions ("I will do X"), on the other. These may be designated, in traditional medieval terms, *judgments of the will* (*arbitria voluntatis*), and distinguished from *judgments of the intellect* ("X is the case"), which terminate theoretical reasonings.[4] Judgments of the will, understood in this way, have special importance for free will because the locus of the will's freedom is to be found in them. That is to say, free choices, decisions, and practical judgments may be viewed as instances of *liberum arbitrium* (literally, "free judgment"), the common medieval designation for free will. Thus, the title of St. Augustine's seminal work *De Libero Arbitrio Voluntatis*, usually translated "Of the Free Choice of the Will," means literally "Of the Free Judgment of the Will." The shift from "judgment" to "choice" is only mildly misleading for our purposes since choices and decisions are among the most important judgments of the will. "Freedom of will" includes "freedom of choice or decision," as many philosophers have supposed, but freedom of the will is also more than freedom of choice or decision. The broader term "judgment of the will" is the first indication of this breadth.

Bramhall, Hobbes, and other writers on free will also refer to choices, decisions, and practical judgments as "acts of will," thereby introducing another controversial expression into free will debates. In what sense, if any, can choices, decisions, and

practical judgments be regarded as acts (or actions) of will? To act is to "bring something about," and an act or action is the bringing about of something. That which by
definition is brought about by an act or action may be called (following Hugh
McCann [1974]) its "result." Thus, the result of my raising my arm is that my arm
goes up, since raising my arm is by definition "bringing it about that my arm goes
up." The result of killing the prince is that the prince is dead, and so on.[5]

If choices or decisions are acts in this sense, what do they bring about, or what
is their result? The answer, I believe, is that choices or decisions normally bring about
intentions to act—intentions are their results. To choose, or decide, to depart on the
evening train is to bring about the intention to depart on the evening train; it is to
bring that intention into existence. This role as formers or creators of intention is
especially important when we view choices or decisions as exercises of free will. For
intentions in turn are related to *purposes*. The "content" of an intention (in the above
example, "to depart on the evening train") is, or at least includes, a purpose or goal
or end. Thus, a choice or decision can be described as both the *formation of intention* and *the creation of a purpose* that subsequently guides action.

This is a first step toward explaining the formula for free will of chapter 1 — "the
power to be the ultimate creator and sustainer of one's own *ends* or *purposes*." This
power is connected to the ability to make choices or decisions by virtue of the fact
that choices and decisions are the formations of intentions. Viewed more generally,
the power of free will also includes the ability to make other judgments of the will
that play a role in the creation of purposes. Practical judgments, for example, are the
formations of normative or evaluative beliefs (e.g., about what ought to be done),
which also play a role, though a less direct one, in the formation of new intentions,
and hence purposes, by way of practical reasoning.

3. Choices or Decisions

The terms *choice* and *decision* are being used here in ordinary senses in which they
designate "settlements of conditions of doubt or uncertainty" about what an agent
will do. (When used in this way, the two terms are nearly always interchangeable
without significant alteration of meaning, and they will be used as such throughout
our discussions.[6]) So understood, choices or decisions normally terminate processes
of deliberation or practical reasoning, but they need not always do so. We need not
rule out the possibility of impulsive, spur-of-the-moment, or snap, decisions, which
also settle conditions of indecision but arise with minimal or no prior reasoning. Yet,
while impulsive or snap decisions can occur, they are less important for free will than
decisions that terminate processes of deliberation in which alternatives are reflectively considered. For, in the latter cases, we are more likely to feel we have control
over the outcome and "could have done otherwise."

Just as choices or decisions normally terminate processes of deliberation, but
need not always do so, they may also immediately give rise to actions, but need not
always do so. Jane may decide to leave her office now, and immediately take steps to
do so, in which case her decision directly initiates action. But she may also decide to
leave three hours from now and will not take action until then (if she does not change
her mind in the meantime). In both cases, an intention is formed by her decision (to

leave now or to leave in three hours) that will guide her action now or in the future. But only in the former case is action immediately initiated by decision or choice. Conversely, actions (including intentional actions) need not always be initiated by choices or decisions. We frequently act out of habit or on the basis of intentions already formed without any need for explicit choice, decision, or prior reflection and reasoning. So choices or decisions may, but need not, immediately give rise to actions; and actions may, but need not, be preceded by choices or decisions.

I make these points in order to emphasize that the terms *choice* and *decision* are used throughout this book in ordinary senses. Specifically, *choice* and *decision* will not designate what a number of contemporary philosophers call *volitions*. According to some modern theories of action, volitions are "tryings" or "efforts," whose role is to "execute intentions" and "initiate actions."[7] The controversial claim of these volition theories is that all actions *qua* actions are necessarily initiated by volitions, even when we are not aware of trying or making an effort to perform them. When used in this way, "volition" is a technical term of action theory oriented to issues that arise about the initiation of action. By contrast, "choice" and "decision," as I shall be using them, are ordinary terms signifying "settlements of conditions of doubt or uncertainty in the mind."

As a consequence, choices and decisions are not controversial in the way that volitions are. In an interesting passage of *The Concept of Mind* (1949), Gilbert Ryle mentions certain familiar processes

> with which volitions are sometimes wrongly identified. People are frequently in doubt about what to do; having considered alternative courses of action, they sometimes select or choose one of these courses. This process of opting for one of a set of alternative courses of action is sometimes said to be what is signified by "volition." But this identification will not do, for most ordinary actions do not issue out of conditions of indecision and are not therefore results of settlements of indecision. (p. 68)

Ryle's "settlements of indecision" are our "choices" or "decisions," and I am claiming that they play a pivotal role in accounts of free will. They normally (though not always) terminate deliberation or practical reasoning, and they sometimes, but not always, initiate action. What they essentially do, however, is form intentions and create purposes that guide actions, now or in the future; and this accounts for their pivotal role with respect to free will.[8]

4. Intention

Choices and decisions are *acts* of mind (or will), and hence events that happen at a time, possibly terminating deliberations and giving rise to intentions. Intentions, by contrast, are *states* of mind that persist through time and guide actions. Our understanding of intention has been enhanced by some excellent philosophical work on the subject since 1970, which aids our understanding of issues relating to free will.[9] For a time, it was widely believed that intention was a dispensable notion in the philosophy of action. Many philosophers held that explanations of action could be adequately given in terms of beliefs and desires (or wants) alone, with the intermediary notion of intention playing no indispensable role.

But the idea that intentions are dispensable has been eroding in recent years, thanks to the work of a number of philosophers, including Michael Bratman (1987), Myles Brand (1984), John Searle (1983), Gilbert Harman (1986), Alfred Mele (1992), and others. Intentions have a number of different roles to play in practical reasoning and action, some of which are unique to them. Mele conveniently lists some of these roles as follows (1992: 140). Intentions (i) explain and motivationally sustain intentional actions; (ii) they function as plans guiding and monitoring behavior; (iii) they help to coordinate agents' behavior over time and the interactions of the agents with other agents; (iv) they prompt, and play motivating roles in, practical reasoning; and (v) they appropriately terminate practical reasonings. In the light of the previous section, we can add a point that is assumed by the other five: (vi) intentions express an agent's purposes or goals (which is a role that desires or wants alone do not perform, since what is desired or wanted is not always selected as a goal).

In a ground-breaking work, *Intentions, Plans, and Practical Reason* (1987), Michael Bratman emphasizes the second and third of these roles of intentions. His thesis is that intentions are most fruitfully viewed as *plans* of action that function, first, to "allow deliberation and rational reflection to influence action beyond the present" by guiding and monitoring future behavior. Second, intentions-as-plans function to "achieve complex goals" by coordinating behavior over time (both intrapersonally and with respect to the plans of other agents) (p. 2). Bratman is not the only philosopher to recognize that intentions are (or involve) plans.[10] But he has done the most to work out this idea and to show how it makes intentions unique among states of mind involved in the explanation of action.

Along with other writers on the subject, Bratman distinguishes two kinds of intentions—present-directed intentions ("concerning what to do beginning now" [p. 4]) and future-directed intentions (concerning what to do in the future). It is with future-directed intentions, Bratman argues, that the coordinating role of intentions comes into its own. "We form future-directed intentions as parts of larger plans which play characteristic roles in coordination and ongoing practical reasoning; plans which allow us to extend the influence of present deliberation into the future" (p. 8). Thus, John's intention to study this evening is part of a larger plan to pass a college course, which is in turn part of his plan to become a lawyer, and so on. These larger plans are also expressible as intentions (to pass the course, to become a lawyer) whose contents represent his broader purposes.

In this manner, intentions can prompt and enter into practical reasoning as well as result from it (which takes us to function [iv] of Mele's list). Intending to pass the course, and believing he is in danger of failing it, John is prompted to deliberate about how to remedy his situation. Jane's decision to vacation in Colorado in the summer may have been influenced by her long-standing intention (or plan) to visit a friend in Oklahoma City, which is on her way to Colorado. Having decided where to go, she must also decide on the best means for achieving her ends—to go by bus or plane or whatever. In these diverse ways, as Bratman says, intentions are "parts of larger plans which play characteristic roles in coordination [of future behavior] and ongoing practical reasoning." In this role, intentions also embody an agent's "commitments" to future goals, as Harman (1986), Moya (1991), and others also emphasize.

A corollary of the coordinating function of intentions is that they often have complex contents. As a result of her deliberations, Jane intends not merely "to go to Colorado," but "to go to Colorado *by* taking a bus through Oklahoma City." The content includes not merely her end or goal, but also the means of attaining it. This was one reason for saying earlier that the content of an intention always is, *or includes*, the agent's purposes or ends. The content may describe an end plus various means for attaining the end, or several coordinated means and ends. But, of course, the intended means are also purposes or ends of the agent, looked at from another point of view. If Jane intends to go to Colorado by taking the bus, then taking the bus is also one of her purposes, which may then function as an end or goal in some future deliberation (about which bus to take and when to take it). What is a means in one context of practical reasoning may be an end in another.

In summary, the discussion of intention in this section complicates earlier claims about the relation between intention and *purpose*, but does not alter the basic point: *intentions express the purposes or goals or ends of agents* by virtue of the fact that the contents of intentions describe these purposes or goals. The complications have to do with the fact that the contents of intentions may have varying degrees of complexity. Only in the case of what might be called "simple intentions" do they describe a single purpose (e.g., intending to go to Colorado). In other cases, they may describe many purposes or goals in complex relations to one another, including means to ends.

Similarly, this discussion of intention does not alter the basic points made about the relation of intention to *choice* or *decision*, though it complicates that relation as well. The complications have to do again with the complexity of the contents of intentions. Bratman has argued, for example, that in some cases the contents of choices and the intentions they form may diverge in subtle ways (1987: 152–64). Some of the means chosen to a given end may not be intended. While this claim is controversial, if such cases occur, they must be accommodated. Their occurrence, however, would not alter the general point about choice and intention that I have insisted upon: *choices and decisions form intentions and thereby create purposes that guide actions,* now or in the future.

5. Three Senses of "Will": Striving Will

We have been talking about the will in only one of its important senses—rational will. In this sense, will is contrasted with intellect and is a faculty, or a set of conceptually interrelated powers, whose focal point is practical reasoning—powers involving such notions as choice, decision, intention, purpose, normative judgment, means to ends, and others. It is now time to mention the two other senses of "will" that also play roles in accounts of free will. One way to introduce these is to reflect on the familiar expression "I can do *what I will* to do," which appears throughout the Hobbes-Bramhall debate and in many other historical discussions of free will. In this expression, "what I will to do" may have different meanings. It may mean

(i) what I *want, desire,* or *prefer* to do
(ii) what I *choose, decide,* or *intend* to do
(iii) what I *try, endeavor* or make an *effort* to do

The second of these meanings represents *rational will*, which we have been discussing. It is will-as-practical-reason, resulting in what agents choose, decide or intend. Meaning (i) represents what is sometimes historically called *desiderative* or *appetitive will*—that is, willing-as-wanting-or-desiring-or-being-inclined to this or that result . Finally, meaning (iii)—willing-as-trying-or-making-efforts—represents what Brian O'Shaughnessy (1980) has aptly called *striving will*. What the three senses have in common (which allows us to speak of kinds of will) is that each signifies an orientation or inclination toward some objective or end that is desired, chosen, or striven for. In other words, the idea of will is essentially teleological, and different senses of *will* and *willing* represent different ways in which agents may be directed toward or tend toward *ends* or *purposes*.

Free will, I shall argue, involves the will in all three of these senses, though in different ways. To see this, consider practical reason once again as a point of focus. Wants, desires, preferences, and other expressions of desiderative will are among the *inputs* to practical reasoning—they function as *reasons* or *motives* for choice or action. By constrast, choices, decisions, and intentions, the expressions of rational will, are the *outputs* of practical reasoning, its products. If there is indeterminacy in free will, on my view, it must come somewhere between the input and the output—between desiderative and rational will. (This is what was meant by saying that the indeterminacy required by libertarian freedom is "in the will" of the agent.) Incompatibilists, I believe, can live with compatibilist accounts of the relation between choice (or intention) and action. What they must insist upon is an incompatibilist account of the relation between reasons, on the one hand, and choice (or intention) on the other. That is at least part of the meaning of Bramhall's thesis—that the freedom of the agent is "from" the freedom of the will.

[margin note: location of indeterminacy]

But it turns out that the third kind of will—striving will—must also be involved if such an account of free will is to be made out. Thus, in the theory to follow, efforts of will of various kinds also play significant roles. The efforts in question are not merely efforts to perform overt actions. I assume that familiar experiences of trying or making an effort are sometimes directed at our mental activities and processes as well as at overt or physical actions. For example, we have to make efforts to think about problems we have been trying to avoid, or to persist in deliberation when we are tired. When choosing to do the morally right or prudential thing, we may have to make efforts to overcome temptations to act immorally or imprudently. At other times, we make efforts to give all of the options a fair hearing or to sustain our intentions or purposes in the face of obstacles or temptations to backslide. In each of these ways and others, striving will plays a role in free will along with desiderative and rational will.

Regarding efforts and tryings, remarks similar to those made about choices and decisions are in order. The terms *effort* and *trying* (and related terms such as *endeavoring* and *striving*) are to be used throughout this book in their ordinary senses. I assume we all have experiences of making efforts or trying when we meet resistance to our mental and physical activities. Whenever I speak of effort or trying hereafter, I shall assume it is made against some resistance or other that agents must overcome. Thus, I remain noncommittal on the view of some volition theorists who identify efforts or tryings with volitions and argue that volitions, so understood, are involved

[margin note: effort only against opposition]

in all intentional actions, though the efforts go unnoticed if their is no resistance to our actions. Volition theories of this kind have been ably defended by O'Shaughnessy (1980), Ginet (1990), McCann (1974), Hornsby (1980), Davis (1979), and others. But they are controversial, and I take no stand on them in this book. As I said earlier, the theory to follow does not require any technical notion of volitions or tryings as initiators of all actions.[11] What the theory *does* require are efforts and tryings as we ordinarily experience them when we *are aware of resistance* to our mental or physical activities. Volitional theories are thus not required, but striving will *is* required.

6. Reasons and Motives

Wants, desires, and other expressions of desiderative will were said to be among the inputs of practical reasoning. As such, they function as reasons for choice or action. A *reason* for choice or action, as we shall primarily use the term, is a psychological attitude of an agent that can be correctly cited in answer to the question of *why* the agent acted as he or she did. Thus, in answer to the question "Why did Jane choose to vacation in Colorado (rather than, say, in Hawaii)?" we may cite, as her reasons for choice, her wants or desires; preferences, factual beliefs and expectations; likes and dislikes; prior intentions; interests and memories; normative and evaluative beliefs; fears, hopes, and other emotions; and so on.

These are, in general, *psychological attitudes* of the agent, each of which may be cited as *a* reason for why she chose or acted as she did. Of course, to be "correctly" or truly cited as reasons, psychological attitudes must play a role in the etiology of choice or action—they must influence choice or action in some manner or other that is not easy to specify. It is one thing to *have* a reason and another to choose or act *for* that reason. Jane may like river rafting and this may have been a reason for favoring Colorado, had she thought of it. But in fact, her mind was focused on skiing and visiting friends, and river rafting never entered into her decision. It was a reason she *had*, but not one *for* which she chose.[12]

Normally, there are many reasons *qua* psychological attitudes that influence an agent's choice or action. In everyday situations, we pick out one or several attitudes that seem crucial in answer to "Why?" questions, while assuming other uncited background reasons. Thus, we may cite Jane's belief that a friend would accompany her as a reason to choose Colorado, assuming she also *wants* the friend to accompany her; and we cite her desire to visit a friend in Oklahoma City, assuming she also *believes* that Oklahoma City is on her way to Colorado. As Aristotle pointed out, practical reasoning requires at least one cognitive premise (expressing what is believed) and one conative premise (expressing what is wanted or desired). In practice, it usually involves many premises of both kinds.

One way to answer the question of why Jane chose to vacation in Colorado is to cite her wants, beliefs, and other psychological attitudes. But another way is to simply cite the *contents* of the psychological attitudes. We could reply "because she *wanted* to do more skiing" or simply "in order *to do more skiing*." Here we have two senses of *reason* for choice or action—a reason *as psychological attitude* and a reason *as content* of that attitude. We may cite the want or what is wanted, a factual belief or what is believed, an intention or the purpose or goal intended, an evaluative belief or the item valued, and so on. Generally, when I speak of "reasons" hereafter without qualification, the psychological attitude sense will be meant. When the content sense of "reason" is meant, the qualification "in the content sense" will be added.

The primary usage of "reasons" as psychological attitudes is common in free will debates and reflects a certain dependence of the content sense upon the psychological attitude sense when it comes to explanations of choice or action. For the contents of wants, beliefs, intentions, and the like can only explain choice or action insofar as they are the contents of psychological attitudes that an agent actually has. It is only by being wanted, intended, and believed that reasons as contents can function in practical reasoning and explain actions—a point of singular importance for discussions of free will in which issues about the psychological springs of action are a major concern.

The term *motive* also appears regularly in free will debates along with *reason*; interestingly, these two terms are often interchangeable in such debates. The wants, beliefs, likes, interests, and other attitudes that are cited as Jane's reasons for choosing to vacation in Colorado can also be cited as her motives for choosing. And *motive*, like *reason*, is also ambiguous as between psychological attitude and content. A motive of Jane's may be described as either "wanting to see a friend" or just as "to see a friend."

Despite these parallels, some authors note that there are slight differences between the ordinary meanings of *reason* and *motive*,[13] which is not surprising, since etymologically the terms come from different directions. Roughly speaking, motives "move," while reasons "explain." Thus, it has been suggested that one can have reasons (but not motives) for choice or action that do not in fact move or motivate. But even this divergence is hard to pin down. Part of what might be meant is connected to the distinction made earlier between an agent's having a reason for choosing or acting and the agent's choosing or acting for that reason. The problem is that *motive* is ambiguous in this way also. One can have a motive for choosing something that, because it is not attended to, does not enter one's deliberation and does not influence one's choice.

If *reason* and *motive* diverge significantly, it is probably with respect to the "externalist" sense of having a reason, which thus far has not been discussed. Jane may have a reason in the externalist sense for going to a party because the man she loves will be there, but she is completely unaware of this and does not believe he is going. *His being there* is no content of any psychological attitude she actually has and therefore does not *move* her to choose or act (though it would, or should, move her *if* she believed it). So perhaps one could say that his being there is a reason for her going, but not yet a motive. By contrast, an "internalist" reason (in the content sense) is part of some psychological attitude (belief, desire, etc.) that the agent actually has and which can therefore at least potentially motivate the agent.

The problem here is that if externalist reasons do not motivate an agent because they are not the contents of psychological attitudes the agent actually has, neither can they be used to *explain* why the agent chose or acted as she did. The presence of the man she loved at the party would not enter into an explanation of Jane's choices or actions that night if she did not believe he was there. This explains why internalist reasons are the ones usually meant in debates about free action and free will, in which the concern is explaining why agents chose or acted as they did in terms of psychological attitudes they actually had. Our uses of "reason" and "motive" will therefore be internalist hereafter unless otherwise indicated.

The tendency toward convergence of *reason* and *motive* when they refer to internalist reasons is, I think, instructive. It has to do with the close connection between *explanation* and *motivation* of choice or action. While reasons "explain" and motives "move," reasons cannot explain actual choices or actions unless they in fact move or motivate the agent toward the choice made or action performed; and, conversely, if motives actually move toward choice or action, they should play a role in explanations of why the choices or actions occurred.

7. "Wills," "Voluntary," and "Involuntary"

As in many traditional writings on free will, we shall have occasion in subsequent chapters to speak of agents doing "what they will to do," and acting "voluntarily" or "willingly." These expressions are to be understood as follows.

> (W) An agent *wills* to do something at time t just in case the agent has reasons or motives at t for doing it that the agent wants to act on more than he or she wants to act on any other reasons (for doing otherwise).

This is a technical meaning for *wills* that turns out to be important for free will because it falls between the three senses of *will* discussed in section 5. On the one hand, according to W, "an agent's willing to do something" implies wanting or desiring to do it (desiderative will), but is stronger than mere wanting or desiring because it implies wanting it more than other alternatives. On the other hand, "intending" and "trying" (rational and striving will, respectively) usually imply "wanting more" in the sense of W, but there are cases of importance for free will in which these implications may fail, as we shall see. So "wills" in the sense of W is situated between the three meanings of *will* in a way that turns out to be important for free will.

"What the agent wills to do" in the sense of W is also related to the familiar distinction between *voluntary* and *involuntary* action. But the voluntary-involuntary distinction adds further considerations. In free will debates dating back to Aristotle, the voluntary is what is done "in accordance with one's will," and the involuntary what is done "against one's will."[14] This implies willing to do what one does, but that is not enough. It also implies doing it *for* the reasons you will to do it and in a manner that is not *coerced* or *compelled*. Thus, in traditional discussions of free will, the primary examples of involuntary actions are actions done under coercion or compulsion. Adding these considerations to W, we get

> (V) An agent acts *voluntarily* (or *willingly*) at t just in case, at t, the agent does what he or she wills to do (in the sense of W), for the reasons he or she wills to do it, and the agent's doing it and willing to do it are not the result of coercion or compulsion.

I want to emphasize that these definitions of *wills* and *voluntary* are not meant to beg any questions about free will and determinism. We shall have more to say about "wanting more" and acting "for reasons" in subsequent chapters, but neither of these notions by itself implies the absence of determinism. Nor, of course, does either imply the presence of determinism. W, for example, describes what it means for an agent to have a "stronger motive" (to want something more) at a given time, but it does not say anything about whether the agent will actually choose or act on that motive at the time or at a later time. Much less does W imply that agents must always choose or act on their strongest motive, a controversial doctrine to be considered later.[15] W merely tells us what it means to say that an agent *has* a stronger motive at a given time.

Similar remarks apply to the terms *coercion* and *compulsion* in V. We shall have more to say about these terms also in subsequent chapters, but the definition V leaves open the question of whether coercion and compulsion are to be interpreted in compatibilist or incompatibilist terms.[16] All that is assumed by V at this stage of our discussion is an ordinary understanding of coercion and compulsion based on typical cases. In typical cases of *coercion*, persons are forced to do something they would not otherwise voluntarily do. If a man hands over money to a thief holding a gun at his head, the man does what he most wants (i.e., wills) to do then and there, given his circumstances. He prefers handing over the money to suffering bodily harm or death. Nonetheless, his handing over the money is coerced, and not voluntary, because handing over the money is not something he would have most wanted to do, if the thief had not forced him into these unwelcomed circumstances against his will. In typical cases of *compulsion* (e.g., compulsive drinking), persons also do what they most want (or will) to do then and there, but their actions are not voluntary because they could not resist acting on the desires they act upon, even if they wanted to resist.

These familiar examples of coercion and compulsion leave open the question of whether the absence of coercion or compulsion implies the absence of determinism. If the man were *not* coerced by the thief, and handed over his money voluntarily as a gift, his action might nonetheless have been determined by his motives, though it was uncoerced. Likewise, if the drinker were not compulsive, he could resist his desire to drink, but whether the "could" of "could resist" is to be interpreted in a compatibilist or incompatibilist fashion remains an open question. So these preliminary definitions of *wills* and *voluntary* do not settle the Compatibility Question. Even if free actions are willed and voluntary, whether they must also be undetermined is a further question. That question is the subject of the next several chapters.

3

Responsibility

1. It Is up to Us (I): Alternative Possibilities

We turn now to the Compatibility Question. I have argued that incompatibilists need not overburden themselves by trying to argue that freedom in every significant sense is incompatible with determinism. They should concede that there are everyday freedoms—from constraint, coercion, and psychological compulsion, for example—that would be preferred to their alternatives even in a determined world. What incompatibilists should say is that these everyday freedoms are not the only ones worth wanting. There is another kind of freedom that cuts deeper than them and is not compatible with determinism. Free willists add that this deeper freedom is the freedom of the will understood as the power of agents to be ultimate creators and sustainers of their own ends or purposes.

Now when we look into the historical literature on free will to get a clearer picture of what this special kind of freedom requires, we find two conditions for free will turning up again and again that have led people to believe it is not compatible with determinism. These two conditions are often intertwined in historical debates and are only rarely distinguished. Often they are treated as different ways of expressing the same requirement. But I suggest that if we learn anything from historical debates about free will, it should be that these two conditions must be distinguished if the Compatibility Question is to be adequately addressed.

The best way to arrive at the two conditions is by reflecting on the expression "it is really up to us," which is often used to describe the kind of self-determination that free will requires. The first of the two conditions is by far the more familiar one to those aware of recent debates: an action is really up to the agent in the sense required by free will only if the agent "could have done otherwise," or, in other words, if there were "alternative possibilities" open to the agent.

Some quotations from different philosophers and periods will illustrate how widely acknowledged this condition is. Aristotle expresses it as clearly and succinctly as anyone by saying that "when acting is up to us, so is not acting" (1915: 1113b6). Plotinus asks whether an act can be "up to oneself" "if it is not [also] up to one to not do [it]."[1] Bramhall insists that free will requires not only the power to act, but "the power to act otherwise" (1844: 41). Thomas Reid says that the "power to produce any effect implies the power not to produce it" (1983: 523), and Kant argues that for true freedom "the act as well as its opposite must be within the power of the subject at the moment of its taking place" (1960: 45).

These are different ways of expressing the condition that an action (or omission) A at a time t is really "up to an agent" in the sense required by free will only if

> (AP) The agent has *alternative possibilities* (or can do otherwise) with respect to A at t in the sense that, at t, the agent *can* (has the *power* or *ability to*) do A and *can* (has the *power* or *ability to*) do *otherwise*.

We shall call this the "Alternative Possibilities (or AP) condition" hereafter, or simply AP. In the condition, the designation of an action A might stand for an omission as well as an action, since agents can also have the power to omit doing things when they could have done them. But actions will be our usual focus of attention when discussing the condition. When an action (or omission) is looked at retrospectively— when it has already taken place—AP implies that the agent "could have done otherwise." This familiar phrase will also be used at times to designate the condition.

Note that AP is stated as a necessary condition for free will, not a sufficient one. There is more to free will than alternative possibilities, as we shall see. But many people have thought that the existence of alternative possibilities is the characteristic of free will that makes it incompatible with determinism. For if determinism were true, it would seem that, given the past and the laws of nature, no alternative to the action performed would be possible; the future would not be open and the agent could not have done otherwise. But whether these implications actually follow depends on the kind of possibility involved in the AP condition and on the meaning of crucial terms such as *power, ability, can,* and *could.* Recent debates about the Compatibility Question have focused on these issues and they will be among the topics discussed in this chapter and the next.

2. It Is up to Us (II): Ultimate Responsibility

But I said that an adequate treatment of the Compatibility Question requires attention to *two* conditions in the historical literature on free will that seem to imply incompatibility. The second condition, which I will call the condition of Ultimate Responsibility, or UR, is less familiar than Alternative Possibilities or AP, and far less frequently discussed. Yet it is, to my mind, of even greater importance. One reason for the comparative neglect of Ultimate Responsibility is that the two conditions— AP and UR—are often intertwined in historical debates. Thinkers who mention one condition usually mention the other without always taking note of their differences.

Consider, for example, the historical figures cited earlier. Aristotle's claim that "when acting is up to us, so is not acting," is a succinct statement of the AP condition. But Richard Sorabji has argued (in a ground-breaking work on Aristotle's views about necessity, cause, and blame published in 1980) that Aristotle usually cites two conditions for an action's being "up to us" in the sense required by genuine responsibility or blameworthiness (pp. 233–4).[2] In addition to passages asserting alternative possibilities, according to Sorabji, there are others in which Aristotle asserts that "the concept of an action being up to us is connected . . . with the concept of our being, or having within us, the 'origin' (*arche*) of the action" (p. 234). This second condition puts the emphasis for being up to us not on the power to do otherwise, but on the *source* or *explanation* of the action that is actually performed; that source must be "in us."

For Aristotle the *arche* is the origin or source or cause of something, but also its explanation; and the passages in which he talks about the *arche* of voluntary actions being "within the agent" make clear that Aristotle is worried about whether agents are responsible for the characters and motives that are the sources (*archai*) of their actions.[3] For instance, while Aristotle holds that it may no longer be possible for a man of ingrained character not to be wicked, he also suggests that if the man is responsible for his wickedness, then he must at one time in the past have been responsible for the conditions that made him the way he is.[4]

In a similar vein, Plotinus states the AP condition, but also says that "noble and shameful actions of each thing must issue *from* the thing itself" and cannot issue from anything else.[5] Bramhall and Reid insist that free agents must be the ultimate sources of at least some the their own character-building choices and actions if they are to be truly responsible agents.[6] And Kant makes reference to this further condition when he says that a "man . . . must make or have made himself into whatever in the moral sense, whether good or evil, he is or is to become. Either [good or evil character] must be the effect of his free choice for otherwise he could not be held responsible for it and could therefore be neither morally good nor evil" (1960: 40).

I think that reflection on these and other historical sources yields a second important condition for free will. In an earlier work (1985), I called it the condition of "Sole or Ultimate Dominion" and argued that it was pivotal to debates about free will, though too often neglected in such debates. In subsequent writings, the condition underwent revision, and I began calling it "Ultimate Responsibility" or "UR," the title that is used here.[7] Though the UR condition has been neglected in recent debates in comparison with the AP, some philosophers have recognized the importance of UR and given it more than passing attention.[8] Two such philosophers worth mentioning among recent authors are Galen Strawson (1986) and Martha Klein (1990). Interestingly, both Strawson and Klein argue that the UR condition is unsatisfiable in principle (as do many other authors who recognize the condition), and they use this result to argue against incompatibilist theories of freedom and responsibility such as mine. But they do recognize the importance of what I call UR for traditional intuitions about free will, and I think they are correct in recognizing this.

Klein calls the condition in question the "Ultimacy-condition" and defines it as follows: "Agents should be ultimately responsible for their morally relevant decisions or choices — 'ultimately' in the sense that nothing for which they are not responsible should be the source [or cause] of their decisions or choices" (1990: 51). Strawson defines a similar condition for what he calls "true responsibility-entailing freedom" (the kind of freedom, he says, "that matters most to people — at least in so far as questions of morality are concerned" [1986: v]). Strawson's "true responsibility" and Klein's "ultimacy" are what I designate as "ultimate responsibility," defined as a condition for free will.

While the above statements capture the general idea of ultimate responsibility, it is not easy to give a precise statement of the condition. I have attempted numerous versions since the 1970s, the latest of which follows. A willed action is "up to the agent" in the sense required by free will only if the agent is ultimately responsble for it in the following sense.

> (UR) An agent is *ultimately responsible* for some (event or state) E's occurring only if (R) the agent is personally responsible for E's occurring in a sense which entails that something the agent voluntarily (or willingly) did or omitted,[9] and for which the agent could have voluntarily done otherwise,[10] either was, or causally contributed to, E's occurrence and made a difference to whether or not E occurred;[11] and (U) for every X and Y (where X and Y represent occurrences of events and/or states) if the agent is personally responsible for X, and if Y is an *arche* (or sufficient ground or cause or explanation)[12] for X, then the agent must also be personally responsible for Y.[13]

This is a complicated condition and we shall be unravelling its meaning throughout the book. To get a initial feel for it by example, suppose a choice issues from, or can be explained by, the agent's character and motives at the time it is made in such manner that, given this character and these motives, the agent's doing anything other than this act would be inexplicable. Then, to be ultimately responsible for the choice, according to U, the agent must be responsible for the character and motives from which it issued, which in turn entails, according to R, that some choices or actions the agent voluntarily or willingly performed in the past must have causally contributed to the agent's having the character and motives he or she now has.

Compare Aristotle's claim cited earlier that if a man is responsible for wicked acts issuing from his character, then he must at some time in the past have been responsible for forming this character. Or, consider Plotinus's argument against the Stoics that if the ultimate source or cause (*arche*) of our actions was not in us, but in some conditions that we did not produce, we would not be responsible for them.[14] Or consider Bramhall's claim that if Hobbes was right in saying that our good or evil deeds were caused by our characters, and God had made us the way we were, then the ultimate responsibility for our actions would be God's, not ours (1844: 30). In such manner, the UR condition is meant to capture the familiar notions that we alone are (to some degree at least) "authors of our own fate" and "captains of our own souls."

3. Responsibility and Ultimacy

UR associates a certain kind of responsibility (called ultimate responsibility) with free will, thereby introducing the complex subject of responsibility into debates about the Compatibility Question. The basic idea is that the *ultimate responsibility* lies where the *ultimate cause* is. This idea is expressed in two parts by UR. The first part "R" (for "responsibility") may be viewed as a base clause of the definition and the second part, "U" (for "ultimacy") as a recursive or backtracking clause (which is not to imply that the definition is recursive in the mathematical sense). U requires for ultimate responsibility that the responsibility required by R must "backtrack" to the sources of the agent's responsible actions.

The responsibility involved in R is designated "personal" responsibility in order to set aside issues about "collective" or "group" responsibility, in which persons are said to be responsible for the consequences of behavior of a group (a nation-state or race or ethnic group) simply because they are part of the group, whether or not they have done anything themselves to cause the consequences.[15] Whether such collective responsibility can exist apart from personal responsibility is a controversial matter. To account for individual blameworthiness, most people would require at least some minimal complicity on the part of the individual in the group behavior (e.g., not speaking out against atrocities or injustice). But this would mean contributing in some way, however remotely, to the consequences, which is the minimal condition for personal responsibility that R includes.

R also states that the person's contribution must be "voluntarily" or "willingly" performed, which is to be understood in terms of the definitions at the end of chapter 2. An agent acts voluntarily or willingly at a time, according to definition V, just in case, at the time, the agent does what the agent wills to do (in the sense of W) for the reasons the agent wills to do it, and the agent's doing and willing to do it are not coerced or compelled. To be adequate for the personal responsibility intended by UR, the agents' contributions toward making themselves what they are must be voluntary in this sense. They must be made in accordance with each agent's will and not against it.

But note that the "voluntariness" required by R is not of itself meant to settle issues about the compatibility of freedom and determinism. R states a minimal condition of voluntary contribution by agents toward making themselves what they are—a condition required by ultimate responsibility, but not of itself resolving issues that divide compatibilists and incompatibilists. Thus, if UR implies incompatibilism (an issue not yet resolved), it is by virtue of the entire condition, U + R, not by R alone. R says that the agents' contributions to being what they are must not be coerced or compelled, but it is noncommittal about whether coercion and compulsion are to be interpreted in compatibilist or incompatibilist terms. (Recall the related remarks about the definition V of voluntariness in chapter 2.)

Similarly, where R requires that agents "could have voluntarily done" something to make themselves different than they are, the "could have . . . done" may also be interpreted in compatibilist or incompatibilist terms. (For example, it might mean only that the agent would have done otherwise, if something in the past had been different than it was.) This supports the suspicion most readers are likely to have that the backtracking condition U is the pivotal (and most problematic) condition of UR. Nonetheless, U requires a base condition of responsibility to operate upon, and that is what R supplies. Moreover, R does not pretend to give a full account (necessary and sufficient conditions) for personal responsibility. It merely states a minimal condition of "voluntary contribution" by agents to what they are responsible for—a condition that turns out to be important for understanding ultimate responsibility. More will be said about the notion of personal responsibility in UR as we proceed. We shall see, among other things, that if the entire condition UR is satisfied, more is implied about the notion of personal responsibility involved than R alone tells us.

Now let me come clean here and say that I am fully aware that UR—considered now as a whole, U + R—is a highly problematic condition. I do not want to deny this fact for a moment. It is not surprising that Strawson, Klein, and other philosophers who have considered ultimate responsibility, such as Nagel, Watson, Honderich,

Wolf, Double, and Waller, believe it an unsatisfiable condition.[16] For one thing, UR appears to lead to a vicious regress. Indeed, the U (or Ultimacy) part of UR invites such a regress: for *any* X and Y, if you are personally responsible for X, and if Y is an *arche* or sufficient ground of X, then you must also be personally responsible for Y.[17] We shall also have more to say about the notion of an *arche* as we proceed,[18] but the basic idea is this: an *arche* or sufficient ground for an event is any set of conditions that explains why the event occurred here and now rather than not occurring here and now.[19] If our characters and motives (together with background conditions) provide an explanation for our actions in this sense, then we must, according to the U condition, be responsible for forming our characters and motives by earlier actions, and so on indefinitely. The regress would stop with actions that were not explained by our characters and (motives) (or by anything else, for that matter), but then in what sense would we be responsible for *such* actions?

This regress and the dilemma it poses have been recognized in one form or another throughout the history of debates about free will. (Hobbes, for example, made a big issue of it against Bramhall.) In recent philosophy, attempts have been made — the most elaborate by Galen Strawson (1986) — to state the regress more precisely and show why it is vicious. I do not deny that the regress presents serious problems for incompatibilists, and I can sympathize with those like Strawson who feel that as a result of it UR is not a satisfiable condition. Nonetheless, I am firmly convinced (and have been arguing for more than two decades) that UR *is* a necessary condition for free will, so that any attempt to make sense of free will must eventually come to grips with UR and show how it can be satisfied — if it can be satisfied at all. This is one of the tasks undertaken in Part II of this book, in which the Intelligibility Question is addressed.

Meanwhile, in Part I, we have begun our discussion of the Compatibility Question by noting that traditional intuitions about the incompatibility of free will and determinism can be traced to *two* conditions thought to be necessary for free will — namely, AP and UR. There is, to be sure, a great deal more to said about the meaning and implications of both these conditions. But this will be done as we address their relevance to the Compatibility Question in this and succeeding chapters. We must now ask for each of these conditions whether it is in fact necessary for free will and whether it does or does not imply (separately or in combination with the other condition) the incompatibility of free will and determinism.

4. Alternative Possibilities and Responsibility (I): Dennett

We begin with the Alternative Possibilities condition, or AP, and shall return to UR later. AP is by far the more familiar of the two conditions and the one that is most discussed in relation to the Compatibility Question. In contrast to UR, there has been an enormous amount of recent literature on the relation of Alternative Possibilities or "could have done otherwise," to determinism — so much literature, in fact, that the problem in dealing with it is to avoid overload. My main task in this chapter and the next will be to reveal the structure of recent controversies about Alternative Possibilities, trying, as far as possible, to separate the argumentative wheat from the chaff.

The case for incompatibility by way of AP involves two premisses:

1. The existence of alternative possibilities (or the agent's power to do otherwise) is a necessary condition for free will.
2. Determinism is not compatible with alternative possibilities. (It precludes the power to do otherwise.)

Since it follows from these premisses that free will and determinism are not compatible, the case against incompatibility must attack either premise 1 or 2. Obviously, the incompatibility claim 2 is pivotal to the argument, and it has received a great deal of critical attention, as one would expect. But a surprising fact about discussions of the Compatibility Question since 1970 is that premise 1 — which asserts that AP is necessary for free will — has also come under attack.

Well-known arguments by Harry Frankfurt and Daniel Dennett have challenged the claim that the power to do otherwise is in fact a necessary condition for free will. If these arguments are correct, the implications of AP for incompatibilism would be beside the point, because alternative possibilities would not in fact be required for genuinely free and responsible actions. Our first order of business, therefore, is to consider challenges to premise 1 — challenges to the claim that AP is necessary for free will — starting with Dennett's case against it, which is easier to grasp.

At the beginning of chapter 6 of *Elbow Room* (1984), Dennett says, "I have not yet touched the central issue of free will, for I have not yet declared a position on the 'could have done otherwise' principle: the principle that holds that one has acted freely and (and responsibly) only if one could have done otherwise" (p. 131). Dennett argues that this "widely accepted" principle (our AP) is false. Whatever the expression "could have done otherwise" may mean, he says, it is not what interests us "when we care about whether some act was freely or responsibly performed" (p. 132).

In defense of this, Dennett cites the case of Luther. When Luther said "Here I stand. I can do no other," on the occasion of his breaking with the church in Rome, he meant, according to Dennett, "that his conscience made it *impossible* for him to recant" (p. 133). Luther may have been wrong about this, Dennett adds, but that is not the point. For even if Luther was right and he could not have done otherwise, "we simply do not exempt someone from blame or praise for an act because we think he could do no other" (p.133). In saying "I can do no other," Luther was not avoiding responsibility for his act, according to Dennett, but taking full responsibility for it. So if we associate free will with moral responsibility, we cannot suppose that free will necessarily implies that the agent "could have done otherwise." AP would not be necessary for free will.

Dennett adds a personal example. Like most of us, he believes that he could never torture an innocent person for a thousand dollars. His background and character are such that it would be completely out of the question. Yet he sees no reason why his refusing such an offer should not be regarded as a morally responsible act. And so it would also be, he thinks, for the rest of us. Many of our everyday choices or actions flow directly from our characters and motives (as did Luther's), yet we regard them as morally praiseworthy, if they are good, and blameworthy, if bad. So, once again, if we associate free will with moral responsibility, free will does not require that we "could have done otherwise."

What people care about, Dennett says, when they assign free will and moral responsibility is not whether they or others could have done otherwise in particular cases, but whether the consequences of actions are good or bad *and* whether an agent's behavior can be *modified* by praising or blaming, rewarding or punishing. If the behavior of persons is not modifiable in these ways (as in the case of the addict or kleptomaniac), then we do suspect that they are not free and responsible agents. But Dennett thinks that the kinds of freedom that concern us in such cases—the "varieties of free will worth wanting," as he puts it, such as freedom from compulsion—are compatible with determinism.

5. Free Will and Responsibility

Can the Alternate Possibilities condition, or AP, be saved from this kind of criticism? Some critics of Dennett have argued that his account of free will and responsibility in *Elbow Room* is too narrowly pragmatic and consequentialist. For example, Gerald Dworkin (1986: 424) says "I believe that any attempt to forge as close a link between responsibility and modifiability as Dennett wants ignores those ascriptions of responsibility which are not oriented toward the future, but are, so to speak, for the record. And since they are for the record, justice requires that we pay attention to the details of a person's circumstances" and background when the person acted.

Dworkin is speaking from a compatibilist perspective and he thinks that Dennett's account of responsibility is too narrow even for compatibilists. But the point Dworkin is making is especially important for incompatibilist intuitions about responsibility and the AP condition. Dennett focuses on the beneficial consequences of practices of "holding" someone responsible or "accepting" responsibility for one's actions, and he thinks ascriptions of responsibility are justified by these beneficial consequences. But there is a further dimension of responsibility ascriptions, as Dworkin points out, having to do with whether agents *deserve* praise or blame, punishment or reward, for their actions; and this dimension requires that one take account of how the persons got to be the way they are. This further dimension of responsibility is also of critical importance, as it turns out, for understanding incompatibilist attitudes towards AP.

Consider Luther again. Incompatibilists need not deny Dennett's claim that Luther's "Here I stand" might be a morally responsible act, even if Luther "could have done no other" at the time of making it. To decide the issue, however, incompatibilists would insist that we have to know something about the circumstances and background of Luther's action that made him responsible or accountable for it. If Luther's affirmation did issue inevitably from his character and motives at the time it was made, then his moral accountability for it would depend on whether he was responsible *for being the sort of person he had become at that time.*

Those who know something about Luther's biography know about the long period of inner turmoil and struggle he endured in the years leading up to that fateful "Here I stand." By numerous difficult choices and actions during that period, Luther was gradually building and shaping the character and motives that issued in his act. If we have no hesitation in saying that he was responsible for the final affirmation, I think it is because we believe that he was responsible through many past choices and actions for making himself into the kind of man he then was. And, if this is so, the question of whether Luther could have done otherwise shifts backwards from the present act to the earlier choices and actions by which he formed his character and motives. If he is ultimately accountable for his present act, then at least some of these earlier choices or actions must have been such that he could have done otherwise with respect to them. If this were not the case, then what he was would have never truly been "up to him" because *nothing he could have ever done would have made any difference to what he was*.

The AP condition can thus withstand attacks like Dennett's, but only if we put a gloss to it. *Not all* of our morally responsible choices or actions (those for which we are truly praiseworthy or blameworthy) have to be such that we could have done otherwise with respect to them directly. Yet *some* of the choices or actions in our life histories must satisfy AP if we are to be ultimately morally responsible for anything we do. But the remarkable thing to notice about this argument is that it rescues AP as a necessary condition for some free actions *by invoking UR*. When we grant that Luther could be responsible for his final affirmation, despite its being determined, only if he was responsible through past choices and actions for making himself into the kind of man he then was, we are invoking U of UR. And when we say that he could not have been responsible for making himself into the kind of person he then was if "nothing he could have ever done" would have "made any difference" in what he was, we are invoking R of UR.

Rather than hide the appeal to UR in this argument about Luther, I want to bring it out into the open, because I think it is of the utmost importance. I do not believe that the role of AP in discussions of free will can be fully understood apart from UR. Recall the earlier claim that the two conditions were often intertwined in historical discussions of free will. There is a good reason the two conditions have been intertwined—but it is not because there is no distinction between them. Rather, the reason is that both are involved in free will, and their roles are connected. The argument of this section is the first piece of evidence for this claim. It allows us to say that if UR is also required by free will, then free will would not require that *all* responsible actions satisfy AP, but it would require that *some* responsible actions in an agent's life history satisfy AP.

6. Alternative Possibilities and Responsibility (II): Frankfurt

Another challenge to the AP condition was initiated by a paper written by Harry Frankfurt in 1969, which has generated a lot of controversy. Frankfurt attacks the principle that "a person is morally responsible for what he has done only if he could have done otherwise" (our AP), which he calls the "principle of alternative possibilities." The original statement of Frankfurt's argument requires that we imagine some unusual circumstances.

> Suppose someone—Black let us say—wants Jones to perform a certain action. Black is prepared to go to considerable lengths to get his way, but he prefers to avoid showing his hand unnecessarily. So he waits until Jones is about to make up his mind . . . and he does nothing unless it is clear to him . . . that Jones is going to decide to do something *other* than what he [Black] wants him to do. If it does be-

come clear that Jones is going to decide to do something else, Black takes effective steps to ensure that Jones . . . does what he [Black] wants. (p. 835)

To guarantee Black's power, Frankfurt says, we might imagine him having a potion that can be administered to work his will, or imagine him as a neurosurgeon with direct control over Jones's brain and intimate knowledge of Jones's proclivities. The point of the example is this: Jones cannot do otherwise because Black will not let him. Yet Jones might decide on his own to do what Black wants, in which case Black would not intervene. Frankfurt's claim is that if Jones does act on his own and Black does not intervene, then Jones would be responsible for what he did even though he *could not have done otherwise* (because Black would not have allowed it). For Jones would have acted from his own motives and for his own reasons, and no one would have interfered with his choice.

"Frankfurt scenarios" all have this structure. The agent would, like Jones, be prevented from doing otherwise if he was about to do otherwise (say, by a "Frankfurt controller" like Black), but he goes ahead and acts on his own without interference. Even a conscious controller is not necessary to the examples, as David Blumenfeld (1971) has emphasized.[20] For the role played by Black could be played by some natural mechanism (say, in Jones's brain) that would prevent him from choosing otherwise if he were about to do so. Thus, Frankfurt scenarios can be generalized: the controller *or* the mechanism would make Jones do what he did anyway, but Jones does it on his own, and the controller never acts or the mechanism is never activated.

The literature on Frankfurt scenarios and what they prove is now so large that it would take an entire book to do justice to it. But I think we can discern a common pattern in the various responses to the examples that shows how incompatibilists could respond to them.[21] Suppose that A is the action that the controller Black wants Jones to perform (it might be, say, voting for a presidential candidate) and suppose Jones does A on his own without Black's interfering. Many responses to Frankfurt (of which Peter van Inwagen's is the best known) have taken the following general form. If Jones is responsible in this case, it is because he *did A on his own* (i.e., of his own free choice, without interference from Black). But Jones *could* have done other than that: he could have done other-than-A-on-his-own by not choosing or trying to do A and forcing Black to intervene. If Black intervened, to be sure, Jones would still have done A, but he would not have done A-on-his-own. So, responsibility and could-have-done-otherwise are not disconnected after all. Where Jones is responsible (for doing-A-on-his-own), he could have done other than that. And where he could not have done otherwise (with respect to doing-A, simply), he is not responsible.

It seems to me that this response has merit, but gets only part of the picture. Jones is indeed *responsible* for doing-A-on-his own, and that is something with respect to which he *could* have done otherwise. It is also true that he *could not* have done other than A. But the final step in the above argument is problematic. For it is implausible to add that Jones is therefore *not responsible* for doing A even when he does A on his own. This step too artificially separates responsibility for doing-A-on-one's-own from responsibility for doing A. In general, if we are responsible for doing something on our own, we are responsible for doing it. And this seems also to hold in Jones's case. If Jones does A-on-his-own (i.e., if Black stays out of the picture and does not interfere), there is no good reason to say that Jones is not responsible for doing A. But that means Frankfurt's original problem remains: Jones can be responsible for doing A even though he could not have done *other than* A.

Do all responses to Frankfurt examples require an artificial separation of responsibility for doing-A-on-one's-own from responsibility for doing A? An alternative has been suggested by John Martin Fischer (1982), who has contributed as much as any contemporary philosopher to our understanding of the issues of control and responsibility surrounding these examples.[22] Fischer calls responses to Frankfurt that take the form of the argument just given "associationist" responses, by which he means that they insist on associating responsibility and could-have-done-otherwise in a very strong way: if a person is responsible for an action, the person must have been able to do otherwise with respect *that particular action*. Thus, if Jones cannot do other than A, the associationist must (counterintuitively) say that Jones is not responsible for A, even when Jones does it on his own and Black does not interfere.

Fischer argues that this part of the associationist approach does not work, and I agree. We should, as he suggests, simply give up the associationist requirement that moral responsibility for a given action always implies that the agent has the power to do otherwise with respect to that particular action. But notice that, from the point of view of this chapter, *we have already found good reasons to give up this requirement* in the response to Dennett. Luther may be morally responsible for his "Here I stand" even if he could not have done otherwise with respect to *that* action itself, so long as he was responsible for making himself the sort of person he then was by virtue of other actions or choices in his past with respect to which he could have done otherwise.[23]

In short, we salvaged the AP condition in response to Dennett by invoking the UR condition, and I suggest that incompatibilists about moral responsibility should do the same in response to Frankfurt.[24] When acting on his own, Jones would be morally responsible for doing A, even if he could not have done otherwise with respect to A itself, so long as he was responsible for making himself the sort of person he then was by virtue of other choices or actions in his life history with respect to which he could have done otherwise. Black's noninterference is required, of course, but it is not sufficient to establish Jones's responsibility. We also have to know facts about Jones's life: how he acted from his own character and motives, and *how he got to be the way he is*.

If this strategy is followed, AP is saved once again by putting a gloss on it that invokes UR. Not all of the choices or actions for which we have ultimate moral responsibility (in the sense of the UR) have to be such that we could have done otherwise with respect to those choices or actions directly. But some of the choices or actions in our life histories must be such that we could have done otherwise with respect to them, if we are to have ultimate moral responsibility at all. For if this were not so, then nothing we could have ever done would have made any difference to what we had become, whether of good or evil character. The Alternative Possibilities condition would thus be required for free will and ultimate responsibility generally, though every particular act of free will need not satisfy it.

What if a Frankfurt controller were present throughout the entire lifetime of an agent, but never intervened, so that the agent did everything on his or her own, yet never could have done otherwise?[25] Would this undermine the present strategy of salvaging AP for some free actions by way of UR? The answer, interestingly enough, turns out to be no. I shall argue in subsequent chapters that if a controller was present throughout an agent's entire lifetime, but never intervened, *and UR were satisfied*, then *some* of the actions in the agent's life history would be such that the agent could in fact have done otherwise despite the presence of the controller.[26] Conversely, if the controller intervened in these actions, UR would not be satisfied by the agent for those actions, and the controller, not the agent, would be "ultimately responsible" for them. So, whenever UR *is* satisfied for an agent, *some* of the actions in an agent's life history would have to satisfy AP (just as I have been arguing), even on the assumption of an ever-present, nonintervening controller.[27]

7. Conclusion

We began this chapter by discussing two conditions for free will that have led people to believe that it is incompatible with determinism—the Alternative Possibilities condition, or AP, and the condition of Ultimate Responsibility, or UR. After a preliminary discussion of the two conditions, we turned to the task of addressing, for each of the conditions, the question of whether it was in fact required by free will and whether it (either separately or together with the other condition) implied the incompatibility of free will and determinism.

Beginning with the AP condition, we then considered recent arguments by Dennett and Frankfurt that AP is not in fact required by free will. The conclusion drawn from this discussion constitutes the first piece of evidence for an important theme of this book—the interrelatedness of AP and UR in debates about free will and the consequent importance of UR to these debates. For the conclusion was that if UR is also invoked as a necessary condition for free will, then (contra Dennett and Frankfurt) AP is required by at least *some* responsible actions of agents who have free will, though AP need not be satisfied by all of the agents' responsible actions. In other words, if we introduce UR into the debate along with AP, we can concede to Dennett and Frankfurt that responsible actions need not always be such that the agents could have done otherwise with respect to those actions. But we can concede this without also conceding that AP is irrelevant to responsible action generally, or to free will.

If AP is thus retained as a requirement for *some* acts of free will, we can go on to ask (as we shall in the next chapter) whether AP implies the incompatibility of free will and determinism for such acts, evaluating recent arguments claiming that it does. If these arguments for incompatibilism based on AP are correct, free will would require indeterminism for at least some responsible actions and would be incompatible with determinism. But we must also keep in mind that AP has been defended in this chapter as a necessary condition for free will by invoking UR. So we must go on in chapters 5 and 6 to ask whether UR is also necessary for free will, whether it implies incompatibilism, and indeed, whether UR is intelligible at all. Only in this way, I believe, can the Compatibility Question be fully addressed. For I hold—in opposition to many contemporary incompatibilists—that the case for incompatibilism cannot be made on the basis of AP alone. It must also invoke UR.

4

Alternative Possibilities

1. The Consequence Argument: van Inwagen

The most widely discussed argument for the incompatibility of freedom and determinism during the past twenty-five years makes use of the Alternative Possibilities, or AP, condition. It is an attempt to spell out commonly held intuitions that determinism is incompatible with the "power to do otherwise." The argument in question has been formulated in various ways by Carl Ginet (1966), David Wiggins (1973), Peter van Inwagen (1975) and James Lamb (1977), and (in a theological form) by Nelson Pike (1965). Its most widely discussed version is by van Inwagen, who calls it the "Consequence Argument," a title that has gained currency and will be used here. Michael Slote (1982), John Martin Fischer (1988), and others have described the similarities between different versions of the Consequence Argument, suggesting that they are variations of a single line of reasoning and probably all stand or fall together— a view that is widely held.

Van Inwagen, who offers three versions of the argument in *An Essay on Free Will* (1983), regards the three as versions of the same basic argument, which he states as follows:

> If determinism is true, then our acts are the consequences of the laws of nature and events in the remote past. But it is not up to us what went on before we were born, and neither is it up to us what the laws of nature are. Therefore the consequences of these things (including our present acts) are not up to us. (1983: 16)

The best way to proceed with our discussion is to regard *this* as the Consequence Argument and to view the attempts of various authors to refine this line of reasoning as versions of the argument. It is likely that the line of reasoning described in this quotation has fueled incompatibilist intuitions for centuries, and I suspect that a few traditional philosophers had an inkling of the formal structure of the argument itself (Duns Scotus is a possible example).[1] But concerted attempts to formalize the above argument and lay bare its presuppositions were not made until the past twenty-five years, and the results of these efforts have been among the important recent advances in debates about free will mentioned in chapter 1.

We shall focus on a modification of the most widely discussed version of the Consequence Argument by van Inwagen and shall mention other versions in passing.[2] The story of debates about the argument since 1970 is a complex and tangled one, and it is easy to get lost in the details. But if we stick to the main lines of debate, I think we can begin to understand the story's meaning.

The argument attempts to show that if determinism is true, no agent could have done otherwise, which would imply in turn (given the AP condition) that no one has free will. In order to formalize the argument, van Inwagen (1975) introduces a special idiom that is useful for talking about an agent's powers or abilities. Suppose you move your hand at a time t. Then the claim that "you could have done otherwise at t" translates into van Inwagen's idiom as "you could have *rendered false the proposition* that you moved your hand at t." This is an unconventional way of speaking, but it allows one to talk about powers or abilities in complicated cases, which is what the argument requires. We can express the idiom in a general way as follows: where "Q" is a proposition (e.g., "agent a's hand moves at t") and "-Q" its negation ("a's hand does not move at t"),

$P_{at}(-Q)$ = df. agent a at t can (has the power or ability to) render Q false

"$P_{at}(. . .)$" may then be used as a general formula for expressing an agent's powers or abilities at any time. With it, we can also say

$P_{at}(Q)$ = df. agent a at t can (has the power or ability to) render Q *true*

—which ascribes the power to the agent to bring something about, just as "$P_{at}(-Q)$" ascribes the power "to do otherwise." Much of the debate about the Consequence Argument centers upon interpretations of expressions of these kinds—not surprisingly, because they represent the critical terms of the argument, *can, power,* and *ability*.

We now turn to the argument. Let "E" designate the proposition that your right hand moves at t. Let "L" be a conjunction of the laws of nature, and "H" be a conjunction of true propositions describing circumstances (of the history of the world) obtaining prior to your existence.

1. If determinism is true, then the conjunction L & H entails E.
2. If you can do other than raise your right hand at t, then $P_{yt}(-E)$ (you can render E false).
3. If $P_{yt}(-E)$ (you can render E false) and L & H entails E (E is determined), then $P_{yt}(-[L \& H])$ (you can render L & H false).
4. But $P_{yt}(-L)$ is not possible. (You cannot render L [the laws of nature] false.)
5. And $P_{yt}(-H)$ is not possible. (You cannot render H [events in the past] false.)
6. Therefore $P_{yt}(-[L \& H])$ is not possible.
7. Therefore, $-P_{yt}(-E)$. (You cannot do other than raise your right hand at t.)

If this argument is sound, it can be generalized for all agents, times, and events to show that if determinism is true, no one could have done otherwise, and thus, assuming AP, that determinism is incompatible with free will.

Premise 1 follows from the definition of determinism and expresses the intent of the first line of van Inwagen's informal statement of the Consequence Argument—"if determinism is true, then our acts are the consequences of the laws of nature and events in the remote past." Premise 2 simply translates the power or ability to do otherwise (required by AP) into the idiom of "rendering a proposition false." Premises 4 and 5 say, respectively, that you cannot change or falsify a law of nature and cannot alter the past (or falsify a true proposition about the past). Together, 4 and 5 express the claim of the informal argument that "it is not up to us what went on before we were born, and neither is it up to us what the laws of nature are." Premise 6 makes what van Inwagen regards as the noncontroversial claim that if you cannot change the laws of nature and cannot change the past, then you cannot change the conjunction of the laws of nature and the past. And step 7 draws the appropriate conclusion. Premise 3 — perhaps the most controversial of the argument — expresses a principle that will be discussed in the next section.

2. Transfer of Power Principles

Most philosophers who have evaluated this argument for incompatibilism have granted its logical validity. Criticism has focused on the premises, especially 3, 4, and 5 (and occasionally 6). Soon after van Inwagen stated the argument in this form, compatibilists pointed out that the argument would fail if the agent's power to do otherwise (or to render a proposition false) was interpreted in ways that compatibilists tend to favor. Most compatibilists from Hobbes to the present would interpret "You could have done other than move your hand" in a conditional way: "You *would* have done other than move your hand, *if* you had chosen, or wanted or tried to do so."

Such conditional accounts of *can* or *power* were not invented to thwart the Consequence Argument. They were popular among compatibilists long before modern versions of the Consequence Argument came along because they seem to express what compatibilists think it means to be free: being free, they believe, means having the power or ability to do what you will (choose or want or try) to do; and this presupposes the absence of impediments (constraints, coercion, compulsion) preventing you from doing something, if you willed to do it. But, while conditional accounts of *can* or *power* favored by compatibilists were not created to undermine the Consequence Argument, they *would* undermine it, if correct. One way to show this is to focus on the crucial premise 3 of the argument.

> 3. If P_{yt} (-E) and L & H entails E, then P_{yt} (-[L & H]).

This says, "If you can render it false that your hand moves at t, and the laws of nature together with propositions about the past entail that your hand moves at t, then you can render false the conjunction of propositions expressing the laws of nature and describing the past." This premise is a special case of a general principle that van Inwagen states as follows (formulated here in terms of "P_{at} [-. . .]"):

> (TP-) If $P_{(a)(t)}$ (-R) and Q entails R, then $P_{(a)(t)}$ (-Q).

"For every agent a and time t, if a can at t render R false, and Q entails R, then a can at t render Q false." Van Inwagen says that "this principle seems to be analytic. For if Q entails R, then" not-R entails not-Q; and it seems that if an agent can render R false, the agent can render false anything that logically follows from the falsity of R (1975: 53).

But while the principle does seem intuitively true, it has been controversial. We may think of it as a "Transference of Power" (or TP) principle, since it says that the agent's power can be transferred through logical entailment. (Logicians would say the operator "P_{at} [. . .] is closed under logical entailment.) Thus, an equivalent TP principle could be stated in positive form:

(TP+) If $P_{(a)(t)}$ (Q) and Q entails R, then $P_{(a)(t)}$ (R).

"For every a and t, if a has the power at t to render Q true and Q entails R, then a has the power at t to render R true."[3]

On the surface at least, such TP principles are quite plausible, and we may sympathize with van Inwagen's contention that they seem analytic. Consider, for example, an instance of TP+: if you can arrive at Austin by midnight, and your arriving in Austin entails arriving in the capitol of Texas, then you can arrive in the capitol of Texas by midnight. Or, consider this instance of TP-: if you can do something that renders false the claim that nothing can go faster than the speed of light, and the laws of nature entail that nothing can go faster than the speed of light, then you can render the laws of nature false.

But if we interpret "P_{at} (. . .)" — and hence *can* or *power* — in the conditional way favored by compatibilists, these TP principles will fail in some cases, including the case of premise 3 of the Consequence Argument. To see this, consider that the antecedent clause of 3 contains the statement "P_{yt} (-E)" — "you can at t render it false that your hand moves at t" — which, on the conditional account of *can*, becomes

(i) You will render it false that E (your hand moves at t), *if* you choose or want or try to do so (i. e. by refraining from moving it).

But this can obviously be true, even if E is determined. For it may have been true that your hand would not have moved, *if* you had chosen to refrain from moving it, even though it was determined that you did not in fact choose to refrain. So the antecedent clause of premise 3 can be true on a conditional interpretation of *can*. That is to say, it can be true both that "you can render it false that your hand moves, *if* you choose. . ." *and* that "your hand moves is determined." But the consequent clause of 3, by contrast, will remain false *even on* the conditional interpretation of *can*. For on the conditional interpretation, the consequent clause of 3 would say

(ii) You will render a law or nature or the past false at t, if you choose or want or try to do so.

But, as van Inwagen himself concedes, it is doubtful that you or anyone could falsify a law of nature or change the past, *even if* you chose or wanted or tried to do so. As he puts it, "if someone chooses to render false . . . a law" of nature or the past, "then surely he will fail" (1975: 58). But then, on a conditional analysis of *can*, the antecedent clause of premise 3 of the Consequence Argument can be true while its consequent is false, and premise 3 itself is false.[4]

This kind of objection to the Consequence Argument was made by many of its early compatibilist critics.[5] But incompatibilist defenders of the argument, like van Inwagen and Carl Ginet, took a tough line in response. They said that if conditional analyses of *can* and *power* favored by compatibilists invalidate premise 3 of the argument (and invalidate the TP principles on which it is based), *so much the worse for conditional analyses*. In a response to one critic, Michael Slote, van Inwagen put it this way: "It is obvious that if 'can' statements are, as so many compatibilists allege, a certain sort of disguised conditional, then my argument for the incompatibility of free will and determinism is either invalid or has false premises" (1990: 287). But he adds, "so much the worse for" conditional analyses. Van Inwagen and Ginet (1990) think that Transference of Power principles, like premise 3 (in the various forms in which they have stated them) are more intuitively plausible than any compatibilist analysis of *can*. If conditional analyses should falsify intuitively plausible principles about an agent's powers such as premise 3 of the Consequence Argument and the TP principles, they argue, that is further evidence against conditional analyses, which are subject to other well-known objections anyway (objections we shall consider shortly).

Here is the first evidence of an impasse that has plagued discussions of the Consequence Argument for the past two decades. Compatibilists claim the argument fails if you interpret *can* and *power* in the ways they favor. Incompatibilists retort that this is hardly surprising, since conditional interpretations of *can* and *power* favored by compatibilists are designed to render the power to do otherwise compatible with determinism. So incompatibilists charge that compatibilists are begging the question by importing conditional interpretations into the Consequence Argument. But on the other side, numerous compatibilist and other critics of the argument, such as Slote, Watson, Fischer, Lewis, Berofsky, Horgan, Flint, C. Hill, Foley, Gallois, Narveson, Vihvelin, and others charge that incompatibilists are begging the question by *ruling out* compatibilist interpretations of *can* and *power*.[6] As Thomas Flint puts it, while no compatibilist analysis of *can* has gained universal acceptance, it "would . . . constitute the height of unfairness" to assume as a starting point in discussions of the Consequence Argument that "any such [compatibilist] analysis must fail" (1987: 439). Incompatibilists are presenting a logical argument that is supposed to demonstrate the incompatibility of free will and determinism. If there are falsifying interpretations of the premises that cannot be definitively ruled out, it fails as a demonstration.

This impasse has predictably led to heated debates about the meanings of *can* and *power*. But before turning to these debates, we must look at another familiar line of criticism of the Consequence Argument that also raises questions about *can* and *power*.

3. Changing the Laws or the Past: Lewis and Others

The first wave of attacks on the Consequence Argument targeted premise 3 and the Transference of Power principles related to it. The second wave targeted premises 4 and 5. It may seem absurd, on the face of it, to claim that by doing something here and now, an agent can falsify the laws of nature (which is to deny 4) or change the past (which is to deny 5). But again, the whole matter turns on what it means to say that an agent "can" or has the "power" to do otherwise or to render something false (i.e., $P_{at}[-\ldots]$).

In his influential paper "Are We Free to Break the Laws?" (1981), David Lewis raised questions about premise 4 of the Consequence Argument by suggesting that there were two possible meanings of "could have rendered false" relevant to assessing the claim that someone could render a law of nature false.

> Let us say that I could have rendered a proposition false in the weak sense if and only if I was able to do something such that, if I did it, the proposition would have been falsified (though not necessarily by my act, or by any event caused by my act). And let us say that I could have rendered a proposition false in the strong sense, if and only if I was able to do something such that, if I did it, the proposition would have been falsified, either by my act itself or by some event caused by my act. (p. 297)

Lewis concedes that we cannot falsify or break a law of nature in the *strong* sense. Our act cannot directly *be*, or *cause*, a law-breaking event. While there are disagreements about what a law of nature is, he says, there is agreement on the fact that "a genuine law is at least an absolutely unbroken regularity" (p. 292). If a supposed regularity were actually violated by an act, it would not *be* a law of nature. This is why it "seems analytic" to say that you cannot render false a law of nature. But it does not follow, Lewis insists, that you cannot render false a law of nature in the *weak* (or noncausal) sense. For "could render false" in the weak sense would mean only that if you had acted otherwise, some law of nature would have been different. It would not mean that you had made or caused the law to be different by your action.

Lewis therefore insists that, while one cannot render a law false in the strong sense, one *can* render a law false in the weak sense. And he thinks that is all a compatibilist has to say to refute premise 4 and the Consequence Argument. For being able to falsify a law in the weak sense is compatible with determinism, since all it means is that if you had acted otherwise (contrary to fact), the actual world *would* have been different as regards its laws. The intuitive plausibility of premise 4 comes from reading it in the strong sense, according to Lewis, whereas compatibilists can and should read it in the weak sense, in which case it is false.

Meanwhile, premise 5 of the Consequence Argument was subjected to similar attacks by other critics.[7] For example, John Martin Fischer (1983), writing independently of Lewis, argued that a distinction similar to Lewis's distinction between strong and weak senses of rendering false can also be applied to propositions about the past. One could thereby also reject premise 5 without having to accept suspect notions of backward causation or backward time travel. One could concede that we are powerless to falsify the past in the strong sense, which would mean initiating a causal sequence in the present that would actually cause some change in the past. But it would not follow that we could not render false propositions about the past in the weak sense. For that would mean only that we could now perform some action, such that if we were to perform it the past would have been different in some way from what it actually was. The intuitive plausibility of premise 5, according to "multiple pasts compatibilists" (as Fischer [1986] calls those who take this line[8]), comes from reading "rendering false" in the strong (causal) sense, whereas compatibilists can and should read it in the weak (noncausal) sense, in which case premise 5 is false.[9]

4. An Impasse Once Again

These parallel attacks upon premises 4 and 5 of the Consequence Argument have
led to a similar impasse between incompatibilists and compatibilists as the attacks
upon premise 3. One can imagine the following response by defenders of the Consequence Argument (which is a reconstruction of the response some of them have
actually made):[10] "Why should we accept the weak (or noncausal) reading of *can* or
power rather than the strong (or causal) reading? The weak reading is not at all intuitive in the context of the Consequence Argument. If you ask ordinary persons whether
they believe they can change the past or falsify a law of nature, they will surely take
you to mean it in the strong (causal) sense and deny that it is possible. (They may
have thought a little about miracles and may wonder whether God can change the
laws or the past, but they will deny that they themselves can do these things.) Now
you compatibilists say that ordinary persons are confused, or at least unclear, about
these matters and that a proper reading of 'can render false' ought to be the weak
reading. But we incompatibilists see no confusion or unclarity here at all.

"We incompatibilists do understand Lewis's *distinction* between weak and strong
senses, but having taken note of this distinction, it is clear to us that the proper reading of the premises of the Consequence Argument is the strong sense of 'can render
false.' The only thing that could recommend the weak sense to anyone, as we see it,
is a prior commitment to compatibilism. For if determinism were true, then an agent
would have actually done otherwise, only if the past or the laws of nature had been
different in some way—for example, if the agent had chosen otherwise, believed
otherwise, or was otherwise in different circumstances prior to action. In this respect,
the weak sense of 'can render false' accords nicely with compatibilist interpretations
of *can* and *power*. But it has nothing further to recommend it as the proper interpretation of the premises of the Consequence Argument, if one is not already committed to compatibilism. As incompatibilists, our commitment to the argument rests upon
the intuitive plausibility of its premises when read in the natural, *strong* sense of *can*
and *power*—whereby they mean the ability to bring something about or cause something to be by virtue of one's actions."

But Lewis, Fischer, and others have argued that appealing to the strong sense of
"can render false" (or "can do otherwise") will not necessarily save the Consequence
Argument either.[11] To be sure, premises 4 and 5 would be true in the strong sense,
but there would then be problems, they argue, with either premise 3 or 6. If they are
right about this, the Consequence Argument would fail, though for different reasons,
on *either* the weak *or* strong reading of "can render false." But are they right? What
is the problem with premises 3 or 6 of the Consequence Argument, if "can render
false" is read in the strong sense?

Suppose you are able to refrain from moving your hand (E) in the strong sense.
According to the Lewis definition, this means that you "are able to do something
such that, if you did it, E would have been falsified either by your act itself, or by
some event caused by your act." In the present case, if you refrained from moving
your hand, you would falsify E (that your hand moves) *by the very act* of refraining
itself, thus satisfying the strong-sense reading. Now, if premise 3 were also true in the
strong sense—so that power in the strong sense was transferred through entailment—

and if L & H (i.e., statements about the laws and past circumstances) entailed E , it would follow that you could render false the conjunction of the laws and the past *in the strong sense*. But this falsifies premise 6, which says on this reading that you *cannot* render the conjunction of L & H false in the strong sense.

The denial of 6 admittedly seems counterintuitive, for remember that in the strong sense, premises 4 and 5 are assumed to be true. It is assumed that you cannot falsify a law of nature (4) and cannot falsify the past (5) in the strong sense. Therefore it seems odd to say that you *can* falsify the conjunction of the laws and the past (the denial of 6). But suppose we react to this oddness by refusing to accept the denial of 6 when 4 and 5 are true. Then, according to the argument of Lewis and Fischer we are now considering, doubt would be cast *on premise 3*. For the denial of 6 results from the transference of power through entailment allowed by premise 3. That is, it is premise 3 which allows one to say that if you could have done other than move your hand and your hand's moving was determined by laws and the past, *then* you could have rendered false a law of nature or the past (which is the denial of 6). So, if the denial of 6 is wrong, premise 3 must be rejected on this reading, that is, on the strong reading of *can* or *power*. One of the steps, 6 *or* 3, must be false, and the Consequence Argument would fail either way.

This argument is sound, if certain assumptions are made. But it contains an easily overlooked assumption that incompatibilists will not concede. To see this, consider how incompatibilists are likely to react to the above argument. "Note," they will say, "that premise 3 makes two assumptions that lead to the denial of 6. Premise 3 says '*if* (i) you could have done other than move your hand, and (ii) your hand's moving was determined by laws and the past, then you could have rendered false a law of nature or the past' (which is the denial of 6). But to us incompatibilists, assuming *at the outset* that (i) 'you could have done other than move your hand' *under the assumption that* (ii) 'your hand's moving was determined' begs the whole question. For it means that the power to do other than move your hand that is assumed in the antecedent of 3 must be a *compatibilist* power—which means in turn that the argument against 3 succeeds only if one assumes at the outset a compatibilist interpretation of the power to do otherwise.[12] Since we incompatibilists [this response continues] think that Transference of Power principles, like 3, are more intuitively plausible than any compatibilist accounts of 'could have done otherwise,' we would draw a different conclusion from the argument. We would say that if, in the strong sense, 6 is true, and hence the consequent of 3 is false, and if your moving your hand is determined, then it is false *that (i) you could have done other than move your hand* in the strong sense to begin with. And this, of course, is exactly the intent of the Consequence Argument—to show the falsity of 'you could have done otherwise,' in the strong sense, if your action was determined."

It now looks as if we have arrived at the familiar impasse over the Consequence Argument by a different route. On the one hand, its defenders say, like van Inwagen and Ginet, that the critics are begging the question by illicitly assuming compatibilist interpretations of "can do otherwise" (or "can render false") in the argument. On the other hand, critics such as Lewis, Fischer, and Slote insist that they have at least shown how *those who accept compatibilist interpretations* of *can* or *power* may reject the Consequence Argument by rejecting one or another of its premises 3, 4, 5, or

6.[13] The critics have indeed shown this, but an impasse remains about which interpretations of *can* and *power*—compatibilist or incompatibilist—are appropriate for the argument.

Though my intuitions in this debate (not surprisingly) are on the side of incompatibilists such as van Inwagen and Ginet, I have been troubled for a long time by this impasse. It will not do for us incompatibilists to bludgeon our opponents with our intuitions (or for compatibilists to do the same to us). There may be some satisfaction in table pounding and hand waving, but not much progress. A better strategy, it seems to me, would be to look more deeply into the intuitions that lie behind the disagreements in the hope of seeing *why* incompatibilists and compatibilists differ so radically about the meanings of *can* and *power*. To this task I now turn.

5. Conditional Analyses of "Can" (I): Austin

Though other paths might be followed in the complex debates about the Consequence Argument, I am firmly convinced that all known paths lead to the same conclusion as the one we have just arrived at: the Consequence Argument will succeed *unless* some compatibilist account of the power or ability to do otherwise (render false) should turn out to be the correct one. We therefore turn our attention to compatibilist accounts of power, and to recent debates generally about the meanings of *can*, *power*, and "could have done otherwise." Standard compatibilist analyses of these expressions since Hobbes have been "conditional" analyses and they provide a useful point of departure. Conditional analyses of *can* and "could have done otherwise" have been much discussed in the past few decades and have been subjected to some revealing criticisms.

According to the conditional analyses most commonly favored by compatibilists, "can" or "could" statements about powers and abilities, such as

(C) You could have done otherwise

are to be interpreted as "would . . . if" statements, of the form

(WI) You *would* have done otherwise, *if* you had willed or chosen or wanted to do otherwise.

Different terms are used in the "if" clauses of such analyses by different authors—*chosen, wanted, tried, believed, intended, had different motives*, and so on. The likelihood is that different terms would be appropriate for different cases, depending upon the agent's situation, though the analysis would have the same "would . . . if" form in all cases.

Nonetheless, the potential variety of terms in the "if" clauses of conditional analyses makes terms such as *will* and *willed* especially useful for discussing them. Recall that in chapter 2 we distinguished three senses of *will*, which together cover the range of possible terms that might appear in the "if" clauses of conditional analyses: *want, desire, prefer, incline to, choose, decide, intend, try, endeavor, make an effort to*, and so on. The terms *will* and *willed* are therefore useful as stand-ins for the others. A general form of WI would be "You would have done otherwise, if you had willed otherwise," in which "willed" might be replaced by any of the other terms, depending on context. (This is in fact what is often done in the Hobbes-Bramhall debate and in other traditional debates about free will.)

Conditional analyses such as WI appeal to compatibilists because compatibilists generally view varying kinds of freedom as the absence of constraints or impediments preventing agents from doing what they will (or choose or endeavor) to do. If you were paralyzed or tied to a chair, you would not be free to leave the room because circumstances would prevent you from leaving, even *if* you chose or endeavored to leave. If you lived under an oppressive regime and sufficiently feared the consequences of speaking your mind, you would not speak your mind, even *if* you wanted or desired to. If you were a compulsive drug user, you would not be free to resist using the drug because you would not succeed in resisting, even *if* you tried. In such manner, freedoms from physical constraint, political oppression, psychological compulsion and others, take a conditional form: we are free when no impediments would prevent us from acting, if we so chose or desired.

As plausible as this approach may seem for understanding a broad range of everyday freedoms, nonetheless, conditional analyses of power such as WI have serious deficiencies that have led more than a few recent compatibilists themselves to question them (e.g., Keith Lehrer [1976], Robert Audi [1974], and Bernard Berofsky [1987]). In the past few decades, there have been two basic types of criticism of conditional analyses—one suggesting that conditional analyses do not provide *necessary* conditions for the possession of powers or abilities, the other that they do not provide *sufficient* conditions. The first type of criticism, to be discussed in this section and the next, is represented by arguments first put forward by J. L. Austin (1966) and Philippa Foot (1966), and further developed by G. E. M. Anscombe (1971), M. R. Ayers (1968), and others. The second type, to be discussed in section 7, is represented by criticisms made by Roderick Chisholm (1966) and Keith Lehrer (1968), among others.[14]

J. L. Austin's influential essay "Ifs and Cans" is the best known source of the first type of criticism of conditional analyses.[15] Austin established two things in "Ifs and Cans" of great importance for debates about free will. He asked whether or not statements about what an agent "can do" or "could have done" involve a disguised "if." One view about this was that a statement such as our C, "You could have done otherwise," really means something like

(CI) You *could* have done otherwise, *if* you had willed or chosen or wanted to do otherwise.

Unlike WI, this statement CI simply attaches the conditional "if" clause to the original "could" statement, C. Austin's first point was that *this* kind of conditional analysis certainly could not be right. For CI makes the *existence* of a power or ability to do something depend on the agent's willing or choosing or wanting to exercise the power or ability. This has the absurd consequence, as Michael Ayers (1968) later put it, that no one would have any abilities at any time which they did not then actually want or choose to exercise. Thus, if "can" or "could" statements such as C are disguised conditionals, Austin argued, the conditionals could not be "could . . . if" conditionals, like CI, but must rather be "would . . . if" conditionals, like WI.

Having disposed of an obviously wrongheaded conditional analysis such as CI,

Austin turned his attention to conditionals like WI. He argued that while WI is a more promising candidate as an analysis of "You could have done otherwise," WI also fails as an adequate analysis. For it is sometimes true that a person can (or could) do something, but false that the person would do it (or would have done it), if he or she chose or tried. Austin's best-known example illustrating this point was one in which he imagined himself a golfer standing over a three-foot putt. It would be perfectly consistent, Austin argued, to say that he could (or had the power to) make the putt, though he might have missed it. For he has made many putts of this length in similar circumstances of the past—and also missed a few. His power to do it, therefore, does not imply that he *would* do it every time he wanted or tried—from which it follows that the truth of "would . . . if" statements like WI is not a necessary condition for the truth of "can" or "could" statements like C.

6. "Can," Responsibility, and Determinism: Anscombe

Austin noted some interesting consequences of this argument for debates about free will and determinism. We might imagine that when he stroked the putt and was trying his best to make it, a sudden undetermined twitch in his arm (caused, we might further imagine, by a quantum jump in his nervous system) made him miss the putt. In this case also, we might say that "he could have made the putt," though he in fact missed it. For the twitch, being undetermined, *might* not have occurred, and if it had not occurred, he would have made the putt. Or we may suppose conversely that an undetermined twitch in his arm occurred, allowing him to make the putt when he otherwise might have missed it. In this case also, it is true that he *could* have made it—obviously so, because he *did* make it.

These examples show that there are things we can do, even though our actually doing them may depend on chance or indeterminism. We may choose or try to do them, but whether we succeed when we choose or try is not determined. Such examples show what is wrong with a doctrine that goes back to the Stoics and has been favored by many compatibilists and soft determinists for centuries,[16] including Hobbes and Mill, and some twentieth century figures, such as R. E. Hobart (1966), Moritz Schlick (1966) and A. J. Ayer (1954). This is the doctrine that freedom and responsibility not only are compatible with determinism but actually *entail or presuppose determinism*. The idea that seemed to motivate this ill-conceived doctrine was nicely stated in a well-known passage of David Hume's *Treatise on Human Nature*: "Where [actions] proceed not from some cause in the characters and dispositions of the persons who performed them, they . . . can neither redound to his honor, if good, nor infamy, if evil. . . . the person is not responsible for the [action] . . . as it proceeded from nothing in him that is durable or constant" (1960: 411).

There is certainly something right about this claim of Hume's. If our actions did not "proceed from some cause" in our characters and dispositions, but occurred, for example, accidentally or by chance, we would lack the requisite control over the actions required by freedom and responsibility. But the causal influence thus required by power, freedom, and responsibility does not imply that our actions have to be *determined* by our characters and dispositions, as Austin's example shows.

This important point was developed further by Elizabeth Anscombe in her *Causality and Determinism* (1971). Anscombe argued, in a manner reminiscent of Austin, that one can be said to "cause" or "produce" an outcome, even if that outcome is not inevitable or determined, given one's efforts. Suppose a karate master swings his arm down on a thick board, and suppose that there are non-negligible indeterminacies in the motion of his arm that make the outcome (breaking the board or not breaking it) undetermined. If the board does break, the indeterminacy does not prevent us from saying that the motion of the arm *caused* the board to break, or that the karate master *produced* the broken board even though he might have failed to break it. Nor does the indeterminacy lead us to say he did not have the power to break it or was not responsible for breaking it, if it does break when he strikes it.

What we are talking about here is probabilistic causation, and the point is that such causation is often good enough for ascriptions of power and responsibility. It may be true that chance and probability would limit our powers to some degree or mitigate responsibility in some instances, but chance and probability do not eliminate power and responsibility entirely. The thesis that we can, in particular, be held *responsible* for the outcomes of our actions, even when those outcomes depend to some degree on chance, was successfully defended in this way by Philippa Foot (1966) and others (as well as by Anscombe) against the views of Hobart, Schlick, and Ayer.

A telling example I have often used to illustrate this point is the following. Suppose a disgruntled nuclear facility employee plants with evil intent some radioactive material in the drawer of an executive's desk for a few days. Whether the executive actually gets cancer may be genuinely a matter of chance, since that outcome depends on the occurrences of undetermined quantum radiations and mutations, as well as on the length of time the executive spends at his desk. But if the executive does get cancer, there is no question that the employee should be held responsible. It would be no adequate defense for the employee to plead that the outcome was a matter of chance and therefore he is not blameworthy. Such an "indeterminism" defense would be absurd, both morally and legally.

Similarly, a man who aims at and shoots someone from a high building cannot successfully plead that he is not guilty because from that distance there was only a one-in-a-hundred chance he would succeed in hitting anyone. Chance or probability intervening between our intentions and actions (even genuine indeterminacy of the quantum mechanical kind) will not eliminate responsibility (though it might mitigate responsibility, if the chances are remote and difficult to foresee). Even in a world in which there was considerably more real indeterminacy at the macro level than there seems to be in the actual world, one could still impute responsibility to agents to the extent that one could hold them responsible for *raising* or *lowering the probabilities* that certain good or bad things would occur. The nuclear employee intentionally raised the probability that the executive would get cancer from a small percentage to, say, 50 percent, and that was more than enough to charge him with murder when he succeeded.

For reasons such as these, the once popular doctrine that freedom and responsibility *entail* or *require* determinism is now largely discredited. This does not mean, of course, that compatibilism is refuted. The weaker thesis that freedom is *consistent* with determinism is still in the running. Many compatibilists, from the Stoics and Hobbes to Hobart, Schlick, and Ayer, have indeed gone beyond the weaker compatibilist thesis to affirm the stronger thesis that freedom and responsibility require determinism, and this was a mistake. But it was not a mistake universally made by compatibilists, nor one that invalidates compatibilism.

In fact, a basic theme of modern compatibilism, as I suggested in chapter 1, runs counter to the thesis that freedom requires determinism. What many modern compatibilists want to say is that *determinism does not really matter* to issues about human freedom and responsibility; the truth of determinism, as Dennett puts it (1983), would not make any difference with respect to the existence of any kind of freedom worth wanting. Pursuing this line, modern compatibilists could claim that Hobart, Schlick, and Ayer are making the same mistake as incompatibilists, but from the opposite direction. Whereas incompatibilists insist that freedom requires indeterminism, Hobart, Schlick, and Ayer insist that freedom requires determinism. Both are wrong, modern compatibilists may say, because the truth of determinism would not matter to the existence of any freedoms we should care about.

Nor do the arguments of Austin, Anscombe, and others that freedom and responsibility are compatible with *indeterminism* suffice to vindicate incompatibilism.[17] Such arguments help the incompatibilist cause by undermining certain kinds of compatibilist analyses of power and by showing that probabilistic causation is compatible with the ascription of powers and responsibility. But this is not enough to vindicate incompatibilism. For, as we shall see in part II, there are as many difficulties in trying to reconcile free will with probabilistic causation as there are in trying to reconcile it with deterministic causation, and there are many as yet unsolved problems of reconciling the rationality and control required by free will with indeterminism.

Note, for instance, that in the examples of Austin and others, such as the golfer and the nuclear plant employee, chance or indetermism plays the role of a *constraint* intervening between the choices, intentions, or tryings of agents and the success of their actions. The chance factors (such as the twitching of the arm or the radiation-induced mutations) are things the agents cannot control and are as much hindrances or impediments to the agents' intentions, as any causal constraints may be. Compatibilists argue that this is what indeterminism or chance would always be if it entered into human reasoning or action—a nuisance or hindrance or impediment, rather than an enhancement, of freedom. That is why arguments like those of Austin and Anscombe, while they help the incompatibilist cause by showing inadequacies in compatibilist analyses of power, fall short of vindicating incompatibilism.

7. Conditional Analyses of "Can" (II): Chisholm, Lehrer

A second line of criticism of conditional analyses of "can" and "could have done otherwise" is represented by objections of Roderick Chisholm and Keith Lehrer. Chisholm (1966) argued that the truth of a conditional such as WI ("You would have done otherwise, if you had willed or chosen otherwise") would not be sufficient for the truth of C ("You could have done otherwise"), unless one added that

(C') You could *also* have *willed* or *chosen* otherwise.

The need for C' is nicely illustrated by an example from Lehrer (1964). Suppose someone presents you with a tray of red candies. Nothing would prevent you from eating one of the candies, *if* you chose to. But you have a pathological fear of blood and of eating anything the color of blood, so you cannot *choose* to eat the candies; and so you cannot *eat* them.

Note that while Austinian objections say that conditional analyses like WI do not provide *necessary* conditions for the possession of powers or abilities, objections such as Chisholm's and Lehrer's say that they do not provide *sufficient* conditions. One must at least add C' to make WI a sufficient analysis of C. But adding C' introduces the term *could* all over again—the term that WI was supposed to analyze. If the "could" in C' were given a conditional analysis in turn, we would get something like

(WI') You would have chosen otherwise, if you had *willed to choose* otherwise.

And this would require a further C" to the effect that one *could* have willed to choose otherwise, and so on indefinitely.

The result, Chisholm and Lehrer argue, would be an infinite regress that would never allow one to eliminate the term "could"—which shows that something is wrong with conditional analyses of the standard "would . . . if" kind. This regress can only be stopped, according to Chisholm, by a "could" statement that was not further analyzed conditionally—a statement which said that the agent could have done otherwise, with no "ifs" or conditions added concerning further willings. Chisholm, in fact (unlike Lehrer), presents his argument as an incompatibilist who thinks that the correct (i.e., incompatibilist) account of "could have done otherwise" would be *unconditional* or *categorical*. It would say that the agent might have done otherwise, *all past circumstances* (including the agent's motives and willings) *and all laws of nature remaining the same*. Not surprisingly, compatibilists regard that kind of solution to the regress problem as too drastic, not to say question-begging, since it makes the power to do otherwise incompatible with determinism by definition.[18] But, then compatibilists must come up with some other way to stop the regress.

One compatibilist suggestion for stopping the regress was made by Donald Davidson (1973) and Don Locke (1974). They noted that verbs in the "if" clauses of conditional analyses are of two kinds. Some are verbs of action, such as *choose, decide, try,* or *endeavor,* while others are state or dispositional verbs, such as *want, desire, intend,* and *prefer.* Davidson and Locke concede that if one analyzes C ("You could have done otherwise") in terms of a verb of action, as in "You would have done otherwise, if you had chosen otherwise," then a further C' is needed to the effect that "You could have chosen otherwise." But they argue that if one then analyzes this C' as "You would have chosen otherwise, if you had *wanted* (or *desired*) otherwise," the regress terminates. For wants or desires are not further actions the agent could or could not have performed.

This kind of suggestion tends to bring to the surface deep-seated differences between the intuitions of compatibilists and incompatibilists. Some compatibilists think this Davidsonian suggestion neatly solves the problem of Chisholm's regress. Since wants, desires, and other dispositions are not actions we could or could not perform, there is nothing more to ask about what the agent could or could not do. But most incompatibilists (and some compatibilists as well, including Lehrer, Audi, and Berofsky) think that solutions of this kind merely paper over the real problem underlying Chisholm's regress.

Consider Lehrer's example again. It may be true that you would have eaten the candy, if you had not had an aversion to it, and also true that aversions are not actions one could or could not perform. Nonetheless, Lehrer's point remains: if you could not have done anything to control the aversion or overcome it, then you could not have *eaten the candy*. So your power to eat the candy, if your eating it depends upon certain motivations you have, depends on your power to do something that might help you control, resist, or overcome those motivations. The issue, in other words, is not simply whether you "could have wanted otherwise" then and there, but whether you could have done anything to make your existing wants or desires (or aversions) *more or less effective in action*, for example, by making efforts to overcome them, exercising self-control, resisting temptation, acting on other countervailing wants, and so forth. And if you cannot control, resist, or overcome present motivations, the question then becomes whether there is anything you could have done in the past to avoid being in the fix you are now in, such that you cannot resist or overcome these motivations. Any attempt to stop the regress with wants, desires, or other motives will generate further questions of this sort about the past or present power or control agents may have (or have had) over their motivational situations.

8. UR Revisited

There is a significant lesson in these arguments about Chisholm's regress. For it turns out that the kinds of questions we have just asked—about whether agents can resist acting on the motives they do have or could have done anything to avoid being in a situation in which they could not resist—are importantly related to UR. This should not surprise us, because such questions obviously bear on the *responsibility* agents have for their actions. If agents could have resisted acting on the motives on which they acted, then they could have done otherwise, and what they did was "up to them" in the sense of the responsibility condition R of UR. By contrast, if they could *not* have resisted acting on those motives, then the motives in question would be sufficient grounds for their actions in the sense of the U condition of UR. In that case, to be ultimately responsible, the agents would have to be responsible (to some degree) for becoming the sorts of persons who now had such motives they could not now resist.

For such reasons, I believe the deeper problem to which Chisholm's regress points is precisely this problem of the power or control we have over our motives and dispositions and, in general, over the "springs" of our actions. This, I think, is why stopping the regress with wanting in Davidsonian fashion is unsatisfying. Davidson himself put his finger on the problem at one point. After arguing for stopping the regress with state verbs such as wanting, he adds the following revealing comment: "I do not want to suggest that the nature of an agent's beliefs and desires, and the question of how he acquired them, are irrelevant to questions of how free he, or his actions, are. But these questions are on a different and more sophisticated level from that of our present discussion" (1973: 70).

The problem hiding in this concession, as Gary Watson points out (1987: 160), is that these "more sophisticated" questions—about *how we acquired the motives and dispositions* we do have, and to what degree *we* are responsible for having them or for resisting acting upon them—are precisely the questions that generated the free-will debate in the first place and remain at the heart of the debate. When Bramhall objects that Hobbes's compatibilist freedom "to act, if you will" is an inadequate kind of freedom, if agents do not also have *power over their own wills*, he is drawing attention to these "more sophisticated" questions about the origins and resistibility of our wants and other motives.

It is important to recognize that these considerations bring the condition of Ultimate Responsibility, or UR, back into the picture. For UR directs our attention to just such questions about whether we are ultimately responsible for being the kinds of persons we are and for acting or not acting upon the motives we happen to have. I think it important to bring out the involvement of UR at this point, for I believe it lies behind the disagreements over Chisholm's regress and is in fact the key to the larger debate between compatibilists and incompatibilists over the meaning of *can*, *power*, and "could have done otherwise." What I want to suggest (and I will develop this point further in the next chapter) is that the fundamental reason incompatibilists and compatibilists clash over the meaning of "can" and "could have done otherwise"—why they so often scarcely understand each other on these subjects—is that *incompatibilists usually take seriously a condition of Ultimate Responsibility like UR for free will, in addition to AP, while compatibilists do not.* This may not always be obvious because, as indicated in chapter 3, the two conditions—AP and UR—are often not clearly distinguished in historical debates. But I think it becomes clear when clashes of intuitions between compatibilists and incompatibilists over the meanings of *can* and *could* are probed deeply enough.

The role of UR is critical, because I think it can be shown (as the next chapter will also argue) that no compatibilist analysis of "can" or "power"—including recent compatibilist alternatives that do not rely on conditional analyses—will satisfy UR. If this is true, then, while compatibilist interpretations of "can" and "power" may be adequate to account for many significant everyday freedoms, compatibilist interpretations would not be adequate for *free will*—if free will requires UR as well as AP. Moreover, if the Consequence Argument succeeds *unless* some compatibilist account of *can* or *power* is correct, as argued in this chapter, the Consequence Argument would succeed *for free will*, though not for other kinds of (compatibilist) freedoms that do not also satisfy UR.

Thus, as I see it, the topics we have discussed in this chapter, which include the case for and against the Consequence Argument and debates about the correct interpretation of "can" and "could have done otherwise"—indeed, the entire debate over the Compatibility Question—cannot be resolved by focusing on AP alone without also bringing in UR. *Focusing on the power to do otherwise and alternative possibilities alone is just too thin a basis on which to rest the case for incompatibilism.* To get beyond current stalemates about the meanings of powers and abilities, one must dig more deeply into the sources of conflicting intuitions about these meanings. And when that is done, I think one eventually arrives at the topic of our next chapter—UR.

5

Ultimate Responsibility

1. Theses 1 and 2 on UR

At the end of the previous chapter, I suggested that the condition of Ultimate Responsibility, or UR, was the missing link in debates about the Compatibility Question, and I made two claims about UR:

> *Thesis 1 (on UR)*: Persistent disagreements between compatibilists and incompatibilists over the interpretation of contested expressions such as "can" and "could have done otherwise" (and hence over AP and the Consequence Argument) are best understood, I believe, by recognizing that incompatibilists are concerned with a kind of freedom (called "free will") that satisfies UR as well as AP, whereas compatibilists are not concerned with such a freedom. (In other words, for incompatibilists, free will requires AP + UR, not AP alone.)

> *Thesis 2 (on UR)*: Compatibilist analyses of "can" and "could have done otherwise" fail to satisfy UR (if UR is satisfiable at all) and therefore do not adequately account for free will as incompatibilists understand it, though compatibilist analyses may be able to account for everyday freedoms that do not require UR.

These two theses were merely stated at the end of chapter 4. In this chapter, I want to defend them and a series of further theses on UR that address its meaning and relevance to the Compatibility Question and to the other three core questions about free will.

The first part of the chapter is diagnostic. In defense of Theses 1 and 2, I first try to bring to the surface the subliminal role played by UR in post-1970 debates about compatibility. The aim is to show how UR might be involved in the disagreements between compatibilists and incompatibilists that go beyond disagreements about the conditional analyses of power discussed in chapter 4. To show this, I am going to focus on certain compatibilist theories that have played an important role in debates about free will since 1970, in particular those based on so-called hierarchical theories of motivation.

Hierarchical theories are important to our purposes for several reasons. First, they are a definite improvement upon earlier compatibilist accounts of free agency such as we discussed in the previous chapter. Second, hierarchical theories provide a basis for compatibilist accounts of free *will* as well as free action, thereby allowing

60

compatibilists to answer the long-standing charge (made by Bramhall and suggested by Chisholm's regress) that compatibilists can account for freedom of action but fail to account for freedom of will. Third, and most important, hierarchical theories are an excellent vehicle for showing how and why disagreements about UR separate compatibilists and incompatibilists (thereby supporting Thesis 1). A discussion of hierarchical theories will lead to the further theses about UR later in the chapter and eventually to a defense of Thesis 2.

2. Hierarchical Motivation: Frankfurt

Theories of hierarchical motivation, introduced by Harry Frankfurt and Gerald Dworkin and further developed by Wright Neely and others, are among the most significant advances in compatibilist accounts of free agency of the past few decades.[1] A large number of other recent compatibilist views (for instance, "evaluative" views such as Gary Watson's and Paul Benson's, the "reason view" of Susan Wolf, "autonomy" theories such as those of Richard Double and Alfred Mele, the doxastic view of Tomis Kapitan, among others) have either been inspired by theories of hierarchical motivation or have been developed in opposition to them.[2]

The attraction of hierarchical theories is that they suggest a way to remedy one of the chief deficiencies of traditional compatibilism. As we have seen, compatibilists generally view freedom as the absence of constraints or impediments to the will. But, as Watson points out, "classical compatibilists conceived of free agency in terms of external impediments" while neglecting "the more 'internal' impediments" that occur in phobias, obsessions, addictions, neuroses, and other kinds of compulsive behavior (1987: 147). Traditional compatibilists like Hobbes, who thought of the will as expressed by desire, overlooked the fact that, in compulsive behavior, the persons' own desires can sometimes be impediments preventing them from doing what they will.[3]

Frankfurt addressed this problem in an influential paper titled "Freedom of the Will and the Concept of a Person" (1971). This paper did not take an explicit stand on the Compatibility Question, but the ideas presented in it nonetheless laid the groundwork for many subsequent compatibilist accounts of free will.[4] Frankfurt argued that classical authors, by focusing too much on external impediments to freedom rather than on the internal impediments involved in compulsive behavior, were able to account for freedom of action but neglected the freedom of the will. Bramhall, we recall, made a similar complaint against Hobbes about the neglect of the freedom of the will. But Frankfurt's response to this complaint takes a different turn from Bramhall's.

To attack the problem of compulsive behavior, Frankfurt introduces a distinction between first-order and second-order desires. Second-order desires are desires about other desires (p. 8). A drug addict, for instance, may have a first-order desire to use a drug, and a second-order desire not to have the (first-order) desire to use the drug. Frankfurt then defines "second-order volitions" as second-order desires that certain first-order desires be effective in action (p. 10). The addict may want his desire to avoid the drug to be effective in action (i.e., to lead him to actually avoid the drug), but, alas, it does not. His behavior is compulsive. He therefore lacks freedom of will, according to Frankfurt, because he cannot secure "the conformity of his will [first-order desires] to his second-order volitions." He does not "have the will he wants to have" (p. 16).

For Frankfurt, persons are organisms capable of having second-order volitions. They are capable of caring about the kinds of desires they act upon and whether those desires conform to their second-order volitions. A "wanton" is one who has first-order desires but lacks reflective attitudes toward those desires that would generate second-order volitions (p. 11). Such persons lack the conditions for freedom of will. Persons "act freely" in the sense relevant for moral responsibility, according to Frankfurt, when they secure conformity to their second-order volitions (i.e., to their wills), so that their acts are appropriately caused by their second-order volitions (p. 14).

Note that, on this hierarchical view of motivation, it is possible to have third-order (and higher) desires and volitions as well. Frankfurt's general point is that the motivational complexity necessary to have higher order desires and volitions is necessary for creatures capable of free will. This seems to me a correct point that incompatibilists as well as compatibilists should accept, even if incompatibilists like myself do not think Frankfurt's account of free will goes far enough. Though Frankfurt is hesitant to call himself a compatibilist or incompatibilist, it is clear that one of his motives was to offer a demystified account of freedom of will that would not commit one to the excesses of traditional libertarian views like Bramhall's. As a consequence, theories of hierarchical motivation like his have been developed by Dworkin, Neely, and others to defend compatibilist views of freedom and autonomy.

3. Identification and Wholeheartedness

The hierarchical approach does indeed make significant advances beyond classical compatibilism in the treatment of internal constraints and in allowing some measure of freedom of will as well as freedom of action. It also provides a richer conception of personhood in terms of levels of motivation than classical compatibilism provided. But hierarchical theories have also provoked objections from compatibilists and incompatibilists alike.[5]

One problem, first noted by Watson (1975) and subsequently addressed by D. Zimmerman (1981), Shatz (1985), Fischer (1986), Thalberg (1989), Double (1991), and others, is indicated by the following questions: Could one not be wanton with respect to one's second-order desires and volitions as well? "Suppose," says Double, "I decisively identify with my first-order desire . . . to sacrifice my life if my religious leader asks me to. If I do so in a completely nonreflective way, it is difficult to see how I have more freedom than a wanton, despite the fact that according to Frankfurt's . . . account these decisions are clearly mine" (p. 35). Would not free will demand that one also be reflective about second-order desires by bringing some of them and not others into conformity with one's third-order volitions, and so on to higher orders indefinitely? Why stop at the second, or any higher, level?

Frankfurt's answer is that a series of ever higher order volitions can be terminated by appealing to a notion of *identification*, or "decisive commitment," to one or another of the agent's first-order desires. "The fact that [the agent's] second-order volition to be moved by this [first-order] desire is a decisive one," he says, "means that there is no room for questions concerning the pertinence of desires or volitions of higher orders" (1971: 16). The agent has decided that no further questions about higher order desires "remain to be asked." But this answer has not satisfied his critics. As Watson argues, either this reply of Frankfurt's "is lame or it reveals that the notion of higher order volition is not the fundamental one. We wanted to know what prevents wantonness with regard to one's higher order volitions. What gives these volitions any special relation to 'oneself'? It is unhelpful to answer that one makes a decisive commitment where this just means that an interminable ascent to higher orders is not going to be permitted. This *is* arbitrary" (1975: 17).

It is clear that Frankfurt is concerned about this "identification problem," as we might call it, and he has returned to it on a number of occasions, most recently in his perceptive presidential address to the American Philosophical Association (1992). In this address, Frankfurt is concerned to show that the identification with some of one's desires (or commitment to them), which is required by hierarchical accounts of free agency, can escape the dilemma of either being arbitrary or leading to a regress of higher order volitions. To show this, Frankfurt appeals to a notion of *wholeheartedness*. Persons are wholehearted when there are no conflicts among their second- and higher order volitions—when their wills are not divided or ambivalent (p. 10). Ambivalent persons lack the *volitional unity* of wholeheartedness. They are of two (or more) minds about what they want to be and how they want to live (p. 9). Wholehearted persons, by contrast, may face obstacles to their wills; they may be committed to careers, projects, and relationships that involve considerable effort and struggle. But they are not ambivalent about their engagements; they "do not desire to be volitionally different" than they are (p. 11). This is the sense in which they have the wills they want to have.

Frankfurt (1992) thinks this notion of wholeheartedness can help us to understand the "troublesome notion" of identification that is required by hierarchical theories of personhood. For he argues that to be wholehearted with respect to one's motives and projects is to be "fully *satisfied*" with them, to have "no active interest in bringing about a change in them" (p. 12). As a result, he argues that hierarchical accounts need "not presume . . . that a person's identification with some desire consists simply in the fact that he *has* a higher order desire by which the first desire is endorsed. The endorsing higher order desire must be, in addition, a desire with which the person is *satisfied*. . . . Identification is constituted neatly by an endorsing higher order desire with which the person is satisfied" (p. 14).

This explains, according to Frankfurt, "why there is no danger of a problematic regress" of higher order volitions (p. 13). For satisfaction with one's self, he argues, does not require the adoption of any further cognitive attitudes, higher order or otherwise, to support it. "It is a matter of simply *having no interest* in making changes. What it requires is that psychic elements of certain kinds *do not occur*" (p. 13). Furthermore, if identification—conceived as wholeheartedness—does not require a regress of endorsing motives, neither is it arbitrary in any objectionable sense. To be ultimately satisfied with the state of one's will may indeed be a bottom-line condition, Frankfurt argues, but there is nothing irrational or unjustified about it.

4. CC and CNC Control

Frankfurt's solution to the identification problem is partly successful, but it leads
directly to a second (and, I believe, more important) criticism that has been made of
his and other hierarchical accounts of motivation from their inception. This is the
problem of the "origins" or "sources" of the agent's will, or higher order volitions.
"For all [Frankfurt's] account tells us," says Watson, "the person's higher-order preference may be the result of brainwashing, or severe conditioning of the kind which
is plainly incompatible with autonomy" (1987: 148). And as Fischer adds, questions
about how we got the higher order volitions we do have also bear on issues of moral
responsibility that we normally associate with free will (1986: 60). After all, a ruthless dictator and a killer may be "wholehearted" in the pursuit of their life-plans. There
may be no ambivalence in their wills at all. When we wonder about the extent of
their responsibility, wholeheartedness is not the only thing that is relevant. We also
want to know how they got to be the way they are and whether they are responsible
for the will, or higher order volitions, to which they are wholeheartedly committed.
We want to know whether and to what extent *they* are responsible for their
wholeheartedness.

In the margin: Watson & Fischer

If we came to be wholehearted not by our own efforts but by brainwashing or
being manipulated by a cult leader, or conditioned by behavioral engineers, or given
a powerful mind-altering drug, we might be satisfied with the will we had, but would
lack autonomy in the deeper sense of "control over our own wills" that was traditionally associated with free will.[6] Viewed in this light, it is not difficult to see why examples of control and manipulation of the will by other agents (as in brainwashing
and behavioral conditioning) have played an important role, not only in criticisms
of hierarchical theories but also in discussions of the Compatibility Question generally. The examples of behavioral control just given draw attention to a distinction, of
paramount importance for free will debates, between two kinds of control that one
agent can exercise over another. This distinction is worth our attention at this point
because it is the basis for this second objection to hierarchical theories and because
it plays a pivotal role in sorting out core disagreements between compatibilists and
incompatibilists on free will in relation to UR.

The two kinds of control in question, of one agent over another, may be called
(in terms I have previously used) *constraining control* (CC) and *nonconstraining control* (NC).[7] In the case of constraining control, controlled agents are know-
ingly forced to do something against their wills. They are held at gunpoint or threatened with punishment if they do not do the controller's bidding, or they are locked
in a room and simply prevented from doing what they want to do. Constraining or
CC controllers get their way by creating constraints or impediments that thwart
the wills of those they control, preventing other agents from doing what they want
to do.

Nonconstraining (NC) control is another matter. It is exemplified by the cases
of behavioral conditioning and behind-the-scenes manipulation just described. In
such cases, the controllers do not get their way by constraining or coercing others
against their wills, but rather by manipulating the wills of others so that the others
(willingly) do what the controllers desire. The controlled agents consequently do not

feel frustrated or thwarted. They act in accordance with their own wants, desires or intentions. Yet they are controlled nevertheless by others who have manipulated their circumstances so that they want, desire, or intend only what the controllers have planned. In the most interesting cases, such control is a "covert" nonconstraining control—or CNC control, as I have previously called it—in which the controlled agents are unaware of being manipulated or perhaps even unaware of the existence of their controllers.[8]

We are well aware of these two ways to get others to do our bidding in everyday life. We may force them to do what we want by coercing or constraining them against their wills, which is constraining or CC control. Or we may manipulate them into doing what we want while making them feel that they have made up their own minds and are acting "of their own free wills"—which is covert nonconstraining or CNC control. Cases of CNC control in larger settings are provided by examples of behavioral engineering such as we find in utopian works like Aldous Huxley's *Brave New World* or B. F. Skinner's *Walden Two*.[9] Frazier, the fictional founder of Skinner's Walden Two, gives a clear description of CNC control when he says that in his community persons can do whatever they want or choose, but they have been conditioned since childhood to want and choose only what they can have or do (1962: 263).

Utopian versions of CNC control such as Skinner's are an excellent medium for expressing the second objection to hierarchical views of free will such as Frankfurt's. For the citizens of Walden Two, as they are described, are marvelously "wholehearted" in their attitudes and engagements. They are "satisfied" with themselves (almost to a cloying degree) and "have the wills they want to have." As a result, Frazier, the founder of Walden Two, insists that it is "the freest place on earth" (p. 297). And why should it not be? There is no coercion in Walden Two and no punishment. All citizens can have and do whatever they want or choose; and they can *will* to do whatever they *want*—that is, their first-order desires always conform to their second-order volitions. They have maximal freedom of will and action in the hierarchical sense.

Yet most people who look at Walden Two would say—and say rightly, in my opinion—that its citizens lack free will in a deeper sense than being able to do what they want and will what they want. In this deeper sense, their wills are not "their own" because they are not the original creators of their own ends or purposes. Their ends or purposes are created by their conditioners or controllers. Skinner himself is very much aware of this problem. For while his fictional representative Frazier says that Walden Two is the freest place on earth, he also insists that there is no free will in Walden Two (p. 257). This looks like a contradiction. But, as Bruce Waller points out, the apparent contradiction is removed once we realize that the freedom lacking in Walden Two is free will of the traditional kind, which required ultimate creation of one's own purposes (1990: 176). And to *this* freedom Skinner is saying good riddance. We never did or could have such a freedom, he thinks, because it is an impossible ideal that cannot be accommodated by the modern scientific picture of human beings. Meanwhile, the freedoms that Walden Two does maximally provide—to have and do whatever you want and to have the will you want—are all the freedoms that we should care about and can have.

5. Control and Reflection

The Walden Two case shows why covert nonconstraining (or CNC) control is an effective vehicle for explaining the differences between hierarchical views of free will, such as Frankfurt's, that are susceptible to compatibilist analyses and views of free will that are favored by incompatibilists. One might say that, in Walden Two, free will in the hierarchical sense is maximized, while free will in the deeper sense of ultimate control of ends or purposes is minimized. Indeed, *compatibilist free will is maximized* in Walden Two *by minimizing incompatibilist free will*: the citizens have the wills they want *because* they have been conditioned to want and choose only what they can have and do.

Hierarchical compatibilists may respond that persons in Walden Two do lack something that is necessary for the hierarchical view of free agency. Persons in Walden Two do not reflect very much about their ends or purposes, but merely accept their way of life without question. Frankfurt and other hierarchical theorists emphasize that the power to reflect upon and reconsider one's goals to meet new circumstances is a necessary condition for free will.[10] This is an important point that I conceded earlier. But the powers of reflection, important as they may be for free will, do not solve the problem posed by CNC control, because CNC control is consistent with high degrees of reflection and self-awareness. To begin with, the citizens of Walden Two are portrayed as quite reflective by everyday standards. They have plenty of leisure with which to pursue study of the arts and sciences, and they do reflect upon and reconsider many of their everyday goals within the confines of their community. They are more reflective than the majority of citizens of our ordinary world.

It is true that Walden Two citizens do not question the community itself and its way of life, but why should they, by the standards of the hierarchical theory? They are *wholeheartedly* committed to their community and way of life; it makes them happy or *satisfies* them. And if and when it did not satisfy them, Skinner would encourage them to make changes in it. For he emphasizes that Walden Two is an experimental community based on scientific principles. If things go wrong in various areas so that people are not satisfied, efforts will be made to change them. But, as long as things do not go wrong and the members are satisfied and wholly committed to their projects, they have all the freedom they could want. It seems that this must be so in the hierarchical sense as well. I cannot see that their condition fails to satisfy the hierarchical view of free agency and free will in any way; *and yet they are CNC controlled.*

Putting the matter in a more general way, you could imagine any degree of reflectiveness and self-awareness you wish. You may imagine persons so sophisticated that they are thinking about the appropriateness of their fourth- or fifth- or twentieth-order desires. And yet they still might be CNC controlled by more sophisticated beings who have manipulated their highest order desires. (At the very highest level of sophistication one might imagine God doing the controlling, since the problems posed by CNC control have their theological counterparts in problems of divine predestination or foreordination.) But even without such imaginings, we are well aware in everyday life that reflective persons can also be subject to manipulation. Indeed, sometimes reflective persons are susceptible to manipulation precisely because they are reflective, so long as others know enough to predict the lines their reflection will take. All of which means, in summary, that possessing powers of reflection does not by itself solve the problem of CNC control.

6. CNC Control and Determination

It has been noted by compatibilists themselves (e.g., Watson [1987]) that CNC control poses problems for all compatibilist views of free agency, and not only for hierarchical views. It is easy enough to see why. Compatibilists want to define freedom in terms of the "absence of *constraints*" that prevent agents from acting as they want (or also, on hierarchical views, from willing as they want). But CNC control is *nonconstraining*. Its existence is consistent with saying that agents can do what they will and will what they want. Yet CNC control seems objectionable in ways that are recognized by compatibilists and incompatibilists alike. CNC control seems to undermine a kind of freedom that we normally associate with autonomy (or controlling our own lives) and a dignity that goes along with autonomy—in other words, a freedom that is not captured simply by the ability to do what we want and will what we want.[11] The importance of CNC control is that it draws attention to such a "deeper" freedom.

One thing compatibilists might do (and some have done) when faced with the problem of CNC control is to bite the bullet and say that it does not take away any further possible freedom worth caring about so long as we are happy and free from coercion and compulsion. This, in effect, is what Skinner says. Why worry, he asks, about being covertly controlled or behaviorally engineered if it makes us happy? If we could be wholehearted and satisfied, why worry about how we got that way (p. 254)? If we had an effective science of human behavior, it would be senseless, he thinks, to refrain from using it in order to make people happy because of atavistic longings for a mysterious deeper freedom or ultimate control that, in his view, we cannot have anyway (p. 255).

Hobbes bites the bullet on CNC control in a similar way, but in a theological context. Why worry that God has predestined us, he says, for this takes away no freedom that we could otherwise have had in any case. Since we do not know what God has predestined us to do, we must go on deliberating about the best way to live anyway, just as if God had not predestined us (1962: 174). The only freedom we can have, Hobbes says, is the freedom to do what we will, and this freedom we can have even if we are predestined.

I have called views like those exemplified here by Skinner and Hobbes "hard compatibilism."[12] Hard compatibilists believe that freedom in every significant sense is not only compatible with determinism, but is compatible *with CNC control* as well.[13] The designation "hard compatibilism" seems appropriate because this is a hard line indeed, and one that I think is also hard to accept. Predestinationism of the kind defended by Hobbes and by some of his compatibilist successors, such as Jonathan Edwards (1969: 173), is no longer as popular as it once was among theists because it seems to take away a significant freedom from humans while passing ultimate responsibility for evil on to God. Similarly, Skinner's behaviorally engineered world is no more acceptable to most compatibilists today than predestinationism is to theists, because a behaviorally engineered world like Skinner's seems to take away a measure of autonomy and dignity that is worth wanting.[14]

But if hard compatibilism will not do, then compatibilists must take a softer line on CNC control. It is pretty obvious what they must do. They must emphasize the distinction between *CNC control* by other purposeful agents and *mere determination* by natural causes (without purposeful control by other agents); and they must argue that while CNC control takes away freedom in a significant sense, mere determination by natural causes does not do so. (This we might call, by contrast, "soft" compatibilism.) The problem is to locate the relevant difference between the two that makes one of them (CNC control) objectionable and the other (mere determination) not.

This problem turns out to be more difficult than first appearances suggest.[15] First of all, if we look back for a moment at constraining (or CC) control, our powers or freedoms are equally impaired by CC control as by mere determination. Your power or freedom to run or dance is no less impaired if you are paralyzed by natural causes than if some other agent is holding you down.[16] In each case, the significant thing is that you *cannot* do something you want to do. It is true that you might feel resentment against your purposeful controllers, whereas resentment is misplaced against natural forces (though in fact many people do rail against nature or fate). But the point is that your lack of *power* or *ability* to do something is equally impaired by CC control and mere determination, and it is power or ability to do something that is relevant to your *freedom*.

Now, if the distinction between CC control and mere determination by natural causes does not make a difference in our powers, when the results are the same, why should the distinction between CNC control and mere determination by natural causes make a difference in our powers, when the results are also the same? Imagine a possible world W_1 in which every aspect of persons' lives is controlled by invisible gods or spirits. Imagine another world W_2 in which these persons' lives are exactly the same as in W_1 in every detail of thought, belief, and circumstance from birth to death except that in W_2 everything is produced by natural causes rather than by gods or spirits. What *powers* or *abilities* or *freedoms* do the persons have in one world that they do not possess in the other? If one of them is paralyzed in one world, he is paralyzed in the other. If another can sing in one world, she can sing in the other. If one person is strong-willed and another weak-willed in one world, they are the same in the other. If one is wholehearted and another ambivalent in one world, they are the same in the other. In order to find a relevant difference between CNC control and mere determination, we have to look beyond the powers that each might contingently take away, since any contingent power the one might take away, the other might take away as well.

One move that compatibilists can make in response to this challenge is suggested by Bruce Waller (1988: 165). Waller asks why, leaving aside gods (and God) for the moment, we find CNC control by other human agents (such as in behavioral engineering) objectionable in ways that mere determination by natural causes, such as heredity or environment, is not. And he suggests that we fear CNC control because of the potential harm that can be done to us and our interests by CNC controllers (p. 166). After all, manipulators and controllers are more likely to have their own

— What about the case where I am manipulated by a CNC controller who is completely determined by natural causes?

good in mind than ours, and therefore we feel safer knowing that no purposeful agents are covertly controlling us. It is the potential danger to our interests lurking in CNC control and our inability to do anything about it that troubles us.

There is something to this suggestion. But it also cannot fully explain why we object to CNC control, since we have reasons to oppose CNC control even when we believe it is benign and for our own good. This is evident in the negative reaction many people have to Walden Two, even when they concede that persons might be conditioned to be happy there. The problem of benign CNC control is also evident in the case of children who may know that their parents are well-intentioned toward them, yet they resent parental control anyway. As they reach their maturity the children want something over and above the removal of fear that their parents will choose badly for them. They want an autonomy and dignity that they associate with the power to run their own lives, to make and take responsibility for their own choices even at the expense of making mistakes and being worse off than if they had let their parents run their lives.

Such autonomy, of course, is close to the heart of what we want when we want free will in the traditional sense, and it seems to be taken away by CNC control, whether the control is nefarious or benign. Even to a benign controller, one may want to say: "It is a value to me to take control of my own life, even if I should make mistakes and *be less happy* as a result." (Compare St. Augustine's question in Book II of *De Libero Arbitrio Voluntatis* of why God gave human beings free will since they might use it to bring greater sufferings on themselves and others than if they did not have it.)

7. Constraint, Control, Determination

We are now very close to the vital center of the dispute between compatibilists and incompatibilists over free will, where UR is lurking. An additional step will get us all the way there. Compatibilists can make one further move to distinguish CNC control and mere determination as regards freedom. This move is made in a very clear way by Dennett (1984), who asks us to pay more attention to the notion of *control* in discussing these matters. The kind of control that disturbs us regarding our freedom, Dennett argues, is the kind that one agent can purposefully exercise over another (p. 57). In short, objectionable control is exercised by purposeful agents, not natural forces. It is a category mistake to think otherwise, Dennett says. For, while nature may determine us, *nature* ("not being an agent") *does not control us* (p. 61). CNC control is objectionable because we do not want to be controlled by other agents. We may think determination is equally objectionable because we illegitimately transfer these bad feelings about control to nature.

This is a very interesting move from the perspective of the history of free will debates. Classical compatibilists insisted on a distinction between *constraint* and *mere causation* (or determination). The former is objectionable, they said, because it prevents us from doing what we want (it impedes our freedom). But *mere* causation or determination *without constraint* is not objectionable in the same way because it does not impede our will. Incompatibilists go wrong, it was argued, because they fail to recognise this distinction. Ayer (1954), for example, suggested that incompatibilists were caught in the grip of a mistaken image of natural causes or laws of nature "over-mastering" us, or constraining us against our wills, when in fact the existence of laws only indicates that certain events follow others according to regular patterns.

Now CNC control enters the picture. It is interesting because it is non-constraining. It shows that being prevented from doing what you will and willing what you want are not the only things that matter to us concerning our freedom. But then Dennett comes to the rescue. He plays the old compatibilist tune in a new key. Just as classical compatibilists distinguished *constraint* from *mere causation*, he says we must distinguish *control* from *mere determination*. CNC control is objectionable because it is control by others, but natural causes do not control us, *even when they determine us*. Incompatibilists are guilty of a confusion if they think otherwise.

This move is instructive, not because it refutes incompatibilism but because it gets us to the core of what separates compatibilists and incompatibilists about free will. Most incompatibilists never were "confused" about the distinction between constraint and causation, nor are they confused about the distinction between CNC control and mere determination. (A few may have been confused, but that says more about them than the issues.) In fact, these distinctions are fairly straightforward and you have to be pretty dense to miss them. Constraints are causes that impede the will, and all causes do not impede the will; CNC control is by purposeful agents, while mere determination is not. This is not the stuff of which category mistakes are easily made. Something else has to be going on. Nor is it enough to say that incompatibilists are somehow misusing the term *control* when they say that control by natural forces is no different than control by other agents. We have to get beyond the once fashionable, but ultimately superficial, idea that the whole free will dispute results from a "misuse" of ordinary language.[17]

No. Something else is going on here, as I said. When compatibilists and incompatibilists look at CNC control and mere determination, they are interested in entirely different issues. Compatibilists focus on the *controllers* and try to find the relevant differences there. We resent purposeful controllers or fear they may harm us, and these feelings are inappropriate for nature, which does not "control" us. These claims of Dennett's and Waller's are true, but for incompatibilists they represent only half the story. You also have to look at it from the side of the *controlled* agents. What *powers* have they lost when they are CNC controlled? As we saw, they may lose many powers (e.g., to run or dance) depending on the contingencies of how they are CNC controlled. But we also saw (in the "two worlds" example) that for any such powers they might contingently lose by CNC control, they might lose exactly those same powers by mere determination.

Yet there is one other power that persons *essentially* lose by being CNC controlled simply because the control is CNC; and this power is one that especially interests incompatibilists. It is the power to be the ultimate *source* or *origin* of one's own ends or purposes rather than have that source be in something *other than you*. This, of course, is the governing image of free will that we tried to spell out in terms of UR: the origins or sources, or *archai*, of actions should be in the agents themselves and not in something outside the agents, if the agents are to be ultimately responsible for what they do and what they are. And this power to be such a source of your

[margin note: ordinary language]

own ends is one that both CNC control and mere determination take away. For whether the sources of your ends or purposes lie in nature or in other agents, *they do not lie in you.*

Such is the problem that troubles incompatibilists about both CNC control and mere determination. Not only do both CNC control and determination take away this ultimate power over one's purposes, they both do so essentially, just because in each of them the ultimate source is outside the agent. It is not like the power to run or dance, which a particular CNC controller (or a particular heredity or environment) might or might not take away; it is a general power that CNC control and mere determination take away simply because of what they are.

8. UR Again

So when we push the disputes over hierarchical freedom and CNC control to their limits, we again arrive at UR. According to Thesis 1 of this chapter, the fundamental disagreements between incompatibilists and compatibilists can be traced to the fact that incompatibilists take UR, as well as AP, seriously as a condition for free will and compatibilists do not. We can see this exemplified in the dispute about CNC control and mere determination. On the one hand, those who take UR seriously are more concerned with what CNC control and mere determination have in common than their differences. With both of them, the ultimate causes of the controlled agents' ends or purposes lie outside them, not within them. On the other hand, those who are dubious about UR—who suspect it is an unnecessary or incoherent condition— tend to look for some other reason CNC control is objectionable (for example, that we resent, or fear, purposeful controllers), such that mere determination is not objectionable in the same way. In this manner, different attitudes to CNC control of compatibilists and incompatibilists are related to how seriously UR is regarded as a desirable or attainable condition for free will.

Similar remarks apply to the dispute over hierarchical theories. Frankfurt offers an insightful account of free will, spelled out in terms of "identification" and "wholeheartedness," in terms of the conformity of one's desires to higher order volitions, or having the will one wants. But the theory says little about the origins or sources of one's will, or higher order volitions, or wholeheartedness, as critics of hierarchical theories have noted. For all the hierarchical theory says, as Watson puts it, the agent's higher order volitions could have been produced by behavioral conditioning (or, we might add, by any other kind of CNC control).

Looking back upon this debate, we can see that the concern for the origins of our will leads incompatibilists to UR—to the demand that the ultimate source of our wills lies in us and not in something outside us. From this perspective, hierarchical accounts of free will do not go far enough. Having the will you want and being able to act on your higher order volitions may be *part* of what it means to have free will (after all, incompatibilists need not deny that compulsion, in Frankfurt's sense, takes away free will). But having the will you want and being able to act on higher order volitions cannot be the whole story, since they avoid the deeper question of whether you are ultimately responsible for having the will you do have. By contrast, compatibilists are likely again to dismiss these concerns about UR, arguing that questions of ultimate origins are <u>unanswerable and therefore beside the point.</u> They would insist that <u>we must be content with something less,</u> such as having the wills we want.

9. Responsibility (R): Theses 3 and 4

Thus differing attitudes toward UR lie behind the disputes about CNC control and hierarchical theories. But this is not all. According to Theses 1 and 2, differing attitudes toward UR also lie behind the disputes of chapter 4 about the Consequence Argument and the meanings of "power" and "could have done otherwise." To see why this is so, we have to look more closely at UR itself and spell out its implications in terms of some further theses. In order to do this, it will be helpful to restate the condition: A willed action is "up to the agent" in the sense required by free will only if the agent is ultimately responsible for it in the following sense.

> UR: An agent is *ultimately responsible* for some (event or state) E's occurring only if (R) the agent is personally responsible for E's occurring in a sense which entails that something the agent voluntarily (or willingly) did or omitted, and for which the agent could have voluntarily done otherwise, either was, or causally contributed to, E's occurrence, and made a difference to whether or not E occurred; and (U) for every X and Y (where X and Y represent occurrences of events and/or states) if the agent is personally responsible for X, and if Y is an *arche* (or sufficient ground or cause or explanation) for X, then the agent must also be personally responsible for Y.

The condition has two parts: a base condition R ("Responsibility") and a recursive or backtracking condition U ("Ultimacy"). We talked about the implications of each part in chapter 3. But the time has come to look more closely at each of them.

It follows from condition R that in order to be ultimately responsible for being what you are (or for having the character and motives you do have) there must have been something *you could have voluntarily done* (or omitted) at some time or other that would have made *a difference in what you are* (or in the character and motives you now have). Thus, if there never was anything Luther could have done at any time to make himself different than he was, he could not be ultimately responsible for being what he was. It was this line of thought that led in chapter 3 to our saying that while the Alternative Possibilities condition, or AP, does not have to be satisfied by every free and responsible act, it must be satisfied by some actions in an agent's life history if the agent is to have free will. This yields a further thesis about UR. (Hereafter, I designate these theses by "T" followed by an appropriate number.)

> T3 (on UR): UR entails (by way of R) that *some* actions in an agent's life history must satisfy AP. Agents with free will in the sense of UR must be such that they (could have done otherwise) on some occasions of their life histories with respect to some character- or motive-forming acts by which they make themselves into the kinds of persons they are.

But, as also indicated in chapter 3, we must not think that because UR entails AP (for some free actions) by way of R, that R alone settles issues which separate

[handwritten marginal note:] Why isn't it sufficient for them to have believed (albeit mistakenly) that they could have done otherwise?

compatibilists and incompatibilists. For the "could have voluntarily done otherwise" of R is left uninterpreted and might be given a compatibilist interpretation so far as R alone is concerned. Thus, we add:

> *T4 (on UR)*: R of UR entails AP-for-some-free-actions, but R by itself does not entail incompatibilism. R states a minimal condition of responsibility required by UR which entails AP-for-some-free-actions, but is non-committal on the Compatibility Question.

10. Ultimacy (U) and Incompatibility: Theses 5 to 7

If UR entails incompatibilism, it is by virtue of adding the U, or Ultimacy, condition. U goes beyond R by requiring for "ultimate" responsibility that the agent also be responsible for anything that is an *arche*, or sufficient ground, reason or explanation for the agent's responsible actions. It is now time to look more closely at this requirement. It means, for example, that if antecedent conditions and laws of nature (or prior character and motives) provide a sufficient reason or explanation for an action, then to be ultimately responsible the agent must be responsible for at least some of those explaining conditions. Something the agent willingly did or omitted must have made a difference in whether or not these explaining conditions were the case.

This interpretation of U reflects a view to which I have been gravitating for the past decade—that the pivotal notion of an *arche* or sufficient ground in U of UR is to be spelled out in terms of the traditional notion of a "sufficient reason." This means in turn that the notion of ultimate responsibility, so crucial for free will on my accounting, is intimately related to the historically important idea of a sufficient reason. Sufficient reasons in turn come in three varieties (here I partly follow Schopenhauer[18]): they may be (i) (logically) sufficient *conditions*, (ii) sufficient *causes* (i.e., antecedent circumstances plus laws of nature) or (iii) sufficient *motives*. The first two entail the existence of that for which they are reasons. The third, sufficient motive, applies to actions and is sufficient in the sense that, given the motive, the action for which it is a motive would be performed voluntarily or willingly and would not be omitted voluntarily or willingly.

What U thus requires is that if an agent is ultimately responsible for an action, the action cannot have a sufficient reason of any of these kinds *for which the agent is not also responsible*. If the action did have such a sufficient reason for which the agent was not responsible, then the action, or the agent's will to perform it, would have its source in something that the agent played no role in producing. Then the *arche* of the action, or of the agent's will to perform it, would not be "in the agent," but in something else. By requiring that the agent be responsible for sufficient *motives* as well as sufficient conditions and causes, U makes clear something that I believe is crucial for understanding free will—namely, that ultimately responsible agents must not only be the sources of their actions, but also of their *will* to perform the actions. How they will to act, and not only how they act, must be within their ultimate control if they are to possess free *will*.

"Being responsible for any sufficient reason" of one's action does not mean the agent has to be the complete or sole cause of the sufficient reason. If a sufficient reason for a present action consisted of a combination of antecedent circumstances and laws of nature, including character traits and motives of the agent, then to be responsible for it, the agent only has to be responsible for some of the antecedent circumstances, character traits, or motives that would have made a difference to the present action, had they been different.[19] The agent must be responsible for these conditions' not being different than they are. Similarly, the agent's responsibility for a sufficient reason does not have to be due to something done in the present, but may be due to something done at earlier times by the agent to form character or motives or to influence later circumstances. What is not allowed by U is that the action have a sufficient reason such that there is nothing the agent could have ever voluntarily done that would have made it different than it is.[20]

[margin note: but again what if the agent believed he could have done otherwise, but was mistaken]

It should now be evident that the antideterministic implications of UR come from U. If any form of determinism were true (scientific or causal, fatalistic, psychological, theological, or logical), there would be a sufficient reason for the occurrence of every event either in the decrees of fate, or antecedent causes plus laws of nature, or foreordaining acts of God, and so forth. For some of these sufficient grounds, it is clear that *we* would not be ultimately responsible if they existed, for example, the decrees of fate or the foreordaining acts of God. But for other grounds, such as antecedent causes or prior motives and states of character, the case is more difficult. We might have been responsible for them by virtue of earlier acts.

As a consequence, UR does not directly entail incompatibilism. Instead, it entails a disjunction.

[margin note: ✻ either an infinite regress or a denial of PSR]

> T5 (*on UR*): U of UR entails *either* that there is an infinite regress of voluntary actions (and/or refrainings) for which the agent is personally responsible *or* some voluntary actions (or refrainings) in the agent's life history for which the agent is personally responsible were not determined (because they had no sufficient causes). *(not) determined = (no) sufficient cause*

The problem is that the first of these alternatives is not credible, at least for finite agents, requiring as it does an infinite regress of actual voluntary actions or refrainings. (Cf. G. Strawson [1986], Klein [1990], S. Wolf [1990].) A few philosophers have speculated about the possibility of an actual infinite regress as a way to salvage incompatibilist intuitions.[21] But I think we have to agree with the majority view that if this were the only way to salvage incompatibilist intuitions, they could not be salvaged. Thus, we have

[margin note: !]

> T6 (*on UR*): If the infinite regress of T5 is not possible for finite agents, then if UR is satisfiable for finite agents at all, some voluntary actions (including refrainings) of the agents' life histories for which the agents are responsible in the sense of R must be undetermined. Let us call these undetermined actions "self-forming actions" (or SFAs) (taking the liberty of assuming that voluntary refrainings can be called actions).

T6 then yields

> T7 (*on UR*): ("The Incompatibility Thesis"): If free will is exercised by finite agents and entails UR, then some undetermined self-forming actions, or SFAs, exist, and determinism is false.[22]

T5 to 7 represent an argument for the incompatibility of free will and determinism based on UR. The following thesis is commentary on that argument.

> T8 (*on UR*): When we consider the implications of AP alone for determinism, we tend to focus on notions of "necessity," "possibility," "power," "ability," "can," and "could have done otherwise." UR also involves these notions (since it entails AP-for-some-free-actions). But, as Martha Klein has pointed out, an interest in ultimacy adds a different set of concerns about the "sources," "grounds," "reasons," and "explanations" of actions and events—that is, concerns about where they came from, what produced them, and who was responsible for them.[23] It is by focusing on such concerns about origins and responsibility, I would argue, and not merely on alternative possibilities, that one arrives at incompatibilism. AP is part of it, because AP is implicated in responsibility, as we see from T3. But it is the additional theme of responsibility for origins expressed by U that leads to incompatibilism.

11. SFAs, AP, and the Consequence Argument: Theses 9–12

T6 asserts that the idea of Ultimate Responsibility as expressed by UR requires that there be some voluntary "self-creating" or "self-forming" actions (including refrainings) in the life histories of agents for which the agents are personally responsible. At this point, we do not know what kinds of acts these would be, but there are some general things that can be said about them.

> T9 (*on UR*) ("Self-Forming Actions" or SFAs): SFAs (of T6) are the undetermined, regress-stopping voluntary actions (or refrainings) in the life histories of agents that are required if U is to be satisfied, and for which the agent is personally responsible in the sense of R. The agents must therefore be responsible for them directly and not by virtue of being responsible for other, earlier actions (as would be required if they were not regress-stopping). This means that, for SFAs, the "something the agents could have voluntarily done (or omitted) that would have made a difference in whether or not they occurred" is simply *doing otherwise*, rather than doing something *else* that would have causally contributed to their not occurring.

> T10 (*on UR*): Putting Theses 6 and 9 together, it follows that SFAs are both undetermined (by virtue of U) and such that the agents willingly performed them and "could have voluntarily (or willingly) done otherwise" (by virtue of R). In other words, *SFAs satisfy AP in an incompatibilist sense* requiring indeterminism.

From this we can derive the second thesis stated at the beginning of the chapter:

> T2 (*on UR*): Compatibilist analyses of *can, power,* and "could have done otherwise" fail to satisfy UR and therefore cannot adequately account for free will as incompatibilists understand it, though compatibilist analyses may be adequate for other kinds of everyday freedoms not requiring UR.

It was further argued in chapter 4 that the Consequence Argument would succeed unless a compatibilist analysis of "can render false" or "can do otherwise" is the correct one. Adding this result, we get

T11 (on UR): If free will requires UR, the Consequence Argument will succeed
for some free actions for which the agent is ultimately responsible by virtue of
the actions themselves and not by virtue of other actions (that is, for SFAs).[24]

To be sure, this result is no surprise at this point, since we know directly from T6
that SFAs cannot be determined. But T11 does reflect the dialectical situation regarding incompatibility that I described at the end of chapter 4—namely, that AP
alone is too thin a basis for resolving the Compatibility Question. Different accounts
of "could have done otherwise" are possible, so ways must be found for ruling some
of them out of the Consequence Argument and some in. This requires looking more
deeply into intuitions about free will that separate compatibilists and incompatibilists—which eventually leads, I believe, to UR.

Looking at the Consequence Argument through the lens of UR throws light on
some of the disputes of chapter 4. Consider the objections to premises 4 and 5 of the
Consequence Argument ("You cannot render false a law of nature" [or the past])
that were based on Lewis's weak (non-causal) interpretation of "can render false."
On this weak interpretation, "If you had done other than move your hand, it would
have been the case that some law of nature (or some proposition about the past) was
false, though your act itself would neither have been nor caused a law-breaking (or
past-altering) event." Incompatibilists such as van Inwagen and Ginet insist that this
weak reading of "can render false" is simply not what they and most ordinary persons mean when they inquire as to whether anyone can alter a law of nature or change
the past, and they therefore insist that the weak reading is inappropriate for the Consequence Argument.

R of UR throws light on why incompatibilists might think this. Rendering false
a law or the past in the weak sense does not imply being *personally responsible* for
doing so, as required by R, because in the weak sense your act "would neither have
been, nor caused, a law-breaking (or past-altering) event." The laws or the past would
have been different had you done otherwise in the weak sense, but *you would not
have been responsible for their being different*. To the contrary, as Lewis himself notes,
if determinism were true, changes (in the laws or the past) would have been causally
responsible for the difference in your act and not the other way around.

Thus, if one were thinking about the Consequence Argument in terms of the
kind of personal responsibility to which UR directs us, the *strong* (causal) reading of
"could have done otherwise" would seem appropriate for the Consequence Argument—just as incompatibilists usually insist. Premises 4 and 5 (which say you can't
change a law of nature or the past) would then seem plausible, since they are true on
the strong reading, as critics of the Consequence Argument concede. Of course, many
of those same critics also argue that, on the strong causal reading, some other premises of the Consequence Argument would fail, namely premise 3 or 6. To refute
such criticisms, it would not be enough to invoke R of UR. One would also have to
appeal to U of UR to show that compatibilist interpretations of "could have done
otherwise" cannot be imported into the premises of the Consequence Argument *for
SFAs* (T10).

In this manner, a thorough defense of the Consequence Argument should, I
think, lead incompatibilists to UR. When incompatibilists are pressed on why

compatibilist interpretations of "can" and "could have done otherwise" should not be allowed in the Consequence Argument, the only decisive and convincing answer I think incompatibilists can give is to appeal to a condition of ultimate responsibility like UR. Some incompatibilists may say that they are not assuming ultimate responsibility when they think about free will, but are thinking about AP alone: they simply have a basic intuition that compatibilist interpretations of "could have done otherwise" are not adequate and only incompatibilist interpretations will suffice. I do not deny that they have such an intuition. I have it too (at least for free will). But what I am suggesting is that when incompatibilists try to spell out their intuition—to make it clearer in a way that will definitively rule out compatibilist interpretations of "could have done otherwise"—they will come up with something like UR *or fail to make a convincing case*. And this claim brings us back full circle to Thesis 1, with which the chapter began: that persistent disagreements between compatibilists and incompatibilists over the meanings of "can" and "could have done otherwise" are related to differing attitudes toward UR.

12. "Of One's Own Free Will"

The title of this concluding section is the most common phrase in which the expression "free will" still regularly occurs in ordinary discourse. In recent decades, compatibilists have attempted to give accounts of the phrase "of one's own free will" consistent with determinism.[25] The arguments of this chapter suggest an incompatibilist account of it based on the preceding theses on UR. We shall first add a further thesis on SFAs that follows from previous ones.

> T12 (*on UR*): While SFAs are required by UR for there to be ultimate responsibility at all, *SFAs are not the only actions for which we are ultimately responsible*, according to UR. Luther's "Here I stand" would have been an affirmation for which he was ultimately responsible, even if it was determined and even if he could not have done otherwise, so long as it was a willed action (issuing from his character and motives) and he was responsible (as U requires) by earlier undetermined SFAs for the character and motives from which the affirmation issued.[26] In other words, incompatibilists do not have to hold that all actions for which agents are ultimately responsible must be undetermined; ultimately responsible actions form a wider class of actions than undetermined SFAs.

This thesis represents an advance in my own thinking about free will for which I am indebted in part to Peter van Inwagen and Alfred Mele. In my earlier work on free will, I had argued that incompatibilists do not have to claim that all *morally* responsible actions must be undetermined. Agents such as Luther (and ourselves, in many everyday contexts) can be morally responsible for actions determined by their wills, so long as they formed their wills by earlier undetermined actions. In correspondence, van Inwagen indicated that he leaned toward a similar thesis which he later spelled out in an important paper (1989). Some time later, criticisms of my earlier work by Mele (which eventually appeared in his 1995) led me to realize that one could say something even stronger than the thesis about morally responsible actions that van Inwagen and I had both defended: not only might incompatibilists say that not all of our *morally* responsible actions have to be undetermined, they might say (as in T12) that not all of our *ultimately* responsible actions have to be undetermined.

Moreover, this realization led me to another realization concerning the expression "of one's own free will." An act like Luther's can be ultimately responsible, according to T12, though determined by his will, *because* the will from which it issued was a will *of his own making,* and in that sense it was his "own" free will. But this suggests an incompatibilist interpretation of the phrase

> T13 (*on UR*) ("Of One's Own Free Will"): Agents act "of their own free wills" (=it is "up to them what they do in the sense required by free will") just in case their actions are willed and they are *ultimately responsible* for them in the sense of UR. It would then follow from T12 that agents can act of their own free wills in this sense, even when their acts are determined and even when they could not have done otherwise—so long as the wills from which they act were formed by them by earlier SFAs that were not determined. Thus, incompatibilists can also say that acts done "of our own free wills" need not all be undetermined. Often we act freely and responsibly (even in an *incompatibilist* sense) out of a will already formed. What is required by UR is that we ourselves freely formed that will, so that it is "our own" free will.

So Dennett may be right about Luther's having free will—and yet wrong about the need for indeterminism and "could have done otherwise" for free will. Ultimately responsible acts, or acts done of one's own free will, make up a wider class of actions than those self-forming actions (SFAs) which must be undetermined and such that the agent could have done otherwise. But if no actions were "self-forming" in this way, we would not be *ultimately* responsible for anything we did. Nor would we have free will.

> T14 (*on UR*): To have *free will,* according to the formula of chapter 1 is to have the "power to be the ultimate creator and sustainer of one's own ends or purposes." We can now say that *the meaning of "ultimate" in this formula is supplied by UR:* to ultimately create and sustain one's ends or purposes is to create and sustain intentions by acts of will (choices, decisions, judgments and efforts) for which one is ultimately responsible in the sense of UR.

undetermined ⟷ no sufficient cause

undet. / no sufficient cause ⟷ AP

6

Significance

1. The Dialectic of Origination

It appears that UR implies incompatibilism. But why should we want UR, which is, after all, an incredibly strong and problematic condition? The case for incompatibility is far from over if we do not go on to address this question, which is a version of the Significance Question for free will: "Why do we, or should we, want to possess a kind of freedom (called 'free will') that requires UR (as well as AP-for-some-free-actions)—and requires as a consequence the incompatibility of free will and determinism?" What is so important about ultimate responsibility that should make a freedom requiring it "worth wanting"? I believe there is more to say about this difficult question than has been said in the long history of debates about free will. The Significance Question marks one of those areas in which uncharted pathways in the labyrinth of free will abound. In this chapter, we explore some of those pathways.

The image of a kind of freedom that would satisfy UR is a remarkable one, but it is one that I think most of us have had at one time or another (if only to reject it in our more reflective moments). (i) The source or ground (*arche*) of action would be in the agent or self, and not outside the agent. This would mean that (ii) if we were to trace the causal or explanatory chains of action backward to their sources, they would terminate in actions that can only and finally be explained in terms of the agent's voluntarily or willingly performing them (i.e., in self-forming actions or SFAs). (iii) The agent would be the sole author or underived originator of these self-forming actions and would thereby be ultimately responsible to some degree for the self which was formed by them and for subsequent actions issuing from that self. (iv) These self-forming actions would not be determined by anything within or outside the self for which the agent was in no way responsible.

These four conditions describe a kind of "sole authorship" or "underived origination" that many ordinary persons believe they want when they want free will. I know of no better description of such a belief in the recent literature than Thomas Nagel's:

> The sense that we are the authors of our own actions is not just a feeling, but a belief; and we can't come to regard it as pure appearance without giving it up altogether. But what belief is it? . . . Although many of the external and internal conditions of choice are inevitably fixed by the world and not under my control, some

range of . . . possibilities is generally presented to me on an occasion of action —
and when acting I make one of these possibilities . . . actual, the final explanation
. . . is given by the intentional explanation of my action. . . . My reason for doing
it is the whole reason why it happened, and no further explanation is either necessary or possible. (1986: 114–5)[1]

In fairness to Nagel, he has doubts that this belief can be satisfied: "I suspect it is no
intelligible belief at all" (p. 114); "we are apparently condemned to want something
impossible" (p. 113). But he has accurately described the belief in question, which
is a direct consequence of UR. To give the belief a convenient title in this chapter, I
am going to call it the belief in *underived origination* or *sole authorship* — understood
in terms of conditions (i) to (iv) of the second paragraph of this section.[2] In order to
be ultimately responsible for any of our actions, we must be the underived originators or sole authors of at least some of them in this sense, which accords with UR.
The question for this chapter is not Nagel's question of whether this belief has a
coherent content (that is the Intelligibility Question, which is the topic of part II).
Rather, the present question is why so many ordinary persons and traditional philosophers have wanted such an extraordinary thing as underived origination or sole
authorship, and why anyone should want it.

The usual answer given to this question in traditional debates about free will is
that underived origination or sole authorship is necessary for a number of other things
that humans generally desire and are worth wanting. Candidates for these other goods
have included (1) genuine *creativity*; (2) *autonomy* (self-legislation) or *self-creation*;
(3) true *desert* for one's achievements; (4) *moral responsibility* in an ultimate sense;
(5) being suitable objects of *reactive attitudes* such as admiration, gratitude, resentment and indignation; (6) *dignity* or *self-worth*; (7) a true sense of *individuality* or
uniqueness as a person; (8) *life-hopes* requiring an *open future*; (9) genuine (freely
given) *love* and *friendship* between persons (or in religious contexts, freely given love
toward God); and (10) the ability to say in the fullest sense that one acts *of one's own
free will*.

Few would deny that (1) to (10) are desirable in some respect. But do they require
free will in the strong sense of UR and underived origination? Incompatibilist intuitions suggest they do, but compatibilists and agnostics about free will have argued
that we can have each of the things described in (1) to (10) in a measure that is worth
wanting without supposing anything so problematic as underived origination or sole
authorship. What compatibilists generally try to do is to "deconstruct" or "demytholo-
gize" the objects of desire described by (1) to (10) — to provide plausible interpretations of them that do not require underived origination and incompatibilist free will.
Incompatibilists in turn respond by trying to show that the deconstructed or demythologized compatibilist versions of (1) to (10) fall short of what we *really* want by
way of autonomy, moral responsibility, desert, and so on.

The result of these opposing strategies is what I call the "dialectic of (underived)
origination (or sole authorship)." The theses of this dialectic are represented by
incompatibilist intuitions regarding (1) to (10), while the antitheses are the
compatibilist deconstructions of these intuitions (and the substitution of compatibilist
alternatives). Most of the historical and recent debate about whether free will is worth
wanting has involved some aspect of this dialectic of origination. Yet I think it is only

the first stage in the debate about Significance. We begin with it here and then move on to other stages.

2. Incompatibilist Intuitions (I): Creativity, Autonomy, Desert, Moral Responsibility

1. Creativity and Novelty

Incompatibilists have often claimed that the underived origination required by free will is a necessary condition for genuine creativity in the universe. Karl Popper, the distinguished philosopher of science and a staunch incompatibilist, says the following about physical determinism.

> It . . . destroys, in particular, the idea of creativity. It reduces to a complete illusion the idea that in preparing this lecture I have used my brain to create *something new*. There was no more in it, according to physical determinism, than that certain parts of my body put down black marks on white paper. (1972: 222)

Others have expressed similar sentiments. William Barrett says that critics of incompatibilist views of freedom often miss

> one of the main motives in the rebellion against determinism, not only on the part of ordinary people but on the part of those modern philosophers who have been most vigorously opposed to the determinist position, namely the desire for freshness, novelty, genuine creation—in short, an open rather than a closed universe. (1958: 46)

W. S. Anglin argues similarly that creativity in the arts and other human enterprises presupposes the underived origination that is characteristic of an incompatibilist free will. He says that on this

> view of what it is to create . . . one brings forth something that is not implicit in the past. The circumstances of the artist influence him, of course, but they do not supply that particular vision or insight that becomes the work of art. It is not nature or God, but simply the composer who creates the symphony. One need not expect . . . that any person . . . with character and musical abilities similar to those of Beethoven . . . would write down exactly the same notes as Beethoven wrote down [when he composed the Fifth Symphony]. Beethoven himself in that situation, might well have composed a different symphony, or no symphony at all. (1990: 14)

2. Autonomy or Self-creation

Among the creations we wish to be "our own," one stands out as particularly important—our own "self." Free will has been traditionally conceived as a kind of creativity (*poiesis*, in the language of the ancient Greek thinkers) akin to artistic creativity, but in which the work of art created is one's own self. As ultimate creators of some of our own ends or purposes, we are the designers of our own lives, self-governing, self-legislating—masters, to some degree, of our own moral destinies.[3] Incompatibilist intuitions about this notion of self-governance have been expressed by many writers. Sir Isaiah Berlin says, "I wish my life and decisions to depend on myself, not on external forces of whatever kinds" (1969: 131), and Nagel says that our aspiration for self-governance gives us "the sense that we ought to be able to . . . become the abso-

lute source of what we do. At any rate we become dissatisfied with anything less"
(1986: 117–18).

Kant associated such a conception of self-governance with the now-popular
notion of "autonomy" (literally, the capacity to "give a law to oneself," or to be "self-
legislating"). To be autonomous in a Kantian sense is to be able to act in accordance
with laws of one's own choosing (that is, principles or maxims about what we ought
to do) rather than acting merely in accordance with nature's laws, or rules imposed
by other persons (1959: 52). Such autonomy, according to Kant, requires underived
origination by the will—or, as he puts it, "a kind of causality belonging to living beings
insofar as they are rational . . . that . . . can be efficient independently of foreign causes
determining it" (p. 65). Lacking this, Kant argues, the actions of free agents would
be entirely subject to laws not of their own making, namely the laws of nature. He
added that the compatibilist's effort to give us something less than this kind of origination independent of "foreign causes" is a "wretched subterfuge" and "petty word
jugglery" (1956: 99).

3. Desert for One's Achievements or Accomplishments

Imagine a medical researcher who has discovered a potent new antibiotic drug. It is
the greatest achievement to date of her professional career and she is understand-
ably proud of it. There have been some grumblings, however, by colleagues that she
is not deserving. What are they saying? That she was at the right place at the right
time. She discovered the new drug, to be sure, in her laboratory culture, but the circumstances that led up to and determined the discovery were none of her doing. It
was all a matter of luck.

She is indignant at this charge, as most of us would be. But why? Because if *none*
of the circumstances issuing in the discovery were her doing, then her desert is seriously decreased, to the level, say, of a lottery winner who is responsible only for buy-
ing the ticket. So she defends herself, arguing that some of the pivotal circumstances
leading to the discovery were in fact her doing. She prepared the way for the discovery by prior experiments and by looking in places her colleagues had been ignoring.

This pattern of criticism and defense involves the same reasoning that led to UR.
If there were circumstances that *completely* determined and explained her discover-
ing the drug and if *she* were not responsible for these circumstances beyond being in
the right place at the right time, then the outcome would be a matter of luck. She
resists this conclusion by arguing, *as UR would require*, that she was personally responsible for at least some of the pivotal circumstances that determined the outcome.
If her critics respond that such things as her prior experiments which influenced the
present discovery were also completely determined by circumstances for which she
was not responsible, she would again, in defense of her desert, either deny the claim
or argue that she was in turn responsible for some of *those* determining circumstances.

What this pattern shows is that the woman's conception of true desert for her
accomplishments involves the idea that she is, to some degree, ultimately responsible for them. She is willing to concede that her discovery involved some luck. She
was not in control of all of the circumstances. We never are. But she defends her
desert by arguing that some of it was ultimately her doing. And incompatibilists argue
that this is the way most people think about genuine desert before they are corrupted

by philosophical doubts about the possibility of ultimate responsibility and underived origination.

4. *Moral Responsibility*

Suppose now that the act whose desert is in question is not a scientific discovery or artistic creation, but a morally praiseworthy or blameworthy act. A man has just rescued a drowning child. He feels demeaned and insulted by the comments of an envious rival that his act was merely an instinctual reaction to a difficult situation. The charge is not that his action was constrained or controlled by others. He did what he wanted and willed what he wanted, but the claim is that his act was nonetheless determined by internal and external circumstances, none of which were within his control or up to him. The man would undoubtedly react as the woman researcher did. He would interpret the charges as an attack on his moral desert and, if he wished to defend himself, would insist that the act was not entirely caused by circumstances that were not up to him and not ultimately his doing.

Similar points hold for blameworthy and shameful acts—though often in reverse, since most persons wish to exonerate themselves for such acts. A man is involved in an auto accident in which a young bicyclist has been killed. He reports to the police that the accident was caused by circumstances over which he had no control. The sunlight was bright in his face, reflecting off the front window, and he did not see the bicyclist. He was driving within the speed limit and was paying attention. But was it true that all the morally relevant circumstances were beyond his control? Was he really attending to the situation or reaching for a cup of coffee? Did he take suitable precautions in the blinding sunlight? The point is that, in posing and responding to such questions, both he and his interrogators assume that *to be negligent with respect to the act, he must be negligent with respect to at least some of the circumstances determining it,* if it was determined. And this is an application of UR.

Such UR-related questions take on a special urgency when the issue of *punishment* for blameworthy actions is added. In what sense can punishment be justified if there is nothing agents could have ever voluntarily done to make themselves or their circumstances different than they were? In what sense can agents be justifiably punished for negligence or occurrences that were ultimately beyond their control? To be sure, there would remain utilitarian reasons for punishment even if UR were not satisfied, as is often noted—to deter the agents themselves or others from doing similar things in the future. But utilitarian justifications for punishment circumvent rather than address the issue of blame*worthiness* for past actions, or *desert* for punishment, which is the issue that leads to UR-related questions about whether actions or circumstances were ultimately within the agents' control.[4]

3. **Incompatibilist Intuitions (II): Reactive Attitudes**

5. *Reactive Attitudes*

Incompatibilist intuitions are also reflected in our attitudes toward other agents. Much of the discussion of this topic in recent decades has revolved around what Sir Peter Strawson has called the "reactive attitudes," such as gratitude, admiration, resentment and indignation. In his influential essay "Freedom and Resentment" (1962),

Strawson asks whether the belief in determinism would compel us to abandon these familiar reactive attitudes toward other persons. Many philosophers have indeed felt that incompatibilist intuitions are built into the reactive attitudes. For example, Nicholas Nathan (1992: 46) imagines a case in which you are "full of gratitude for a decision" recently made by someone (for example, to lend you money). On learning that the decision was completely determined before it was made, Nathan says, you would naturally tend to be less grateful (unless, of course, the decision was determined by the agent's own character and motives, or by other circumstances for which the agent was responsible). And the same would be true, he adds, if someone had done you a wrong you resented.

Strawson's argument in "Freedom and Resentment" presents an interesting challenge to such intuitions. He claims that the reactive attitudes are so deeply embedded in our form of life that we would not, and could not, abandon them, even if we became convinced that determinism was true. We would go on having and appealing to these attitudes as before. Thus, for all practical purposes, he concludes, determinism does not matter to the reactive attitudes. Their existence or importance does not depend upon the belief that people's choices and actions are undetermined.

Strawson's view amounts to a pragmatic solution to a metaphysical quandary—a solution that has been attractive to many philosophers.[5] But many other philosophers believe the metaphysical quandary cannot be so easily dismissed. Their reasons are nicely expressed by Nagel:

> When we first consider the possibility that all human actions are determined by heredity and environment, it threatens to defuse our reactive attitudes as effectively as does the information that a particular action was caused by the effects of a drug—despite all the differences between the two suppositions. . . . Some of the externally imposed limitations . . . on our actions are evident to us. When we discover others, internal and less evident, our reactive attitudes toward the affected action tend to be defused, for [the action] seems no longer attributable in the required way to the person who must be the target of those attitudes. (1986: 125)

Such incompatibilist intuitions about the reactive attitudes are widespread, and I certainly share them. My own thoughts on this matter were inspired by a local trial of a young man who had raped and murdered a sixteen year old girl. I imagined myself as a relative of the victim attending the trial on a daily basis. My initial thoughts of the young man were filled with anger and resentment. But as I listened daily to the testimony of how he came to have the mean character and perverse motives he did have—a sordid story of parental neglect, child abuse, bad role models, and so on—some of my resentment toward him decreased and was directed toward other persons who abused and influenced him. Some resentment was indeed left for the young man, but it was due to my continuing belief that he had *some* residual responsibility for what he became, despite the abuse and bad influences. In such manner, the changes in reactive attitudes, *as well as* the residual resentments, are related to beliefs about ultimate responsibility. Judging by media reports of similar trials, such reactions are very common and, as Nagel argues, quite reasonable.

One might argue that since reactive attitudes are person-directed, they could be transferred from the young man to other persons, but not to impersonal forces like heredity, environment, or nature, assuming determinism were true. This may be correct, but it does not affect the main point. If resentment against the young man could not be *transferred* to impersonal forces, it still might be *transformed* into something else, such as bitterness, sadness, or frustration, if I became convinced that his character and motives were completely determined by factors he could not control. Or, some reactive attitudes might be transferred and some transformed. But in either case, they would have *changed* in some ways for UR-related reasons.

In summary, reactive attitudes are not so easily detachable from incompatibilist intuitions as Strawson supposes. Another philosopher who makes this point is Galen Strawson, the son of Sir Peter Strawson, whose more recent work *Freedom and Belief* (1986) contains an interesting critique of his father's position in "Freedom and Resentment." The younger Strawson points out that the reactive attitudes cannot be so effectively divorced from our cognitive beliefs as the elder Strawson supposes. For instance, in the above example, the decrease in my resentment toward the young man was not something I wanted to happen. But my resentment did decrease, despite myself, because it could not be entirely divorced from my beliefs about how the young man came to be the kind of person he was. Galen Strawson makes this point, and then adds:

> The fact that the incompatibilist intuition has such power for us is as much a natural fact about cogitative beings like ourselves as is . . . our . . . commitment to the reactive attitudes. . . . What is more, the roots of the incompatibilist intuition lie deep in the. . .reactive attitudes . . . [that] enshrine the incompatibilist intuition. The notion of true responsibility comes easily to the non-philosophizing mind and is not found only in (or behind) what Strawson [the elder] calls the "panicky metaphysics" of philosopher libertarians. (p. 88)

I think this disagreement between the two Strawsons represents more than a domestic dispute that has been going on for many years. It exemplifies a generational change in attitudes toward traditional philosophical problems that has taken place in the English-speaking world in the past few decades. The elder Strawson's "Freedom and Resentment" appeared in the heyday of ordinary language philosophy of the 1960s, when it was common to say that ordinary language should stand on its own, undisturbed by the mischievous speculations of philosophers. In contrast, by the 1980s, when the younger Strawson's *Freedom and Belief* appeared, philosophers were less likely to assign the last word on philosophical issues to ordinary language and more likely to take traditional metaphysical problems seriously. Doubts persist about whether metaphysical problems such as free will are solvable (as we see in both Nagel and Galen Strawson). But there is less a tendency to treat problems like free will as pseudo problems or to think that the deep-seated intuitions that provoke such philosophical problems are easily dismissed as confusions.

4. Incompatibilist Intuitions (III): Individuality, Dignity, Life-Hopes

6. *Individuality and Uniqueness*
A number of philosophers have argued that the underived origination or sole authorship required by free will is also connected to views about our individuality and

uniqueness as persons. One philosopher who makes this point is Ted Honderich (1988)—an interesting advocate because he is not a libertarian or free willist, but one of the best-known modern defenders of hard determinism—a philosopher who believes that all human actions are determined (or near-determined) by natural causes. Yet hard determinists, like Honderich, also believe that freedom is incompatible with determinism; and Honderich has written perceptively about incompatibilist intuitions that would have to be forsaken if determinism were true.[6]

Among these intuitions, he thinks, is the notion that if all of our actions were determined, something important to our sense of individuality would be lost. "What I have in mind," he says, "is only this": that if all of a person's actions are determined, then "what [the person] did is *explained* by something that is not individual to, or peculiar to," the person (1988, vol. 2: 68). Our sense of importance as individuals depends in part on the belief that some of our actions are uniquely our products, which means "they are not to be explained . . . in such a way that it would follow that another person of like dispositions would in the same situation perform a like action" (p. 68). Thus, we think it demeaning to be told that *anyone* with the same upbringing and background as ourselves would have accomplished exactly the same things, no more, no less. We think this takes away the uniqueness of our own contribution. Honderich admits that this is a "vague conception," but he thinks it is one we cannot easily shake (p. 69).

Another philosopher who agrees with this point is F. H. Bradley.[7] In response to J. S. Mill, Bradley says that if the "plain man" were to be told that all of his actions were determined and could have been written down in a book before he was born, he "would be most seriously perplexed and in a manner outraged" (1927: 15).[8] He would feel that "he himself might just as well have been anyone else from the first, since nothing remains which is specifically his. The sanctum of his individuality is outraged and profaned" (p. 20). Notice that the feeling Bradley and Honderich describe is not a reaction to CNC control or some kind of coercion or manipulation. It is a reaction simply to the possibility that one's actions and accomplishments be entirely predictable by being subsumed under general laws.

But why should anyone think that a problem? The answer, I believe, is that persons would thereby be treated as instances of types rather than as unique individuals. Sir Isaiah Berlin expressed the same thought in his well-known essay "Historical Inevitability" (1969) when trying to explain why so many people are troubled by the deterministic presuppositions of much contemporary psychological, historical, and social research. There is more to the concern about determinism in the human sciences, according to Berlin, than the fear of being manipulated by behavior modification squads hired by corporations or governments to influence one's behavior. Beyond such practical concerns, there is also a concern about one's status as a person: most people want to ascribe a uniqueness to themselves that would make it impossible for others to treat them as types, subsuming all of their behavior under general laws. They want to say, "Don't type me. Pay attention to *me* and not to your physiological, psychological, or social formulae, because I will surprise you, no matter how comprehensive your knowledge is. To deal with me as a person, you must wait to see what I will do and then react accordingly." (Similar sentiments were expressed by Dostoyevsky's "Underground Man.")

7. Dignity

Needless to say, this conception of individuality or uniqueness is related to human dignity. The same is true of many of the other goods previously considered — autonomy, desert for one's achievements, moral responsibility, and so on. They all have some connection to dignity, understood as the "worthiness for respect from others for one's personhood, values, and purposes." The indignation of the medical researcher and of the man who saved the drowning child, as well as the outrage of Bradley's plain man, are reactions to perceived threats to a sense of personal worth that we associate with the ultimate sources of our actions and achievements. Kant expressed this connection between dignity and ultimacy by asserting that rational beings should be treated as "ends in themselves" because they are "the ultimate creators of their own ends" (1959: 52).

The connection Kant envisaged between dignity and ultimacy can be explained as follows. To treat others as moral agents is to assume that, on some matters, the buck stops with them. They, and they alone, are ultimately accountable for their purposes and actions. (As James Felt has put it, the libertarian intuition is that "the buck-stops [here] because it started [here]" [1994: 82].) But there is another side to this coin. If I am to be held responsible for my purposes and actions *because I am their ultimate source*, then I likewise want those purposes and actions to be respected *because I am their ultimate source* — and not merely because what I do is useful to others. In other words, I want to be treated as an end in myself (with dignity), because I acknowledge ultimate responsibility for my own ends.[9]

8. Life-Hopes and an Open Future

Our views about the origination of action are related to the way we view the future as well as the way we view the past and other agents. Honderich has introduced the useful term *life-hopes* in order to draw attention to this fact. He says "Talk of [our] initiating, . . . bringing about [or] producing . . . implies an activity that is not itself a product [and] . . . secures to us open futures" (vol. 2, p. 19). To view actions in this way, he says, generates certain kinds of life-hopes. To have this "sort of life-hope, whether about being an actress, surviving a battle, or whatever, is to have a hope best characterized" as the "hope for an unfixed future . . . in which we are not creatures of our environment and our dispositional natures" (p. 22). Honderich is, of course, well aware that we would go on hoping that things turn out well, even if determinism were true (as he believes it is). But he argues that our life-hopes would have an unmistakably different flavor if we believed in a closed (deterministic) universe rather than an open (indeterministic) one. In the former kind of universe, it is simply that we don't know how things will turn out, whereas in the latter we believe that we can rise above the conditioning and influence of the past to produce something new by our own efforts.

This creates an attitude toward our present and future that was aptly described by another incompatibilist, William James, in his well-known essay "The Dilemma of Determinism." "The great point" about the incompatibilist view, James says, "is that the possibilities are really *here*. . . . At those soul-trying moments when fate's scales seem to quiver," we acknowledge "that the issue is decided nowhere else than *here* and *now. That* is what gives the palpitating reality to our moral life and makes it tingle

. . . with so strange and elaborate an excitement" (1956: 183). It may be easy to ridicule James's assertion that a certain passion and excitement would be taken out of
present and future choice situations if we believed their outcomes were determined.
But many ordinary persons and philosophers, myself included, would say that it is
true.[10] The point is not that our life-hopes would be different as to their specific contents in a deterministic universe, but rather that all of them would be seen in a different light because of altered beliefs about our contribution to their realization.

9. Love and Friendship

Another claim sometimes made about incompatibilist free will is nicely expressed
by Anglin. Suppose, he says,

> we could . . . press a button and thereby make someone love us. . . .That person
> would then perhaps show us great signs of affection. . .but would they really love
> us? . . . Moreover, even if the sufficient cause of the "love" is not something easily
> identifiable like button pressing but something more subtly embedded in the causal
> structure of the world, it still seems that the love is not authentic. (p. 20)

Anglin may be going too far in suggesting that a love which is merely the result of
instinct or biological determination could not be real or authentic love. A mother's
love or romantic passion would be quite real instances of love, even if determined.
But there is nevertheless a point to his remarks. There is a *kind* of love we desire
from others—parents, children (when they are old enough), spouses, lovers, and
friends—whose significance is diminished, as he says, by the thought that they are
determined to love us entirely by instinct or circumstances beyond their control or
not ultimately up to them. (Galen Strawson [1986: 309] makes a similar point about
a love of this kind and its relation to incompatibilist intuitions.[11]) To be loved by
others in this desired sense requires that the ultimate source of others' love lies in
their own wills.

This thought is also pertinent to theological debates about free will, which are
of special concern to Anglin. "God might have created us in such a way," he says,
"that it was prearranged that we 'love' both him and each other. This would not really be love. For no one can love truly unless, at some time or other, he is free not to
love, and in a sense which precludes an arrangement which would be a sufficient
cause of love-like behavior" (p. 20). This is a common theological theme in the West,
at least from St. Augustine onward: free will was given to human beings not only to
allow for moral responsibility and "desert in the nature of things," but also so that
the love returned to God by creatures would be freely given and have its source in
them. This theological theme in turn reflects the all-too-human belief that if the love
others bear us were to turn out to be determined, it would have diminished worth.

10. "Of One's Own Free Will"

At the end of chapter 5, I offered an incompatibilist interpretation of this expression
which implies that we act from a will that is ultimately of our own making. As a final
step in their initial contribution to the dialectic of origination, incompatibilists would
insist that this ultimate sense of acting "of one's own free will," defined by Thesis 13

of chapter 5, is the one required by genuine creativity, autonomy, desert, moral responsibility, and other goods described in (1) to (9).

5. Compatibilist Deconstructions (I)

Few people, as I said earlier, would deny the importance of most of the goods listed under (1) to (10). But do these goods really require ultimate responsibility and underived origination, and hence indeterminism, as the preceding arguments of incompatibilists assert? Compatibilists say no; and as their contribution to the second phase of the dialectic of origination, they proceed to give accounts of such things as autonomy, desert, moral responsibility, creativity, dignity, and the like in ways that do not require incompatibilist freedom.

Consider (1), creativity and novelty. "By virtue of denying underived origination," compatibilists might say, "we do not have to deny the existence of novelty and creativity within the universe in perfectly ordinary senses of these terms. Even if determinism were true, Beethoven's Fifth Symphony would have been something new in human history in the obvious sense that nothing like it had ever been produced before. And Beethoven would be artistically creative in the obvious sense that he had produced something novel and magnificent. Thus, the claims of Popper, Barrett, and Anglin that 'genuine' creativity or novelty require the falsity of determinism are utterly question begging—however appealing they may be to the untutored imagination. One may, of course, define 'genuine novelty' so that it requires an indeterministic future (as Barrett seems to do); or 'genuine creativity' so that it requires underived origination (as Popper and Anglin do). But this settles nothing, for it simply amounts to assuming incompatibilist interpretations of the words 'creativity' and 'novelty.'

"A similar point can be made about other items on the list, like (6), individuality and uniqueness. Compatibilists do not have to deny individuality and uniqueness in perfectly ordinary senses of these terms. Our uniqueness as individuals is the consequence of our time and place of origin, our genetic code, and the physical and psychological histories of our development. Even identical twins with the same genes have unique histories beginning in the fetal stage and consequently different pasts and ways of seeing the world. This is all the individuality and uniqueness we can, and should, reasonably desire as beings in the natural order, and it is perfectly consistent with determinism. One could, of course, define 'genuine' individuality and uniqueness so that they require underived origination, as Honderich and Bradley seem to do in the above quotes. But this simply amounts to assuming incompatibilist interpretations of the terms 'individuality' and 'uniqueness.'

"Incompatibilists may respond that our ordinary (compatibilist) senses of 'creativity,' 'novelty,' 'individuality,' and 'uniqueness' are understandable, but mundane. They want a more exalted kind of creativity (or novelty or individuality or uniqueness).[12] But when one deconstructs what incompatibilists want (or say they want)— namely 'genuine' or 'true' creativity or novelty—it turns out to be just the kind of creativity or novelty that requires ultimate responsibility and underived origination. They are begging the question."

6. Compatibilist Deconstructions (II)

Similar criticisms can be made by compatibilists with respect to the other goods of (1) to (10). The terms *genuine* and *true*, compatibilists may say, "are used in the same question-begging way by incompatibilists to characterize autonomy, dignity, love, friendship, desert, life-hopes, and the like. In each case, interpretations of these notions can be given that do not require ultimate responsibility or underived individuation. To illustrate, consider a central item on the list—moral responsibility (4). Compatibilists may, and often do, argue as follows.

"In everyday affairs, we hold people morally responsible or accountable for their actions unless some excusing or mitigating conditions are present.[13] Were they coerced or acting under threats? Were they capable of knowing the difference between right and wrong? Were their actions intentional or inadvertent? Could they have reasonably foreseen the consequences and did they take suitable precautions? Were they subject to hallucinations or delusions? Did they have the capacity to understand the gravity of their acts? Did they act from irresistible desires caused by phobias, obsessional neuroses, or addiction? Were they manipulated in ways they could not have reasonably resisted (e.g., by subliminal advertising, or brainwashing, or hypnosis)? Was their reasoning or other capacities temporarily impaired in ways they could not have prevented? and so on.[14]

"Compatibilists hold that these are the considerations that do and should enter into everyday judgments of moral and legal responsibility or accountability. And they hold that it would be absurd to suggest that, if determinism were true, we should stop asking such questions or stop using the answers to them to excuse or mitigate moral responsibility. The differences between being or not being psychotic, addicted, mentally impaired, manipulated, ignorant, or coerced would be as significant in a determined world as in an undetermined one. To be sure, no philosopher or legal theorist has ever provided an exhaustive list of responsibility-excusing or mitigating conditions, but there is a good reason for this. The meanings of expressions such as 'moral responsibility' and related terms such as 'accountability,' 'praiseworthiness' and 'blameworthiness' are normative, as well as factual. Their application can vary depending on the standards to which we choose to hold people responsible. Whether an agent took reasonable precautions, or could have resisted a threat, or should have foreseen consequences, depends in part on what we normally expect of persons in similar circumstances or what standards we regard as reasonable for others similarly circumstanced.

"If moral responsibility can be thus understood in compatibilist terms, so can such notions as desert (3), dignity (7), and the reactive attitudes (5), all of which presuppose moral responsibility. As for autonomy (2), there have been a number of cogent accounts of it by recent philosophers that do not require incompatibilist freedom.[15] There is general agreement that autonomy requires the capacities (i) to *reflect* upon and critically *evaluate* one's reasons or motives for action, (ii) to *revise* them in the light of these reflections, (iii) to *identify* with some of one's reasons and motives as expressive of one's 'real' self, and (iv) to act upon reasons one chooses to identify with in a manner that is not coerced, compulsive, or manipulated. But none of these capacities, we compatibilists claim, requires the falsity of determinism. In a determined world we could, and would want to, distinguish persons who possessed the capacities to reflectively evaluate, revise, identify with, and act upon various of their reasons without constraint from persons who lacked such capacities.

"Once again, incompatibilists may respond that compatibilist notions of moral responsibility, desert, dignity, and autonomy are understandable but mundane. We may want responsibility, desert, dignity, and autonomy in compatibilist senses and might well prefer them to their opposites even in a determined world. But that is not all we want, according to incompatibilists. We also want to be responsible, autonomous, and deserving in more 'exalted' senses that are not possible in a determined world. Yet when one deconstructs what incompatibilists mean by a more exalted ('genuine' or 'true') responsibility, desert, or autonomy, this also turns out to be just the kind that requires ultimate responsibility and underived origination, and hence indeterminism. They are begging the question once again."

7. The Dialectic of Selfhood (I)

So goes the dialectic of origination. Incompatibilists argue that free will (in a sense requiring UR and underived origination) is necessary for the possession of many other goods such as genuine creativity, autonomy, desert and the like. Compatibilists counter that these goods can be attained in a measure worth wanting without requiring free will as incompatibilists understand it. Incompatibilists respond that the demythologized or deconstructed compatibilist versions of these goods fall short of what people *really* want; compatibilists, they say, fail to give us genuine or true versions of the goods. Compatibilists counter that the references to genuine versions of these goods are question begging, because what incompatibilists have in mind are just the versions that satisfy conditions of ultimate responsibility and underived origination. We are back to the original question: what is so important about ultimate responsibility and underived origination in the first place?

This is another one of those junctures at which free-will debates so often end in stalemate. And I think that here, as elsewhere, the only way to make progress is to dig more deeply into the conflicting intuitions that lie behind the disagreements—a project that once again leads into uncharted territory. In the history of philosophy, debates about the Significance Question do not usually get far beyond the dialectic of origination. Intuitions on both sides are repeated, but that is as far as it usually goes. To go farther, I think we have to look more closely at the notions of ultimate responsibility and underived origination themselves. Why *are* they so important? What lies behind the widespread conviction not only among ordinary persons (Bradley's "plain men"), but among many philosophers as well, that ultimate responsibility and underived origination confer greater value on each of the goods (1) to (10)?

This question is baffling, I think, because we underestimate how "metaphysical" one has to become in order to answer it. Aristotle held that metaphysics—*sophia* or "wisdom" or "first philosophy," as he called it—was the study of the ultimate sources and explanations (*archai kai aitia*) of things. The free will issue is metaphysical in just this sense. It is about the ultimate sources and explanations—*archai kai aitiai*—of some special things in the universe, namely responsible human actions. We should therefore expect debates about the significance of free will to delve rather deeply into the metaphysical depths—and that is what they must do. Such debates are not simply about practical questions that arise in everyday life or law courts concerning responsibility, blameworthiness, and desert. Compatibilist accounts of free and responsible agency are often adequate to such questions. But <u>debates about free will go beyond the practical concerns of the law courts and everyday conflicts. They are about the human condition broadly conceived, about our place and importance in the scheme of things.</u> Hence, the concern is not merely with desert from this or that point of view, but desert "in the nature of things": not merely responsibility with respect to this or that set of norms, but "ultimate" responsibility in the nature of things.

When we do take seriously the metaphysical depths of the free will issue, I believe we are propelled beyond the dialectic of origination to what I call the "dialectic of selfhood."

Imagine a baby several months old lying in an infant seat, propped up at a 60-degree angle. The baby's arms and legs shake with uncontrolled and undirected energy as she surveys the room around her. This shaking comes from her nervous system, and ultimately from the brain, which soaks up 80 percent of the energy-producing glucose of the body. It is for good reason that we call young children "bundles of energy." (Nietzsche would undoubtedly say it is the "will to power" in them, which he regarded as the desire to exhibit one's share of the energy of the universe.) Our baby doesn't quite know what to do with all that energy yet; her task is to gradually learn to get more control over it.

One of the earliest steps in the process of gaining control is a step that many parents have observed. Objects pass in front of the infant and she follows them with her eyes. She has no control over most of them and simply observes them pass by. But one passing object has a special fascination—her own hand. It is different, for it seems that she can control it. One day she actually learns to hold the hand still in her visual field, make a fist with it, and then open it again. This turns out to be utterly fascinating. When she first discovers it, the act is repeated over and over again, and she smiles with delight at each success. She has discovered that this passing object—her hand—is something special. It is part of her, and she can control it by an act of will. She has discovered the phenomena of *action* and *will* simultaneously by recognizing that she can control and direct some things out there in the world by attending to them and willing them to happen in her mind. No wonder she is fascinated.

Not surprisingly, this discovery is also connected with the distinction the infant is learning to make between herself and the world. Some things, like her hands and feet and other parts of her body, are more intimately hers because they are directly under the control of her will. By contrast, she cannot make the toy that passes in front of her eyes obey her will, though she can move it by pushing it with her hand. In other words, she is learning to see her self as a *source* of motion or activity in the world distinct from other such sources. The ancient Greek thinkers employed the term *psyche* (meaning "soul") in this manner: Each living thing had a psyche by virtue of its power to "move itself." The infant in these early acts recognizes that she has a psyche and is beginning to distinguish herself accordingly from other things in the world, including other psyches. Other human beings are of special interest, of course, but babies also take a special delight in animals. They see animals as independent sources of motion like themselves, and delight in this kinship.

Imagine now what it would be like if this will/action barrier were never crossed. The baby observes things passing by, but can never *do* anything that would have an effect on the passing scene. Even the baby's inner life is just a passing scene. Everything just happens, and she is purely an experiencer or observer, living in what might be called a "womb with a view." In a certain sense, the baby would then no longer be "in" the world, but merely observing it from outside. Her hands and arms are objects like any others passing by. At times one gets the impression that this is the way David Hume describes the self, as something that experiences and observes things, including its own inner life, as if it were in a womb with a view (1960: 633–6).

Perhaps that is also why Hume could never find "himself" in the passing show, but always came upon this or that experience. For our ordinary conception of a self in the world distinct from other selves is more than the conception of a passive observer. It is also the conception of an active being whose willing can have effects on the passing scene. Our full sense of *being a distinct self is tied up with the conception of our being a distinct source of motion or activity in the world,* such that what goes on behind the screen of our mind can have effects out there in the world. This is a crude picture, to be sure. The dialectic of selfhood is still in its infancy at this stage, like the baby herself. But what it suggests is that there is a close connection between the phenomena of will and action, on the one hand, and selfhood, on the other.[16]

8. The Dialectic of Selfhood (II)

In part I of the dialectic of selfhood, just described, we come to view ourselves as distinct sources of motion or activity in the world, separate from other things (animate or inanimate), which are moved by forces independent of our wills. We see our *selves*, on the one hand, as independent sources of motion over against the *world*, on the other, with its myriad sources of motion that are not directly under the control of our wills. And insofar as we come to value our selfhood, we take delight in what we are able to produce or accomplish as sources of motion. Thus, the baby smiles at her ability to open and close her fist. Later, like all children, she will hunger for appreciation and praise for her accomplishments, whatever they may be—crawling, walking, or painting a picture.

All parents know this inexhaustible craving in children for appreciation and acknowledgment for what they do. When the appreciation and acknowledgment are not forthcoming, as in dysfunctional families, the effects on the developing psyches of children are devastating. According to A. O. Lovejoy (1961), eighteenth-century philosophers referred to this craving as the desire for "approbation," and regarded it as a fundamental human need throughout life. This desire for approbation, I suggest, is part and parcel of a more fundamental need to affirm our selfhood as independent beings in the world who are sources of activity (i.e., as psyches or souls in the ancient sense). It is an affirmation of selfhood that will later attach to such things as desert for our acomplishments, taking responsibility for our actions, dignity, individuality, and being a fit object of gratitude and other reactive attitudes—all of them part of the dialectic of origination.

In its first phase, this affirmation of selfhood is crude. There is the self as such a source of motion over against the world, understood as whatever is other than one's self. Self and world (or self and not-self) are conceived as separate, independent sources of motion. But something happens to this simple picture when we begin to understand more about the world. It turns out that we are not separate from the world, as if we were in a womb with a view and able to influence the world from outside it. We find out that we are in the world and are influenced by it in many different ways. Behind the window to the world—where *we* are supposed to be—is the brain, and it is a physical object, like the body itself, which is part of the world and is causally influenced by the world.

This awareness that we are part of the world and are causally influenced by it provokes a spiritual crisis that is phase 2 of the dialectic of selfhood.[17] Perhaps we are not really independent sources of motion in the world at all, but are entirely products of the world, or of the not-self. Perhaps we only *seem* to "move ourselves" in a primordial way, when our motions are in fact caused by forces in the world of which we are unaware. This thought takes many forms in the history of ideas, but in all its forms it poses a similar threat to the human self-image and a corresponding crisis in human thinking. Such is the case when we learn that much of our character and behavior is influenced by factors of heredity and environment of which we were unaware. Such is the case when we learn that our behavior can be determined by subconscious motives traceable to long-forgotten experiences in our past, or when we learn that our thoughts and behavior can be influenced by subtle chemical imbalances of the neurotransmitters or hormones in our brains or endocrine systems.

One crude reaction, at this stage, in defense of our psyches (or ourselves as independent sources of activity) is to insist that we are not in the natural world at all. The self behind the window is outside the natural world altogether, looking in on it. It can influence the external world by intervening in the natural-causal order but is not entirely determined by that natural order. This reaction is, of course, mind-body dualism of the Cartesian kind. I do not wish to defend such a view here, for I believe, along with most contemporary philosophers, that it is too crude a reaction to the dialectic of selfhood, and creates more puzzles than it solves. (In part II we shall also see that dualism cannot resolve the deepest mysteries about free will.) But I think it is important to understand why dualism is a natural reaction at a certain stage in the dialectic of selfhood. It is an attempt to salvage the self or psyche as an independent source of activity by placing it beyond the subversive influences of the "world" or "not-self."

Another reaction is possible in phase 2 of the dialectic of selfhood that does not place the self entirely outside the world. We can concede that we are part of the natural world and influenced by it in many ways, but not completely. Of all the data that comes to us from the outside world through our senses and is processed by our brains, we ourselves are capable of determining to some degree what gets in and what is screened out—what influences our thought and action and what does not. In other words, we have the final say about the *way* the world influences us.

A useful image here is the membrane of a cell. It is the dividing line between the cell and world, or not-cell. The purpose of the membrane is to let in things that are useful to the cell and to keep other things out. Biologists generally view the presence of such a membrane or device for screening input and output as an essential characteristic of life. David Hawkins suggests that living things did not have to learn to reproduce themselves. Rather, life began when things that could reproduce themselves (DNA molecules) learned to live (1967: 324). That is, they acquired membranes around them which distinguished them from the world and allowed them to *selectively* interact with their environment.

Imagine our self now as a much more sophisticated living thing with such selective powers. It is subject to myriad influences from the outside world, but has the power to select some of the things that will influence it and reject others. Many influences permeate the membrane that separates it from the world, but the self remains an independent source of activity within its membrane. Within its inner sanctum or citadel,[18] it is able to decide to some degree what influences it. In such manner, independent selfhood is preserved from being overwhelmed by the world in the second phase of the dialectic of selfhood.

9. The Dialectic of Selfhood (III)

Unfortunately, the preceding solution can only temporarily quell doubts about the influence of the world upon us. If we have already learned that we are influenced by many things of which we were unaware, how can we be sure that the very selections we make from within our inner sanctum are not determined by influences in our past that we are unaware of, and are not in our control? What if our choices about *how* the world will influence us are themselves determined by the world? This is phase 3 of the dialectic of selfhood, where we encounter full-fledged threats of deterministic doctrines in all their guises—physical, fatalistic, psychological, and so on. What I am suggesting here is that we view the threat of determinism, not as an isolated phenomenon, but as *a stage of the dialectic of selfhood*—the process of self-understanding about the relation of our self to the world, or not-self. At each stage, we are trying to preserve a remnant of the idea that we are independent sources of activity or motion in the world against the threat that we are mere products of forces coming wholly from the world—forces that are not the products of our own wills.

Keeping in mind this general pattern, we can see what the natural reaction would be to the challenges posed in phase 3. To the charge that choices emanating from our inner sanctum might be completely determined by forces (perhaps unknown to us) coming from the world and not from our wills, we might respond: "This cannot be so for *all* of our choices, if we are to be independent sources of activity in the world at all. Some of our choices must not be completely determined by forces coming from the world and not from our wills. Or, if our choices *are* so determined by the world, then at least some of the determining circumstances must at some time have had *their* source in our wills." But this response is an expression of UR: if our choices had their complete source or explanation in certain circumstances, then to be responsble for the choices, we have to be responsible for at least some of those circumstances. And, like UR, this response leads either to a regress or to the supposition that at least some of our self-forming actions must have had their ultimate source (or *arche*) in us—in the self, not in the world or not-self.

In this manner, the dialectic of selfhood propels us toward notions of ultimate responsibility and underived origination as a response to more sophisticated threats to our status as distinct selves over against the world. Historical debates about free will are a consequence of this dialectic. For, as I see it, *free will is a higher stage response to the dialectic of selfhood*. It emerges as an issue when we realize how profoundly the world influences us in ways of which we are unaware. *The advent of doctrines of determinism in the history of thought is an indication that this stage of self-understanding has been reached.* This is why free will issues typically arose in human history in response to doctrines of determinism and why it is appropriate to begin a discussion of free will with historical threats of determinism, as we did in chapter 1.

But the idea of free will, once attained, takes on a significance of its own that goes beyond the determinist threats which provoke it. It emerges as an extension of the basic desire to be selves or psyches with the power to be independent sources of activity in the universe. This requires that not all of what we are can be determined by the world. At least some of what we are, whether praiseworthy or blameworthy, must have its underived origin in us, so that we are ultimately responsible for it. The power to be "self-" creating in this way *is* free will.

Perhaps we cannot have such a power. Perhaps it is impossible or unintelligible, as so many modern thinkers believe. But we want it, I am suggesting, for the same reason that children and adults take delight in their accomplishments—from making a fist or walking upright to composing a symphony. And the want is no arbitrary one. It is related to the fact that we first distinguish ourselves *as selves* distinct from the world by virtue of our ability to control some things by our wills, as the baby did her fist. Thereafter, we associate being a self in the full sense with *doing* things— making, producing, creating, bringing about; as effecting changes in the world by our wills. And we resist attempts to undermine the belief that we are the ultimate sources of what comes from our wills because we believe our independence as selves *in* the world is tied up with our independence as actors and willers *from* the world. (When the baby first walks, she says, "Unhand me. I want to do this on my *own*.")

Bradley, Honderich, Nagel, and others are onto something, therefore, when they say that free will is connected to our sense of our importance and uniqueness as persons. Bradley's "plain man" was outraged by the thought that determinism might be true. He felt that thereby the inner sanctum of his personhood would be profaned. In general, the greater depth that attaches to each of the goods (1) to (10), if one assumes free will, comes from the fact that the individual is the ultimate source of his or her actions and attitudes. In a primitive state of consciousness (phase 1 of the dialectic of selfhood) this is what we thought we were all along—namely, independent sources of activity over against the world or not-self. When greater knowledge of the seditious influences of the world threaten this belief, we do what we can to retrieve it. For it represents what we wanted from the moment we realized that we could get out of the womb with a view, and could *be* somebody.

Perhaps this desire for independent selfhood is perverse, as some Eastern philosophies assert.[19] This is an issue worth discussing and we shall return to it shortly. But, for better or for worse, I am suggesting that free will is deeply implicated and intertwined with the idea of being such an independent self. If the latter is valued (or disvalued), the former will be also, and vice versa. Nor should we trivialize the connection by supposing that independent selfhood implies selfishness. For we know from ethicists that self-concern is consistent with concern for others. Independent selfhood need not imply selfishness, any more than free will does. In fact, the possession of independent selfhood, like the possession of free will, is a precondition for moral agency in the fullest sense—for being selfish *or* having moral concern for others in a way that emanates ultimately from us.[20] In this manner, the dialectic of selfhood completes the dialectic of origination.

10. Objective Worth

There is one final step in this account of the significance of free will. I believe that ultimate responsibility, and hence free will, are also related to another notion, which I have elsewhere called "objective worth."[21] To understand what objective worth is, consider a story about Alan the artist. Alan has been so despondent that a rich friend concocts a scheme to lift his spirits. The friend arranges to have Alan's paintings bought by confederates at the local art gallery under assumed names for $10,000 apiece. Alan mistakenly assumes his paintings are being recognized for their artistic merit by knowledgeable critics and collectors, and his spirits are lifted. Now let us imagine two possible worlds involving Alan. The first is the one just described, in which Alan thinks he a great artist, and thinks he is being duly recognized as such, but really is not. The other imagined world is a similar one in which Alan has many of the same experiences, including the belief that he is a great artist. But in this second world he really is a great artist and really is being recognized as such; his rich friend is not merely deceiving him to lift his spirits. Finally, let us imagine that in both these worlds Alan dies happily, believing he is a great artist, though only in the second world was his belief correct.[22]

We begin to understand what objective worth is when we ask whether it would make any difference to Alan which of these worlds he lives in. To say that there is an important difference in value in the two worlds for Alan, even though he would not know it and would *feel* equally happy in both, is to say he endorses a notion of *objective* worth. One of the consequences of this notion is that a person's subjectively felt happiness is not the only measure of value. To understand what objective worth means to Alan, we must ask him to imaginatively stand outside the worlds—taking what Nagel calls the "objective" viewpoint—and compare the two. Of course, we could imagine a third world in which Alan is deceived as in the first, but finds out he is being deceived. And that would be clearly the worst of all three worlds. Yet the fact that the third imagined world is the worst of the three for Alan in no way changes his judgment that the first world, in which he is deceived (and never knows it), is worse than the second, in which he is not deceived. And this shows that objective worth means something to Alan, as it would to most of us who would find it demeaning to be told, "Your paintings (or writings or causes or other accomplishments) are really worthless, but so what—you are having a good time making, or engaging in, them, and that's all that matters."

I want to suggest that the notion of ultimate responsibility is of a piece with this notion of objective worth. If, like Alan, we think that the objective worth of our acts or accomplishments is something valuable over and above the felt satisfaction the acts have or bring, then I suggest we will be inclined to think that a freedom requiring ultimate responsibility is valuable over and above compatibilist freedoms from coercion, compulsion, and oppression. When these compatibilist freedoms are maximally present, there are no constraints or impediments preventing us from having or doing whatever we please. Such freedoms would be enough, if we did not care about more than what pleases us—namely, if we did not care in addition, like Alan, about our "worthiness" or "deservingness" to be pleased. Are our acts or deeds, our accomplishments and we ourselves, objectively worthy of recognition, respect, love, or praise, as Alan wished for his paintings or might wish for himself? It is this concern for the objective desert of our deeds and characters that leads naturally to a concern about whether those deeds and characters have their ultimate sources in us rather than in someone or something else (fate or God, genes or environment, social conditioning or behavioral controllers). Do they ultimately redound to us or not? The answer to this question does not have to do merely with subjective happiness, but with the objective worth of our selves and our lives.

By contrast, if objective worth means little to us, or makes no sense—if we believe that the final perspective Alan or anyone should take is *inside* the worlds, in which subjective happiness is all that counts (even if it is based on deception)—we are likely to see no point or significance as well in ultimate responsibility and incompatibilist freedom. Both ultimate responsibility and objective worth require us to stand back and take an objective view of the universe and our place in it. We imagine our deeds as having worth "from the point of view of the universe," and we imagine ourselves as buck-stopping originators of those deeds from the point of view of the universe. Both require an objective point of view, and if we no longer believe there can be any such point of view or no longer think it matters, both objective worth and ultimate responsibility will tend to fade into insignificance.

This is a great divide on free will, and our standing on one side or the other of it is more a question of attitude or (what I have elsewhere called) "aspiration" than of knowledge.[23] Those for whom objective worth is unimportant or unattainable will naturally wonder what all the fuss over ultimate responsibility is about, while those who think objective worth is important and attainable will wonder how others could be indifferent to issues of ultimate responsibility. Dennett is right in saying that the question is about what kind of free will is "worth wanting." But in answering that question, he and others compatibilists put the emphasis on "wanting," whereas incompatibilists such as myself put the emphasis on "worth."

11. Attitudes and Values

I have argued that when one traces the desires we have for incompatibilist free will to their roots, by way of UR, one eventually arrives at two elemental (and I think interrelated) desires—(i) the desire to be independent sources of activity in the world, which is connected, I maintain, from the earliest stages of childhood to the sense we have of our uniqueness and importance as individuals; and (ii) the desire that some of our deeds and accomplishments (such as Alan's paintings in my example) have objective worth—worth not just from one's own subjective point of view, but true (i.e., nondeceptive) worth from the point of view of the world.

I have suggested that both desires play a role in libertarian intuitions, and that in this role they are related. The objective worthiness that concerns libertarians comes not merely from having in fact lived a good life or accomplished certain goals, but from the fact that you yourself were the independent source of the living of that life and of accomplishing those goals.[24] So the objective worth in question presupposes independent selfhood. But, conversely, being an independent source of activity in the world is wanted *for* the sake of *doing* something that will make an objective (i.e., nonillusory, nondeceptive) mark upon the world, and in this sense, independent selfhood is directed toward objective worth; it seeks to express itself through activity that has objective, nonillusory, significance in the world.[25] I think these desires, thus linked together, lie behind and help to explain libertarian intuitions about genuine desert, responsibility, creativity, and others involved in the dialectic of origination.

Does this mean that all persons must have the desires for independent selfhood and objective worth, or must make them paramount in their lives, or think that their objects are attainable — on pain of irrationality? No, it does not; nor do I think demonstrations are possible on such matters from premises that no rational person could reject. Some philosophers thought, like Kant, that you could compel assent to the value of incompatibilist freedom by reasoning (transcendentally, in Kant's case) from premises that no one could rationally reject, and many modern libertarians still approach the problem in this way. But I do not. The reason is that differences about fundamental values are too contestable, given what we know, to allow such facile demonstrations, and the free will issue involves issues about fundamental values by way of the Significance Question. Thus, in chapter 1, I noted that disagreements about free will involve not only conceptual and factual disputes, but disagreements about values as well; and although these value disagreements are discussable, they cannot be conclusively settled by conceptual analyses and factual appeals alone.

Kant

What one *can* do with value disagreements about free will (and what I have tried to do in this chapter) is to show why a freedom requiring ultimate responsibility is valued by incompatibilists, and has been valued for centuries; how it can be traced to certain basic desires that many of us have about the significance of our lives and of what we may accomplish in the scheme of things; and *then*, on the basis of what is thus shown, *commend* this kind of freedom as something "worth wanting" to others who must make their own judgments about it. Some persons will acknowledge that the objects of these desires are important to them and are worth wanting; others will disagree. There is a point here at which argument finally gives out. But there is much to be done before that point is reached, as I have indicated, in trying to figure out just what one is committed to when one is committed to incompatibilist free will, why one is committed to it, and why it cannot be captured by compatibilist reconstructions of autonomy, responsibility, desert, and so on.

As an example of why it is so difficult to compel assent on these matters by arguing from premises no one could rationally reject, consider the case of the Buddhists mentioned earlier. Theravadin Buddhists regard the desire for "independent selfhood" not only as unimportant, but as perverse. For them, the evils of the world flow from our attachment to our independent (finite) selves (*tanha*) and to the worth of personal actions and achievements; these attachments chain us to continuous rebirth. The goal is to extinguish the individual self and all attachments to personal action and achievement, thereby gaining enlightenment (*nirvana*, which in Sanskrit literally means "extinction," as of a candle flame). This Buddhist view shows, as clearly as any view could, why it is so difficult to compel assent in these matters from incontestable premises. How do you settle the matter of whether the desire to be autonomous and independent selves is a good thing, as many in the West would say, or a destructive perversion, as these Buddhists say? I don't think one can settle it in a final and definitive way. Yet, I also think it would be senseless for those who *do* value independent selfhood (and other things that go with it, such as individual responsibility and dignity) to abandon their belief in its importance and their desire for it on the grounds that they cannot conclusively refute Buddhists. Similarly, I think it would be senseless for those who value the objects of the desires for independent selfhood and objective worth to abandon their belief in the importance of what they value on the grounds that they cannot conclusively refute those for whom independent selfhood is unimportant, or those who may believe that subjective value is all that can matter or is worth caring about.[26]

But, again, it is worth emphasizing that there is much to argue about beyond these bottom-line disagreements. Compatibilists might deny, for example, that (i) independent selfhood and (ii) objective worth as described in this chapter are *possible* or *attainable* goals (can we gain such independence from nature? Can there be objective worth, or is all worth subjective?). And these challenges must eventually be addressed by defenders of incompatibilist free will. I do not take up the challenge to objective worth in this volume. To do so would require a full-scale discussion of the problem of objectivity of value, which would require another book at least as long as this one. I have, in fact, discussed this problem in another book (along with the notion of objective worth).[27] But I *do* take up the challenge to independent selfhood in this book. Indeed, the aim of part II is to show that the ideal of being an independent source of activity in the world of the sort required by ultimate responsibility and incompatibilist free will is an intelligible and attainable ideal, and one that can in principle be realized in the natural order.

In conclusion, then, why do we want free will? We want it because we want ultimate responsibility. And why do we want that? For the reason that children and adults take delight in their accomplishment from the earliest moments of their awakening as persons, whether these accomplishments are making a fist or walking upright or composing a symphony. This delight is no arbitrary feature of what we are. It is related to the fact that we first distinguish ourselves *as selves* distinct from the world by virtue of our ability to control some things by our wills, as the baby did her fist. Thereafter, we associate being a self in the full sense with imagining ourselves doing things — making, producing, creating, bringing about — as effecting changes in the world by our wills. And we resist attempts to undermine the belief that we are the ultimate sources of what comes from our wills because we believe our independence as selves *in* the world is tied up with our independence as actors and willers *from* the world; we resist the idea that the activity we direct back *upon* the world, which is, after all, the expression of our independent selfhood, has merely illusory and not real significance or worth *for* the world.

When the child learning to walk says, "Unhand me, I want to do this on my own," I believe she is expressing a primordial desire that inevitably arises in creatures who attain a certain level of intelligence and self consciousness: the desire to be "somebody" whose contribution to the world is her own. That is to say, creatures of higher consciousness such as we are have an unquenchable thirst for individual-ity and personhood (which I think are inextricably linked). Belief in free will is a higher order expression of that thirst in response to the seditious influences of the world. Whether that thirst can be fulfilled and what its ultimate significance may be are matters of continuing debate. But I believe the thirst goes with the territory of self-reflectiveness and is connected to higher aspirations in human beings toward a worth for their existence that transcends transitory satisfactions. If these aspirations matter, free will matters.

II

THE DESCENT PROBLEM: INTELLIGIBILITY AND EXISTENCE

7

Plurality and Indeterminism

1. The Intelligibility Question

In chapter 1, I described the free willist's task as one of ascending a mountain and descending on the other side. The ascent consists in answering the Compatibility and Significance questions in an incompatibilist or libertarian way. You may not be satisfied with the answers given to these questions in part I. But I ask you now to suppose, for the sake of argument, that we have successfully made our ascent and stand atop the mountain. Unfortunately, the case for an incompatibilist or libertarian free will is far from over, and in many respects the most difficult part lies ahead. Mountain climbers say that descents can be more precarious than ascents, and this is the case here. On the ascent, we have to establish whether a significant kind of freedom is incompatible with *determinism*. On the descent, we have to establish whether a kind of freedom that requires *indeterminism* can be made intelligible, and where it might exist, if it does at all, in the natural order. These are, respectively, the Intelligibility and Existence questions.

Most writing on free will since 1970 has dealt with the Compatibility Question. Indeed, this has been the case throughout much of the history of free will debates. The Intelligibility Question receives some treatment, but it is too often a perfunctory treatment that consists of putting labels on mysteries. As indicated in chapter 1, my initial interests in free will drew me toward the Intelligibility Question. It was neglected and yet pivotal for dealing with other issues about free will, including Compatibility. That I was not alone in this belief was made clear by an essay written in 1973 by David Wiggins. Near the end of that essay, Wiggins wrote:

> One of the many reasons I believe why philosophy falls short of a satisfying solution to the problem of freedom is that we still cannot refer to an unflawed statement of libertarianism. Perhaps libertarianism is in the last analysis untenable. But if we are to salvage its insights we need to know what is the least unreasonable statement the position can be given. Compatibilist resolutions to the problem of freedom must wear an appearance of superficiality, however serious or deep the reflections from which they originate, until what they offer by way of freedom can be compared with something else, actual or possible . . . which is known to be the best that any indeterminist or libertarian could describe. . . .

> Whether or not it is our world . . . we must continue to press the question, "What is the possible world which could afford the autonomy of thought and agency the libertarian craves in this one?" (pp. 33; 53–4)

This was a clear expression of the problem I had been working on for several years before reading Wiggins's essay and one that has engaged me since. Is a libertarian or incompatibilist free will possible? Can we show that such a freedom is coherent and give a clearer account of it than libertarians have offered in the past, an account that might show how such a freedom could exist in the natural order?

2. Indeterminism

For those who believe a libertarian free will is not intelligible, the culprit is indeterminism. If free will implies ultimate responsibility and underived origination, then it requires that some free actions must be undetermined. They must be capable of occurring or not occurring, given *exactly the same past and laws of nature*. There is no easy way around this troubling "indeterminist" condition; it seems to be a simple consequence of denying that free actions are determined. But why is the indeterminist condition a problem?

A simple way to answer this question is to imagine, as we did in chapter 1, how the indeterminism required by free will might occur in the natural order. Suppose it involved quantum jumps or other quantum uncertainties in the brain. How would the occurrence of these events enhance an agent's freedom, since they would be chance events, occurring unpredictably and not under anyone's control, including the agent's own control? Images of this sort suggest that indeterminism would not enhance, but would rather undermine, the rationality, control and responsibility normally associated with free choices and actions. These images have in turn led critics of libertarian theories to charges that undetermined actions would be "arbitrary," "capricious," "random," "irrational," or "inexplicable."[1]

These familiar charges often put an end to further discussion of free will. But they are, in fact, only a first stage of the debate about indeterminism. For the charges that undetermined actions would be arbitrary, capricious, random, irrational, and inexplicable can be effectively answered, at least in their simplest forms, by incompatibilists. To see this, we have only to return to the arguments of Austin (1966), Anscombe (1971), and others discussed in chapter 4. Those arguments showed that actions can be undetermined without being arbitrary, capricious, or irrational. Take Austin's three-foot putt or the sniper intending to shoot his victim, two examples in chapter 4. Suppose quantum uncertainties in their nervous systems made it genuinely undetermined whether Austin would hole the putt or the sniper would hit his victim. Still, if they did succeed in what they aimed at, their acts would not have been arbitrary, capricious, or irrational, since they had reasons for the actions and were intending and trying to perform them for those reasons.

To put it another way, the reasons or motives of Austin and the sniper "inclined" them to hole the putt and kill the victim, respectively, but did not "necessitate" or "determine" their doing so. The idea that "reasons may incline without necessitating"—to use Leibniz's familiar dictum—has played a significant role in free will debates, and it is not difficult to see why.[2] That reasons may incline without necessitating allows one to say that actions (like holing the putt or killing the victim) can be rational and explicable by reasons, rather than merely capricious or arbitrary, even though they are undetermined.

So, libertarians can, and often do, invoke Leibniz's dictim that reasons may incline without necessitating to respond to the initial charges of arbitrariness, irrationality, and the like made against indeterminist theories of freedom. But the debate does not end at that point, because these initial charges of arbitrariness and irrationality are only the first step in a more complicated exchange. It turns out that the familiar objections about arbitrariness and irrationality are pointing to a deeper problem for indeterminist theories of freedom that is more difficult to resolve. I described this problem in an earlier work (1985) and have since referred to it as the problem of "dual rationality." Under that title it has been the subject of recent discussions on free will.[3] But I have since come to see dual rationality as but one aspect of a more general "problem of plurality" for all indeterminist accounts of freedom, and as a consequence I now prefer the expression "plural rationality" (or, alternatively, "plural motivation") to "dual rationality." I have also come to believe that the more general problem of plurality (which includes the problem of plural rationality) is the deeper issue lying behind all historical charges of arbitrariness, capriciousness, irrationality, and inexplicability made against indeterminist theories of freedom. When these familiar charges are traced to their roots, they lead to the problem of plurality in one or more of its aspects. While plural rationality (or plural motivation) is only one aspect of the problem of plurality, it provides a good introduction to the general problem.

3. Plural Rationality or Motivation

The best way to understand plural rationality is by example. Consider Jane, who was deliberating about where to spend her vacation. Should she vacation in Hawaii or Colorado (or Europe, or wherever)? The matter is important to her and she has been thinking about it for days. She has considered various consequences of each option, imagined contrasting scenarios, consulted brochures and bank accounts, and considered her desires, interests, and broader purposes. In the end, she gradually comes to believe that Hawaii is the best option, all things considered, and chooses it.

Now if the choice were not determined, then Jane could have chosen otherwise (e.g., she could have chosen Colorado), given exactly the same past circumstances (and laws of nature) preceding the actual choice of Hawaii. This means that *exactly the same prior deliberation* up to the moment of choice, through which she came to believe that Hawaii was, all things considered, the best option, may have issued in the choice of Colorado—exactly the same prior thoughts and reasonings, the same imagined scenarios and considered consequences, the same prior beliefs, desires, and other motives that led to the choice of Hawaii—not a sliver of difference—would have issued in the choice of Colorado instead. This is strange, to say the least. Even if it *may* have happened, say critics of indeterminist freedom, the choice of Colorado in such circumstances would have seemed a fluke or accident, capricious and irrational, given the same prior deliberation which led her in fact to favor Hawaii.

Of course, one can imagine Jane choosing differently in a noncapricious and rational way *if* something in her past deliberation had been different—if she had had different beliefs or desires, imagined different scenarios, or considered other consequences that favored Colorado over Hawaii. This is what compatibilists usually demand—that something relevant to the choice in one's past have been different in some way. But compatibilists are not committed to the indeterminist condition, which requires that the alternative choice occur given exactly the same prior circumstances. That condition, say critics of indeterminism, *would* render free choices "capricious," "arbitrary," or "irrational" in objectionable ways. Perhaps we sometimes do make capricious (or spontaneous, or spur-of-the-moment) choices against the grain without having good reasons for them. But if all our free choices had to be irrational in this way (as Dostoyevsky's "Underground Man" imagined), would that be what we mean by freedom of choice?

To put the problem in perspective, notice that it is the choosing "otherwise" that is the source of the difficulty. While it would have been capricious, arbitrary, or irrational to choose Colorado given exactly the same deliberation that led to the choice of Hawaii, the actual choice of Hawaii need not have been irrational, capricious, or arbitrary. Indeed, it is *because* the choice of Hawaii was the reasonable one for Jane, given her deliberation, that the choice of Colorado would have appeared capricious and irrational. Indeterminism therefore does not rule out *one-way* rationality and noncapriciousness. The problem of indeterminism is with *plural* or *more-than-one-way* rationality and noncapriciousness. What we seem to want in free choice is the power to go more than one way (to choose Hawaii *or* Colorado *or* Europe, or whatever we choose) rationally and deliberately, rather than flukishly, given exactly the same prior deliberation and thought processes. We want the choice to be rational, *whichever way it goes.*

Notice that Leibniz's dictum—"reasons may incline without necessitating"—will not help with *this* problem. Jane's reasons incline her, all things considered, to the choice of Hawaii. But precisely because her reasons do incline her to Hawaii, the choice of Colorado or some other option (which might take place, since the outcome is undetermined) would be irrational in the circumstances. Leibniz's dictum explains *one-way* rationality or motivation, but, *for that very reason*, it poses a problem for *plural* rationality or motivation. If reasons or motives incline one to the choice of A (Hawaii) rather than B (Colorado) or some other option—so that A is the reasonable outcome of one's deliberation—then the choosing otherwise in exactly the same circumstances would be "arbitrary," "capricious," "irrational," and "inexplicable" *relative to the psychological history of the agent* prior to choice (including the agent's prior deliberation and reasons). Likewise, if the choice of B had been the reasonable conclusion of a deliberation, the choice of A would have been arbitrary relative to that prior deliberation. This is the problem of plural rationality (or plural motivation, if one substitutes "motives" for "reasons" in the above argument).

Plural rationality is a problem whether the reasons incline to A *or* B, or to any option over all the others. Of course, reasons do not have to incline to any one option over all others. There is another possibility that should be familar to those who know the history of free will debates: the agent may be equally attracted to more than one option. At the terminus of deliberation, one's reasons may not incline to A rather than B, all things considered, or to B rather than A. This is a case of what medieval thinkers called the "liberty of indifference" (*liberum arbitrium indifferentiae*), sometimes represented by the notorious example of Buridan's ass, which starved between two equidistant bales of hay.[4] The example of the ass is perhaps wrongly attributed to Buridan, since it is not found in his writings. But there are similar examples of the liberty of indifference in other medieval sources, like Dante's *Divine Comedy* (1932: *Paradiso*, 4): "Between two foods, equally tempting, placed/ Equally near, a man, though free to choose/ Would starve before deciding which to taste." Such examples have a long history: Schopenhauer (1960: 61) traces them back to Aristotle's *De Caelo* (295/32).

It is not difficult to see why the idea of a liberty of indifference frequently appears in free will debates, if one reflects upon the problem of plural rationality. But it is also not difficult to see why the liberty of indifference fails to solve the problem of plural rationality, and why the liberty of indifference has indeed been an object of ridicule by critics of libertarian theories of freedom, like Hobbes, Hume, and Schopenhauer, throughout the centuries.[5] A man who was not an ass would certainly not starve when placed between two equally tempting foods. But if his reasons were exactly equal, his choice of one rather than another would be arbitrary *relative to* his reasons (though his choice of one of them rather than nothing would not be arbitrary). But this means that the liberty of indifference does not solve the problem of plural rationality either. Indeed, it makes matters worse. Instead of one choice (A or B) being arbitrary relative to the prior deliberation, both would be arbitrary in the case of a liberty of indifference. The deliberation would not provide the agent with good reasons for choosing A *rather than* B or B *rather than* A. Hobbes, Hume, Schopenhauer and other critics were therefore right to suppose that if all libertarian free choices reduced to a liberty of indifference, libertarianism would not give us the nonarbitrary outcomes that genuine free choice seems to require.

4. Plural Voluntariness and Control

We have thus far traced the initial charges of arbitrariness and irrationality against indeterminist theories of free will to the problem of plural rationality. But I said that plural rationality is but one aspect of a general "problem of plurality" for indeterminist theories. Plural rationality, as it turns out, is only one of several "plurality conditions" affected by indeterminism. Another one of these conditions is plural voluntariness.

As described in chapter 2, voluntary actions are done "in accordance with the agent's will" (i.e., predominant desires or motives) and are not coerced or compulsive. Thus, one thing required by *plural* voluntariness is that the agent can act in more than one way and the act will not be coerced or compulsive, whichever way it goes. If a man meets a panhandler on the street, he may choose to give the panhandler money or not. If no coercion or compulsion is involved either way, the choice is plural voluntary. But if the panhandler threatens him with a knife, the situation changes. The man may still have a choice of sorts (he may still refuse to hand over his money and take his chances). But if he does hand over his money in these circumstances, it will be involuntarily (or "against his will") because of the coercion. So the choice left him by the coercer is no longer plural voluntary.

Plural voluntariness also fails when something happens by mistake or by chance that agents did not want or try to make happen. Suppose that, standing in front of a coffee machine and having decided to press the button for black coffee, I mistakenly press the button for coffee with cream. My doing so was involuntary. It was not what I wanted, intended, or even tried to do. Such cases have special relevance for issues about indeterminism. If my mistake at the coffee machine was due to a chance occurrence in my brain or nervous system, the case would be like Austin's missed putt or the sniper missing his victim. If Austin holes his putt, he does so in accordance with his will, but if he misses, it would be against his will. He may hole it or fail, but not both voluntarily, just as I may press either button of the coffee machine, but not either one voluntarily. Our acts are one-way voluntary, but not plural voluntary. Similarly, if the sniper misses his target due to an undetermined jerking of his arm, it would be against his will. Had he shot his victim, he would have done so voluntarily, but he does not *miss* voluntarily. It is of some interest that in such cases we are also inclined to say that missing the target is not something he "freely" does, even if his doing it is undetermined.

acts are not plural voluntary

undetermined ≠ free

We should not be misled here by the thought that actions like the sniper's that are only one-way rational and voluntary cannot be *responsible* actions. They can be (at least one-way) responsible. If the sniper hits and kills his victim, he is guilty of murder. The problem, once again, is with the doing *otherwise*—that is, missing the target. If he can be blamed for hitting the target, he cannot be praised for missing it, for that is not something he voluntarily did. Rather, he would be blamed for the *attempt* to murder, which *was* voluntary. Similarly, Jane's actual choice of Hawaii may be voluntary and responsible. What would be problematic regarding responsibility would be her failure to choose Hawaii flukishly and involuntarily, by virtue of an undetermined occurrence in her brain. Indeed, we would rightly question whether such an occurrence was her "choice" at all rather than something that happened *to* her.

control

This brings us to a third plurality condition related to the other two, but involving the further notion of *control*. Indeterminist accounts of agency have also been criticized on the grounds that they undermine the voluntary control agents are supposed to have over their free and responsible actions. Undetermined actions are not controlled by anyone, it is said, including the agents themselves. In this vein, indeterminist theories have been caricatured by critics such as Schopenhauer, who imagined a man whose legs suddenly began to move by chance when he wanted to sit still (1960: 47). Or, critics have imagined a deliberator who, like Jane, has come to favor one option in a deliberation, yet inexplicably finds herself selecting another, owing to a chance occurrence in her brain. Of course, defenders and critics of libertarian agency disagree about whether these examples are fair to libertarians or are mere caricatures. But both sides agree that these examples do not describe the kind of control over acting otherwise that genuinely free and responsible agency requires.

What kind of control is that? It is not enough that the man's legs can both move or stay still at a given time, as chance would have it. Rather, *he* must be able to move them or keep them still, *as* he chooses. It is not enough that Jane's brain might or might not register a selection of Colorado at a given time due to a chance occurrence. Rather, *she* must be be able to select or not select Colorado at the time in accordance with her will. These would be instances of what I shall call "plural voluntary control" (or simply "plural control"). To have such control over a set of options at a given time is to be able to *bring about* any one of the options (to go more-than-one-way) *at will* or *voluntarily* at the time. That is to say, it is to be able to do *whatever you will* (or most want) to do among a set of options, *whenever you will to do it*, for the reasons you will to do it, and in such manner that neither your doing it nor willing to do it was coerced or compelled.[6]

Jane lacks such control if she cannot prevent an undetermined occurrence in her brain from selecting some other option when she favors Hawaii. I lack such control at the coffee machine if I cannot prevent myself from pressing the wrong button against my will. The sniper lacks it to the extent that he may miss his target by virtue of an uncontrolled twitch in his arm. His missing would not be something over which he had voluntary control; it would not be something done "at will." Now, of course, the sniper *might* have missed at will, *if* he had wanted or intended to miss; Jane might have chosen Colorado at will, *if* she had favored it; and I might have pressed another button at will, *if* I had intended to. Compatibilists may account for plural voluntary control in this way, but not incompatibilists, because the indeterminist condition allows no such "ifs." The indeterminist condition makes the stronger requirement that the sniper could have missed the target *at will* given *exactly the same prior circumstances* in which he in fact hit the target at will, that is, given that he wanted, and was trying, to hit it (and similarly for Jane's choosing Colorado, given that she favored Hawaii, or my pressing the wrong button, given that I intended otherwise). Doing otherwise in such circumstances, say the critics, *would* be "flukish," "accidental," "arbitrary," or "capricious."

5. Why Plurality? The One-Way Solution

In summary, when one traces to their roots the familiar charges of arbtrariness, capriciousness, randomness, irrationality, and inexplicability against indeterminist theories of freedom, one comes upon the problems of plural rationality, voluntariness, and control, three aspects of what I have called the "problem of plurality." The first step leading to this result was recognizing that the familiar charges of arbitrariness are easily answered in their simplest forms. Actions can be undetermined without being arbitrary, capricious, and irrational. To show this, one has only to consider examples in which indeterminism may be involved, but the agents nonetheless succeed in doing what their reasons incline them to do or what they were intending or trying to do. Such are the examples of Austin, the sniper, Jane, the coffee machine, and the nuclear employee who plants radioactive material in his boss's desk—whenever the agents in question succeed in their aims (though their actions might have gone awry by virtue of undetermined occurrrences).

But these examples—which show that actions can be undetermined without being arbitrary, capricious, and irrational—also reveal a deeper problem for indeterminist theories to which these familiar charges are pointing. The problem is with the agents' doing otherwise in the same circumstances in a manner that is undetermined, such as Jane's choosing Colorado at the end of exactly the same deliberation that led her to choose Hawaii. This is a problem of being able to choose or act in *more than one way* rationally, voluntarily, and with voluntary control when the choices or actions are undetermined. The underlying problem about indeterminism—the problem of plurality—is that it seems to undermine these plurality conditions.

But if this is the difficulty lying behind the familiar charges of arbitrariness, why couldn't incompatibilists defuse their critics by simply rejecting the plurality conditions? "What is so important about more-than-one-way rationality, voluntariness and control?" they might say. "Why aren't one-way rationality, voluntariness, and control good enough for free will? We know from Austin-style examples that the one-way versions can be reconciled with indeterminism, and we know from cases like the sniper and the nuclear plant employee that one-way rationality, voluntariness, and control may be good enough for responsibility and blameworthiness. It is true that indeterminism *diminishes* even one-way control, and incompatibilists who took this one-way line would have to concede that point. To the extent that the sniper might miss his target or a person might press a wrong button owing to undetermined occurrences, they would not only lack plural voluntary control, they would also have less one-way control over their actions. (They could not be sure of hitting the target or pressing the right button.) But incompatibilists who took this one-way line might respond that diminished one-way control is a price incompatibilists might be willing to pay in order to get the indeterminism they require, so long as that indeterminism does not undermine one-way control and responsibility altogether. Meanwhile, by rejecting the plurality conditions and going with one-way rationality, voluntariness, and control, incompatibilists could defuse their critics in one fell swoop."

Unfortunately, this simple "one-way" response to critics of indeterminism is too easy. It has not usually been regarded as adequate by incompatibilists *or* their critics. Why not? It seems that we have strong intuitions about the plurality conditions in relation to indeterminism. It would be odd, to say the least, if all free choices and actions were such that the agent's power to do otherwise was always merely the power to do otherwise irrationally, involuntarily, and not under his or her own voluntary control. This is not the power to do otherwise that people usually have in mind when they think about free and responsible actions, as Patricia Greenspan has pointed out (1978: 238), and the fact that it is not what people usually have in mind shows that intuitions about the plurality conditions in relation to freedom and responsibility have a powerful hold upon us. But why do we have such intuitions about plurality and why are the intuitions so important? These questions are all too rarely asked. But they need to be asked, if incompatibilists could defuse their critics by denying plurality and accepting this easy one-way solution.

6. Plurality and UR

Why cannot incompatibilists so easily dismiss the plurality conditions? The answer to this question, I believe, is especially revealing and has something to do with the roots of our intuitions about free will in UR. The surprising fact is that *the plurality conditions are entailed by UR* for undetermined actions. This means that these conditions are deeply embedded in our intuitions about free will and that incompatibilists, in particular, cannot easily dismiss them. To see the connection between plurality and UR, we have to look again at the pivotal U- or Ultimacy-condition of UR: "For any X and Y, if an agent is personally responsible for X, and if Y is an *arche* (or sufficient ground or cause or explanation) for X, then the agent must also be personally responsible for Y." In chapter 5, I described the *arche*, or sufficient ground, of this definition as a "sufficient reason" of any one of three kinds—(i) a (logically) sufficient condition, (ii) a sufficient cause (antecedent circumstances plus laws of nature), or (iii) a sufficient motive. UR, of course, does not claim that every action or other event must have a sufficient reason of one or more of these kinds for its occurring. That would be to assert the historically important but highly controversial "principle of sufficient reason,"[7] and UR asserts no such principle.[8] What UR does say is that *if* an agent is to be ultimately responsible for an action and *if* that action has a sufficient reason for occurring, then the agent must also be responsible for that sufficient reason.

To understand how the plurality conditions get into the picture we have to focus on the third of the kinds of sufficient reasons presupposed by UR: sufficient motives. Sufficient motives are sets of reasons or motives (wants, beliefs, etc.) that explain actions. An agent has a sufficient motive for doing something A at a time t when the agent's reasons or motives are such that, given them, if the agent did A at t, it would be *voluntarily* or *willingly*, and if the agent did other than A at t, it would not be voluntarily or willingly. According to the definitions of chapter 2, agents act voluntarily or willingly (the terms are used interchangeably throughout this book) when the agents act for reasons they want to act on more than they want to act on any reasons for doing otherwise, and their having those reasons and acting on them are not the result of coercion or compulsion. The sniper has a sufficient motive in this sense to shoot his victim. If he succeeds he will do so voluntarily or willingly, but if he misses, it would not be voluntarily or willingly. I have a sufficient motive when standing before the coffee machine to press the button for black coffee. I will press the button for coffee with cream only unwillingly or by mistake.

By requiring that agents be personally responsible for sufficient motives of their actions, as well as for sufficient causes and conditions, UR requires not only that agents be the ultimate sources or grounds of their actions, but also that they be the ultimate sources or grounds of their *wills*—of their willing to perform the actions. This is crucial for ultimate responsibility. For it may be that, although nothing else made you act as you did, someone or something else (e.g., a devil, a behavioral controller, or a neurological defect) produced in you a sufficient motive for acting as you did.[9] You would then be able to control your act in accordance with your will, but would not have ultimate control over your will. You would have freedom of action, but not freedom of will.

Now cases of "one-way" rationality, voluntariness, and control (such as the sniper, the three-foot putt, the coffee machine, and the like) are cases in which there is a sufficient motive for the agent to go one way rather than another. The agents may act in more than one way, but they most *want* to act, or are *intending* or *trying* to act, in only one of those ways. In other words, their wills are "set" in one direction and they are diverted to another direction only if something happens that is not under their voluntary control; for example, if they are causally prevented or chance occurrences interfere. To determine "ultimate" responsibility in such cases when the will is set in one direction, we have to determine *how the agent's will got that way*. Are the *agents* responsible for the one-way wills (i.e., the predominant motives or intentions) they now have, or was something or someone else responsible for their having the wills they do have? Is the sniper ultimately responsible for the fact that his predominant motives and intentions are now set on killing a man, so that he will miss only unwillingly?

When we think about the sniper's guilt, in other words, we think about the origins of his evil motives and intentions. They are the sources of his guilt, even if by chance he fails to succeed in acting on them and is guilty only of attempted murder.[10] And if these motives should turn out to be sufficient for his presently willing to kill the victim, then UR requires for ultimate responsibility that something he did or could have omitted in the past must have been capable of making a difference in whether or not he had these motives. In general, when the agent's will is "set one way," we have to backtrack to find the ultimate source *of its being set that way* rather than some other way. If an infinite regress is to be avoided, there must be actions somewhere in the agent's life history for which the agent's predominant motives and the will on which the agent acts were *not already set one way*.

Such regress-stopping acts would be the SFAs of T6 required by UR. To say that *these* self-forming acts could not be such that the agent's predominant motives and will were set one way when they were performed is to say that SFAs must be more-than-one-way rational or motivated. Moreover, we know that SFAs must also be plural voluntary from the R condition of UR, which requires that "something the agent voluntarily did, and for which the agent could have voluntarily done otherwise" made a difference in the agent's current motives and dispositions; and we are going to learn in the next chapter that if all the conditions of UR are to be satisfied (U + R), SFAs must be plural-voluntarily controlled as well.[11] Thus,

> T15 (*on UR*): The "self-forming actions" (or SFAs) required by UR must satisfy the plurality conditions. They must be more-than-one-way rational, voluntary, and voluntarily controlled. In the case of plural rationality or motivation, if this were not so, the wills of agents (their reasons, motives, intentions, etc.) would already be "set one way" when SFAs occur, and UR would require further backtracking to determine whether the agents were responsible for having the wills they do have. In other words, to play their buck-stopping roles, SFAs *must be "will-setting" and cannot presuppose a will already set*. Some free and responsible actions might be merely one-way rational, voluntary, and voluntarily controlled, but not all of them could be, if agents are to be ultimately responsible for forming their own wills.[12]

There is no doubt that most people have deeply rooted intuitions about the plurality conditions. They are inclined to think that our freedom would be seriously deficient if we could never do otherwise *except* irrationally, involuntarily, and in a manner we could not voluntarily control. I am suggesting that the depth of these intuitions is traceable to UR. It is noteworthy that AP alone is not sufficient to support the plurality conditions, nor does indeterminism alone support them. For, as Austin pointed out about his three-foot putt, he "could have done otherwise" than hole it and his holing it may have been undetermined. But what he could *not* have done in *those* same circumstances is miss the putt *willingly*—as a result of wanting, intending, or trying to miss it.[13] This ability—to do otherwise willingly—is something more than being able to do otherwise simply; and it is something more that is required by ultimate responsibility *for one's own will*.

7. The Free Agency Principle

If the plurality conditions are required for free will, then the simple one-way solution to the problems of indeterminism will not work. Libertarians must come up with more radical proposals for reconciling indeterminism and free will. And this is precisely what libertarians have done throughout the history of free will debates. The difficulties they have to deal with, let us remind ourselves, are caused by the indeterminist requirement that agents must be able to willingly do and do otherwise, "all past circumstances and laws of nature remaining the same." If Jane's free choice of Hawaii or Colorado satisfies this condition, she must be able to choose *either* option rationally, voluntarily, and under her voluntary control, given the same past and laws of nature. The problem is to explain how this can be so.

[margin note: But I don't see how Jane's case could satisfy this condition]

The nearly universal libertarian response to this problem in the history of philosophy has taken the following form. There must be some explanatory factors, libertarians have conjectured, *over and above* the past circumstances and laws of nature to account for the agent's choosing one way rather than the other rationally, voluntarily, and under the agent's control. For something must be different to explain the difference in choice (C_A or C_B), and that something cannot be the past circumstances and laws (P), which are the same. Such a strategy of looking for "additional explanatory factors" beyond P to account for the difference in C_A or C_B is nearly universal among libertarians, but the strategy is also dangerous. For it has been all too tempting for libertarians to look for those additional factors in mysterious sources outside of the natural order or to postulate unusual forms of agency or causation whose manner of influencing events is at best obscure.

[margin note: the typical response]

In this vein, libertarians have traditionally invoked factors such as noumenal selves; transempirical power centers; Cartesian egos; special "acts of will"; "acts of attention" or "volitions" that cannot in principle be determined; mental events that exist outside of (but can also intervene within) the natural order; special forms of agent, or nonoccurrent, causation that cannot be accounted for in terms of familiar kinds of event or occurrent causation; the "Will" conceived as a kind of uncaused homunculus within the agent; and so on. How these special causes or agencies are supposed to operate, or how they are supposed to explain why one choice occurs rather than another, is never well enough explained to allay suspicions that libertarian accounts of free agency are mysterious. These suspicions, as I indicated in chapter 1, have grown in the twentieth century to a point where belief is more widespread than ever that an old-fashioned incompatibilist free will is unintelligible and has no place in the modern picture of human beings that is emerging in the natural, social, and cognitive sciences.

[margin note: mysterious solutions]

In chapter 1, I promised in response to this situation to try a new approach to the Intelligibility Question in part II that would attempt to avoid traditional libertarian appeals to special forms of agency or causation and would try to put the libertarian view into more meaningful dialogue with modern science. The time has come to describe this aim in more precise terms by way of a further thesis on UR:

T16 (on UR) ("The Free Agency Principle"): In the attempt to formulate an incompatibilist or libertarian account of free agency that will satisfy the plurality conditions and UR, we shall not appeal to categories or kinds of entities (substances, properties, relations, events, states, etc.) that are *not also needed by nonlibertarian* (compatibilist or determinist) *accounts of free agency satisfying the plurality conditions.* The only difference allowed between libertarian and nonlibertarian accounts is the difference one might expect—that some of the events or processes involved in libertarian free agency will be indeterminate or undetermined events or processes. But these undetermined events or processes will not otherwise be of categories or ontological kinds that do not also play roles in nonlibertarian accounts of free agency (such as choices, decisions, efforts, practical judgments, and the like)—the difference being that in nonlibertarian theories, these events or processes need not be undetermined. Such differences as there are between libertarian and nonlibertarian theories should flow from this difference alone, and the task will be to make sense of a libertarian freedom satisfying the plurality conditions, given this difference.

The Free Agency Principle counsels against libertarian appeals to special kinds of entities or causes that are not needed by other, nonlibertarian accounts of free agency. Thus, if Kant or others appeal to a noumenal self that is outside of space and time to account for incompatibilist free agency, the Free Agency Principle counsels us to ask, is this postulate also necessary for accounts of free agency that do not require indeterminism? If the answer is no, the Free Agency Principle tells us not to rely on such a postulate, that is, to do without appeals to a noumenal self outside of space and time. If the answer is yes, then we would need such a self to account for free agency in *any* form—libertarian or nonlibertarian—and the Free Agency Principle would allow it.

Now, in the case of a Kantian noumenal self, most philosophers (Kant included) would agree that, whatever reasons we may have to postulate such an entity, it is not needed by nonlibertarian accounts of free agency. Kant was aware of compatibilist and determinist views of free agency in their Hobbesian forms—that is, being able to do what you will and being determined by your motives. These Hobbesian freedoms did not impress Kant, who regarded them as poor substitutes ("wretched subterfuges," in his words) for free will (1956: 99). But Kant was also clear that if freedom *did* mean only what Hobbesians thought it meant, then it would not require a noumenal self. Hobbesian freedoms could be explained in Kantian terms by antecedent desires, beliefs, or other psychological states of (what Kant called) the "phenomenal (or empirical) self" alone. Free will, by contrast, could not for Kant be subject to "causes determining it in time" and required the assumption of a noumenal self beyond space and time as its source (1956: 100).

But if this is the purpose for which noumenal selves are invoked, then the Free Agency Principle counsels us to avoid appealing to them, if we can. In general,

T17 (on UR): The Free Agency Principle functions as a methodological rule preventing us from postulating special kinds of entities, or special forms of agency or causation, that are invoked specifically to salvage libertarian intuitions and are not needed to account for free agency generally—whether libertarian or nonlibertarian. The motivation behind the principle is this: if the Free Agency Principle could be satisfied then, any unsolved problems remaining about incompatibilist free will (such as problems about the nature of consciousness) would be problems confronting all persons, *whatever their positions on free will*, and not problems *specifically created by libertarian theories*. Residual mysteries surrounding free will would be mysteries for all of us and not mysteries created by libertarianism. Life is full of mysteries, we might say, but they should be created by the world, not by our theories.

(The point is not simply to assume that the Free Agency Principle is true or satisfied, but rather to try our best to see if it can be satisfied, thereby answering charges of mystery that are exclusive to libertarianism.) I needn't tell you that the Free Agency Principle imposes heavy burdens on libertarian theorizing. Many philosophers whom I respect, compatibilists and incompatibilists alike, questioned the wisdom of undertaking a project based upon it.[14] It may be, as they warned, that indeterminist theories of freedom cannot hope to get off the ground without postulating one or more of the traditional libertarian strategems ruled out by the Free Agency Principle. I am willing to entertain this possibility. But we cannot know until we try. And since there is widespread skepticism about traditional libertarian strategies anyway, it may be worth trying to see if we can do without them—especially if a by-product of such an effort would be to put traditional debates about free will into greater dialogue with twentieth-century developments in the sciences and other fields. One can therefore view the next three chapters as a thought experiment in this direction. There are obvious benefits if it succeeds; and if it should fail, we may learn more about what is needed to make sense of free will—or why it cannot be made intelligible at all.

[Handwritten margin note: The reason for adopting the Free Agency Principle]

8. Libertarian Strategies

Kant's noumenal self is only one example of a traditional libertarian strategem ruled out by the Free Agency Principle. In the remainder of this chapter, I want to consider other examples that shed further light on the principle and on what may, and may not, be assumed in the coming chapters. First, consider Sir John Eccles's appeal to a "transempirical power center" to account for libertarian free will.[15] Eccles argues that incompatibilist freedom requires indeterminism somewhere in the brain. But he also argues that the relevant neural indeterminacy can only provide gaps in nature that make room for free will. These gaps must be filled by the operation of a transempirical power center intervening in the physical processes of the brain to account for the agent's doing one thing rather than another, given the same physical past.

The Free Agency Principle counsels us to ask the same question of Eccles's transempirical power center we asked of Kant's noumenal self: Is the appeal to such an entity also necessary for nonlibertarian accounts of free agency that do not require indeterminism? If the answer is no (as even Eccles seems to believe, since he requires such an entity to fill *undetermined* gaps in the physical order), then the Free Agency Principle counsels us to avoid appeals to transempirical power centers, if we can. "See if you can do without them," it says. Of course, if Eccles or anyone could show that transempirical power centers were needed for other metaphysical reasons, and not just to salvage libertarian intuitions, the Free Agency Principle would allow, and indeed require, them.

The same argument could be run through for traditional libertarian theories that speak of the "Will" as the source of undetermined free choices and view the Will as a kind of special power source or homunculus within the agent. Now we certainly need to refer to the will in some sense to account for free will. But the Free Agency Principle counsels against turning the will into another "agent within the agent," if such a postulate is not also needed to account for nonlibertarian notions of free agency. By contrast, the term "will" in the three traditional senses discussed in chapter 2 — desiderative, rational, and striving — designates *powers* or capacities of the agent to which we must indeed refer. But these powers or capacities are familiar ones (to choose or decide, to reason practically, to make efforts, and so forth) that also play roles in nonlibertarian theories of free agency.

Still other libertarian theories have postulated special "acts of will" or "acts of attention" that cannot in principle be determined by antecedent causes. Again, we need to ask whether such entities are also required by nonlibertarian theories, and if the acts in question must be undetermined by their very nature, the answer will be no. Now, "acts of will," *in some sense*, are also needed to account for free will. But the acts of will required are such familiar things as choices, decisions, efforts, and practical judgments, discussed in chapter 2, which are also involved in nonlibertarian theories of free agency. Such acts might be undetermined, but we are not to assume that they cannot be determined in principle merely by virtue of the kinds of acts they are. Indeed, some of our everyday choices and other acts of will may in fact be determined, even for incompatibilists (T12). Whether or not they are determined is not to be settled by armchair speculation or a priori assertion alone. Similarly, I shall later argue that "acts of attention" also have a role to play in some exercises of free will. But these acts are also not defined so that they cannot be determined in principle. In sum, the Free Agency Principle does not rule out acts of will and acts of attention *simpliciter* from libertarian theories. What it rules out is the postulation of *sui generis* acts of these — or any kinds — that are undetermined in principle.[16]

Perhaps the most popular traditional libertarian strategy for dealing with free will is to assume some sort of dualism between mind and body, as Descartes did.[17] Many ordinary persons, as well as philosophers, believe the only way to make sense of undetermined free actions is to assume some kind of intervention of mental phenomena (thoughts, volitions, reasonings, etc.) in the physical order. Agents might then act or act otherwise, all past *physical* circumstances remaining the same, but mental events would not be included among the same past circumstances because they are not physical. Mind/body dualists of this sort would thus reject a crucial assumption made throughout our discussion of the plurality conditions — that the past circumstances of the indeterminist condition include "the entire *psychological history* of the agent" prior to choice. If some parts of the agent's psychological history could be exempted from this requirement, the exempted parts might then explain the difference in action, given the same *physical* past.

The Free Agency Principle counsels the same attitude toward mind/body dualisms of this sort as it does to other libertarian strategies. If a case could be made for saying that an interactionist dualism (or any dualist view) provides the most plausible solution to the mind/body problem—whatever view one takes of free will—then the Free Agency Principle would sanction dualism. But if dualist views of mind and body are invoked specifically to save libertarian theories of free agency from incoherence and have little beyond that to recommend them over alternative solutions to the mind/body problem, then the Free Agency Principle counsels us not to rely on them. (If the only recommendation for a strategem is that it would get libertarians off the hook, try to do without it.)

9. Reasons Explanations and Causal Explanations

Other familiar libertarian strategies draw attention to the fact that free actions must be explained in terms of reasons or motives. These strategies then try to make a case of one kind or another that (E) "explanations in terms of reasons are incompatible with explanations in terms of causes."[18] This claim, E, if true, would provide a direct route to incompatibilism that Gary Watson has dubbed "explanatory incompatibilism" (1982: 12). On such a view, one would not need the Consequence Argument or UR to argue for incompatibilism. It would follow from the mere fact that free actions must be explained "teleologically"—in terms of reasons—that they could not be antecedently caused (and hence could not be determined).

The problem is that E is highly controversial. It is not obvious that merely because some events can be explained in terms of reasons, they cannot also be caused or determined. Compatibilists, who are probably in the majority among contemporary philosophers, obviously reject E and find the arguments for it unconvincing.[19] But even many incompatibilists are suspicious of E (and I include myself among them). E seems an altogether *too* easy route to incompatibilism. This is not to say that the first part of the explanatory incompatibilist view is wrong. One may concede that explanations in terms of reasons or motives are needed to account for free agency satisfying the plurality conditions without going on to assume, as E does, that causal explanations are *thereby* ruled out.

Indeed, satisfying the plurality conditions requires saying that the agent could have acted either way *rationally* and *voluntarily*, which involves acting for reasons; and that much seems true for incompatibilist (*and* compatibilist accounts) of free agency. But E is another matter. If distinctive structures are present in the agents' brains when they have desires, beliefs, intentions, emotions, and other reasons or motives—structures that influence their behavior when they act for reasons—then teleological explanations of behavior in terms of reasons may be compatible with causal, and even deterministic, explanations in terms of brain function. This is the way compatibilists and determinists view the matter; and I see no good reason to rule out such a possibility in principle, as E does.

Another reason I am suspicious of E, as an incompatibilist, is this. On my view, not all acts done of our own free wills and for which we are ultimately responsible have to be undetermined (only SFAs have to be undetermined). Thus, Luther's "Here I stand" might have been determined by his character and motives and still have been an ultimately responsible act done of his own free will, if his character and motives were formed by prior SFAs. Yet Luther's act, if determined, would still have been explicable by his reasons or motives. Indeed, it would be necessary to say that the act did issue from *his* character and motives (formed by earlier SFAs), rather than from some other causes, to establish that he was ultimately responsible for it. Yet E requires that no rationally explicable actions could in principle be determined. Not only Luther's act, but numerous everyday actions, such as answering a telephone, when the agent has every reason to perform the action then and there and no reasons not to perform it, would have to be undetermined, if E were true. I agree with Peter van Inwagen (1989) that such an extravagant position is unacceptable even for incompatibilists. An adequate account of incompatibilist free will should allow that some (and potentially many) everyday acts explicable by reasons may be caused or determined by characters and motives already formed. The possibility of such actions, as I see it, is part of a complete theory of *ultimate* responsibility.

What, then, does the Free Agency Principle counsel with regard to explanatory incompatibilism? We have to distinguish the two claims made by this view. The first is the claim that free actions satisfying the plurality conditions must be explained in terms of reasons or motives (desires, beliefs, intentions, etc.). Since this seems to be true for incompatibilist and compatibilist accounts of rational and voluntary action alike, the Free Agency Principle allows such explanations. But it is otherwise with the second and pivotal claim of explanatory incompatibilism, namely E. Nonlibertarian accounts of free agency do not require that explanations in terms of reasons be incompatible with explanations in terms of causes (and there are further reasons, I have argued, why incompatibilists should not require this as well). The Free Agency Principle therefore counsels us to do without E, but not to do without explanations of actions in terms of reasons or motives.

10. Agent, or Nonoccurrent, Causation

The final libertarian strategy to be considered involves appealing to a special kind of "agent or nonoccurrent causation" in order to account for free will. The term *nonoccurrent causation* comes from C. D. Broad (1962), who used it to characterize the causation of action by a *thing* or *substance* (the self or agent) that cannot be explained as the causation of occurrences or events *by other occurrences or events* (i.e., by "states" or "changes"). Agent-causation of such a kind (hyphenated hereafter to indicate this special meaning) is unusual, as even its defenders acknowledge. Causation of events (or occurrences) by things is commonplace, but it can usually be interpreted as the causation of events by other events. "The stone broke the window" is elliptical for "The stone's striking the window caused it to break"; "The cat caused the lamp to fall" is elliptical for "The cat's jumping on the table caused the lamp to fall." But no such paraphrasing in terms of events or occurrences is possible in the case of agent-causation of the nonoccurrent kind. An agent nonoccurrently causes something to happen, not by virtue of doing something else or as a result of being in some states or undergoing some changes that cause that something to happen. According to agent-cause theorists, in order to account for undetermined free agency, we must recognize another kind of causation alongside the usual causation of events by other events. We must recognize the possibility of direct causation of an event or occurrence by an agent or substance.

Unusual as such a notion of agent-causation may be, many philosophers believe that it alone captures basic incompatibilist intuitions about underived origination. Roderick Chisholm, one of the best-known defenders of agent-causation of the past few decades, argues that libertarians cannot assert that every free "act is caused by some other event" because of their commitment to indeterminism (1982, p. 28).[20] But they also cannot assert that a free act "is not caused at all" or they will have simply identified freedom with indeterminism. "The possibility that remains," Chisholm adds, is that some free acts are caused, "not by any other events, but by something else instead. And this something else can only be the agent" (p. 28). It is by virtue of agent-causation, which Chisholm has sometimes called "immanent causation," that we can, in his terms, be "prime movers unmoved"(p. 26) of our own actions. A similar point is made by Richard Taylor, another well-known defender of agent-causation, in the following words: "some . . . causal chains . . . have beginnings, and they begin with the agents themselves" (1974: 56).

Given such references to "prime movers unmoved," it is not surprising that critics of libertarian views such as Broad find the notion of nonoccurrent causation mysterious, and argue that it is essentially mysterious. Many agent-cause theorists themselves acknowledge its obscurity. "One can hardly affirm such a theory of agency with complete comfort," Taylor says, "and wholly without embarrassment, for the conception of men and their powers which is involved in it is strange indeed, if not positively mysterious" (p. 58). Broad and other critics of agent-causation, such as Carl Ginet (1990: 12), point out that if the cause of an action is the agent, and not an event, the cause cannot explain even elementary features of the action that we would expect causes to explain, such as why the action occurred at one time rather than another. How could the mere existence or presence of the agent explain an act's occurring now rather than at some other time when the agent also existed or was present at that other time as well?[21]

Nor does nonoccurrent causation help to explain what most needs explaining for indeterminist theories of freedom, namely how the plurality conditions are satisfied: Why did the agent rationally and voluntarily do A here and now rather than doing otherwise? Other libertarian theories, such as dualist theories or explanatory incompatibilism, try to answer this question by citing the agent's reasons, motives, volitions, or other mental states or changes. But agent-cause theories deny that adequate answers to plurality questions can be given in terms of *occurrences* alone of any kinds, physical *or* psychological, past *or* present, involving the agent or not. What agent-cause theories add is that the agent (nonoccurrently) caused A at t rationally and voluntarily, and if the agent had done otherwise, the agent would have (nonoccurrently) caused something else (or nothing at all) at t rationally and voluntarily. But this adds no further information about why the agent did it. One can understand why Hobbes thought agent-cause theories were "empty" of explanatory content and why modern critics such as Gary Watson, John Bishop, and Bernard Berofsky argue that agent-causation is at best a "label" for "what libertarians want," rather than the theory they need.[22]

What does the Free Agency Principle say about agent- or nonoccurrent causation? Is such a notion needed to explain free agency, libertarian *or* nonlibertarian? If the answer is yes, the Free Agency Principle allows (and indeed requires) nonoccurrent causation. If the answer is no—if nonoccurrent causation is needed only to account for undetermined or incompatibilist free agency—the Free Agency Principle would tell us not to rely on such a notion. Now some agent-cause theorists, such as Richard Taylor, have in fact answered yes to this question. They hold that a notion of nonoccurrent causation is required to explain the very notion of *action* (which is defined as an agent's bringing something about), whether the actions are free or unfree, determined or undetermined. If this were true, then any account of free agency, libertarian or nonlibertarian, would require some notion of nonoccurrent causation by agents, and the Free Agency Principle would require it.

But only a minority of agent-cause theorists accept Taylor's view that non-occurrent causation is required to account for action in general, whether determined or undetermined. Most defenders of agent-causation, including Chisholm, and other recent defenders, such as C. A. Campbell (1967), John Thorp (1980), William Rowe (1987), Randolph Clarke (1993), and Timothy O'Connor (1993a), invoke a special relation of nonoccurrent causation specifically to account for undetermined or incompatibilist free actions, not for action in general. On this majority view, agent- or nonoccurrent causation is specially invoked to make sense of libertarian free agency, and it is just such an appeal that is disallowed by the Free Agency Principle. If nonoccurrent causation is needed for free agency generally, then we need it, too. But if it must be invoked only to make sense of libertarian freedom, then the Free Agency Principle counsels us to try to avoid it.

Let us be clear, however, that doing without agent-causation in the nonoccurrent sense does not mean denying *agent causation* (unhyphenated) in the ordinary sense that agents act, bring things about, produce things, make choices, form their own characters and motives, and so on. Any theory of free agency, libertarian or otherwise, must give an account of what it means for agents to do things and to bring things about, and this means giving an account of what it means to be an agent or self that is (in the language of chapter 6) a "source of motion or activity" in the world. In this ordinary sense of agent causation, the notion is needed in any account of free agency, libertarian or nonlibertarian; and part of the task of the next three chapters will be to give an account of it. The idea is to see whether such an account can be given for libertarian free agency *without* invoking a special notion of nonoccurrent causation or any other libertarian strategem ruled out by the Free Agency Principle. Then, if mysteries or unsolved problems remain about how agents can act or bring things about in the world, they will be mysteries or problems about the nature of action and agency generally, and not mysteries or problems created specifically by libertarian theories of free agency.

In conclusion, readers will have noted that I have not mounted a full-scale attack on traditional libertarian strategies that are ruled out by the Free Agency Principle. Apart from comments on standard objections to some of these strategies, I have merely explained why they are ruled out and why they will be avoided in the following chapters. There are two reasons for proceeding in this way. First, there already exists an enormous critical literature on traditional libertarian strategies showing their limitations, and I myself have criticized them in earlier works.[23] But, second, and more important, my main objection to all traditional libertarian strategies ruled out by the Free Agency Principle is a general one and can be stated as follows.

T18 (on UR): The argument of succeeding chapters will be that traditional libertarian strategies ruled out by the Free Agency Principle (T16) (such as appeals to noumenal selves, mind/body dualism, agent-causation, or explanatory incompatibilism) are not necessary for an account of incompatibilist free will. Simply put, I am going to argue that strategies not satisfying the Free Agency Principle are not needed by libertarians. Whatever *can* be done to make sense of a free will satisfying UR can be done without them. And whatever *can't* be done to make sense of incompatibilist free will *can't be done with them either.*

8

Moral and Prudential Choice

1. Self-Forming Willings

The task before us was aptly described in an earlier quote from Wiggins: "Whether or not it is our world . . . we must continue to press the question, 'What is the possible world which could afford the autonomy of thought or agency the libertarian craves in this one?'" I do not think an answer to this question is going to be found merely by analyzing ordinary notions like *can*, or *power*, *reasons*, or *choice*. If a coherent libertarian account of freedom were already embodied in some existing human language or conceptual scheme, we would have found it long ago. What is called for is not mere analysis, but theoretical construction out of diverse materials, old and new, ordinary and not-so-ordinary—a thought experiment, if you like, that is meant to produce what Plato called a "likely story," though not necessarily a familiar one. Moreover, the experiment must be carried out within the constraints of the Free Agency Principle, with the hope that the account of free will arrived at will provide some clues about the place free will might have in the natural order in which it must be exercised. Or, to put it in another way, we are looking for an answer to the Intelligibility Question that might also throw light on the Existence Question.

Like any theoretic construction, the one to follow proceeds in stages. An account of free will is built up step by step over the next few chapters. To emphasize the more important steps, I designate them "theses" on free will. We already have eighteen theses on UR, and since the argument is that UR is a necessary condition for free will, the theses on UR may be regarded as the first eighteen theses on free will. We now begin to build upon them.

The first thesis to be added was introduced in chapter 2 and is definitive of the free willist view I want to defend. We are now in a position to restate it in terms of prior theses on UR.

T19 (on FW) ("Bramhall's Thesis"): "The freedom of the agent is from the freedom of the will." We have seen that, while actions in general, and not only acts of will, can be performed "of the agent's own free will" (T13), the *having* of a free will requires some regress-stopping, undetermined actions (SFAs) in the life histories of agents by virtue of which they are the ultimate creators of some of their own purposes (T6). These prior theses allow a more precise statement of Bramhall's thesis. It amounts to the claim that the self-forming actions (SFAs)

"willings" or "acts of will" of one sort or another (the
[...] out in subsequent theses). In sum, *SFAs are SFWs*

[...]rtant to the theses on UR. UR requires undetermined
[...]me kind or another, but does not say what form they
[...] are acts of will or willings is a further step that is
[...]ifying. Its justification comes from the role that
[...]tical construction to follow (of which it is an initial
[...]nsition from theses on UR to theses on free will,
[...]ee willist." I favored the term "incompatibilist"
[...]npatibility Question in Part I, and the term "lib-
[...]ng traditional incompatibilist theories. Hereaf-
[...]opriate.
[...]ng willings."

[...]n the theory to follow, the "self-forming willings," or
[...] (also called "undetermined free willings") include acts of the following kinds: (1) Moral choices or decisions, (2) prudential choices or decisions,
(3) efforts of will sustaining purposes, (4) attentional efforts directed at self control and self modification, (5) practical judgments and choices, and (6) changes
of intention in action. The first, second, and fifth of these are examples of the
libera arbitria voluntatis or "free judgments of the will" discussed in chapter 2.
The other three are examples of what was called in chapter 2 "striving will" (following O'Shaughnessy).

I do not want to say that these six categories are exhaustive of undetermined free
willings because I do not know that to be so.[1] There is room for expansion of the
theory. But these six, as we discuss them over the next three chapters, will amply
illustrate what is meant by "self-forming willings" and the role they play in the
theory.

> *T21 (on FW)*: The SFWs of T20 include such things as choices, decisions, judg-
> ments, formations of intention, and efforts or tryings, all of which are mental
> "acts" or actions of one sort or another as defined in chapter 2—the bringings
> about, or sustainings, by agents of various states of affairs. They are called acts
> "of will" because what they bring about or sustain are intentions, purposes, and
> normative or evaluative beliefs that in turn guide action. Indeed, we shall see
> that all three senses of "will" defined in chapter 2 (desiderative, rational, and
> striving will) are involved in every SFW. SFWs of each kind are motivated by
> desires and other inclinations; they involve the formation, alteration, or sustain-
> ing of intentions or beliefs that guide action; and they involve some element of
> trying or effort.

In this chapter, we are going to focus on the first two kinds of free willings mentioned in T20, namely, (1) moral and (2) prudential choices. They have much in
common, and together provide a vehicle for introducing basic features of the theory.
Accounts of other kinds of free willings are added in chapters 9 and 10.

2. Moral and Prudential Conflict

Moral and prudential choices, as understood here, differ from practical choices (the fifth category of free willings of T20) in the following respect. Moral and prudential choices involve conflicts between what an agent believes ought to be done and what the agent wants or desires to do. In the moral case, the *oughts* express moral obligations that are in conflict with self-interested desires. In the prudential case, they concern future or long-term interests that conflict with desires for present or near-term satisfactions (such as the desire to lose weight versus the temptation to have one more beer). Practical choices, by contrast, are not defined by conflicts between perceived obligations and inclinations. If you are deliberating about which restaurant to dine at, or deliberating (like Jane) about where to vacation—and if neither option is perceived as the one you ought to choose for moral or prudential reasons— then the choice is practical.

Some libertarians, such as C. A. Campbell (and also Kant, on some interpretations of his view), have limited the exercise of incompatibilist free will to moral and prudential choices.[2] As I see it, these thinkers correctly emphasize the importance of moral and prudential choice for an adequate theory of free will, but wrongly limit free will to such choices. Any adequate account of free will ought to be able also to accommodate practical choices and a broad spectrum of other kinds of free willings (as T20 does). Nonetheless, moral and prudential choices are pivotal for an adequate account of free will, and we shall begin with them.

Consider a woman on the way to an important sales meeting who witnesses an assault or mugging in an alley. Should she stop and call for help or press on to avoid losing a sale crucial to her career? Or consider an engineer who is a recovering alcoholic trying to repair his marriage. Working late at night under great stress, he is tempted to have a drink in order to go on. The businesswoman faces a moral conflict, the engineer a prudential one. But both are torn by conflicting motives and must make mental efforts to get their ends or purposes sorted out—to "set" their wills in one way or another. They are strongly tempted to act from self-interest, in the one case, or to relieve present tensions, in the other. But they are also committed to moral beliefs and long-term plans, and are making efforts to overcome temptations that threaten these commitments.

Resolutions of such moral and prudential conflicts may only be temporary. The woman may pass beyond the alley, then decide to return and yell for help, only to lose her nerve before she gets there in fear for her own safety. The engineer may reach for a bottle of bourbon in his drawer, but decide at the last second not to drink from it. Backsliding and changes of intention are always possible, and temptations may recur. But the resolutions of such conflicts—whether temporary or long-term— involve settings of the will in one direction or another that may initiate action immediately or at some time in the future (if the agents do not change their minds).

3. The Divided Will

On the free willist view I want to defend, resolutions of such moral and prudential conflicts in the life histories of agents could be (and many would be) "self-forming" in an incompatibilist sense (i.e., SFWs). By choosing one way or another in such cases, the agents would be strengthening their moral or prudential characters or reinforcing selfish or imprudent instincts, as the case may be. They would be "making" themselves or "forming" their wills one way or another in a manner that was not determined by past character, motives, and circumstances. But saying this creates a problem. For, if moral and prudential choices are not determined in such cases, the agents might choose either way, all past circumstances remaining the same up to the moment of choice. If the businesswoman's choice satisfied this condition, she might have decided to walk on and ignore the mugging, given exactly the same motives and effort that preceded her decision to return and call for help.

How can this be made intelligible? Her choice terminated and was preceded by an effort to resist the temptation to act selfishly, which effort may have succeeded or failed. Assuming that success or failure was not merely a matter of chance, what may have explained the effort and its resulting success or failure? Not necessarily some other effort. The woman's effort may have been explained by her prior character and motives, which accounted for the conflict in her will and the struggle to overcome it. But then one might argue that if the prior characters and motives explained the effort, UR would require that she be responsible for having formed her prior character and motives by virtue of earlier choices or efforts. A familiar and potentially vicious regress would ensue.

This regress might be stopped, however, if one could make sense of the following scenario. The choice in moral and prudential conflict situations terminates an effort (to resist temptation) in one way or another. What is needed is a situation in which the choice is not explained by the prior character and motives alone, or by the prior character and motives plus effort, *even if the prior character and motives can explain the effort*. If such a condition were satisfied, the agent's past character and motives would influence choice without determining it. But how can such a condition be satisfied, and how would the resulting choice be explained?

The answer is in two parts. The first part consists in saying *how* prior character and motives would explain the effort in cases of moral and prudential choice. Prior character and motives would do so by providing *both* (i) the reasons and dispositions that account for the agent's trying to resist moral or prudential temptation and (ii) the self-interested reasons or present inclinations that account for why it is *difficult* for the agent to resist temptation. In other words, the complex of past motives and character would explain the *conflict* within the agent's will *from both sides*. It would explain why the agent makes an effort to resist temptation and why it is an *effort* (because there is also resistance in the will that has to be overcome). Thus, the businesswoman is torn between self-interested motives on the one hand, and her moral conscience on the other; and the engineer between his craving for alcohol on the one hand, and his desires to save his marriage and career on the other.

It is because their efforts are thus a response to inner conflicts embedded in the agents' prior character and motives that their characters and motives can explain the conflicts and why the efforts are being made, without also explaining the outcomes of the conflicts and the efforts. Prior motives and character provide reasons for going either way, but not decisive reasons explaining which way the agent will inevitably go. By contrast, if prior reasons on one side or the other were decisive, the agents would not be experiencing the kinds of inner conflicts and struggle they are in fact experiencing. Thus,

> T22 (*on FW*): Self-forming willings (SFWs) of a moral or prudential kind are characterized by inner conflicts within the wills of agents and a consequent struggle by the agents to get their ends or purposes sorted out. In such conditions, the agents' wills are divided by conflicting motives, requiring an effort to act morally or prudentially against natural inclinations toward self-interest or present satisfaction. The old adage "no pain, no gain" applies to such SFWs. The self-creation characteristic of free will emerges by way of inner conflict within the will through which, to paraphrase James Joyce, we "forge in the smythies of our souls" our as yet uncreated selves.[3]

> T23 (*on FW*): In the moral and prudential situations described in T22, the complex of past reasons or motives explains the conflict and struggle within the agent's will from both sides. Some of the agent's reasons or motives (the moral or prudential ones) explain why the agent makes an effort to resist temptation, while others (self-interested motives or desires for present satisfactions) explain why it is such an *effort*. The inner conflict, in other words, is embedded in the prior reasons or motives themselves and it is owing to this fact that prior reasons or motives can explain the conflict and the struggle within the agent without necessarily explaining the outcome.

4. Efforts and Indeterminacy: Chaos, Nonequilibrium Thermodynamics, and Neural Networks

We now turn to the second part of an answer to the question of how prior reasons or motives can explain the effort to resist temptation without also explaining the choice that terminates the effort. We must now look at this "effort of will" (to resist moral or prudential temptation) that intervenes between prior reasons or motives, on the one hand, and the resulting choice, on the other.

> T24 (*on FW*): Let us suppose that the effort of will (to resist temptation) in the moral and prudential choice situations of T22 and T23 is (an) *indeterminate* (event or process), thereby making the choice that terminates it *undetermined*.

Consider a quantum analogue. Imagine an isolated particle, such as an electron, moving toward a thin atomic barrier. Whether or not the particle will penetrate the barrier is undetermined. There is a probability that it will penetrate, but not a certainty, because its position and momentum are not both determinate as it moves toward the barrier. Imagine that the choice (to overcome temptation) is like the penetration event. The choice one way or the other is *undetermined* because the process preceding it and potentially terminating in it (i.e., the effort of will to overcome temptation) is *indeterminate*.

But this quantum analogy is merely that—an analogy. Our efforts of will most likely correspond to complex processes in our brains that are macro processes involving many neuron firings and connections. Since we know that the effects of quantum level fluctuations are usually negligible at the macro level, how can these efforts be indeterminate? One way to begin thinking about this issue is to imagine that the neural processes occurring when the efforts are being made are chaotic processes, in the sense of what is nowadays called "chaos theory." In chaotic systems, very minute changes in initial conditions grow exponentially into large differences in final outcome, a phenomenon called "sensitivity to initial conditions." The ubiquity of chaotic systems in nature is now widely recognized, and there is growing interest in the chaotic behavior of the brain at many levels, from the transmission of impulses along individual nerve fibers, to the functioning of neural networks, to general patterns of brain waves.[4]

But chaotic behavior, though unpredictable, is not necessarily indeterministic. In fact, chaos theory has shown that one can have determinism without predictability.[5] Yet chaos theory may nonetheless be significant for discussions of human freedom, if quantum indeterminacy is also brought into the picture—as recently noted by scientists and philosophers such as Henry Stapp (1990), George P. Scott (1991), Jesse Hobbs (1991), James Garson (1993), and James Kellert (1993).[6] As Garson puts it,

> Chaotic systems are, by definition, perturbation amplifiers. They can override the general rule that quantum mechanical indeterminacies cancel out at the macro-level. Since chaotic events are exquisitely dependent on the very small, the doings of subatomic particles in a very small region of space-time may be reflected in massive differences in global behavior. If we view the brain as a chaotic system that amplifies the nondeterministic sub-atomic events, then chaotic unpredictability is no longer epistemological; it is metaphysical (or rather physical)." (p. 4)

Jesse Hobbs argues similarly that

> because [the] equations [governing chaotic systems] display sensitivity to initial conditions . . . they threaten to eliminate [the] ontological distinction one may wish to draw between the quantum level and higher levels. . . . It seems likely that [chaotic systems] magnify quantum-level indeterminism throughout their range, which as mentioned, may dwarf the range of deterministic systems lacking sensitivity to initial conditions." (p. 143)

That range of chaotic systems, Hobbs adds, "arguably [includes] virtually everything in the biosphere."

Stapp discusses these possibilities in relation to the human nervous system. "The brain is a highly non-linear system with feedback," he says. "Classical computer simulations show that the macroscopic state into which it will evolve is very sensitive to small variations at the synaptic level" that could effect the excitory or inhibitory potential of neurons to fire when receiving incoming charges from other neurons. These neural firings might then be further amplified chaotically to have global effects in the nervous system (p. 10).

Physical chemist Scott relates these possibilities to recent developments in nonequilibrium thermodynamics pioneered by Nobel laureate Ilya Prigogine. Energy dissipating chemical systems (so-called "dissipative structures") reach unstable bifurcation points in far-from-equilibrium thermodynamic conditions—bifurcation points at which the systems can evolve differently as a result of minute changes in their environment. Such systems can occur in physical chemistry, but, as Scott points out, the nonequilibrium thermodynamic conditions that make them possible are ubiquitous in living things (p. 265). In particular, he says, "the action potential waves on the bubble thin membranes of the nerve cells [which] are the most fundamental control activity in human behavior" are nonequilibrium thermodynamic phenomena of the sort that could chaotically amplify indeterminate events at the micro level.[7]

Of special interest are the potential effects such chaotic amplification might have on neural networks, which are systems of many functionally interconnected neurons.[8] The operation of such networks is holistic in the sense that, as Gordon Globus (1995) puts it, "the influence of the whole net" of neurons affects each "individual node [i.e., each neuron] and the influence of the individual node [affects] the whole net" (p. 6). As a consequence, such networks can be sensitive to variations of firings of individual neurons. As Globus says, "Make a few changes in the connection weights [the excitory and inhibitory potentials of neurons] and functionally everything changes [in the neural network] via non-linear interactions. . . . The net spontaneously and probabilistically self-organizes" (p. 8). Similarly, the self-organization of the network can effect the firing potentials of its individual nodes. There are reciprocal influences of parts to whole and whole to parts. The flexibility that such reciprocal influences afford in neural networks makes it possible for the brain to respond creatively to an ever-changing environment and is one of many reasons for current research interest in neural networks.

As a working hypothesis, then,

If SFWs are experienced as efforts of the will but are still just random events when considered physically, then free will is an illusion.

T25 (*on FW*): Imagine that the indeterminate efforts of will of T24 are complex chaotic processes in the brain, involving neural networks that are globally sensitive to quantum indeterminacies at the neuronal level. Persons experience these complex processes phenomenologically as "efforts of will" they are making to resist temptation in moral and prudential situations. The efforts are provoked by the competing motives and conflicts within the wills of the persons described in T22 and T23. These conflicts create tensions that are reflected in appropriate regions of the brain by movement further from thermodynamic equilibrium, which increases the sensitivity to micro indeterminacies at the neuronal level and magnifies the indeterminacies throughout the complex macro process which, taken as a whole, is the agent's effort of will.[9]

T26 (*on FW*): In effect, conflicts of will of the kinds described in T22 and 23 stir up chaos in the brain and make the agents' thought processes more sensitive to undetermined influences. The result is that, in soul-searching moments of moral and prudential struggle, when agents are torn between conflicting visions of what they should become (that is, on the occasions of self-forming willings, or SFWs), the outcomes are influenced by, but not determined by, past motives and character. The uncertainty and inner tension that agents feel at such moments are reflected in the indeterminacy of their neural processes.

5. Efforts and Weakness of Will

These suggestions give rise to a host of objections that I will try to address in some reasonable order, beginning with the most obvious. From this point onward, objections will be put into the mouth of an imagined compatibilist, or a skeptic about incompatibilist free will. *Objection 1*: "If these indeterminate efforts truly are macro indeterminate processes in the brain, as you suggest, it is difficult to see how the choice outcomes that result from them could be in the agent's control rather than merely matters of chance."

The first thing we have to remind ourselves here is that the indeterminate processes in the brain of T25 are *also* physical realizations of the agents' efforts of will and are experienced by the agents as something they are *doing*—that is, trying or struggling to resolve inner conflicts by overcoming temptations to act selfishly or imprudently. If the woman resolves her conflict by choosing to return to the alley and yell for help, she will have done so *by* making the effort to act morally, even if the outcome of her effort was not determined and hence not certain or guaranteed; and if the engineer suppresses his thoughts about the bourbon and gets back to work, he will have done so by making an effort to do so.

If we were able to inspect these agents' brains and found that the processes going on there when they were making these efforts involved non-negligible indeterminacies, that would not mean that the outcomes were not the result of their efforts and not therefore *their* doings. To deny that the efforts and outcomes were theirs on such grounds would be as absurd as saying that our reasoning processes and their outcomes would not be our doings if they turned out to involve indeterministic chaotic processes in the brain (as well they might, according to some recent suggestions[10]). The indeterminacy involved would mean that the outcomes that did occur were not guaranteed to occur, not that they were not our doings.

Objection 2: "But what if the agents' efforts to overcome temptation *fail*? You say that if the businesswoman and engineer succeed in acting morally or prudently they will have done so *by* their efforts (even if the efforts might have failed). Suppose, however, they succumb to temptation instead. This would not have been the result of their effort, but a failure of their effort—a failure that, since it was undetermined, was beyond their control. How is this unlike the 'one-way' examples of the sniper and Austin's putt, in which the agents are *trying* to do one thing, but fail and do otherwise *by chance*?"

The comparisons with the sniper and Austin are indeed relevant and especially revealing at this point. For there is a significant difference between those earlier examples and the cases of moral and prudential choice described in T22 and 23. In the moral and prudential situations of T22 and 23, the wills of the agents are deeply divided by conflicting motives. This is not the case for Austin and the sniper. Austin wants to make the putt, but does not also want to miss it. The sniper wants to kill his victim, and does not want to miss. Any motives that might incline them in a different direction have insufficient strength to create a conflict in their wills. It could be otherwise. We might imagine a different example in which the sniper has moral qualms before he shoots. In this case, his will would be torn in different directions about whether or not to shoot at all and his situation would be more like that of the businesswoman or engineer. Thus,

> T27 (*on FW*): The moral and prudential choices of T22 and 23 are unlike the one-way willed examples of Austin's putt or the sniper discussed in earlier chapters. If Austin or the sniper fail to hit their targets, it is merely by chance and not

an expression of their wills, because they do not in any sense will to fail. But in the moral and prudential cases, because the agents are moved by powerful competing motives, the resistance or impediment to their efforts to act morally and prudentially is *coming from their own wills* (the self-interested or present-oriented desires they are trying to resist). Though the outcome is not determined, they do not fail merely by chance. In one sense, they "will" (or want) to succeed (in overcoming temptation), but in another sense, they also "will" (or want) to fail (and succumb to temptation). As a consequence, unlike Austin and the sniper, either outcome is willed by the agents, though from a different point of view and by virtue of different motives.

Objection 3: "This is still troubling for many reasons. For one thing, in moral and prudential choice situations, the competing sets of motives are not on a par in the minds of the agents before they choose. If the agents really are making efforts to overcome moral and prudential temptation, then they believe in some sense that the moral or prudential reasons *ought* to prevail over reasons of self-interest or present satisfaction, and are trying to make them prevail. If this were not so, the agents would be mere wantons or psychopaths and would experience no moral or prudential conflict. But then the moral and prudential cases *are* like Austin's and the sniper's after all. Failing to overcome temptation may happen by chance contrary to what the agent is trying to do."

It is true that if agents never believed in some sense that moral (or prudential) reasons ought to override reasons of self-interest (or present satisfaction), there would be no moral or prudential conflict. But that is only half the story. Believing "in some sense" that moral or prudential reasons "ought" to override their competitors does not imply that moral or prudential reasons do in fact override or outweigh their competitors in the minds of the agents. If moral and prudential convictions were always unshakeable and were never seriously threatened by countervailing motives, there would *also be no inner moral or prudential conflict.* The agents would be moral or prudential robots never tempted to do otherwise. By contrast,

> T28 (*on FW*): When there is genuine conflict of the kind described in T27, desires on one side seriously compete with desires on the other. Whatever the agents may consciously believe or avow about the priority of moral or prudential reasons, the fact is that if we look more deeply into their full psychological profiles (conscious and unconscious motives alike), there is some doubt and indecision in their minds about this priority. If not, there would be no genuine conflict. The agents may believe some reasons ought to outweigh others *from* a moral or prudential point of view, but in these conflict situations their moral or prudential points of view *are not their only points of view* that matter. And insofar as the conflict between different internal points of view is real, it is uncertain whether moral or prudential reasons really do outweigh their competitors "in the minds of the agents" considered as the total psychological profile — no matter what the agents may consciously believe or avow. This uncertainty in the minds of the agents, I suggest, is reflected in the indeterminacy of their efforts to

overcome temptation and in the consequent indeterminacy and unpredictability of the outcomes.

T29 (*on* FW): When in such conflict situations agents do decide, and the indeterminate efforts become determinate choices, the agents will *make* one set of reasons or motives prevail over the others then and there *by deciding*. It is true that the "strong-willed" options (overcoming temptation) and the "weak-willed" ones (succumbing to temptation) are not symmetrical, if the agents are trying to overcome temptation. Nonetheless, both options are wanted and the agents will settle the issue of which is wanted *more* by deciding. If the businesswoman and engineer overcome temptation, they will do so by virtue of their efforts. If they fail, it will be because they did not *allow* their efforts to succeed. They chose instead to make their self-interested or present-oriented inclinations prevail, and they may subsequently feel regret, remorse, or guilt for doing so.

Some philosophers have argued that acting out of weakness of will in such situations must always be compulsive. If the engineer gives in and has the bourbon while believing that it is in his long-term best interest to do otherwise, then the desire for drink must have overmastered him; it must have been irresistible. Such reasoning is one basis for historical skepticism about the possibility of weakness of will, or *akrasia*, that goes back to Socrates and Plato.[11] The problem is to explain the possibility of acting against one's better judgment freely or voluntarily (i.e., noncompulsively). It is a problem that has troubled compatibilists and incompatibilists alike, and a solution to it must be found, whatever position one takes on free will. T28 and 29 suggest an incompatibilist solution.

T30 (*on* FW) ("Weakness of Will"): For choices of the kind described in T28 and T29, if the effort of will to overcome moral or prudential temptation is indeterminate, then the outcome either way is not determined. The agent may succeed in overcoming temptation or may fail. But this means that the weak-willed motives (of self-interest or imprudence) are *resistible*, even if the agents should act upon them. And if the motives of self-interest or imprudence are resistible, the weak-willed choice is not compulsive. Where the efforts to resist temptation are indeterminate and their outcomes undetermined, the agents could have succeeded in overcoming temptation, and thus "could have done otherwise" in a strong indeterminist sense of "could." Similarly, if the agents succeed in overcoming temptation, they also could have done otherwise in a manner that is undetermined. The motives of duty and prudence are also resistible, and the agents are not moral or prudential robots either.

6. Voluntariness and Control: The Plurality Conditions

Objection 4: "It is still far from clear that you should be allowed to say the agents 'could have *done* otherwise' in these circumstances, rather than saying that some outcome merely 'happened.' For surely the fact that the efforts are indeterminate takes away, or at least diminishes, one's *control* over the resulting choices. By making choice outcomes depend upon indeterministic efforts, are you not limiting the power or control that agents have over their free choices, and in particular over those very self-forming choices (SFWs) that are supposed to carry the burden of ultimate responsibility?"

Well, the agents cannot guarantee one outcome rather than the other *beforehand*. But

> T31 (*on* FW): It does not follow that because you cannot guarantee which of a set of outcomes occurs beforehand, you do not control which of them *occurs, when* it occurs. Having plural voluntary control over a set of options implies being able to bring about *whichever* one (of the options) *you will, when you will* to do so; and the choices in moral and prudential situations described in T27 through 30 satisfy this condition because they are willed by the agents, whatever way they go when they are made.[12]

Objection 5: "But there is more to plural voluntary control by your own account of it than being able to do whichever of the options you will when you will to do it, even if that is necessary. Other conditions have to be fulfilled, including that you do it *for* the reasons you will to do it rather than accidentally or merely by chance, and that you do it without being coerced, compelled, or otherwise controlled by anyone or anything else in doing it."

This is correct. T31 is only the beginning of an account of plural voluntary control for SFWs of moral and prudential kinds. We must add to it, and to do so the first step is to consider the other two plurality conditions, plural rationality and voluntariness, since they provide some of the further conditions. We can then return to plural voluntary control itself.

> T32 (*on* FW): "Plural voluntariness" (or absence of compulsion or coercion either way) for moral or prudential SFWs follows from what was said in theses T27 through T30, together with a few additional considerations. From T30, it follows that the choices either way are not compulsive. If the agents might act from one or the other competing sets of motives and the outcomes are undetermined, then the motives from which they acted either way would not have compelled them to act as they did; they might have acted from the other motives. Coercion presents further complications and must be treated differently from compulsion. For it might be argued that the businesswoman and engineer are like the coerced man who has a gun held to his head in an important respect: they are placed in circumstances they would rather not be in and are faced with choices they would rather not have faced. Nonetheless, there is a crucial difference between cases of coercion such as that of the man with the gun held to his head and the circumstances of the businesswoman and engineer. The attractions for the man with the gun held to his head of handing over his money are entirely created by the robber's actions, while the attractions of helping the crime victim for the businesswoman who is passing by are not wholly created by the actions of the mugger, but by his actions *and the urgings of her moral conscience*. The mugging taking place at a certain distance in an alley precipitates a conflict in the businesswoman, but the conflict precipitated is in her own will, between her moral conscience and her career ambitions; and she will settle that conflict

voluntarily either way, by following her conscience or her self-interest. It would be different if someone pointed a gun at the woman's head and said "Go back and help or else." Then she would go back involuntarily, just as the man hands over his money to the robber involuntarily. The primary conflict would then be between *her* will and the *coercer's* will, rather than a conflict within her own will prompted by the circumstances.

Similarly, the engineer is not happy about the situation in which he has been placed by having to work late under great stress. But the primary conflict precipitated is within his own will, between desire to drink on the one hand, and desire to save his marriage on the other; and he will settle that conflict voluntarily either way.

7. Rationality and Choosing for Reasons

There is one other aspect of plural voluntariness not covered by T32, but it is dealt with by the third plurality condition.

> T33 (*on FW*) ("Plural Rationality" or "Motivation"): Self-forming willings (SFWs) of the moral or prudential kinds described in T22 through 32 are also plural, or more-than-one-way, rational, or motivated in the following sense. Whether the agents overcome temptation (and act on moral or prudential reasons) or succumb to temptation (and act on reasons of self-interest or for present satisfactions), the agents (r_1) will in each case have *had* reasons for choosing as they did; (r_2) they will have chosen *for* those reasons; and (r_3) they will have made those reasons the ones they wanted to act on more than any others *by* choosing for them.[13]

Regarding condition r_1 of this thesis, we should recall from T23 that the agents had reasons of both competing kinds before they chose. The existence of competing reasons in their psychological histories accounts for both the prior conflict in their wills and the effort to overcome that conflict. The agents do not therefore create their reasons for choosing by choosing. Rather, the reasons are ones they already have. What they do by choosing is to make one set of reasons prevail over others then and there as motivators of action. Regarding condition r_3, the relevant thesis is T29: "In cases of moral and prudential conflict . . . both options are wanted" by the agents for different reasons, "and the agents will settle the issue of which is wanted *more* by deciding. If the businesswoman and engineer overcome temptation, they will do so by virtue of their efforts. If they fail, it would be because they did not *allow* their efforts to succeed. They chose instead to make their self-interested or present-oriented inclinations prevail."

This leaves condition r_2 of T33 to be dealt with—that the agents choose either way *for* reasons. I noted in chapter 2 that choosing or acting "for reasons" is something more than merely having reasons for choosing or acting. Jane may have had several reasons for vacationing in Hawaii—for example, she likes beaches and a friend lives there whom she had wanted to visit. But the second reason never entered her deliberation because she forgot that the friend now lives in Hawaii. Her wanting to visit the friend was a reason she had, but not one for which she acted. Now I think it is evident that in the moral and prudential cases we have been discussing, like those of the businesswoman and the engineer, the reasons the agents have for either choice *do* influence their choices one way or the other, much as Jane's liking beaches influenced her choice. If the engineer chooses not to drink, it will be because he wanted to save his marriage and career, and if he chooses to drink it will be because of his strong (though resistible) desire to relieve tension. These are the reasons "for" which he acts and not just reasons he has. They are not idle, or out of the loop, like Jane's unconsidered desire to see an old friend. In such manner, r_2 of T33 would also be satisfied for moral and prudential choices of the kinds described in T22 through 32; and the case for plural rationality would be complete.

A question remains, however, about the nature of this "influence" that reasons are supposed to have on actions when agents act "for" the reasons. Many recent authors who have written perceptively on the notion of acting for reasons, such as Donald Davidson (1980), Myles Brand (1984), Robert Audi (1986), Alfred Mele (1987; 1992), Fred Dretske (1988), and John Bishop (1989) believe that this influence must be spelled out in causal terms.[14] If agents act for reasons, then the reasons (or, more precisely, the agent's having the reasons) must play a role in the causal "etiology of the action," as Mele puts it (1992:3). I think libertarians can accept this assumption so long as the causal connections between reasons and actions are allowed to be probabilistic, as well as deterministic.[15] Most of these authors do in fact concede this possibility. While their accounts of "acting for reasons" are designed to make it compatible with determinism, they concede that nothing in the ordinary understanding of acting for reasons requires that the reasons must determine action (as opposed to causally *influencing* action).

But even the staunchest causalists do not believe that causal influence is *sufficient* for saying the agents "choose for reasons." There is also a teleological element involved in choosing for reasons. The choices must connect the reasons in a certain way to future actions chosen and intended. Thus, if the engineer chooses to avoid drinking because he wants to save his career and marriage, these reasons for choosing also become his reasons for acting (i.e., for his actually avoiding the drinking) by virtue of his choosing for the reasons. To say that the reasons for choosing become his reasons for acting is to say that his *persistence in doing what he chooses* will thereafter be sensitive to alterations in the reasons. For example, the engineer's ability to sustain the intention not to drink rather than backslide will be affected by changes in the strength of his desires to save his career and marriage and by his ability to keep these desires in the forefront of his thinking when tempted to drink. The reasons thus come to play distinctive roles in his future behavior by virtue of his choosing for them. As a consequence,

> T34 (*on FW*) ("Choosing For Reasons"): When agents choose for reasons in the sense required by the plural rationality of T33, there is a reciprocal influence of reasons on choice and choice on reasons. The reasons play a role in the causal etiology of the choice (though they need not determine it), while the choice itself, once made, connects the reasons to the intention formed so that the "reasons for choosing" also become "reasons for acting." Thus, a choice once made for moral or prudential reasons connects those reasons to subsequent

behavior so that the agent's ability to persist in acting morally or prudentially is sensitive to variations in the agent's attitudes toward the moral or prudential reasons. The same is true if agents choose immorally or imprudently. Persistence in immoral or imprudent action depends upon variations in the strength of, and focus upon, self-interested or present-oriented motives, such as the business-woman's desire to get to her meeting or the engineer's desire to have a drink.

Relating this to the model presented in T24 and 25 of what might be going on in the brain when moral and prudential SFWs take place, we can add that

> T35 (*on FW*): As a consequence of T34, choosing A for reasons R (e.g., moral or prudential reasons) does more than create an intention to A or initiate events leading to the doing of A. It reorganizes the motivation structure of the brain, creating connections between the neural patterns corresponding to the agent's having reasons R and neural patterns corresponding to the intention created by the choice. By virtue of these newly created neural connections, the agent's reasons for choosing play a teleological as well as causal role in behavior, influencing future behavior in the manner described in T34. Moreover, the creation of such connections between reasons and intention amounts to the agent's making the reasons for which the choice is made "the ones he or she wants to act on then and there more than any other reasons by choosing" (which is condition r_3 of T33). If the choice had gone the other way—if the agent chose for self-interested reasons or reasons of present satisfaction instead—the motivational structures of the brain would have been reorganized differently.

[margin note: reasons and the brain]

T34 and 35 complete the account of plural rationality (or motivation) of T33. Self-forming willings of the moral or prudential kinds are plural rational, or motivated, in the following sense. Whether the agents act on moral or prudential grounds or succumb to temptation, the agents in each case (r_1) have reasons (or motives) for choosing as they do; (r_2) choose *for* those reasons; and (r_3) make those reasons the ones they want to act on more than any others then and there by choosing for them. Self-forming willings of moral and prudential kinds thereby reorient the agent's motivational life in the direction of one form of behavior rather than another.

8. Purpose and Agency: The Self-Network

Plural voluntariness (T32) and rationality (T33) provide some of the further conditions for plural voluntary control, but not all of them. In the broadest sense, one has plural voluntary control over a set of options when "one is able to do or bring about whichever of the options one wills, when one wills to do it, for the reasons one wills to do it, rather than accidentally or by mistake or merely by chance, and without being coerced, compelled, or otherwise controlled by anyone or anything else in doing it or willing to do it (such as a Frankfurt controller or mechanism, or a CNC controller or mechanism)." Not all of these conditions are dealt with by prior theses, but some are. Thus "doing whichever of the options you will (i.e., most want) to do, when you will to do it" is covered by T31 plus r_3 of T33 (plural rationality). "Doing it *for* the reasons that you will to do it" is covered by r_2 of T33 along with the commentary on choosing for reasons in T34 and 35; and "doing it and willing to do it without being coerced or compelled" is covered by T32 (plural voluntariness) plus r_3 of T33.

This leaves two further conditions of plural voluntary control to deal with: not doing it "accidentally or by mistake or merely by chance," and doing it "without being controlled by any other agents or mechanisms" such as Frankfurt or CNC controllers. Regarding the first of these conditions, it may appear that since moral and prudential SFWs are undetermined, they must be done "accidentally," or "by mistake," and hence "merely by chance." But this is not so.

> T36 (*on FW*) ("On Purpose" [I]): Moral and prudential SFWs are very much unlike cases in which agents do things accidentally or by mistake, and hence merely by chance, such as my pressing the wrong button on the coffee machine or the sniper missing his victim by accident (T27). Note, first, that if I press the *right* button at the coffee machine, the one I was trying to press, I do not do so accidentally, by mistake, or merely by chance, even though the outcome was not determined and I might have failed (and similarly for the sniper if he hits the victim he was aiming at). It is only if we fail in such attempts that we do so accidentally, by mistake, or merely by chance. But with moral and prudential SFWs, *either way*, the agents do *what* they will to do *when* they will to do it (T31), they do it *voluntarily*, that is, without being coerced or compelled in doing it (T32) or in willing to do it (T33 [r_3]), and they do it *for the reasons* that they will to do it (T33 [r_2]), so that the reasons (moral or immoral, prudent or imprudent, as the case may be) do not influence their choices merely accidentally, but rather the agents choose for the reasons in the manner described by T34 and 35. But it is the fulfillment of *just such conditions* as these that leads one to say something was done intentionally or "*on purpose*" rather than "by accident," "by mistake," or "merely by chance." For example, when I press the right button on the coffee machine, all the above conditions are satisfied (I do what I will to do then and there, for the reasons I will to do it, without being coerced, etc.); and when I press the wrong button accidentally, the above conditions are *not* all satisfied (I do not act voluntarily or do what I will). Hence, we say the right button is pressed "on purpose" but the wrong one only "by mistake."

By contrast, in the cases of the businesswoman and the engineer (and other moral and prudential SFWs), the above conditions are satisfied *either way*. So when the businesswoman chooses to help the victim or go on to her meeting, she does so intentionally or on purpose. To say this, of course, is not to say that the businesswoman must have a *prior* intention to make just the choice she does make. Writers on intentional action warn us not to assume that intentionally (or purposefully) doing some A always requires a prior intention to-do-A (Bratman (1987:112–16), Mele (1992: 131–5). Cases of deliberation and choice are especially interesting examples in which this assumption fails. Suppose an agent is deliberating about whether to choose A or B. The deliberation is intentional in the sense that the agent intends to-choose-either-A-or-B. But it is not yet true—so long as the deliberation is in progress—that the agent intends to-choose-A or intends to-choose-B. The agent will choose one or the other, and if the choice is intentional, it will be by virtue of the general intention to resolve the matter *in one way or the other*, not by virtue of the prior intention to make just *that* choice.

This point applies to choices or decisions generally. They are made intentionally or on purpose not by virtue of a specific prior intention to make the particular choice made but by virtue of the general intention to resolve indecision in one way or another.

This observation in turn allows us to expand upon the account of choosing for reasons in T34 and 35. It was said in T34 that when one chooses for reasons, there is a reciprocal influence of reasons on choice and choice on reasons. The reasons for which one chooses causally influence the choice (without determining it), while the choice, once made, reorganizes the motivational structures of the brain so that the reasons come to have a special role to play in future behavior. This is part of what is meant by saying that a choice is made "on purpose," but only part. One has to also look at the broader purposes and motivational system of the agent of which the specific reasons for acting are a part. The businesswoman may resolve her conflict by choosing to help the assault victim (A) for moral reasons (R), or by choosing to go on to her meeting (B) for selfish reasons (R'). But, *qua* agent and practical reasoner, she has the general purpose of resolving the conflict in one way or the other and thereby deciding (for the present at least) what sort of person she wants to be—which of her internal points of view (T26) she wishes to have prevail. The conflicting reason sets, R and R', are, after all, both *hers*; they are parts of her general motivational system.

Further insight into purposive agency beyond T34 and 36 must therefore come from understanding the role played by the general motivational system of the agent in the economy of practical reasoning and behavior. On this topic, I think interesting clues are available in the recent research of cognitive and neuroscience.[16] Whatever view one eventually takes on the mind/body problem, or on the relationship of consciousness and selfhood to the brain, I do not think recent research in these scientific fields can be ignored if one hopes to arrive at an adequate understanding of free agency. When we say that the conflicting reasons sets R and R' motivating the businesswoman are both *hers*—parts of her general motivation system—this corresponds, in neural terms, to saying that the neural connections representing R and R' are embedded in a more comprehensive network of neural connections representing the general motivational system in terms of which she defines herself as agent and practical reasoner. I propose to call this comprehensive network representing her general motivational system the "self-network."

In a recent work, *Consciousness Reconsidered* (1992), which surveys some of the scientific research referred to in the previous paragraph, Owen Flanagan refers to what I am here calling the "self-network" in the following way:

> A person's higher-order self is one of the many models contained in his brain. Once acquired and in operation, this model is part of the recurrent brain network causally responsible for the life a person lives and how he thinks and feels. . . . Even though the self is not *the* control center of the mind—the mind may well have no single control center—in setting out plans, aspirations and ideals, it plays an important role in a person's overall psychological economy. (p. 207)

The "recurrent brain network" to which Flanagan refers, which sets out the "plans, aspirations and ideals" of the agent and embodies the motivational structures of the brain that influence and guide practical reasonings and action is what I am here calling the "self-network."

To suppose there is such a thing, one does not have to suppose, as Flanagan notes, that the self-network controls everything in the brain, or that it has a specific location rather than being distributed widely throughout the brain. On the question of what may give unity to this network, clues are provided in the recent work of Francis Crick and Christof Koch (1990), Rudolfo Llinas, D. Pare and U. Ribary (1991; 1993), among others.[17] Crick and Koch suggest on the basis of recent research that visual awareness occurs when neurons in many cortical areas "cooperate to form some sort of global activity" (p. 267). The underlying mechanism is the synchronous firing of diverse groups of neurons forming distinctive oscillations or wave patterns through-out the network. Llinas and Pare (1991) note that magnetoencephalograph data reveal similar wave patterns in wakefulness and dreaming, and they suggest that the fundamental organization subserving the unity of self-awareness involves coupled or causally interacting oscillations or wave patterns of certain types throughout the brain.

These suggestions are speculative, but the existence of the synchronized and causally interacting oscillations or wave patterns to which the hypotheses refer is not speculative.[18] On the basis of current research, it seems that the best place to look for the unity of the self-network is in the dynamical properties of neural circuits and connections that make such synchronous patterns of neural firings possible.[19] These circuits would not always be activated (in deep sleep they would shut down altogether), but when activated they would be the basis for the awareness that the motivational system they subserve is that of a single self or agent (barring pathological conditions such as multiple personality disorder). With this in mind, I suggest the following further thesis.

> *T37 (on FW)* ("Self-Network"): The feeling that certain events in the brain, such as those corresponding to our efforts and choices, are things we are doing rather than things that are merely happening has its basis in the superposition of the synchronized wave patterns (or patterns of oscillations of neural firings) of the self-network upon those neural events. The suggestion, in other words, is that the neural events corresponding to our efforts and choices would be overlaid by the wave patterns unifying the self-network—so that the wave patterns and the effort or choice events are coupled, causally influencing and interacting with each other. The effort and choice events would occur, so to speak, "within" the self-network whose distinctive patterns of oscillations were superimposed upon them. In turn, the superimposed patterns of oscillations of the self-network would be contributing causes to choice, pushing one competing reason-network over the top, so to speak, so that A is chosen for reasons R rather than B for reasons R' (or vice versa)—thus supporting the belief that the efforts and choices are our doings, the products of our selves.

These claims are meant to apply to mental action and agency in general, whether deterministic or nondeterministic, compatibilist or incompatibilist. Many people think that only libertarian theories have problems explaining "agency" in naturalis-tic terms. If actions are not determined by reasons, they think, then some further account of agency is required, whereas if actions *are* determined by reasons, nothing more is required to account for agency. But this conclusion is altogether too hasty.

T38 (*on* FW): There are good reasons to believe that something like the self-network of T37 is needed to account for agency, whether actions are undetermined *or determined*. For the mere fact that a mental event is determined — even determined by reasons — does not guarantee that it is something the *agent* does, as Fred Dretske (1988) and David Velleman (1992) have rightly pointed out.[20] First, there is the further question of what makes the *reasons* reasons *of* the agent. (The reason-networks would also have to be inside the self-network, coupled to its patterns of oscillations.) Second, there is a further problem about the possibility of "causal deviance," which is to say that the reasons may cause the action through some wayward causal chains (that circumvent the self-network) such that the action is not brought about by the agent for the reasons, though it is determined by the reasons. So, even when choice is determined (as in Luther's case on Dennett's account of it), the fact that the choice is the *agent's* doing rather than a mere happening means that something playing the role of a self-network is needed to link the reasons to the action and the agent in appropriate ways.

It would follow that the self-network, as described here, or some other structure in the brain playing a similar theoretical role, is needed to account for free agency, whether actions are determined or not. That is, some such postulate would be needed to account for free agency in general, as the Free Agency Principle requires, not merely for libertarian free agency. In that case,

T39 (*on* FW): The crucial differences for *undetermined* free willings (or SFWs) needed for libertarian free agency would be these: (a) the contributing patterns of oscillations of the self-network would *involve chaotic indeterminacies* as described in T25 and 26, so the choice outcome would not be determined, and (b) there would be more than one feasible option (A for R or B for R') that the patterns of the self-network might push over the top, thus triggering the choice outcome. Whichever outcome is pushed over the top, however, would be the product of the self-network whose distinctive oscillations would be crucial to its coming about.[21]

We now combine theses 36 to 39 in order to get the following thesis.

T40 (*on* FW) ("On Purpose" [II]): To say that moral and prudential conflicts such as those of the businesswoman and engineer are resolved on purpose either way and not by accident, mistake, or merely by chance is not only to say, as T36 does, that (i) the agents do what they will to do either way, for the reasons they will to do it, without being coerced, and so forth. It is also to say that (ii) the resolution either way is causally influenced by the self-network by way of superposed oscillations (in the manner described in T37 and 38), (iii) in fulfillment of one or another of the *purposes* of the self-network (to resolve indecision in *one way or another*), (iv) by one of the *feasible* options or *means* allowed by the self-network, that is, by choosing either A *or* B (but not, say, C or D) (T39).

Prior to resolving her conflict, the businesswoman does not have the specific purpose of going back to help the assault victim (A) or of going on to her meeting (B). But she does have the general purpose of resolving the conflict in one way or another (iii); and these options, A and B, are the feasible options or allowable means by which that purpose may be fulfilled (iv). If, in addition, the resolution one way or the other is causally influenced by the self-network (ii), as described in T37 through 39, and is willed for reasons, as described in T36 (i), then it is not merely accidental or done by mistake. We thereby designate it a "choice" rather than a merely accidental occurrence, such as Jane's selecting Colorado due to a quantum jump in her brain when she favored Hawaii, or my pressing the wrong button on the coffee machine due to a chance occurrence in my nerve pathways.

9. Plural Voluntary Control

This brings us to the final condition not yet discussed concerning plural voluntary control. The choice or action over which one has such control cannot be controlled by *other* agents or mechanisms, like Frankfurt controllers, implanted drugs, hypnotic suggestion, or covert nonconstraining (CNC) controllers of any kind, such as behavioral engineers or other behind-the-scenes manipulators. The absence of such controllers or mechanisms is a crucial requirement for free will generally, as we learned in chapters 3 and 5; and satisfying it is *not* guaranteed by fulfillment of the other conditions thus far discussed for plural voluntary control. Agents may will to do what they do for reasons, and they may act intentionally or on purpose, while their actions, wills and purposes are nevertheless under the control of other agents or controllers. The absence of such control is therefore an important further condition for free will. So, it is a fact of some significance that this requirement also turns out to be satisfied for SFWs of the kinds we have been describing.

> *T41 (on FW)* ("SFWs and Frankfurt or CNC Controllers"): Imagine what must be done to exercise Frankfurt control over a person's choice. The controller, Black, plans to make Jones do A. But he waits to see if Jones is going to do A on his own and only intervenes if Jones is about to do B instead. But if A is an SFW (say, a choice), the controller faces a dilemma in carrying out such a strategy. Since the SFW is preceded by an indeterminate effort, it is undetermined whether choice A or B will occur until one or the other of them actually does occur. The controller cannot know which one is going to occur beforehand unless he predetermines one of them to occur. He can therefore wait until he finds out whether the agent will do A or B, but then it is too late to control the choice. Or he can intervene in the brain, shutting down the indeterminacy or its effects before either choice occurs, thereby determining the outcome he wants. In the latter case, the choice will be determined by the controller and the controller, not the agent, will be *ultimately responsible* for it. It will not be an SFW. By contrast, if the controller does not intervene to predetermine the outcome and the indeterminacy remains in place until the choice is made—so that the outcome *is* an SFW—then the agent, and not the controller, is ultimately responsible for it. But then it is also the case that the agent *could have done otherwise*.[22] So the "Frankfurt divergence" between (ultimate) responsibility and could-have-done-otherwise fails to hold for SFWs. If the agent is ultimately responsible because the controller does not intervene, the agent could have done otherwise; and if

the agent could *not* have done otherwise because the controller did intervene, then the controller is ultimately responsible and not the agent. Similar conclusions can be drawn about CNC controllers, or any other kinds of controllers or mechanisms. If they tamper with our brains, shutting off the indeterminacy prior to choice, they can control our choices, but not if the efforts remain indeterminate and the choices undetermined up to the moment they occur.[23]

This thesis allows us to answer the objection raised in chapter 3 about a Frankfurt controller that was present throughout the entire lifetime of an agent, but never intervened. The objection was that if such an ever-present, nonintervening controller existed, the controlled agent would never have been able to do otherwise throughout an entire lifetime because the controller would never have allowed it. Yet, the agent might have been responsible for many actions in that lifetime since, if the controller never in fact intervened, the agent would have often acted on his or her own. Thus, responsibility would not require that the agent *ever* could have done otherwise. But we can see from T41 that if the controller (though ever-present) never intervened, *and* some of the actions in this agent's life history were SFWs, as UR requires, then the agent *could* have done otherwise with respect to those SFWs; and the agent, not the controller, would be ultimately responsible for them. Thus,

T42 (*on FW*): T41 allows us to retain a powerful intuition we feel that if a Frankfurt controller never actually intervened throughout an agent's entire lifetime, so that the agent always acted on his or her own, then the *mere presence* of the controller should not make any difference to the agent's ultimate responsibility. This intuition can and should, I think, be retained. But it is also the case that if some of the actions the agents perform on their own throughout their lifetimes (with the controller never intervening) are SFWs, as must be so if UR is satisfied, then it will also be true, according to T41, that the agents could have done otherwise with respect to those actions. The mere presence of a nonintervening controller would not change the fact that ultimately responsible agents must have been able to have done otherwise with respect to *some* actions in their life histories.

Finally, with theses 41 to 42 added to the others, we have an account of

T43 (*on FW*) ("Plural Voluntary Control"): SFWs of moral and prudential kinds described in previous theses satisfy the conditions of plural voluntary control in the following sense. The agents have plural voluntary control over a set of options (e.g., choosing morally or prudentially, or vice versa) when they are able to do whichever of the options they will to do, when they will to do it (T31), for the reasons they will to do it (T33 through 35), on purpose rather than accidentally, by mistake, or merely by chance (T36 through 40), without being coerced or compelled in doing it (T32) or in willing to do it (T33), or otherwise controlled in doing or willing to do it by any other agents or mechanisms (T41 through 42). These conditions can be summed up by saying, as people sometimes do, that the agents can choose either way *at will*. Or, alternatively, when these conditions for plural voluntary control are satisfied, one can say that it is "up to the agents" what they will do when they act.[24]

But if all this is correct, why does the intuition persist so strongly in us that agents simply *couldn't* really have control over the outcomes if they are undetermined? I confess that I, too, have felt, and still do feel, the pull of this intuition. But intuitions, however powerful, should not go unexamined; and I think this one needs to be put on a rack until it yields its secrets.

intuitions

> *T44 (on FW)* ("Antecedent Determining Control"): I believe the reason intuitions persist that choices or actions could not be in the agent's control if they are undetermined, even if they should fulfill the conditions of plural voluntary control just given in T43, is that there is a *kind* of control that *is* lacking in SFWs and would be lacking in any actions that are undetermined. This is the ability to be in, or bring about, conditions such that one can guarantee or determine which of a set of outcomes is going to occur *before* it occurs, whether the outcomes are one's own actions, the actions of others, or events in the world generally. No doubt, such "antecedent determining control" as we might call it, is valuable in many circumstances; and we cannot help but value it by virtue of an evolutionary imperative to seek security and get control of our surroundings. But it does not follow that antecedent determining control is the only kind of control we can have. For, as argued in T31, it does not follow that because you cannot determine which of a set of outcomes occurs *before* it occurs, you lack control over which of them occurs, *when* it occurs. When the conditions of plural voluntary control are satisfied, agents exercise control over their future lives *then and there* in a manner that is not antecedently determined by their pasts.

This does not mean that antecedent determining control has no role to play in the exercise of free will. Quite the contrary: it has an important role to play, since many actions done of our own free will (T13) may be antecedently determined by us, given our past characters and motives—like Luther's "Here I stand." But if all control had to be antecedently determining in this way, we would not be ultimately responsible for anything we did.

Now if someone insists that the inability to guarantee an outcome before it occurs is a limitation of voluntary control even if it does not imply the absence of voluntary control, then I grant it. But I would insist that this limitation is a requirement for free will. Rather than hide this fact, I think incompatibilists should bring it out into the open.

> *T45 (on FW)*: Paradoxical as it may seem, in order to have *ultimate* control over their destinies, possessors of free will must relinquish another kind of control at pivotal points in their life histories, namely, an antecedent determining control that would guarantee how things will turn out in advance.[25] Free will, for this reason among others, is not an unlimited or absolute power. All free choices, including SFWs, are limited by heredity, environment, and conditioning; and SFWs are further limited by not being antecedently determinable. But this does not mean that agents possessing free will do not have voluntary control over their destinies; it only means that when they engage in self-formation, what they choose is not determined by their *already* formed characters and motives.

10. Value Experiments, Responsibility, and Teleological Intelligibility

Objection 6: "Noble sentiments, perhaps, but I am still not convinced. Maybe it is my caveman yearnings for antecedent determining control, but I think we shall have to circle around these issues about control many more times before I become convinced. Let's try to go around once more in a different way. Even if one conceded, for the sake of argument, that the choices could be 'willed' either way and made 'for reasons' either way in the senses you define for the plurality conditions, it still seems that the willing one way rather than the other, or choosing for one set of reasons rather than the other, would be arbitrary, given that the choice is undetermined and issues from an indeterminate effort of will. In short, do you really escape the charges of *arbitrariness* for choices that terminate indeterminate efforts? Isn't the choosing for one of the competing sets of motives rather than another merely arbitrary, even if the agent does want to choose by that set more than by any other *when* he or she chooses?"

I agree that we must keep circling around these issues, and the question of arbitariness is one that must be forthrightly addressed. I grant that free choices are arbitrary in the sense that they are not fully explicable in terms of the past. But that is because their full meaning or significance does not lie in the past. In order to explain this point in an earlier work (1985: 94), I connected the existence of free will to what may be called

> T46 (*on FW*) ("Value Experiments"): Every free choice (which is an SFW) is the initiation of a "value experiment" whose justification lies in the future and is not fully explained by the past. It says, in effect, "Let's try this. It is not required by my past, but it is consistent with my past and is one branching pathway my life could now meaningfully take. I'm willing to take responsibility for it one way or the other. It may make me a (morally) better or worse person, a (prudentially) happier or sadder person, but I will be aware that it was my doing and my own self-making either way—guided by my past, but not determined by it."

Imagine a writer in the middle of a novel. The novel's heroine faces a crisis and the writer has not yet developed her character in sufficient detail to say exactly how she will react to this new situation. The author makes a judgment that she will react one way rather than another and thereby gives greater detail to her character from then on. But the author's judgment was not determined by the heroine's already formed past. For that past was not clear enough in the author's mind to give unique direction. In this sense, the judgment of how she would react in the new situation was "arbitrary," but not entirely so. It had input from the heroine's fictional past and in turn gave input to her projected future.

> T47 (*on FW*) (*Liberum Arbitrium*): It is worth noting in this connection that the term "arbitrary" comes from the Latin *arbitrium*, which *means* "judgment"— as in *liberum arbitrium voluntatis* or "free judgment of the will" (the medieval designation for free will). I have argued elsewhere that there is a kernel of insight in this etymological connection for understanding free will (Kane 1985: 112). For the point of focusing on the author's narrative "judgment" in the ex-

ample of the novel just given is to bring out the fact that free agents are both authors of, and characters in, their own stories all at once. By virtue of their free choices (*arbitria voluntatis*), they are "arbiters" of their own lives—"making themselves" as they go along out of a past that (if they are truly free) does not limit their future pathways to one.

T48 (on FW) ("Teleological Intelligibility" or "Narrative Continuity"): What is required of free choices, then, is not that they be completely explicable in terms of the past, but that they possess a "teleological intelligibility" or "narrative continuity," which is to say the choices can be fit into "meaningful sequences," as Wiggins has put it (1973: 52), or fit into a coherent narrative for which the agents themselves are at least partly responsible and in which they take responsibility for the novel pathways they initiate. It is for this reason that I have called my theory of free will in the past a "TI" or "teleological intelligibility" theory (borrowing this expression from Gary Watson [26]) to contrast it with other libertarian theories such as those that rely on notions of nonoccurrent causation (AC theories) or those claiming that explanations in terms of reasons are not compatible with explanations in terms of causes (explanatory incompatibilism). TI theories do not rely on such assumptions, but they do require that the events comprising the lives of free agents have some sort of teleological or narrative intelligibility over and above merely physical descriptions and causal relations.

other forms of libertarianism [margin note]

The idea of a "narrative conception of the self" and of self-representation has been gaining currency in recent decades among diverse writers in different fields, including psychologist Jerome Bruner (1986), literary critic Frank Kermode (1967), and philosophers as different in orientation as Alasdair MacIntyre (1981) and Daniel Dennett (1988; 1991).[27] None of these thinkers adapts the narrative theme directly to the free-will issue, as I have done, much less to an incompatibilist view. Indeed, Dennett (who has written perceptively on this narrative theme in recent years) is very much opposed to an incompatibilist view, as we have seen. Nonetheless, I believe this theme of a "narrative self" has a role to play in an incompatibilist view of freedom, as spelled out in theses 46 through 48. It is one of many smaller pieces of the larger puzzle of free will.

11. Chance, Folk Psychology, and the Brain

Objection 7: "This is all interesting, but remains far from satisfying. All this talk of 'narrative continuity' and being 'author of one's life' still seems idle if the alleged choices issuing from indeterminate efforts merely 'happen' and are not in the agent's control. And it remains difficult to shake the conviction that the choices would not be in the agent's control if the efforts preceding them really are indeterminate. Consider, for example, what is supposedly going on in the brain, on your free willist account, when moral or prudential conflicts arise. When neuroscientists inspect the brain they will find nothing more than an interconnected set of neuron firings in which micro indeterminacies are not negligible. The process will in turn terminate either in some definite sequence of nerve firings that corresponds to the 'choice' to overcome temptation or in another set of nerve firings corresponding to the 'choice'

This has been my objection since p. 130 [margin note]

to succumb to temptation. But why one of these outcomes occurs rather than another will be inexplicable in terms of the preceding process. Probabilities can be assigned, but that is all."

I agree that if the physical descriptions of these events were the only legitimate ones, then free will would look like nothing more than chance or probability. When neuroscientists described it in physico-chemical terms, all they would get are indeterministic chaotic processes with probabilistic outcomes. In short, when described from a physical perspective alone, *free will looks like chance*. But the physical description is not the only one to be considered. The indeterministic chaotic process is also, experientially considered, the agent's effort of will; and the undetermined outcome of the process, one way or the other, is, experientially considered, the agent's choice. From a free willist point of view, this experiential or phenomenological perspective is also important; it cannot simply be dispensed with.

T49 (*on FW*): On the view presented here, you do not have to be a Cartesian dualist about mind and body to affirm free will, but you cannot be an extreme *eliminative* materialist either.[28] You cannot say that the phenomenological or folk-psychological descriptions of human thought and action (in terms of desires, beliefs, choices, intentions, efforts, and the like) can be lopped off the top of one's worldview, leaving only physico-chemical descriptions of the brain and behavior (at least as physics and chemistry are currently constituted).[29] You cannot say, for example, that the description of efforts as indeterministic chaotic brain processes is the *only* correct description of them, ignoring or dispensing with everyday descriptions of them as *efforts* the agents are making to resolve uncertainties in their minds—and hence something the agents are doing. For then free will *would* be written out of the world picture; but so would many other valued things, such as consciousnes, purpose, and mental action in general, that are needed to account for *free agency* generally, libertarian *or* nonlibertarian. (Recall the requirement of the Free Agency Principle [T16] that we cannot dispense with categories needed to account for free agency in general, whether compatibilist or incompatibilist, libertarian or nonlibertarian.)

I am not going to engage here in the debate over eliminative materialism and the relation of consciousness and folk psychology to the brain. What I want to emphasize is that free will issues are deeply implicated in these debates. Every aspect of common-sense psychology does not obviously have to be retained in the final accounting, but the folk-psychological language of desires and beliefs, as well as consciously experienced processes of reasoning, effort, and choice—or some suitable surrogates for them—cannot be dispensed with in the final accounting if free will is to survive.

T50 (*on FW*): Folk psychological descriptions may be transformed in some future scientific psychology. They may be "reconfigured as time and cognitive neuroscience proceed," in the words of Patricia Churchland (1994: 26). But the reconfigurations cannot be so radical as to eliminate the explanatory roles currently played by desires and beliefs, processes of reasoning, efforts, choices, and distinctions between mental *actions* and mere happenings—all deeply embedded in current folk psychology.[30] If such roles and distinctions go by the boards, *one would not be able to describe free agency at all*—libertarian or nonlibertarian. So, while the Free Agency Principle (T16) does not require mind/body dualism to account for free will, neither does it allow one to describe deliberations, efforts, choices, and other mental goings on *merely* as physico-chemical processes, whether they are undetermined *or* determined.

12. Mind, Body, and Consciousness

Objection 8: "But now the suspicion arises that you are exchanging one mystery for another. In place of the usual libertarian stuff, such as agent-causes, noumenal selves, or mind/body dualism, you are giving us the mysteries of indeterministic efforts of will—described physically as indeterminate processes that are happening in the brain, but phenomenologically as something the agents are doing. On this score, your view is reminiscent of Brian O'Shaughnessy's 'dual aspect' account of the will (1980).[31] For O'Shaughnessy, 'tryings' or 'making efforts' have physical aspects. They may be neural processes that initiate and constitute the first stages of physical movements. But, on the other hand, tryings or efforts are also psychological, according to O'Shaughnessy, because we experience them directly or immediately and are therefore related to them epistemically as we are related to our own sensations (vol. 2: 127). Perhaps dual-aspect theories of this kind are an improvement over substance dualisms, but they are scarcely without their own mysteries. How *can* a physical process of the brain be at the same time a consciously experienced effort of will?"

Well, this is a puzzle, all right, but it is part of the larger riddle of consciousness, which is troubling no matter what position is taken on free will: how can thoughts, sensations, perceptions, or any other conscious events—*including* efforts of will and choices—be at the same time physical processes of the brain? This is a problem whether you are a compatibilist or incompatibilist, or whether you think brain processes are determined or not.

T51 (*on FW*) ("Consciousness"): As I said earlier, the goal of these chapters is not to eliminate all mystery from free will. Rather, it is to eliminate mysteries that are created by taking a *distinctively libertarian view* of free will—as opposed to mysteries that confront everyone, no matter what their position on free will (T17). Indeterministic efforts are mysterious because they partake of several deep cosmological problems that are problems for everyone, not just libertarians. One of these problems is "the mind/body problem," including at its core the "problem of consciousness": how can thoughts, perceptions, and other conscious experiences—including efforts of will—be brain processes? But this is a problem whether you are a compatibilist or incompatibilist, libertarian or nonlibertarian. It is no less mysterious how neural firings in the brain could be conscious mental events if they are *determined* than if they are undetermined, or if they involve undetermined chaotic processes than if they do not.[32]

Suppose future neuroscientists should inform us that the efforts of will we were making to overcome temptation in everyday moral and prudential choice situations actually corresponded to indeterministic chaotic processes in our brains such as I have described. Prior to learning this, let us suppose, we accepted without question the common-sense view that when engaging in everyday struggles over whether to help someone in distress, take an extra drink, or perform a difficult task, we were making efforts to resolve these conflicts and resolved them one way or another by our choices. At the same time, we were unsure what was going on in our brains when all this was occurring and may have had different opinions about that. How should we react to this new information about indeterminacy in our brains provided by the neuroscientists? Should we say, as a result of it, that the efforts we thought we were making to resolve everyday moral and prudential conflicts were not really *our* efforts after all, and the choices we thought we were making to resolve these conflicts not really *our* choices? As indicated earlier, I think such a reaction would be as absurd as saying that our reasoning processes and their outcomes were not our doings if they turned out to involve indeterministic chaotic processes in the brain, as well they might, according to some recent suggestions.[33]

Objection 9: "But there is an ambiguity in your use of the expression '*our* choices' when you argue this way—an ambiguity that is relevant to the dispute about control. Perhaps it would be odd in the above circumstances to deny the choices were 'ours' *in the sense that* we would continue to experience them phenomenologically as our choices despite what the neuroscientists had told us about their being undetermined. And if the phenomenological perspective is to be given its due in reality along with the physical perspective (as O'Shaughnessy and others insist against the eliminativists), then you might have a point. But, even if this is granted, there is another sense of 'our choices,' in which it would be perfectly reasonable to deny that the choices were ours if it turned out they were the results of indeterminate processes in our brains. We might still be making choices (phenomenologically speaking) to resolve moral and prudential conflicts, but we would not have *control* over our making of them; and in that sense they would not be 'ours.' If one distinguishes between *choosing* and having *control over one's choosing*, the above arguments are much less plausible, because the choices would not be ours in the sense we should care about for freedom and responsibility."

This point is well taken. The distinction between doing something and having control over your doing it is important and has to be discussed. Some people think this is no real distinction—that doing something and having control over doing it are the same thing. After all, they might reason, if you *do* it, then you are *able* to do it, and so have the *power* to do it; and having power over something is having control over it. But this reasoning is fallacious, for there are many circumstances in which doing and having control over one's doing diverge. These circumstances are ones in which (i) choices or actions are compulsive (you drink but have no control over your drinking); or (ii) actions are forced or constrained by factors the agents cannot control (missing an appointment because one is locked in a room); or (iii) actions are done by mistake or accidently or inadvertently (when I press the wrong button on the coffee machine); or (iv) the actions are controlled by other agents or mechanisms, such as Frankfurt controllers, drugs, or hypnotic suggestion; or (v) are controlled by CNC controllers, or behind-the-scenes manipulators, from behavioral engineers to devils, spirits, or God.

But note that none of these ordinary and nonordinary ways in which persons may act without having control over their actions *applies to SFWs*, according to earlier theses.

> T52 (*on FW*) ("Control"): Each of the varied ways in which agents may act without having control over their actions—(i) compulsion, (ii) constraint or force, (iii) mistake, accident, or mere chance, (iv) control by other agents or mechanisms, such as Frankfurt controllers, (v) or by CNC controllers or mechanisms of any kinds—is ruled out for SFWs according to T31 through 42. Indeed, with regard to self-forming willings in moral and prudential contexts, theses T31 through T42 successively eliminate each of the conditions for saying that agents *do them*, but do not *control their doing of them*. These conditions are then summed up in the condition of plural voluntary control in such manner that to say agents control their own actions is to say that they *perform* them *with plural voluntary control*.

does this satisfy objections?

13. Two Cosmological Problems

In T51, I said that the view presented here does not attempt to eliminate all mystery from free will, but only such mysteries as are created by taking a distinctively libertarian view of it. And I added that the indeterministic efforts required by free will are mysterious because they partake of several deep cosmological problems that are problems for everyone, not just libertarians. I can now say that I think there are at least two such cosmological problems with which free will is deeply implicated, both of which have been central to philosophical discussions throughout much of this century. The first is the problem of consciousness already mentioned in T51. I now add that

> T53 (*on FW*): "The Second Cosmological Problem" of which free will partakes is the problem of genuine indeterminacy-in-nature, which is pretty mysterious as well. How can wave/particles such as electrons have indeterminate trajectories in which their position and momentum cannot both be exact at the same time? How can physical systems in general have indeterminate properties? We know that great scientists, some of whom were in on the founding of quantum physics, such as Planck, Einstein, and De Broglie, could not accept the inexact trajectories, the indeterminacy, and other related mysteries of the quantum world. They hoped by way of hidden variables or some new theory to get back to the exactness and determinacy of the classical picture. I suggest that we should expect the same resistance and puzzlement over indeterminate efforts of will in free will debates as indeterminate trajectories received from skeptical physicists when they were first introduced. Indeterminate efforts force us to view human actions and life histories in unaccustomed ways, just as indeterminate trajectories and properties force us to view the physical world in strange and novel ways.

Igor Stravinsky was fond of reminding people who did not like his music that when Beethoven's late string quartets were first heard, with their strange harmonies, many even knowledgeable listeners insisted that "this was not music." The Beethoven quartets required some getting use to, and when people got used to them, their ideas about music changed. So it is with indeterminate trajectories in physics; and so it should be, I am suggesting, with indeterminate efforts of will. When I first began to think about indeterminate efforts in the late 1970s, I thought they were too strange to take seriously. But now, fifteen years later, I am as comfortable with them as I am with quantum wave particles and Beethoven's late quartets—which is to say, only moderately comfortable, for I am well aware that they require looking at the world in strange and novel ways. But I think understanding free will requires a similar kind of initial conceptual dissonance. "To solve the problems of philosophers," Wittgenstein said, "one must [learn to] think even more crazily than they do" (a task which has become even more difficult after Wittgenstein than it was before him).[34]

There is a further difficulty, to be sure, about the fact that indeterminate efforts are macro indeterminate processes involving chaotic amplifications. This might suggest something like the following picture. Genuine indeterminism at the micro level is followed by deterministic amplification to get macro indeterminism. The indeterministic efforts are therefore a combination of indeterminism followed by determinism; and the agent lacks ultimate control of both successive stages of the process, the indeterministic part and the deterministic part. It was to forestall this kind of objection that I emphasized in T25 that the indeterministic effort of will corresponds to the entire chaotic process in the brain, including the micro indeterminacies and their amplifications. I call this

T54 (on FW) ("The Fusion Principle"): As long as effort is being made and the will is in tension, the micro indeterminacies are being fed upward to the neural net as a whole, which is continually reorganizing in response to micro indeterminacies and is in turn influencing individual neurons. There is an ongoing mutual feedback from the net to its parts and back, and this continuing process *taken as a whole* is the experienced effort. One does not therefore merely have indeterminism or chance (at the micro level) *followed by* a determinate effort, or a determinate effort *followed by* indeterminism or chance. Rather, the indeterminism and the effort are "fused": the indeterminacy is a property *of* the effort and the effort *is* indeterminate.[35] To fully understand how this fusion could take place would be (as William Hasker [1995] has suggested) to understand the nature of conscious experience and its unity (our first cosmological problem), as well as to understand how consciousness and mind are related, if at all, to the indeterminacy of natural processes (our second cosmological problem). In other words, it is possible that the ultimate understanding of this fusion may lie in the *connection* between the two cosmological problems—between consciousness and quantum reality.[36]

T55 (on FW): So I concede that indeterminate efforts are mysterious. But I want to suggest that their mysteriousness partakes of the difficulties of understanding (i) consciousness and (ii) quantum indeterminacy—two of the central cosmological problems of the age. And these two problems, we should note, are problems for everyone; they are not problems specifically created by libertarian theories of freedom (thus satisfying the Free Agency Principle). Nor should it surprise us that free will (which Kant regarded as *the* central "cosmological" problem) should be intimately related to these two other cosmological enigmas.

9

Efforts, Purposes, and Practical Reason

1. Efforts Sustaining Purposes

In this chapter, the theory is further developed by adding accounts of the other four kinds of undetermined free willings or self-forming willings (SFWs) of T20—namely, efforts of will sustaining purposes, attentional efforts involved in self-control and self-modification, practical choices and judgments, and changes of intention in action. In the next chapter, further objections are addressed and refinements are made to the theory.

When these other kinds of self-forming willings are added, we see that the range of undetermined SFWs in human life is much wider than one might have expected from the theory thus far developed. Keep in mind that SFWs are not the only *actions*, generally speaking (including willings), that can be free—in the sense of being done of one's own free will (T13) and for which the agent can be ultimately responsible (T12), as the Luther example indicated. Many everyday actions may be free and responsible in these senses, even if not undetermined, so long as the will from which they issued was formed by prior SFWs. Still, it is important to realize that undetermined SFWs themselves need not be rare occurrences. Self-formation of the kind required by SFWs is more common than expected in all but the most underdeveloped of life histories.

We turn initially to the third category of SFWs of T20—efforts of will sustaining purposes. The first thing to note in connection with this category is that our efforts of will need not only be directed at forming new intentions or purposes by way of deliberation. Our efforts are also, and even more often, directed at sustaining or carrying out intentions or purposes already formed in the face of obstacles to their realization. In chapter 1, free will was defined as the "power of agents to be the ultimate creators *and sustainers* of their own ends or purposes." We create ends or purposes through choices or decisions (and indirectly through deliberation and practical judgment). We sustain purposes by making efforts to carry them out in the face of impediments and countervailing inclinations. When these impediments are coming from the agent's own will, then efforts sustaining purposes can also be SFWs.

A vivid example of such sustaining efforts was suggested to me by philosopher/musician Teed Rockwell from his own experience. For many years, he says,

> I have been playing a musical instrument called the Chapman Stick, which has something called "ambiguous intonation"—if you don't touch the strings exactly

right it doesn't play in tune. It requires a tremendous effort of will to play it in tune.
... This instrument is evidence against the common assumption that willing is
only needed while learning something new, and that once a physical skill is learned
it then becomes unconscious and effortless. My experience has shown that there
is a certain kind of emotional "tautness" that one must maintain at all times to play
cleanly and expressively. (Perhaps I should say "tension" but this kind of tension is
not always entirely unpleasant. It can be magnificently exhilarating.) If one relaxes
this tautness for even a second, mistakes in tuning and in other things are sure to
follow. When I feel lazy and don't focus awareness as tightly, my tuning goes out.
I therefore take credit for the fact that my intonation is as good as it is and, conversely, feel responsible when, relaxing my will, the intonation becomes sloppy.[1]

This is a clear example of what is meant here by "efforts of will sustaining purposes."
Rockwell's purpose when he sits down to play is to stay in tune. He does not have to
form the purpose at every moment as he plays. It is the content of an already formed
intention that is guiding his activity. But he must make efforts throughout the playing to sustain the purpose against inclinations to become lazy or to allow his mind to
wander.

> T56 (*on* FW) ("Efforts Sustaining Purposes"): Efforts of will required to play an
> instrument in tune or to exercise other skills or perform tasks demanding effort
> in the face of obstacles and difficulties provide further examples of SFWs (com-
> prising category 3 of T20). This category includes efforts involved in activities
> (physical or mental)—in arts, crafts, work, sports, games, spiritual meditation,
> or rational inquiry—requiring effort to counteract inclinations toward laziness
> or loss of focus. It also includes efforts required to carry out tasks or projects for
> which one has an aversion, fear, or dislike (from doing household chores to study-
> ing for an exam or scaling a mountain). It thereby includes heroic and coura-
> geous acts of saints and heroes who must overcome fears and anxieties in order
> to fulfill their purposes, as well as the more mundane efforts by which we (some-
> times) manage to get through difficult tasks. And this category also includes ef-
> forts to carry out moral and prudential intentions already formed, but difficult
> to execute.

The businesswoman of our earlier example may decide to return to the alley and
render assistance. But fear may threaten her resolve as she walks back to the alley,
requiring further effort to fulfill the purpose already formed.

> T57 (*on* FW): Efforts of will sustaining purposes of the kinds described in T56
> may also be conceived as indeterminate. The "tautness" or "tension" described
> by Rockwell may be viewed as the result of conflict in the wills of agents who are
> trying to sustain their purposes, which is like the conflicts described in T22 and
> 23. On the one side are desires to carry out a certain purpose; on the other side,
> fears, aversions, anxieties, inhibitions, and other countervailing inclinations that
> must be overcome to carry out the purpose. In the case of physical skills and
> activities, this conflict may be between desires to train the body to do something
> which is at first unnatural or difficult and desires to move or act in ways that are
> more natural or less difficult. In other cases, different conflicting motives may
> be involved. But, whatever the sources of conflict, one could imagine the result-

ing tension to be reflected in the brain by movement further from thermodynamic equilibrium (such as is described for moral and prudential conflict in
T25 and 26) with consequent indeterminacy in the effort to carry out the purpose in the face of conflicting fears or aversions.[2]

T58 (*on FW*): Drawing a further parallel with moral and prudential conflict
(from T29), one may say that, in at least some of these cases, if the agents succeed in sustaining their purposes, they would have made the purposes prevail
by their efforts; and if they fail, it would be because they willingly allowed their
conflicting aversions or desires to prevail. In such instances, the agents would
have willed the outcomes either way and may have willingly done otherwise,
whichever way they go.

Not all efforts sustaining purposes necessarily fulfill these conditions. Some may
be compulsive or otherwise unfree. The conflicting desires may *not* be resistible due
to compulsion or other causes. Or it may be that the agents do not will themselves to
fail, but fail because of obstacles or impediments that are unwilled or beyond the
control of their wills. Rockwell may fail to play in tune because he cannot move his
fingers in the way his instrument requires or because his desires to move the fingers
in a more natural way are irresistible. But, then, in such cases his failings would not
be free in the sense required by SFWs; and these cases would not be of the kind
envisaged in T57 or in his example, in which he willed his sloppy play and feels responsible for it because he could have willfully done otherwise.
    Some people may contend that cases of willed failure of this kind are not pos-
sible in principle. But such an assumption simply begs the question. It is akin to the
assumption that genuine weakness of will (in contrast to compulsion) is never possible in moral and prudential choice situations. It is one thing to say that immoral or
imprudent actions are often compulsive, quite another to say that agents can never
freely and voluntarily act against their better judgment. Similarly, it is one thing to
say that failure to sustain or carry out purposes may often be compulsive, quite another to say this must be so in all cases. Rockwell may be wrong in thinking his case
is as T57 describes. But the point is that he may also be right. I see nothing incoherent in the idea that agents can sometimes willfully *allow* their fears, aversions, or
countervailing desires to triumph over their efforts when they could have willingly
done otherwise. T57 explains how this might be so in cases of efforts sustaining purposes, just as T30 explained how it might be so for weakness of will in moral and
prudential situations. Recall that the task of this part of the book was to say what
incompatibilist free will would be like, if we had it; and T57 attempts to do this for
efforts sustaining purposes, just as earlier theses attempted to do it for moral and
prudential choice.
    Finally, we may add that

T59 (*on FW*) ("Plurality Conditions"): If efforts sustaining purposes fulfilling
the conditions of T56 through 58 were to occur, they would satisfy the plurality
conditions. The agents would have reasons for which they acted either way and
would make one or another of these reasons prevail at any moment by willing to
succeed or fail at that moment. Their doing so would not be coerced or compulsive or controlled by other agents or mechanisms, since going either way

would not be determined (owing to the indeterminacy of the effort to sustain the purposes); and so they would be able to go either way "at will" during the period when the effort was being made

2. Failures, Points of View, and Omissions

We must add, however, that there are some noteworthy differences in the way that the plurality conditions would be fulfilled for efforts sustaining purposes by comparison with moral and prudential choices. Most notably, when persons are attempting to sustain purposes already formed they are not also intending to fail. Rockwell intends to play in tune; he does not intend to fail. Yet the claim being made is that he may nonetheless fail willingly or voluntarily. How can this be? The answer is that what persons *intend* to do at given times may not always be what they *most want* to do at those times (cf. Mele, 1992: 124), and willing to do something at a time (according to definition W of chapter 2) is wanting to do it at the time more than you want to do otherwise.

> T60 (*on FW*): To understand how free will can be exercised in sustaining purposes as well as in creating them, we must understand that the wills of agents at given times may not be in conformity with one or another of their *purposes* or intentions at those times, just as we saw earlier that the wills of agents may not always be in conformity with their *better judgments*. In cases of moral and prudential failure or weakness, what agents will (or most want) to do then and there goes against, or is contrary to, their better (moral or prudential) judgments. Analogously, in cases of failure to sustain purposes, what the agents will (or most want) to do then and there goes against, or is contrary to, one or another of the agents' avowed purposes or intentions. In both cases, there is a tendency to think that failure or weakness must be compulsive or determined, since otherwise weak-willed action seems inexplicably perverse and even irrational. Yet I think that a full account of free will requires the recognition that failures or weakness of both these kinds can occur and need not always be compulsive or determined.

> T61 (*on FW*): To be sure, weakness in the presence of avowed purpose or better judgment *is* motivationally perverse and irrational from one point of view. But the possibility of such "motivational perversity" — of having powerful motives to act against better judgments or to fail in sustaining purposes already formed — is, I think, the price to be paid for free will. Weakness of this kind is also irrational *in a sense*. From one perspective, it is irrational to act against avowed purpose or better judgment; and yet, from another perspective, the agents may have good reasons for doing what they do (so that plural rationality is fulfilled in the sense of T33). When self-deception and rationalization are involved — as they often are in these cases of what David Pears (1985) calls "motivated irrationality" — the behavior is only irrational from one point of view. From another point of view, the agents have powerful reasons to deceive themselves or rationalize, and do it willfully. In sum, those who have free will are no longer motivationally simple creatures, but are capable of either nobility or perversity. They live somewhere east of Eden, having gained dignity, but lost innocence.

To understand this resulting motivational complexity for cases of efforts sustaining purposes, we have to remind ourselves that

> T62 (*on FW*) ("Internal Points of View"): In all cases of SFWs (including efforts sustaining purposes), agents are experiencing inner conflicts between competing *internal motivational points of view* (T28); and they resolve these conflicts by making one of the points of view prevail—making it the one they most want to act upon then and there (T29). What is different about efforts sustaining purposes is that one of the internal motivational points of view supports a purpose that the agent is trying to sustain. Yet, because of the inner conflict, *that* internal point of view is not the only one capable of expressing what the agent *wills* during the time when the effort is being made (just as in moral and prudential conflict, the internal point of view expressing moral or prudential judgment is not the only one capable of expressing the agent's will then and there). In the language of T40, the internal point of view supporting the purpose is not the only "feasible motivational option" of the self-network during this time. Agents may have purposes that, from other points of view embedded in their self-networks, they are reluctant to fulfill.

A second point worth noting about the way efforts sustaining purposes satisfy the plurality conditions is this. Failure to sustain or carry out a purpose need not always be an alternative *action*; it may simply be an *omission* or failure to act. John intends to call Jane this evening to apologize for his rudeness during the day. But he is embarrassed and generally has difficulty making apologies, so he fails to call her. His failure to sustain the intention to apologize is an omission, not an action; yet it may well be a *voluntary* omission satisfying the other plurality conditions (done at will, not under compulsion, and so forth); and he may justly feel guilty and responsible for his failure.

Voluntary omissions of such kinds may also be involved in moral and prudential choice situations, a complication not discussed in chapter 8. Failing to choose morally or prudentially may mean making an alternative choice, as in the examples of chapter 8 (to go on to a business meeting or have a drink of bourbon). But it may also mean simply not choosing or postponing choice. We imagined the businesswoman hesitating at the corner, deciding to help the assault victim or to go on to her meeting. But we could imagine her hesitating at the corner, unable to decide one way or the other, until the assault had taken place or other persons had intervened. In this case, doing "otherwise" (than choosing morally) for that time period would be an omission or failure to choose rather than a choosing otherwise. Yet it might also be a willed failure satisfying the conditions of T59, so that the woman could have chosen to help in time, but did not; and she would consequently be blameworthy for this failing (though no doubt less blameworthy than if she callously chose to go on to her meeting.)

> T63 (*on FW*) ("Omissions"): The account of self-forming willings, or SFWs, of chapter 8 must be expanded to include voluntary omissions satisfying the plurality conditions as well as voluntary actions. In particular, failures to sustain or carry out purposes that are difficult for the agent to sustain or carry out may be

omissions or postponements of action rather than alternative actions. These include cases in which the actions in question are choices (including moral and prudential choices) that are difficult for agents to make. Such cases of failure *to choose* or postponement of choice are "mixed cases" of failure to *sustain* a purpose and failure to *create* a new purpose, since the purpose one fails to sustain (i.e., settling indecision) is the purpose to create some new purpose or other.

As a final example of the motivational complexity that may be involved in failing to sustain purposes, we may cite St. Ignatius of Loyola, whose view it was that people come in three varieties. The best know what they should do and do it; the worst know what they should do and do the opposite. But a third class of human beings, he noted, often do not do either what they should or what they should not, but rather some third thing. Thus, John's wife insists that he mow their overgrown lawn before he watches the football game on TV. He fully intends to comply, but when the time comes he cannot bring himself to do the loathsome task. Yet he also feels guilty about watching the football game. So he fritters away the afternoon doing some third thing such as reading the newspaper or doing a crossword puzzle. He fails to carry out the intention to mow the lawn by doing something else that is not even what he would have most wanted to do, other things being equal (and he may well be doing this of his own free will in the sense of T56 through 59). Ah, humanity!

3. Acts of Attention

Self-forming willings of the fourth kind were described in T20 as "efforts to focus attention for purposes of self-control and self-modification."[3] It turns out that these are also "sustaining" efforts, like those in the third category. But efforts to attend are special kinds of sustaining efforts deserving separate treatment because of the roles they play in self-formation, and hence in the exercise of free will generally. Here is an example. A man who is trying to stop smoking finds that his resolve is strengthened whenever he focuses attention on the image of his father dying of lung cancer. It takes an effort, however, for the man to focus upon that painful scene; and only a strong desire to control and modify his behavior could lead him to do it.

> T64 (*on* FW) ("Attentional Efforts or Acts of Attention in Self-control and Self-modification"): In exercises of self-control and self-modification, we often find it helpful, and sometimes necessary, to focus attention on some image or memory in order to strengthen our resolve. Without such assistance we could not resist intemperate desires or bring ourselves to modify our behavior. But the focusing of attention may itself be difficult and require effort, not only because it may be difficult to concentrate, or the object of attention may be unpleasant (as in the example of the smoker just given), but also, and more generally, because there may be resistance in the will toward doing anything to temper or control what the agent otherwise strongly wants to do (i.e., to act incontinently or *not* to modify his or her behavior). Acts of attending for such purposes would be examples of agents exercising their wills in self-formation. During periods when the agents are making such efforts to attend against resistance within their wills, the efforts could be conceived as indeterminate efforts along the lines of T57 and 58; and

success or failure in focusing attention for purposes of self-control or self-modification would represent yet another class of SFWs. When the effort to attend
and the resistance to it are both coming from the agent's will, the plurality conditions would be satisfied in the same manner as for other sustaining efforts
described in T59.

Frequently, what we attend to in our minds is a key to how we act and how we
form our characters or motives (by sustaining or creating purposes). And our mental
efforts of will are often directed toward attending to this or that image or memory.
William James was so impressed by this aspect of willing that he made "acts of attention" the primary acts of will by which agents exercised their freedom (1907: 447–8).
I would say that James was on to something in this connection—insofar as efforts
directed at attending are an important category of self-forming willings (as is amply
shown by recent psychological and philosophical literature on self-control and self-
modification.[4]) But I also think it would be a mistake to limit all undetermined acts
of will to acts of attention. Such a view is as unsatisfactory as other incompatibilist
views that limit acts of free will to moral and prudential choices. An adequate free
willist view should accommodate a variety of undetermined acts of the will, including moral and prudential choices and acts of attention, but not be limited to them.

4. Practical Choice

We now turn to the fifth category of self-forming willings—practical choice and judgment. This category introduces several entirely new themes that are critical for understanding free will in general. Recall how practical choices differ from moral and
prudential ones. In moral and prudential choice situations, there are conflicts between what agents believe they ought to do (morally or prudentially) and what they
are inclined to do for self-interested reasons or near-term satisfaction. By contrast,
merely practical choices do not involve such conflicts between perceived obligations
and inclinations. Agents in practical choice situations are not trying to do what they
think they ought to do for prudential or moral reasons. Rather, they are trying to decide
what is best from among a number of options, none of which is prudentially or morally
obligated or forbidden—as in the example of Jane's trying to decide where to vacation.

Practical choices can become moral or prudential in different circumstances.
Suppose Jane has just received a law degree and is trying to decide between offers to
join a small law firm in Austin or a large firm in Dallas. This choice is practical, if
neither option is morally or prudentially obligated or forbidden. But if she suspects
one of the firms of unethical practices, yet is strongly attracted by its power and prestige, the choice becomes a moral one for her. Or, if she becomes convinced through
discussions with a mentor that starting in a small law firm is the best long-term move
for her, yet is strongly attracted by the instant prestige of the larger firm, the choice is
prudential. By contrast, when neither option is yet perceived as the one she ought to
choose for moral or prudential reasons (as we shall suppose in the cases of Jane's
choices of vacation and law firm), the choices are practical.

Though practical choices are different from moral and prudential ones, they can
also be important "self-forming willings" in the life histories of agents. Which law
firm Jane chooses can make a major difference in her life and in the kind of person

she will become. Not all practical choices are that important. They vary in significance, from momentous decisions about careers or marriage to less momentous ones
about where to vacation or whom to visit. Yet practical choices of all varieties influence what we become in large and small ways. They set us upon different branching
pathways that lead to alternative experiences and life histories.

It should be obvious that the free willist account of moral and prudential choice
given in the previous chapter cannot be transferred without change to practical choice.
Since in practical choice situations agents are not making efforts to do what they think
they ought to do against prevailing inclinations, such efforts cannot play the same
role in practical choice as they do in moral and prudential choice — or, for that matter, in the efforts sustaining purposes just discussed. As a consequence, indeterminism cannot enter into practical choice in the same way it enters into other categories
of SFWs. Self-forming practical choices turn out to have a somewhat different structure than other categories of SFWs. Yet it is a structure in which indeterminism can
also play a creative role in self-formation. Moreover, I think this different structure
of practical choice is important for understanding the nature of free will generally. It
provokes interesting questions not previously considered about the relation of free
will to creativity, evolution, and other topics.

5. Practical Deliberation and Creative Problem-solving

When we described Jane's attempts to decide where to vacation, we imagined her
narrowing the options to viable ones (Hawaii, Colorado, or Europe), considering the
consequences of each option, constructing scenarios in her mind about them (e.g.,
scenes of swimming versus skiing), factoring in her other goals or intentions (to visit
a friend in Colorado), considering her resources (cost and time), and weighing all
these considerations against her desires, beliefs, likes, dislikes, interests, and other
psychological attitudes.

Viewed in this way, ordinary practical reasoning or deliberation is not a simple
process of deductive reasoning, though it may involve deductive reasoning. It is more
like the trial-and-error processes of "thought experimentation" that are characteristic of scientific discovery and creative problem-solving. The reasoner must consider
various presuppositions and consequences of proposed lines of action, which usually involves the use of imagination to construct probable scenarios exemplifying those
presuppositions and consequences. Of vital importance is what gets considered in
such a process and what does not get considered; what associations are made between
thoughts, images, and memories; what comes to mind; and which of the reasoner's
desires, beliefs, likes, fears, hopes, and other motives are brought to bear on the deliberation. As with instances of creative problem-solving, there are no fixed rules about
what to consider, when one has considered enough consequences, and so on.

There are many ways that undetermined occurrences could play a role in such
a deliberative process and influence what is or is not considered without undermining the rationality of the process. In fact, random search procedures for new relevant
considerations may enhance the deliberative process, as researchers in artificial intelligence have found in designing intelligent machines capable of creative problem-
solving.[5] It is true that randomizing processes programmed into problem-solving

machines are not usually generated by indeterministic processes. But there is no reason they could not be so generated without altering the role the randomizing processes play in trial-and-error learning and creative problem-solving. In human beings, as opposed to machines, one can imagine that nature provides the randomization necessary for creative problem-solving and practical deliberation by way of indeterministic processes in the brain (perhaps chaotically amplified) that introduce new considerations into reasoning. In the case of machines, those natural processes would be simulated by randomizing algorithms introduced into machine programs.

inspiration and creative thinking

T65 (*on FW*): "Practical Deliberation and Creative Problem-solving" have much in common, since both are trial-and-error processes involving thought experimentation about possible outcomes and their consequences. The similarities suggest that if indeterminism plays a positive role in practical deliberation, the role would be like that of inspiration for the creative thinker. Undetermined occurrences would influence the stream of consciousness of the reflecting agent, suggesting new options, new consequences of the options, and new ways of viewing the consequences. Inspiration in creative problem-solving is not totally within the control of the reflecting agent. Yet its effects do not undermine the rationality or responsibility of the process, since the agent must interpret the effects of inspiration and accept or reject them as guides to further reasoning. Undetermined influences in the stream of consciousness of reflective agents could play a similar role in practical deliberation.

We would not begrudge Newton his accomplishment if we learned that a chance collocation of images and thoughts in his mind led to the insight about gravitation when he saw an apple fall from a tree. We would be forgetting the struggles that preceded the insight and those that would follow as he worked with it. We are all inspired, Ned Rorem said of himself and his fellow musicians, but we are not all great. Similarly, practical reasoners may not be in control of what chance-selected considerations come to mind, but they are not helpless with regard to the influence these chance-selected considerations exert on their reasonings.[6]

the un-conscious

One can assume that, in practical deliberation as well as in creative problem-solving, some of the chance-selected considerations may well up from the unconscious mind. Great scientists such as Kekulé and Poincaré have indicated as much in their descriptions of their creative processes. It is true that Freud and other theorists of the unconscious have often taken a determinist or compatibilist line on free will. But, in reality, when it comes to free will, theories of the unconscious are a two-edged sword. The unconscious may be source of compelling desires and fears. But it may also be the source of novel insights resulting from chance associations of thoughts and images. It is odd, as I remarked in an earlier work, that in theories of scientific and artistic creation, the unconscious is given the role of multiplying and expanding the inventive activities of human beings, while in theories of freedom of choice the unconscious is usually viewed as limiting our options by way of compulsions or obsessions, determining them to one only.[7] The alternative role of multiplying and expanding the agent's creative capacities is, I think, the role free willists must focus on in accounts of practical reasoning.

6. Evolution and Learning

T65 suggests further features of the libertarian account of practical choice we are seeking, which may be brought out by another analogy:

> T66 (*on FW*) ("Practical Deliberation and Natural Evolution"): Natural evolution, conceived in Darwinian terms, is a trial-and-error process in which the results of chance mutations in the genetic makeup of individuals are tested and selected through interaction with the natural environment. In practical deliberation, as described in T65, the role of chance-selected considerations entering the deliberative process would correspond to the role of chance mutations in natural evolution, while the role of reasoning would correspond to that of the selecting environment. Undetermined occurrences would influence the stream of consciousness of the reflecting agent suggesting new options and considerations bearing on the options; and the relevance of these considerations would then be tested by way of further thought experimentation about their consequences.

Viewed in the manner of T66, practical human freedom would be conceived as an extension of the evolutionary process allowing analogues of genetic mutations to occur in the mind and then be subject to selection within the mental environments of deliberating agents.

> T67 (*on FW*) ("Practical Reasoning and Value Experiments"): The result would be a qualitative change in the evolutionary process, by which ways of living and acting within a single species are indefinitely multiplied, and the importance of individuals of a species in the selection process (each with his or her own *internal* rational environment) would be immeasurably enhanced. Ways of living and acting could be tested and rejected internally without requiring actual experimentation and possible harm or death to the individual. This may be viewed as an extension of the idea of a "value experiment" of T46, in which it was said that every self-forming willing is the initiation of a value experiment, or an experiment in living, whose justification lies in the future and is not fully explained by the past. The present thesis adds that such value experimentation can take place "in the mind" through practical reasoning before being tried in reality, thus allowing a qualitative change in the processes of evolution by which ways of living and acting are tested and selected.

This evolutionary theme has been emphasized by a number of thinkers in recent decades, and I think it is an important piece of the overall puzzle of free will. One such thinker is Karl Popper, as evidenced in his provocative A. H. Compton lecture "Of Clouds and Clocks" (1972). The problem for indeterminists, according to Popper, is to explain "how freedom is not just chance, but rather the result of a subtle interplay between *something almost random or haphazard* and *something like a restrictive or selective control*" (p. 237). But this, according to Popper, is the problem of evolution and life itself. Random or chance mutations are trial balloons subjected to the selective control of the environment. And "each organism is all the time engaged in problem solving by trial and error . . . it reacts to new and old problems by more or less chance-like . . . trials which are eliminated if unsuccessful" (p. 245). Human problem-solving and deliberation are extensions of this process, with human reasoning added. "Deliberation always works by *trial and error*, or more precisely *by trial and error elimination*, by tentatively proposing various possibilities and eliminating those that do not seem adequate" (p. 234).

Similar conclusions are arrived at by psychologists Donald Campbell (1960) and Dean Simonton (1988), who have developed psychological theories of creative thinking that parallel Popper's ideas. Analogous themes are also evident in the writings of neuroscientists such as Gerald Edelman (1987) and William Calvin (1990), with reference to the emerging paradigm of "neural Darwinism," and in the writings of philosophers such as Daniel Dennett (1978), Robert Nozick (1981), and Alfred Mele (1995). Dennett approvingly quotes the poet Paul Valery's assertion that the essence of invention is intelligent selection from among chance-generated candidates, and he goes on to suggest a model of decision-making based on this idea (p. 294). Imagine, says Dennett, that "when faced with an important decision, a consideration generator whose output is to some degree undetermined produces a series of considerations, some of which may of course be immediately rejected as irrelevant by the agent (consciously or unconsciously). Those considerations that are selected by the agent as having a more than negligible bearing on the decision then figure in the reasoning process" (p. 295). Dennett suggests that such a model might serve the needs of libertarians, though he is skeptical about whether it would give them everything they want (and he is also skeptical, as we have seen earlier, about whether what they want is "worth wanting").

Independently of Dennett and the other thinkers mentioned, I had come to the conclusion that the idea of intelligent selection from among chance-generated considerations must be a *part* of any adequate libertarian account of free *practical* choice, and I made this idea a feature of my account of practical choice in an earlier work (1985). But I was also convinced that selection from among chance-generated considerations could not be the whole story of incompatibilist free will. For one thing, it could not provide an account of moral or prudential choice (as Dennett himself had pointed out). If responsibility is to be captured, then choosing morally or prudentially rather than from weakness of will could not merely be a matter of chance-generated alternatives. Moreover, regarding practical choice itself, there are good reasons for thinking that chance-generated considerations are not the whole story, as we shall see in a moment. Nonetheless, I believe the idea of intelligent selection from chance-generated considerations is part of the story of free practical choice, and hence a piece of the larger puzzle of free will. By adding other pieces to it, we may be able to construct an adequate incompatibilist account of practical choice to go along with earlier accounts of moral and prudential choice and other self-forming willings.

7. Endorsement of Reasons or Motives

Suppose when Jane is deliberating about where to vacation she remembers an evening walk along the beach on her last visit to Hawaii, and the memory reminds her of how much she likes to walk by the ocean in such reflective moments. Or she pictures herself dining in a favorite Hawaiian restaurant, thus reminding herself of how much she likes the variety of Polynesian and Asian foods on the islands. Reflecting similarly about Colorado, she conjures up images of ski slopes and sitting by a fireside on snowy evenings, or past happy or sad occasions with a friend whom she would visit if she goes to Colorado. In such ways, remembered experiences and imagined scenarios enter into her deliberations and are assessed in the light of her wants, preferences, and other psychological attitudes in order to determine which option is most preferred, all things considered.

Following the suggestions of T65 through 67, we now suppose that some of the thoughts, memories, images, and associations that enter into such a deliberative process are chance-selected. The agent is searching for relevant considerations that may weigh for or against one or another option and is open to new thoughts, memories, and associations that may come to consciousness and have a bearing on the deliberation. Many of the resulting chance-selected considerations are passed over as irrelevant, but some—like memories of evening walks by the beach or images of sitting by a fireside—are seen to be relevant to the deliberation and are included in it. The relevant considerations are separated from the irrelevant by cognitive and volitional background attitudes that the agent already has—beliefs, desires, likes, dislikes, and so forth. What is interesting is that just as background beliefs, desires, and other reasons pick out chance-selected considerations as relevant, so do the chance-selected considerations pick out cognitive and volitional background reasons as relevant to the deliberation. Jane's sudden recollection of dining at a favorite Polynesian restaurant in Hawaii reminds her of how much she *likes* that restaurant's menu, for which there is no equivalent in Colorado. This particular liking had not previously entered her deliberation, but henceforth it plays a role, giving further weight (though not necessarily conclusive weight) to the choice of Hawaii.

We may speak in such instances of the *endorsement* of reasons or motives for choice, meaning by this the acknowledgment on the part of the agent that certain reasons or motives (e.g., Jane's liking for this restaurant) are relevant to deliberation in ways not previously recognized. Agents do not necessarily first come to *have* the reasons or motives at the moment they are endorsed. Jane liked this restaurant all along, but had not thought about it until the recollection occurred. Likings, wants, desires, and preferences are not the sorts of things we usually get or lose suddenly (though this may sometimes happen). But these and other psychological attitudes that agents already have may be given new relevance by chance-selected considerations and thereby play new roles in deliberation.[8]

T68 (*on* FW) ("Endorsement of Reasons or Motives"): If undetermined occurrences play a role in deliberation leading to practical choice, they do so by initiating processes of thinking about, or imagining, remembering, or attending to various facts, memories, images, and scenarios that may be relevant to deliberation. We refer generally to the items thus thought about, remembered, or attended to as "chance-selected considerations." Some of them are passed over as irrelevant to deliberation, but others are acknowledged by the agent as relevant. This acknowedgment of relevance amounts to the adoption into the preference set for one or another option of reasons not previously regarded as relevant to the deliberation, or not previously seen as relevant in this way. In either case, we speak of the "endorsement of reasons or motives" for choice.

Note that

> T69 (*on* FW): Such endorsements of reasons or motives can be plural rational
> in a certain sense, even when they are chance-initiated. Some of the new con-
> siderations that come to mind are rejected by Jane as irrelevant; others (such as
> imagined walks on the beach or remembered restaurants) are acknowledged as
> relevant. But, in either case, her response is rational. For if she judges that a con-
> sideration is irrelevant because she lacks reasons that would make it so, or judges
> it relevant because she has reasons that make it relevant, her response is rational
> either way—as is her endorsing or not endorsing the corresponding reasons. In
> this way, indeterminism may play a creative role in the process of practical de-
> liberation without undermining the rationality of the process.

Objection 10: "But, while responses to chance-selected considerations may be
rational in these ways, they fall short of fully satisfying the plurality conditions. For
the deliberating agents are only *reacting* to the chance-selected considerations when
the latter come up. Though the reactions may be rational, the agents do not have a
choice about which option (endorsement or not) is rational, given the chance-
selected consideration and the agents' already existing motives. If a chance-selected
consideration is not relevant to the deliberation, it is rational to reject it but irrational
to acknowledge it as relevant; and if it is relevant, it is rational to endorse it, but irrational to reject it. This falls short of the plural rationality described for moral and
prudential choices in which the agents make one or another outcome the rational
one *by* choosing it. The agents cannot do that in the present case. They are constrained
to act as the chance-selected considerations and their reasons stipulate, if they want
to act rationally."

This objection is well taken. It was on grounds of this kind that I originally came
to believe that chance-selected considerations in practical deliberation could not be
the whole story of incompatibilist free will—*even for practical choice*. The problem
is that chance-selected considerations occur and the agents simply react to them in
a manner constrained by their reasons. Such a process can indeed enhance deliberation and creative problem-solving by introducing novelty. But it gives limited
voluntary control and responsibility to the agents, who lack the freedom to respond
either way rationally once the undetermined events have occurred. It was my view
that, for a fuller picture of free practical choice, further ideas would have to be added
to give agents a more significant role in the process.[9]

8. Taoist Efforts

These additional ideas (which first appeared in Kane, 1985, and are further developed here) involve giving agents a more active role in practical deliberation by way
of efforts of will through which the agents might exercise greater control over the
deliberative process—*without* eliminating the creative role of chance-selected considerations. These efforts of will would be of varying kinds, but they would eventually be interpreted as indeterminate efforts, along the lines suggested for other SFWs.

The first of the efforts involved in practical deliberation I call a "Taoist effort."
The meaning of this unusual designation will become clear as they are described.

[handwritten margin note: It seems to me that we control what comes to mind to some extent by controlling what kinds of thoughts we are open to.]

By definition, reflecting agents cannot control exactly which "chance-selected" considerations are going to come to mind at any moment. But they can willfully put themselves in a frame of mind that is *receptive* to new chance-selected considerations. There are times, both in creative problem-solving and practical deliberation, when it helps to relax the mind—freely associating, letting things flow, opening oneself to new thoughts that may well up from the unconscious. It often takes an *effort* to open one's mind in this way, because there is a natural tendency to stick with familiar modes of thought. Yet such an effort may be just what is demanded to solve a problem or successfully conclude a deliberation.

But notice that this effort to relax the mind and freely associate is a curious one. It is a kind of effort-not-to-make-an-effort, an effort to relax the control of existing modes of thought in order to let new considerations come to mind in a manner that one does *not* control. This is the point of the designation "Taoist effort." A central theme of some Eastern philosophies, especially Taoism (and strands of Buddhism influenced by Taoism, such as Zen Buddhism), is that only when the conscious mind relaxes and does not try to have complete control over its thinking does the agent become truly creative and truly free.[10] Related to this theme is the Taoist ideal of *wu wei* (meaning literally "actionless activity" or "creative inactivity"), which is very much like what goes on when we break off from normal modes of thought and association and put our minds in a relaxed, meditative state that allows for free association and novel thoughts.[11] One does not have to accept every aspect of this Eastern philosophy to see that creativity and freedom can sometimes be enhanced in this way.

> T70 (*on* FW) ("Taoist Efforts"): Practical deliberators, like creative problem solvers, do not have to wait for chance-selected considerations to occur in a manner that is completely uncontrolled and unbidden. When engaging in reflection about what to do, they can make efforts to relax their minds, freely associating and opening themselves to new thoughts and images that may well up from the unconscious. I call efforts of these kinds "Taoist efforts" because they are efforts to temporarily relinquish conscious control over thought processes in order to be receptive to new considerations that may come to mind—that is, efforts-not-to-make-an-effort to control one's thoughts. Doors are thereby opened in deliberation that can free the mind from present commitments and ways of thinking.

[handwritten margin note: Why libertarians should buy into some Eastern philosophy]

In Western thought, reason usually appears as the controlling element of the soul, according to Plato's image, the source of freedom and creativity. Eastern philosophies tell a more ambiguous story about reason. They emphasize its limitations and argue that true freedom and creativity can only be obtained at the price of sometimes relinquishing total rational control by the conscious mind. As I see it, incompatibilist theories of freedom must buy into some of this Eastern wisdom without entirely giving up the controlling function of reason. Where reason relaxes control (to allow for chance-selected considerations) there is room for indeterminism in the process of practical reasoning. This indeterminism makes possible "new beginnings" in practical deliberation that cannot be determined by reason, but can be used by it.

T71 (*on FW*): We now suppose that the Taoist efforts of T70 are indeterministic efforts like those described in earlier theses. In particular, they are further examples of "efforts sustaining purposes," since the agents are making them in order to further their deliberative goals. Insofar as these efforts involve resisting natural tendencies to go along with present commitments and familiar modes of thought, they are made against resistance (like other efforts sustaining purposes), and we can imagine that they are similarly reflected in the brain by movement further from thermodynamic equilibrium, thereby making the agents' deliberative processes sensitive to undetermined influences. Success or failure of the efforts would then be undetermined, but would be willed either way, so that the plurality conditions could be satisfied as in T59 for other efforts sustaining purposes. These Taoist efforts, however, would be playing a unique role of "opening windows" in conscious deliberation through which new thoughts, images, and memories might enter into the agent's reasoning processes.

[margin handwritten note:] Don't we have selective control over which "windows" we open?

T72 (*on FW*) ("The Juror Analogy"): The aim of thus opening one's mind to new considerations is to make the best choice possible by taking into account as many relevant considerations as one can and thereby giving each of the options a fair hearing in deliberation. Jane does not want to overlook anything that might make her Hawaiian vacation an unexpected disaster or some as-yet-unconsidered factor that might weigh heavily in favor of Colorado or Europe. In this regard, the deliberator's situation might be likened to that of a jury member listening to the testimony at a trial. At any time during the trial, the juror may be leaning toward one verdict over the other. But in the interest of not deciding too hastily and giving all options a fair hearing, the juror may make an effort to remain open to new evidence that might sway her or him to the other side. Similarly, in the course of Jane's deliberation, she may at one time or another be leaning toward going to Hawaii. But in the interest of making the best "all-things-considered" decision, she makes an effort to keep her mind open to further considerations that might sway her toward Colorado or other options. This is the role of the Taoist effort.

T73 (*on FW*) ("Openness" and "Fairness"): In this way, the indeterminacy introduced into the deliberative process serves the interest of "openness" of mind to relevant evidence, and "fairness" to competing options in the reception of evidence. Both these features, openness and fairness, in turn serve the needs of practical freedom by allowing for maximally informed practical decisions. Of course, not all agents make such efforts or succeed when they make them. They may decide hastily or on the basis of too little or biased evidence—and may as a consequence choose poorly, unless they are lucky. The point is not that Taoist efforts must be made or always are made in practical deliberation. Rather, they can be made and their purpose (which may not always be realized) is to make the "right" (best-informed) practical decisions, just as the efforts to overcome temptation in moral and prudential situations (which also may fail) are directed at making the "right" moral and prudential decisions.

T73 has interesting implications for free will generally. Note that if Jane treats her options in the manner of T73 prior to choosing among them, she treats them as what might be called "incommensurable alternatives." Hawaii and Colorado (as vacation spots) are such alternatives for Jane if the following conditions are satisfied: that she favors each of them over all other options (e.g., Europe), but for different and (from her point of view) noncomparable reasons; and that she does not *yet* have an all-things-considered preference for either one of them over the other.[12] When such conditions obtain, the alternatives are incommensurable and the different reasons inclining toward them constitute "incommensurable reason sets." This suggests the following thesis, which I defended in an earlier work and believe to be central for understanding free will generally.[13]

> T74 (*on* FW) ("The Incommensurability Thesis"): <u>Exercises of free will by way</u> <u>of SFWs typically involve incommensurable alternatives and incommensurable</u> <u>reason sets (as defined in the preceding paragraph) in one manner or another.</u> In moral cases, the incommensurable reason sets are motives of duty versus self-interest; in prudential cases, desires for long-term goals versus present satisfactions; in cases of efforts sustaining purposes, desires to perform tasks or fulfill goals versus fears, inhibitions, aversions, and other countervailing inclinations. We now add that, in practical deliberation also, agents are torn between competing and not easily comparable reasons for choosing between alternatives, as Jane is torn between reasons for vacationing in Hawaii or Colorado. The sets of reasons favoring each of the alternatives in various SFWs, the "incommensurable reason sets," comprise different and competing visions of what the agent wants to do or become.

9. Practical Judgment and Further Efforts in Practical Deliberation

I have been arguing that an incompatibilist account of practical reason should be expanded by adding various efforts of will through which agents may influence practical deliberation and through which indeterminacy might also enter the process. Taoist efforts are an example of such efforts, but they represent only one example.

> T75 (*on* FW): In addition to Taoist efforts to open one's mind to new considerations, practical deliberation may be influenced by other indeterministic efforts at various stages, including (1) efforts <u>not to quit deliberating too soon</u> or not to choose too hastily, (2) efforts <u>to focus attention</u> on considerations that have come to mind in order to <u>determine all their consequences</u>, (3) to avoid <u>suppressing</u> <u>relevant considerations</u> that one may be resistant to considering, (4) <u>to galva-</u> <u>nize oneself to pursue relevant sources of new information,</u> and (5) <u>to avoid</u> <u>deceiving oneself</u> (or rationalizing about) the relevance of various considerations or their consequences.

This list may not be exhaustive. But it does illustrate the variety of ways in which deliberating agents can influence and control their practical reasoning by their efforts. Jane may be tired of deliberating about her vacation, but, recalling a previous disastrous vacation, she may make the effort (1) to go on deliberating rather than decide too hastily. She may have to make efforts of kind (2) to focus attention on relevant scenarios involving her friend in Colorado in order to be sure whether another visit with this friend is something she really prefers. Thoughts about Hawaii's

varied restaurants may provoke thoughts of overeating and reminders of recent attempts at dieting, which she is inclined to suppress. But if the final decision is to be
in her best interest all-things-considered, efforts of kind (3) must be made to avoid
suppressing such thoughts—as well as efforts to avoid rationalizing (5) about her
doctor's recent warnings against getting too much sun. Finally, the best decision will
require her to make efforts of kind (4) to gather further information about costs, ac-
commodations, and other details that might be relevant to her decision—tasks easily
postponed out of aversion and for lack of time.

It will be noted that all of these additional efforts are "prudential" in nature, since
they are motivated by the long-term goal of making the best all-things-considered
decision in opposition to inclinations to be lazy, hasty, or self-deceptive. But we must
not think there is a contradiction in saying that the efforts are "prudential" while the
choice to be made is "practical." For the goal at which these efforts are directed is
to make a choice *of a practical kind*, and it is in terms of their goals (the kinds of
choices they aim at) that practical, prudential, and moral deliberations have been
distinguished. In fact, it is not difficult to see that

> T76 (*on FW*): Efforts of the kinds described in T75 may play a role in delibera-
> tions of all three kinds—prudential and moral, as well as practical. Thus, T75
> not only extends the account of practical deliberation; it suggests further refine-
> ments to the accounts of moral and prudential deliberation. In moral and pru-
> dential, as well as practical, deliberations, agents may have to make efforts to
> attend to relevant consequences, avoid resisting unpleasant considerations, and
> especially avoid rationalizing or deceiving themselves about the consequences
> of what they are doing. Through such varied efforts, indeterminacy may enter
> into moral and prudential deliberation, as well as practical deliberation, *during
> the process of deliberation* and not only at its termination.

In summary, returning to practical deliberation, we can say that

> T77 (*on FW*) ("Practical Deliberation"): The general picture of practical delib-
> eration presented in T65 through 76 is one in which indeterminacies may occur
> throughout the process of deliberation by virtue of Taoist efforts leading to chance-
> selected considerations, as well as by indeterministic efforts such as those of T75,
> through which the deliberation is advanced. These varied efforts lead to a gradual
> accumulation of reasons for one or another option until one option (Hawaii, Colo-
> rado, etc.) outweighs the others in the mind of the agent and is chosen. The final
> step of this process, the choice itself, may be determined by the accumulation of
> reasons when it occurs, but it may also, and often will, be undetermined when-
> ever uncertainty remains up to the moment of choice about whether to choose
> the presently favored option now, or to go on deliberating. Moreover, whether the
> final step of the process is determined or not, it will have been the result of a pro-
> cess of deliberation whose outcome was undetermined throughout most of its
> duration to the extent that the agent was making Taoist and other efforts to reach
> a "fair," "informed," "nonhasty," "prudent," or "undeceived" decision. To the extent
> that we succeed (or fail) in our efforts to make such decisions, we exercise control
> over our practical deliberations throughout their duration.

It follows, finally, from T77 that insofar as indeterminism appears throughout the process of practical reasoning rather than at its end,

> T78 (*on FW*): The proximate products of undetermined SFWs in practical reasoning will often be *practical judgments* of evaluative and normative kinds rather than choices or decisions proper. In response to chance-selected considerations, the deliberating agent may, like Jane, judge that one option (say, Hawaii) is "better than" others for certain reasons (its Polynesian restaurants). Or she may judge, as the result of efforts of the kinds described in T75, that she "ought to" go on deliberating or ought not to suppress qualms about overeating or getting too much sun. These "better than" and "ought to" judgments are practical judgments of evaluative or normative kinds and they are respectively the proximate products of chance-selected considerations in practical deliberation and of indeterminate efforts of the kinds described in T75. Along with choices or decisions, such judgments are the *libera arbitria voluntatis* or "free judgments of the will" of traditional accounts of free will.

10. Changes of Intentions in Action

The final category of SFWs I want to discuss has to do with a phenomenon that may be called "strict akratic action" or "last ditch" *akrasia*. Here is a striking example, offered by Alfred Mele, of this type of action: "A man who, after careful deliberation, forms the here-and-now intention to shoot his injured horse, may, while taking aim at its head, catch a glimpse of its doleful eyes and decide, due to weakness of will" (and not compulsion) to refrain from shooting it (1987: 19). If the man intentionally refrains, while "still thinking that it would be best to shoot" the horse, then Mele calls this a case of strict akratic action. As with other kinds of weakness of will, the possibility of free strict akratic action may be doubted. I did not include it in my earlier accounts of free will, but have since become convinced through arguments and examples of Mele, David Pears (1985), Robert Dunn (1987), and others, that strict akratic action is possible.[14] Without attempting to reproduce all the relevant arguments and examples, I merely want to show how strict akratic action might be accommodated by the theory of this book, if examples like the above do in fact exemplify it.

Note that situations like that of the man attempting to shoot his horse lie somewhere between efforts sustaining purposes, on the one hand, and moral or prudential choices, on the other. As with efforts sustaining purposes, the man enters the situation with an already formed intention, which he fails to execute. Yet, according to the example, the man *intentionally* refrains from killing the horse at the last moment, which means, as Mele notes, that the prior intention is abandoned or changed, at least for the time being. That makes the situation more like choice or decision. But such instances of strict akratic action are not exactly choices or decisions either, or, at best, they are limiting cases of choice or decision without prior deliberation or reflection. Whether we call them choices or decisions, I think, is less important than recognizing their uniqueness. The man's intention to kill the horse is changed, not as the termination of prior reflection or deliberation, but as the initiation of an alternative action, that is, in and by his willfully lowering his gun and turning away from the horse (hence the designation of these cases as "changes of intention in action").

The controversial issue for our purposes is whether such last-ditch changes of intention can be free (in the sense that the agent could have done otherwise) or whether they must be due to irresistible impulse or compulsion. As Mele argues, the fact that the change of intention was last minute and not preceded by conscious deliberation is not reason enough to say that the agent could not have done otherwise in *all* such cases. Of course, one has to say what "could have done otherwise" means in these contexts, and Mele offers a compatibilist account of "could have done otherwise" (in the work in which the example of the man and the horse appears). My purpose here is to say how an *incompatibilist* account might be given for cases of this kind, assuming some of them may be genuine cases of weakness of will rather than compulsion.

Somehow indeterminism must get into the picture just prior to the change of intention.

> T79 (*on* FW) ("Changes of Intention in Action"): Suppose that, in the case of the man and his horse, as the man is raising his gun and sees the doleful eyes of the horse, a tension suddenly builds within him brought about by a conflict in his will that had been temporarily suppressed until that moment. He must now make an effort to pull the trigger (it is no longer an easy or automatic action) because the look in the horse's eyes has strengthened his inclinations not to do so. The effort to resist these suddenly strengthened inclinations would then be indeterminate, like previous efforts required to overcome countervailing inclinations. The appropriate regions of the brain move further from thermodynamic equilibrium because of the tension that has suddenly arisen within him. This inner tension or conflict will in turn be settled by him one way or the other, though which way is not determined beforehand. If he refrains from shooting the horse at the last minute (thereby changing his intention), he will have allowed his countervailing inclinations to prevail then and there, and if he goes ahead with his plan and shoots the horse he will have overcome those countervailing inclinations by his effort.

Even if we should think of these last minute changes of intention as limiting cases of choices or decisions without prior deliberation, I think they deserve separate treatment because of the special philosophical problems often associated with strict akratic action or last-ditch *akrasia*. What T79 shows is that, if free strict akratic action is possible at all, a place can be made for it in the account of free will offered in the last two chapters.

10

Objections and Responses

1. Indeterminacy and Possible Worlds: Waller

In this chapter, the theory of the previous two is further developed by answering additional objections that have been made, or could be made, against it. In many instances, the objections are those of astute and persistent critics of my view to whom I am indebted for waking me from many a dogmatic slumber. In all cases, the objections throw light on free will issues generally, as well as on the preceding theory.

Objection 11: This objection was first made by Bruce Waller (1988) in a critical study of Kane, 1985. Other versions of it were later made by Mark Bernstein, Thomas Talbott, David Blumenfeld, Galen Strawson, and Richard Double.[1] "Suppose two persons had exactly the same pasts and made exactly the same efforts of will," says Waller, but one does the moral or prudential thing while the other does not. Given that their pasts were exactly the same up to the moment of choice, as indeterminism requires, wouldn't that mean that the outcome was a matter of luck? One of them got lucky and succeeded in overcoming temptation, the other failed. Would there then "be any grounds for distinguishing between [them], for saying that one deserves censure for a selfish decision and the other deserves praise for generosity? If they are really identical, and the difference in their acts results from chance, then it seems irrational to consider one more praiseworthy (or more blameworthy) than the other should be" (p. 151).

The first point to be made in response is that the two persons resolve the uncertainties in their minds in different ways and they have voluntary control over their doing so when they do it (T31). So the outcomes are anything but matters of luck. Matters of luck are in the same category as events that occur by accident, by mistake, or merely by chance; and we saw that SFWs are unlike events in that category (T36 through 40). But there is a second response to this objection that goes beyond these previously mentioned considerations. I would also argue that one cannot assume to begin with that the pasts of these agents are *exactly the same* or that they are "really identical."

> T80 (*on FW*): With indeterminate efforts, exact sameness is not defined. Nor is exact difference either. If the efforts are indeterminate, one cannot say the efforts had exactly the same strength, or that one was exactly greater or less great than the other. That is what indeterminacy amounts to. So one cannot say of

two agents that they had exactly the same pasts and made exactly the same efforts and one got lucky while the other did not. Nor can one imagine the same agent in two possible worlds with exactly the same pasts making exactly the same effort and getting lucky in one world and not the other. Exact sameness (or difference) of possible worlds is not defined if the possible worlds contain indeterminate efforts or indeterminate events of any kinds. And there would be no such thing as two agents having exactly the same *life histories* if their life histories contain indeterminate efforts and free choices.[2]

T81 (*on* FW) ("Uniqueness"): This is how free will is related to the uniqueness of persons as emphasized by authors like Bradley, Honderich, Nagel, and others mentioned in chapter 6. On my view, this uniqueness is radical. It does not mean being exactly different from everything else. It means not being exactly the same as, or different from, everything else. Each life history is unique and cannot be exactly the same as any other if the psychological histories involve indeterminate processes, as they must for free will. The conflicts and struggles within the wills of free agents that give rise to these indeterminacies are reflected in consciousness by the belief of the agents that they are unique persons experiencing their freedom in a way that cannot be exactly duplicated. Their consciousness of this reflects the widespread intuition that we are most uniquely ourselves when we engage in creative activity and "self-making" that is not determined by anyone or anything outside ourselves. In such manner, the uniqueness of persons often associated with free will is not accidentally related to the indeterminacy required by free will. The indeterminacy is connected to the fact that the efforts of will we are making at times of inner struggle are experienced as ours in a unique and irreplaceable way.

2. Epicurean and Non-Epicurean Worlds: The Indeterminist Condition Revisited

T80 and 81 recall a theme mentioned earlier that deserves further discussion. I said in T53 that introducing indeterminacy into one's account of free will means more than simply allowing for chance events in nature. It requires an entirely new way of looking at the life histories of free agents, just as quantum theory requires a new way of looking at the trajectories of physical particles. At issue in this new way of looking is a distinction between two separable features of classical doctrines of determinism (of the kind that is incompatible with free will). "Determinism" (of this kind), as Clark Glymour has said, "requires both the determinateness of quantities and the impossibility of forks in history" (1971: 745). That is to say, it requires (i) determinateness or exactness of the values of properties defining the state of the world at any given time (e.g., the positions and momenta of all particles in classical Newtonian physics as envisaged by LaPlace) and (ii) uniformity of evolution of systems through time, so that a determinate past is consistent with only one (determinate) future.

These two requirements suggest two ways of understanding *in*determinism. First, one can imagine an indeterminist world in which all quantities are "determinate," but "forks in history" are possible. This would be a world in which (as in the classical Newtonian world) all properties of physical sytems, such as position and momentum, are determinate at all times, but in which (unlike the classical Newtonian world, as usually envisaged[3]) the laws allow different (determinate) futures given the same (determinate) past. Such a world would be an "Epicurean world" that allowed for chance "swerves" of the atoms even though their positions and momenta were at all times determinate—a world of *chance* but not of *indeterminacy*. Second, one can imagine an indeterminist world like the quantum world of modern physics (on standard interpretations of it) that allows for both indeterminateness of physical properties and the possibility of forks in history. Indeed, the two conditions are connected in this second world. From its laws, one cannot infer with certainty (but only with probability) that a moving particle will or will not penetrate an atomic barrier (a fork) because the position and momentum throughout the prior trajectory of the particle cannot both be assigned precise values at the same time. In this second kind of indeterministic world, chance or indeterminism is a consequence of indeterminacy.[4] Let us call worlds of the first of these two kinds—with chance (or forks), but not indeterminacy of properties—"Epicurean worlds," and worlds of the second kind—with chance and indeterminacy (like the quantum world)—"non-Epicurean worlds."

> *T82 (on FW)* ("Non-Epicurean Worlds"): My view is that free will requires the second kind of indeterministic, or non-Epicurean, world. Historically, incompatibilists have held that the universe must involve some chance or indeterminism—the atoms must swerve in Epicurean fashion—if there is to be room in nature for free will. This is true, but it does not go far enough. An Epicurean world in which undetermined events occurred given an entirely determinate past—a world of chance without indeterminacy—would be a world of mere chance, not free will. There would be no indeterminate "gestation period" for free acts, so to speak; they would just pop out of a determinate past one way or the other without any preparation in the form of indeterminacy-producing tension, struggle, and conflict. Free will requires a world that is more radically indeterminist than such an Epicurean world—a world like the second (or quantum) world described in the preceding paragraph, in which there is both chance and indeterminacy. To imagine such a world, it is not enough to imagine a classical world of determinate properties and then add undetermined forks to it. One has to imagine a different kind of reality altogether—one in which physical systems are described in ways (say, in terms of multidimensional vector spaces or quantum wave functions) that translate into observable properties only probabilistically—not a familiar world with chance added, but a world in which indeterminacy is woven more deeply into the fabric of reality.[5]

One of the reasons free will is difficult to understand is that it requires just such an unfamiliar indeterministic world (T53). The other reason, also mentioned earlier (T51), has to do with the problem of consciousness (and the two reasons might be connected, as suggested in T55, since consciousness may also require a non-Epicurean, or quantum, world[6]). With T82 in hand, we are now in a position to draw an important conclusion about the "indeterminist condition" of chapter 7.

> *T83 (on FW):* In an indeterminist world of the Epicurean kind described in T82, undetermined free willings would have to satisfy the indeterminist condition as stated in chapter 7: the agent must be able to willingly do and willingly do other-

wise, "all past circumstances and laws of nature remaining exactly the same."
We labored over this condition in chapter 7, showing how it caused problems
for libertarian accounts of free will. What T82 suggests, however, is that libertarian theories of freedom may not in fact require the indeterminist condition
in this strong form. Such a condition would be required for indeterminist worlds
of an Epicurean kind. But Epicurean worlds of mere chance without indeterminacy are not hospitable to free will in any case. By contrast, if free willings were preceded by indeterminate efforts, as in non-Epicurean worlds, agents
would not have to be able to willingly do and do otherwise, all past circumstances remaining exactly the same, because the past circumstances never
would be exactly the same. They would be similar in the sense of belonging
to a class of events governed by the same (probabilistic) laws, but not exactly
alike.[7]

3. Explanation and Probability: Double, Clarke

A different kind of criticism of my view has been made by Richard Double in several
articles and in a widely read book, *The Non-reality of Free Will* (1991). Double's
criticisms raise questions of another kind—about explanation and probability—that
are also deserving of further treatment. I mentioned earlier that the view of free will
presented in earlier chapters is compatible with probabilistic or nondeterminstic
explanations of self-forming willings (T34), though obviously not compatible with
deterministic explanations of them. But little has been said since then about probabilistic explanation and how it is related to reasons-explanations of choices or actions.
Double's criticisms are related to this topic.

It is an important topic because many libertarians (and their critics) have held
that incompatibilist free choices or actions cannot be given causal explanations of
any kinds, deterministic or probabilistic. Even probabilistic explanations of the kinds
sought in behavioral and social science, it is often said, are incompatible with the
uniqueness of libertarian free choices or actions. Only reasons-explanations or agent-
causal explanations can be given of them. I think this familiar libertarian view is wrong,
and I have resisted it throughout this book, because I think it stands in the way of
understanding the place of free will in the natural order in which causal explanations of deterministic or probabilistic kinds hold sway. Causal explanations cannot
be the whole story of free will, but they must be part of the story if free will is to have
a place in the natural order. And since deterministic causal explanations are ruled
out for undetermined free willings, it is important to ask how explanations of them
in terms of reasons are related to probabilistic or nondeterministic causal explanations. This question in turn leads to further issues not previously addressed that are
nicely brought out by Double's arguments.

Objection 12: To lay the groundwork for this objection, I begin by quoting Double
(1991: 203–4):

> The question of what constitutes an adequate explanation is, of course, one of the
> foremost topics in the philosophy of science. . . . [But] there is a minimal prin-
> ciple that I believe is so weak that [most] sides of the debate would accept it. I call
> it 'The Principle of Rational Explanation':

(PRE): Citing a person's deliberative process [and/or reasons or motives] P rationally explains a choice C only if the probability of C given P is greater than the
probability of not C given P.

For example, if citing Smith's deliberative process concerning smoking is to truly
explain Smith's decision to smoke a cigarette, then a very minimal condition needs
to be met, viz., that the deliberative process make it more likely that Smith decide
to smoke than decide not to.

In a later paper (1993), Double explains that his intuition when first formulating this
principle PRE "in response to Kane's [view]. . . . was that although it would be easy
to confabulate explanations for each of two contradictory indeterminate choices, and
to convince ourselves that we had chosen rationally whichever way they went, I did
not see how there could be any *insightful* objective explanation of a choice unless
that explanation entailed that the choice was at least slightly more probable than its
not occurring" (p. 134).

Double goes on to argue that this "highly plausible" principle PRE creates difficulties for libertarian theories, mine included, in reconciling undetermined free
choices with probabilistic explanation. To illustrate, he uses an example of van
Inwagen's in which an agent is faced with a choice between robbing a poor box (A)
and keeping his promise to his mother not to steal (B) (1988a: 433). If either of these
outcomes was determined, its probability would be 1, and the probability of the
alternative 0. Of course, this cannot be the case for either alternative if the choices
are undetermined. But if it is not the case, problems ensue about the probabilities to
be assigned. On the one hand, Double argues, if the probabilities of choosing A and
choosing B are equal and exhaustive (each is .5), as van Inwagen assumes in his example, then PRE will be violated whichever outcome is chosen. Any prior process
of deliberation that is cited in order to rationally explain why that choice was made
would not make the occurrence of that choice more probable than the occurrence
of its alternative. On the other hand, if one outcome is more probable than the other,
say the probability of A is .7 and of B .3, then PRE is satisfied for the more probable
outcome but not for the alternative. The choice of the more probable outcome could
be "rationally explained," according to PRE, but not the choice of the less probable
outcome. But this would mean that *plural* rationality would fail, contrary to earlier
claims.

My response to Double's criticism was, and is, straightforward. PRE would indeed cause problems for libertarians if it were a true principle about rational explanation. But it is a far more problematic principle than first appearances suggest; and
it ultimately fails, I believe, as a general principle of rational explanation.[8] To see
why, let us first consider an argument made against PRE by Randolph Clarke (1992),
who joined the debate between Double and me in a paper criticizing Double's em-
ployment of PRE. Clarke takes issue with Double's assumption that PRE is "so weak
a principle" that most philosophers of science would accept it no matter what their
general view of explanation. This claim, Clarke says, is "certainly mistaken" (p. 3).
To show why, he asks us to "consider a variation of PRE that is not concerned specifically with rational explanation but concerns causal explanation in general." Clarke
calls this analogous principle PCE: "Citing a prior event E causally explains a later
event F only if the probability of F given E is greater than the probability of not F

given E" (p. 4). Double says that he also endorses PCE "because it is a generalized version of PRE, motivated by the same intuition" (1993: 135). But Clarke notes that

> Most philosophers of science . . . reject PCE. . . . The following example has been found by many [of them] to tell against any principle like PCE. Paresis is a condition that results only from untreated tertiary syphilis; absent that prior condition, there is no chance of contracting paresis. Yet, only a small percentage of those with untreated tertiary syphilis ever contract paresis; the chances of getting it given this prior condition is approximately .28. When an individual does contract paresis, it is clear what has caused that outcome, and citing the presence of untreated tertiary syphilis appears to explain the outcome. Hence explanation appears possible even where the explanandum event is relatively improbable given the explanans. (1992: 4)

One thing that is clear from well-known examples of this sort is that uses of the term "explanation" are less clear-cut and well-regimented when probabilities and nondeterministic causation are involved. The general lesson of such examples is nicely stated by Clarke: "Where a causal process is . . . nondeterministic, the mechanism or causal process that produces the highly probable result on one occasion is the same one that produces the improbable result on another occasion. We know as much about how the effect is produced in one case as we do in the other" (p. 4). (Similar claims about nondeterministic explanation have been made by Jeffrey [1971], Salmon [1984] and Lewis [1986, vol. 2: 230].[9])

This is a important point worth dwelling upon. Consider, by way of illustration, a radioactive nucleus that emits alpha particles (helium nuclei) at various times in a manner that is not determined. Quantum laws may tell us that the emission of at least n particles over a time span t is highly probable (say, .99) whereas the emission of, say, n + 5 particles during the same time span is highly improbable (.0001). But these same laws, being probabilistic, do not tell us exactly when a particular emission will occur or exactly how many will occur during t, allowing that even the less probable result (n + 5 emissions in the present case), however improbable, may occur during a comparable time span. Moreover, if and when the less probable result did occur, it would result from the same causal mechanisms (the forces inside the nucleus) that would have produced the highly probable result, had it occurred. In other words, as Clarke says, when a causal process is nondeterministic, it can produce either outcome in a particular instance; and the probabilistic explanation tells us as much or as little about how it does this in the improbable case as in the probable one.

4. Characters, Motives and Probabilities

This argument obviously has important implications for PRE as well as for PCE, as Clarke notes. If either the choice of A or the choice of B might result from an indeterminate process, and either outcome could be explained by reasons if it occurred, there would be no grounds for saying (as PRE does) that one outcome was rationally explained but the other was not, *simply* because one of them was more antecedently probable than the other.[10] The reason is that while the probabilistic explanation tells us which outcome is more likely to occur, it does not tell us why one occurs rather than the other *in the particular case*; and this is true whether the outcome that occurs in the particular case is more probable *or less probable*. We might add that, for similar reasons, the probabilistic explanation does not tell us which outcome is more rational. It tells us which outcome is more likely to occur, but there is no reason antecedent likelihood of occurrence has to match up with rationality. It may be that the antecedent likelihood of occurrence of an action has to do with features other than rationality, such as the agent's strength or weakness of will. Probabilistic and rational explanations would then be on different tracks, one informing us about antecedent likelihoods of occurrences in terms of strength of will, the other about the rationality of the occurrences; and then "greater probability" would not always match with "greater rationality," in the manner required by PRE.

This is the line I took on the relation of probabilistic to rational explanation in my initial response to Double[11] — a response that is spelled out with further elaboration in the following theses. The first step is to clarify what the probabilities signify in undetermined free-choice situations and what values they may take. To do this, a common misconception must first be set aside.

> T84 (*on FW*): Libertarians and their opponents have often assumed that when undetermined free choices or actions occur, the viable alternatives must be equally probable. Thus, if there are two alternatives, each must have a probability of .5. But there is no good reason to require this overly constraining assumption about outcomes. The equiprobability assumption is as misleading as another assumption often associated with it in people's minds—that indeterminist free will must always be a "liberty of indifference" of the kind that confronted Buridan's ass.

[margin annotation: alternatives need not be equally viable or probable]

Van Inwagen has informed me in correspondence that when he made the equiprobability assumption in his example of the poor box mentioned by Double, he meant it only as an illustration and did not mean to be claiming that the options in every incompatibilist free choice had to be equiprobable. This is an important addendum, for a general assumption of equiprobability, as I see it, would ill serve the free willist cause. On my view,

> T85 (*on FW*) ("Probabilities"): The initial settings of the probabilities in free choice situations are related to the agent's prior character and motives and may be anywhere between 0 and 1 (e.g. [.7, .3], [.56, .44], [.2, .8]) depending upon the *strength or weakness of the agent's will* with respect to the options, that is, depending upon the comparative strengths of the agent's inclinations to act, say, from moral motives (A, in the example of the poor box), or from self-interested motives (B). The equiprobability setting [.5,.5] is thus only one of many possible ones. In this way, we can accommodate the point made by Aristotle, J. S. Mill, and many other thinkers that, given the agents' present characters and motives (which may have been built by way of their own past choices and actions), some agents are stronger-willed than others, more likely than not to act morally or prudentially, or to sustain their purposes, in given situations (e.g., A [.7], B [.3]), while others are more weak-willed and more likely to succumb to temptation or fail to sustain their purposes in similar situations (e.g., A [.2], B [.8]).

T86 (*on FW*): But these probabilities do not, of course, guarantee one or another outcome in the particular case. In situations of conflict and struggle characteristic of undetermined free willings (i.e., SFWs) there is always the possibility that even the strong-willed may succumb to temptation and the weak-willed may conquer it. The less likely outcome *may* occur; and just because it was antecedently less likely given the agent's prior motives and character does not mean it was less *rational* given the agent's prior motives and character. Indeed, for SFWs, each outcome is rational for different and incommensurable reasons. Whether the agents resolve their conflicts one way or the other, they have reasons for doing so, they do so for those reasons, and want to do so for those reasons more than for any others when they act. This means that the prior character and motives that create the inner conflict in the agent allow for a rational resolution of it in more than one way *even when the probabilities of its being resolved are not equal*. Under such conditions, PRE fails when the less probable, but still rational, outcome occurs.

Double's response to this argument is to say that it presupposes a different notion of "rational explanation" than he intends (1993: 138). The argument of T85 and 86 assumes that an action is rationally explained when the agent has reasons for doing it (r_1 of T33), does it for those reasons (r_2), and wants to do it for those reasons when it is done (r_3). But this is an explanation of the rationality of the action when and if it occurs. It says that, *if* the action occurs here and now rather than at some other time, it will be *rational*. But it does not explain, as Double rightly notes, why the action actually occurred at this time rather than some other in terms of the reasons the agent had (r_1) before the action occurred—which is the kind of rational explanation he has in mind.

I acknowledge this difference in notions of rational explanation and have acknowledged it throughout the development of the theory of this book (T31, 33, 46, 59, and 74). The kind of rational explanation Double has in mind is not possible for free will (at least for SFWs) because it would mean that one could explain why one action actually occurs rather than another then and there by citing the agent's *prior* reasons alone. No libertarian theory can do that for all actions, as I have repeatedly said. To make such a strong requirement on rational explanation begs the question against libertarians. And to add that this stronger kind of explanation is what an "insightful" rational explanation would amount to is tendentious (cf. Clarke, 1992). It all depends upon what kind of insight you are looking for.

If, on the one hand, you want to know what is going to occur before it occurs in terms of the agent's reasons, then Double's kind of rational explanation is insightful and mine is not. I do not deny the importance of such insight and I can see why Double and others put so much emphasis on it. It is the kind of insight psychologists and social scientists are looking for when they try to explain human behavior—the kind that leads to prediction and potential control of behavior. But free will by its very nature puts limits on such prediction and control (at least for SFWs). And when you cannot predict or explain with certainty when choices or actions will occur, there are other things you may still want to have explained about their rationality.[12] You may want to know whether agents acted *for* reasons they *wanted* to act on *when* they acted, rather than doing something by mistake, or accidentally, inadvertently, or against their wills. This is another kind of rational explanation and it is important because, along with further information to the effect that the agents were not coerced or compelled or otherwise controlled when they acted, this kind of rational explanation is relevant to questions of responsibility of the kind one is interested in with regard to free will.

5. Moral Responsibility

Double's final sally in this debate in his 1993 paper is important enough to be stated as a further *Objection 13*: He says that while my interpretation of plural rational explanation is a possible one, it is not robust enough to account for moral responsibility (p. 140). Similar reservations about the adequacy of my view for moral responsibility have been expressed by Talbott (1986), C. Williams (1986), Blumenfeld (1988), Miles (1988), Waller (1988), Bernstein (1989), Gensler (1989), Tracy (1990), Posth (1990), O'Connor (1993a), and G. Strawson (1994). While some of these criticisms about responsibility were addressed in chapters 8 and 9, it is a topic of sufficient importance and contention to deserve further discussion here.

In one sense, I agree with the above objection as Double states it. Plural *rationality* alone (and hence plural rational explanation, as I understand it) is not sufficient to account for more-then-one-way responsibility. One must add plural voluntariness and plural voluntary control to it. My argument has been that when free choices (and other self-forming willings) satisfy all three plurality conditions as described in T32, 33, 43, and 59, the agent is personally and ultimately responsible for the choices, whichever way they go, in the sense required by conditions R and U of UR. When the choices (or other self-forming willings) in turn bear on the *moral* character of the agent (i.e., when the "self-forming" is of the agent's moral character), then the ultimate responsibility defined by UR becomes ultimate *moral* responsibility. All of the arguments for these claims obviously cannot be repeated here. Suffice it to say, in summary, that,

> *T87 (on FW)* ("Moral Responsibility"): If the plurality conditions are satisfied for SFWs, when the agents choose (or otherwise will) either way, they have reasons for choosing as they do (T27, 33); they choose for those reasons (T34 through 35), rather than by mistake or accident or merely by chance (T36 through 40); they want to choose for those reasons more than any others when they choose (T29); they are not coerced or compelled in so choosing (T32) or in most wanting to so choose (T33); and they are not controlled or made to choose by other agents or by any other things or circumstances (T41 through 42). These conditions (which jointly describe what it means to satisfy the plurality conditions) fulfill the requirement for an agent's being "personally responsible" for something's occurring in the sense of R of UR: "something the agent voluntarily did or omitted, and for which the agent could have voluntarily done otherwise, either was, or causally contributed to, the outcome's occurring and made a difference to whether or not it occurred." Since condition U of UR is also satisfied for SFWs that fulfill the above conditions (T6), we have for them a personal

responsibility that is also ultimate in a strong sense: the agent *and no one and nothing else* has ultimate responsibility for the resolution of the conflict in his or her will. When this conflict bears on the moral character of the agent (such as the businesswoman's choice to render assistance to the assault victim or the engineer's choice to avoid drinking to save his marriage) we speak of the ultimate responsibility as "*moral* responsibility."

To be sure, condition R of UR states only a necessary condition for responsibility. Determining praiseworthiness or blameworthiness in everyday moral and legal contexts often requires the application of additional normative criteria that may be contestable. For example, it is usually required that the agent could have reasonably foreseen the consequences of his or her action; and there may be disagreement about what can reasonably be expected of agents in this regard. But if R of UR, and the plurality conditions that entail it, are not the whole story of moral responsibility, they are nonetheless critical conditions for responsibility that bear specifically on the *freedom* of agents to do what is required of them morally. These conditions rule out coercion, compulsion, physical restraint, and other conditions usually associated with the familiar principle that "'ought' implies 'can.'"

[margin note: Condition R is nec. but not necessarily sufficient for responsibility]

We have now reached a point at which this earlier account of moral responsibility can be expanded by putting T87 together with T85. As T85 asserts, the initial settings of the probabilities in free-choice situations are related to the agent's prior character and motives and may be anywhere between 0 and 1 (e.g., [.7, .3], [.56, .44], [.2, .8]), depending upon the strength or weakness of the agent's inclinations to act upon one or another of the options. In this way, we accommodated in T85 the point that, given their present characters and motives, some agents are stronger willed than others, more likely than not to act morally or prudentially in given situations, or to sustain their purposes, while others are more weak-willed and more likely to succumb to temptation or fail to sustain their purposes. The implications of these points for moral responsibility can now be seen by adding that

> T88 (*on* FW) ("Character Building"): The probabilities for strong- or weak-willed behavior are often the results of agents' own past choices and actions, as Aristotle and other thinkers have insisted. Agents can be responsible for building their moral characters over time by their (moral or prudential) choices or actions, and this character building will be reflected by changes in the probabilities for strong- or weak-willed behavior in future situations. Each time the engineer resists taking a drink in difficult circumstances, he may strengthen his will to resist in future; and conversely, when he succumbs, his will to resist may lessen (or crumble altogether, as sometimes happens with alcoholics). In the former case, where his will is strengthened, the probability of resisting in similar circumstances may rise over time from, say, .6 to .8; in the latter case, it may fall from .6 to .4, or even to 0. If the probability falls to 0, this amounts to the engineer's no longer being able to resist at all. He drinks compulsively. But he may still be responsible for getting himself into that state by succumbing in past situations when the probability was not 0 and he could have resisted. Similarly, if the probability rises to 1, he is no longer tempted to drink. But it may be to his moral credit that he brought himself to that state by strengthening his will through resistance to past temptations.

T89 (*on* FW) ("Saints and Monsters"): The same may be said for other temptations of moral or prudential kinds—temptations to lie, to steal, to neglect onerous tasks because of laziness or aversion, and so on. Thus, we said that Luther may have been ultimately responsible for his "Here I stand," even if it was determined (had probability 1), to the extent that he had made himself into the kind of man he then was by past choices and actions (T12). Moral saints and heroes are not made in a day—nor moral monsters, either—as Aristotle reminded us. And so, <u>moral responsibility is not just a matter of doing the right thing here and now, but also of character-making over time—of building virtuous and vicious dispositions through one's own efforts, choices, and actions.</u>[13]

Thus, it follows from T87 through 89 that

T90 (*on* FW): Moral responsibility *for* SFWs has a twofold source—first, in the present willing itself, as T87 describes, and second, through the input of prior character and motives formed by past choices, efforts, and actions, as T89 describes. To be sure, past character and motives do not determine the outcome in the case of SFWs, but they influence the outcome, and that influence is measured by the antecedent probabilities for strong- or weak-willed behavior, which in turn may reflect past efforts of the agent in resisting or succumbing to temptation. As T89 says, moral saints are not made in a day, nor moral monsters either. Moral responsibility accumulates over time—a theme that the Indian traditions capture in their doctrines of Karma.

T90 expresses one of the reasons we commonly think of adults as more responsible than children. Adults have had more time for character building; and it is normally assumed they have had more input into their present characters and motives (though it may not always be so in fact). In the first SFWs of childhood, the bulk of the responsibility lies in the SFWs themselves; none or little has yet accumulated from the past. This gradually changes over time as character and motives become the products of prior self-forming willings—and moral responsibility then accumulates for what we *are* as well as for what we *do*.

6. Choice, Responsibility, and Indeterminism: Strawson, Bernstein

The difficulties that critics like Double (and others just mentioned) have with this account of moral responsibility—not surprisingly—have to do with indeterminism. They remind us that the moral choices and other SFWs spoken of in T87 through 90 are, after all, *undetermined* occurrences that are assumed to be outcomes of indeterminate processes in the brain; and this indeterminism presents continuing problems about responsibility. As Galen Strawson has put it (*Objection 14*): "In Kane's view, a person's 'ultimate responsibility' for the outcome of an effort of will depends essentially on the partly indeterministic nature of the . . . process of the effort of will. But . . . how can the fact that my effort of will is indeterministic in such a way that its outcome is indeterminate help to make me truly responsible for it?" (1994: 21) Or, as Mark Bernstein says, "How can agents be personally responsible for outcomes that are undetermined and result from indeterminate processes in their brains? In what sense can such outcomes be called *choices* at all, much less morally responsible choices?" (1995: 154).

These criticisms about moral responsibility were addressed in various guises in chapters 8 and 9. But they are important enough to return to one more time in the light of the fuller account of moral responsibility just given. Let me therefore try to pull together the threads of my response to these criticisms in previous chapters and expand upon it. Consider the paradigmatic case of moral choice of chapter 8: the businesswoman responds to the stirrings of conscience by choosing to return to an alley to render assistance to a victim of assault. This choice at least temporarily resolves a conflict in the woman's mind, since she had powerful self-interested motives for going on to her business meeting. I suggested the following thought experiment in the woman's case. Suppose future neuroscientists should find that the relevant processes going on in the woman's brain just prior to choice, which she experienced as inner conflict and effort, involved chaotically amplified indeterminacies as described in T24 through 29—as the theory supposes.

How should we respond to this new neurological information? Critics of indeterminist theories such as Bernstein might insist that, as a result of this evidence, we should say that the resolution of uncertainty and conflict in the woman's mind was not really her "choice" at all, but rather something that merely happened to her. And after a visit to the neurologists she herself would have to say this also, if she was to speak truly. She thought she was *choosing* or resolving the conflict, but now that the real happenings in her brain are known, we (and she) must say that she was mistaken. In response, I argued that there is no good reason whatever to accept such a conclusion from the neurological evidence alone. We have no more reason to do so, I suggested, than to conclude that our thought processes and their conclusions are not really our doings if it should turn out that they involved some indeterministic chaotic processes in the brain, as well they might, according to some recent suggestions.[14] When the woman exits the neurologists' office, rather than say, "These neurologists have discovered that I didn't really choose to help that poor assault victim yesterday," a more sensible response, as I see it, would be for her to say, "These neurologists have discovered that when I chose to help that poor assault victim yesterday, my choice was not determined!"

Now indeterminism may in some instances undermine choice. Consider the example of an undetermined choice of Jane's that was discussed in chapter 7. We imagined that Jane had reached a point in her deliberation at which she favored vacationing in Hawaii when, owing to a quantum jump in her brain, she found herself intending to vacation in Colorado. The case was odd because she did not have the sense of voluntarily doing anything. Rather, the change came upon her involuntarily, like an epileptic seizure, much like the man in Schopenhauer's example, who inexplicably found his legs moving when he wanted them to be still. If a case like Jane's were to occur, she might suspect someone was tampering with her brain or that something had gone wrong requiring neurological consultation. But one thing seems clear: she would be reluctant—and we would be reluctant—to say that she *chose* anything in such a case.

So indeterminism can sometimes undermine choice. But there is no legitimate reason to generalize from cases like Jane's and say it must always do so. Consider the businesswoman by contrast. Her experience, unlike Jane's, is of consciously and voluntarily choosing to follow her moral conscience and to return to help the vic-

[handwritten margin note: There is a premise missing that links phenomenology to cause in such a way that prevents the experience from being epiphenomenal. We need to be able to say what just that we feel like we, as persons/agents are doing - the causal work, but that IN FACT we ARE]

tim, thereby resolving a preceding uncertainty in her mind. Also, in the business-woman's case, unlike Jane's, the indeterminate process discovered by the neuro-scientists immediately preceding the choice was <u>experienced by her as her own ef-</u><u>fort of will</u>, not merely as a random occurrence in her brain that happened to influence the outcome. Given these differences, it would be hasty, to say the least, to lump the two cases together and draw conclusions about the businesswoman's case from Jane's.

When Jane learns from the neurologists that an undetermined occurrence in her brain led to her experience, she may appropriately react by saying that now she knows why this bizarre thing "happened" to her. But there is no corresponding rea-son for the businesswoman to react in the same way because, unlike Jane, her expe-rience was not of something happening to her, but rather of voluntarily doing some-thing—resolving uncertainty in her mind by choosing to help the victim (or by deciding instead to go on to her meeting). Why should the businesswoman conclude that she did not really choose in such circumstances (rather than that her choice was undetermined) just because, *under very different circumstances*, Jane did not really choose? *[handwritten: — But the important question is "why shouldn't she conclude this?"]*

7. Determinism and the Existence Question: Honderich, Weatherford, and Others

Remember that the present issue is not *yet* about whether the businesswoman's choice was a "free" or "responsible" choice, but simply whether it could be called a "choice" at all if it is undetermined. (We have to take these issues one at a time: if it could not be a choice at all, we could not go on to ask what makes it a responsible choice.) Another line the philosophers could take to convince us it was not a choice might be this. "Don't you see," they might say, "that if what she experienced as a choice was preceded by an indeterminate process (as the neurologists have discovered), it was undetermined by antecedent circumstances, and (1) if an event is undetermined by antecedent circumstances, it must be something that merely happens, and cannot be somebody's choice." But why should we believe that (1) is generally true? When we consider that (1) is equivalent to (2), "If an event is somebody's choice, and not something that merely happens, it must be determined by antecedent circumstances," *[handwritten: ok]* (1) appears to be nothing more than the question-begging assumption that all choices must be determined.

Perhaps the plausibility of (1) and (2) is supposed to rest on the more general assumption (3), "If an event is undetermined by antecedent circumstances, it must be something that merely happens, it cannot be something an agent *does* (it can-not be an *action*)." But when we consider that (3) is equivalent to (4), "If an event is an *action*, it must be determined by antecedent circumstances" (i.e., "all actions are determined"), then (3) appears even more question begging than (1) and (2). Now, <u>it may turn out that all choices and actions are *in fact* determined or near-</u><u>determined, as modern determinists such as Honderich (1988), Weatherford, and</u><u>others claim</u>.[15] To question (1) through (4) is not to question *that* possibility. When the neuroscientists look into the brain, they may not in fact find the relevant inde-terministic processes in the appropiate places, as we imagined in the business-woman's case.

But (1) through (4) go well beyond the claim that determinism or near-determinism of all actions and choices might turn out to be empirically true. I said earlier that I think libertarians must accept the empirical challenge of determinism (that it might turn out to be true), if libertarians are going to be serious about finding a place for free will *in the natural order* where we exist and exercise our freedom. This is the "Existence Question" for free will, and, as I said in chapter 1, it cannot be finally settled by armchair speculation, but only by future empirical inquiry. What philosophers can do with regard to the Existence Question is to suggest models about how free will might work in the brain so that future researchers have some idea of what to look for when they search for it; and this is what I have tried to do in preceding chapters.

But (1) through (4) are quite another matter. They are not claiming that all choices and actions may, or will, turn out to be determined, or near-determined, when we learn more about the brain and the physical world. Rather, (1) through (4) are making a priori claims that all choices and actions must be determined—that if any events were undetermined they could not in principle *be* choices or actions. If this were so, any indeterminacy that future neuroscientists should find in the brain just prior to experienced choices (such as we imagined in the thought experiment about the businesswoman) would not be allowed to count as evidence for undetermined choices or actions on a priori grounds. The compatibilist-incompatibilist debate would be over before it began, by fiat.

8. Action and Indeterminism

There is more to be said about (3) and (4)—the claims that no undetermined events could be *actions* and that all actions are determined. Not only are (3) and (4) question begging, there are counterexamples to them. We encountered some of these counterexamples in the arguments of Austin, Anscombe, and other philosophers in chapter 7—one being Austin's holing his three-foot putt when he could have missed by chance. Austin and Anscombe wanted to show, and successfully showed, by such examples that the *power* to act was consistent with the acts being undetermined; but they showed this by also showing that actually performing the acts was consistent with their being undetermined. Now the Austin-Anscombe examples are not entirely relevant to cases such as the businesswoman's because the indeterminism occurs *during* the performance of the actions rather than at their initiation. But the Austin-Anscombe examples are also only the tip of the iceberg when it comes to counterexamples to the claims that undetermined events could not be actions. Athletic competition, artistic creation, and other exercises of skill provide other potential counterexamples.

Consider the giant slalom event at the Winter Olympics of 1994 in Lilliehammer, Norway. The upper part of the course was especially icy that day and many of the finest skiers in the world were unable to navigate it. The great Olympic veteran Alberto Tomba was one of the first to run the course, and he was surprised by the severity of the ice. He had to call on his considerable experience and skill to navigate the icy turns without falling. Reporting the experience afterward, he said that he had to make numerous spur-of-the-moment decisions in response to the unusual conditions. Often he reacted on hunches and several times he almost fell. Skiers in such situations have to react instantaneously to new information coming from outside and inside their bodies at every moment—slippage of their skis on the ice, the positions of their legs, visual information about the course, and so on. Let us imagine that future neuroscientists should find (as they did for the businesswoman) that the processing of information by the brain in such circumstances—especially when it presents new and unusual data calling for novel responses—involves indeterministic chaotic processes such as those described in T24 through 29. This is not an unrealistic supposition in view of the way connectionist neural networks are designed to flexibly react to new data and in view of the possible role that chaotic behavior may play in such reactions.[16] For present purposes, however, it is sufficient to treat this as a possible scenario, in the manner of the Austin-Anscombe examples.

On this supposition, the indeterminate information processing in Tomba's situation would be produced by the novelty of the data to which his nervous system is feverishly attempting to adapt on the icy course, and the attempt to adapt in turn would be producing a tension and uncertainty in his mind about how to react. He might react by tensing the muscles in his legs or shifting his weight slightly to one side. But the reactions in any case would be responses on his part to indeterministic processes in his brain through which the incoming data was being filtered, and the instantaneous responses to this data would be undetermined. But these responses would not on that account cease to be Tomba's actions, since they would be *purposeful* initiations on his part of overt behavior such as tensing muscles in his legs or shifting his weight *in response to* the incoming data *with the intention of* avoiding a fall. Whether we want to call these reactions "choices," given that they were exercised without significant prior deliberation, is perhaps a matter of dispute. (Tomba himself spoke of "spur-of-the-moment decisions.") But, if not choices, Tomba's reactions are at least volitions in the sense in which the term "volition" is normally used—that is, to designate basic mental actions that execute intentions (in this case, the intention to avoid falling), and initiate overt or other actions. The point is that something is no less an action of an agent, whatever term we use to designate it ("volition," "spur-of-the-moment decision," etc.), *if it is a purposeful response to indeterminate data than if it is a purposeful response to determinate data*. The difference in the indeterminate case is that there is a greater likelihood of getting it wrong, as Tomba realized as soon as he became aware of the conditions of the slopes that day.

We often say that great athletes act on "instinct" in such situations—that they display instinctual skills developed through many years of experience. This is true enough. But it is a mistake to assume that instinctual responses displaying skills must always be determined or habitual. Good instincts and skill may be needed to respond quickly to indeterministic data arising from novel situations as much as from deterministic data arising from familiar situations. Tomba's undetermined responses could have gone in different directions and he experienced uncertainty about them. He was not on automatic pilot—not on that day, on that course. If he chose one false move among those available to him, it was curtains. Under such conditions, in which responses are not determined or habitual, good "instincts," experience, and skill are even more necessary than at other times, and the ability to get it right under such indeterminate conditions *more often than not* is what distinguishes great athletes from good ones.

Similar remarks hold for other kinds of creative activity. Picasso described his painting in terms remarkably similar to Tomba's account of negotiating the slopes. Picasso described making "decisions" instantaneously, "with his hands," to place a brush stroke here or there in response to the look of the partially painted canvas. We can imagine that in Picasso's case, as well as in Tomba's, some of these responses might be to indeterministically filtered data without denying the skill involved and without denying that Picasso's reactions were purposeful *responses* he was *making* to the indeterminate data. The potential role of indeterminacy in creative problem-solving was a theme of T65—a theme that can be extended to creative activity of all kinds, like Picasso's, as well as athletic competitions.

Returning, finally, to the businesswoman, on my account she also reacts to indeterminacy in her nervous system that is resolved by initiating the action of returning to help the assault victim or proceeding onward to her business meeting. Like Tomba and Picasso, she responds to an indeterminate situation and her response is a purposeful initiating of one or another overt action. Though the initiating event one way or the other is immediately preceded by and causally influenced by an indeterminate process in her brain, it can nonetheless be an action, because it is her *purposeful response* to the indeterminate process. Moreover, since the response in her case was preceded by reflective and deliberate consideration of options and was the explicit formation of an intention to do one thing rather than another, it fulfills the further conditions for being a "choice."

9. Control and Responsibility

There is one final line of argument that may be used to support the view that undetermined events cannot be choices, and hence not responsible choices. It may be argued that while undetermined events may be *actions* (and even actions that conclude deliberations), they could not be actions that are in the agents' *control,* since "choices" are by definition actions that are in an agent's control. This line of argument goes beyond the questionable claim that undetermined events cannot be actions *simpliciter* and gets closer, I think, to what really troubles people about undetermined choices. After all, it is an old cliché in free-will debates that undetermined events cannot be controlled by anything, and so they cannot be controlled by the agents themselves. At first blush, claims like (1) and (2)—that no undetermined events could be choices and that all choices must be determined—appear question begging. But if one thinks that undetermined events cannot be controlled by anyone, (1) and (2) may be taken more seriously.

This line of argument about control, however, is one I *did* address at some length in chapters 8 and 9. My general point was that familiar assumptions about indeterminism and control are as much in need of rethinking as other familiar and normally unquestioned assumptions about free will. (I am not alone among contemporary philosophers in thinking that a reexamination of familiar assumptions about indeterminism and control is in order. See Ginet [1990], Clarke [1995], and the papers in O'Connor, ed. [1995].) One of the assumptions about indeterminism and control discussed in chapter 8 that is the source of much of the confusion, as I see it, is the belief that all control must be antecedent determining control (T44). I think the time has come in the history of free will debates when this pernicious assumption must be subjected to greater scrutiny. To have antecedent determining control over an action or other event is to be able to bring about conditions that will determine or guarantee its occurrence in advance. If all control had to be of this type, then undetermined free will would be manifestly impossible. For if an action is the result of antecedent determining control then it is determined by prior circumstances. It does not matter if some of these prior circumstances are the agent's own character traits, motives, efforts, or choices. The action would then be determined by the agent's character, motives, efforts, or choices, but determined nonetheless. If all control had to be antecedently determining, then no free action could be agent controlled and undetermined. The case for incompatibilist free will would be over before it began.

My argument (in T31, 43, and 52) was that this assumption about antecedent determining control can and should be questioned. It does not follow that because you cannot determine or guarantee which of a set of outcomes will occur beforehand, you do not have control over which of them *occurs*, when it occurs (T31). To have plural voluntary control over a set of options means at least to be able to bring about whichever one (of them) you will, when you will to do so, which means in turn that in exercising incompatibilist free will, agents have control over their actions then and there, when they are occurring, even if the actions are not determined by prior events. In addition, I argued (T52) that the various reasons we have for saying that agents do *not* have control of their actions when they perform them—compulsion, constraint or force, mistake or accident, control by other agents or mechanisms, and so forth—all fail for SFWs satisfying the conditions of plural voluntary control (T43). Indeed, the conditions of plural voluntary control for SFWs systematically exclude circumstances that are normally taken to undermine agents' control over their responsible actions (T31 through 42; T53).

Now, if someone insisted that inability to guarantee an outcome *before* it occurs is a limitation of control, then I granted it. But I argued that this limitation is the price we pay for free will. In order to have *ultimate* control over their destinies, possessors of free will must relinquish antecedent determining control at pivotal points in their life histories. In order for their contributions to the world to be truly (i.e., ultimately) theirs, they have to relinquish a kind of control over those contributions that would guarantee in advance how they will turn out. This does not mean, as I argued, that possessors of free will do not have voluntary control over their destinies; it only means that when they engage in self-formation, what they choose is not determined by their already formed characters and motives. They become initiators of "value experiments" whose justification lies in the future and are not fully explained by the past (T46). But they take responsibility for setting themselves on one or another future branching pathway—making themselves as they go along out of a past that does not limit their future pathways to one.

10. Agent Causation

The objections so far considered to the free willist view presented in chapters 8, 9, and 10 have chiefly come from compatibilists, determinists, and others who are skeptical about the existence and intelligibility of libertarian free will. Objections to my view by other libertarians, in contrast, have mainly come from those who believe that some kind of "agent-causation" of a nonoccurrent kind is necessary to account for incompatibilist freedom. Most libertarians feel that no libertarian theory that fails to appeal to nonoccurrent causation by agents can be adequate. These libertarian critics may accept much of what I say about free will, but they would argue as follows (*Objection 15*): "Take everything you have said about undetermined free willings in theses 1 through 90. All of it is either inadequate or it does not make sense unless you add to it that (N) 'agents nonoccurrently cause their undetermined free actions or willings.'"

But what exactly are we adding if we add claim N? What exactly does N explain that cannot be otherwise explained or is not explained in theses 1 through 90? We are told that agent-causation of the nonoccurrent kind (hyphenated earlier to signify its special nature) is the causation of an action or other occurrence by a thing or substance that cannot be explained in terms of the causation of occurrences or events (states or processes) by other occurrences. But this is mainly a negative characterization. It tells us that what makes causation by agents "nonoccurrent" is that it cannot be explained in a certain way (i.e., in terms of occurrences or events). But if we are to add to our ontology a special relation of nonoccurrent causation between an agent and an action that is to do some explanatory work, we have to know something more positive about the relation than that it cannot be described in a certain way and that it exists between an agent and an action whenever free actions are not (occurrently) determined. For the question is whether this postulated additional relation explains whatever it is that cannot otherwise be explained in terms of occurrences or events involving agents — or whether it explains anything at all.

Yet agent-causalists are in a bind when it comes to saying something more positive about what agent-causation is or how it operates. For they cannot say what is distinctive about it or its operation in terms of occurrences or events of any kinds, including states or changes involving the agents, physical *or* psychological. Agent-causalists can, of course, agree with many of the things I have said in theses 1 through 90 about the role of reasons or motives, character traits, physical circumstances, deliberation, and so forth, in free choices and actions. But no mention was made in these theses about the need for a special kind of nonoccurrent, or nonevent, causation. So the question is, what are we *adding* to all that we can say about the agent's physical and psychological circumstances by adding that (N) the agents nonoccurrently cause their undetermined free actions?

One suggestion is that we are adding something that seems simple enough, yet cannot be said occurrently, namely that agents *cause* their own actions. In other words, if one does not add that agents nonoccurrently cause their actions, one cannot say they "cause" their actions at all. But this is too strong a claim.[17] Agent-causation is unusual not simply because it is causation of an event or action by a substance or agent. Causation of events by substances or agents is commonplace, but it can usually be interpreted in terms of causation of occurrences by other occurrences. Thus (to use examples of chapter 7) "the stone broke the window" is elliptical for "the stone's striking the window caused the window to break," and "the cat caused the lamp to fall" is elliptical for "the cat's jumping on the table caused the lamp to fall." By con-

[margin notes:]
def. of agent-cause.
?

This is similar to my gripe w/ Kane about the mind-body problem

trast, no such paraphrasing in terms of occurrences or events is possible in the case of agent-causation of the nonoccurrent kind.

Note that the point of such occurrent paraphrases about the stone's striking the window or the cat's jumping on the table is not to deny that the *stone* broke the window or the *cat* caused the lamp to fall (it is not a denial of causation by substances); much less is it to deny that there are stones or cats. The point of such paraphrases is rather this: when you say a thing or substance caused an event or occurrence, you *explain what this means* by saying what it is *about* the stone (its being heavy and its striking the glass) and its situation (the fragility of the glass), and, similarly, what it is about the cat, such that the stone and the cat here and now caused these occurrences. And so with human agents, the point of occurrent descriptions is not to deny that the *agent* caused the action, but to explain what this means by saying what it is *about* the agent and the situation at the time such that the agent caused this action (for example, that the agent was in such-and-such circumstances, had certain reasons and character traits, engaged in practical reasoning, etc.). To reject agent-causation is therefore not to deny that there are agents and that they cause things in ordinary senses of the term—that they make telephone calls and messes, cause harm, produce things, make choices, form their own characters and motives, and so on. To deny agent-causation is rather to deny that we need a special relation of nonoccurrent causation to explain all this.

Most agent-causalists would in fact concede that we do not need nonoccurrent causation to explain agency and action in general. The more common view among agent-causalists is that nonoccurrent causation is specifically needed to explain *un-determined* free actions.[18] If Luther's action is determined by his character and motives, then, although it is his action—something he does—it is not agent-caused by him in this special sense. What, then, does nonoccurrent causation explain about undetermined free actions that cannot be otherwise explained? One suggestion is that, if we do not assume that agents nonoccurrently cause their undetermined free actions, we cannot answer the question "Why did the agent perform this action here and now *rather than* some other?" The problem with such a suggestion, however, is that we cannot do any better answering *this* question by postulating nonoccurrent causation than we can do without it. If the agent freely does A at t and A is undetermined, agent-cause theories inform us that the agent nonoccurrently caused A at t rather than B, and if B is done, that the agent nonoccurrently caused B at t rather than A. Or, they inform us that, in the first case, a special relation of nonoccurrent causation exists between the agent and A at t, and in the second case such a relation exists between the agent and B instead. But these claims do not help at all in answering the original question of *why* the agent did A at t *rather than* B (or vice versa).

In fact, we know that no libertarian answer to such why-questions for undetermined free actions can in principle be complete in the way that a deterministic answer would be complete. What libertarians can and must show, nonetheless, is how it can be rational and responsible for the agent to do A rather than B or B rather than A, despite the fact that neither action is determined. But I think one shows this by appealing, as I have done in theses 1 through 90, to reasons for choice or action that agents may have and for which they may act and by showing how such acts can be voluntary and voluntarily controlled despite being undetermined. If there is something left over by such explanations about why the agent did A rather than B in comparison to what deterministic explanations would explain, then one thing is clear: appeals to a special relation of nonoccurrent causation do not supply what is missing, for reasons given in the preceding paragraph. They provide no further illumination about *why* the agent did A *rather than* B, or vice versa, that cannot be supplied without them.

This result nicely illustrates the claim of T18 about traditional libertarian strategies (including agent-causation) that are ruled out by the Free Agency Principle (T16): "Whatever can be done to make sense of incompatibilist free will, can be done without such strategies . . . and whatever *can't* be done without them . . . *can't be done with them either.*"

11. Self-determination: Rowe, O'Connor, Clarke

A more promising suggestion about why agent-causation is needed comes from philosophers such as William Rowe (1987), Timothy O'Connor (1993), and Randolph Clarke (1993), who have attempted in recent years to revive what O'Connor calls the "beleaguered" theory of agent-causation. O'Connor and Clarke are two very capable younger philosophers whom I count among those persistent critics of my view mentioned at the beginning of this chapter who have awakened me from many a dogmatic slumber. Not a few of the improvements in the theory of this book are the result of their careful reading and persistent criticisms of my earlier writings, as indicated at certain points in chapters 8, 9, and 10. Rowe's efforts to revive interest in agent-causation has taken the form of some important historical studies of eighteenth-century figures, especially Thomas Reid, who appealed to agent-causation to defend libertarian free agency against its critics, like Hobbes.

Rowe, O'Connor, and Clarke believe that agent-causation is needed not so much to explain the rationality of free actions as to explain the *control* or *determination* that agents exercise over their free actions. When we add a claim such as N, "agents nonoccurrently cause their undetermined free actions," we are not necessarily adding further information about why the agent performed one action rather than another that cannot be otherwise provided by appealing to reasons, character traits, and so forth. But we are nevertheless adding something important that cannot be captured without appealing to nonoccurrent causation, namely that it is the agents themselves who have control over their free actions in the sense that they, and they alone, *produce* or *bring about* the undetermined outcome that occurs. As Rowe puts it in his seminal study of Thomas Reid, using Reid's language, free agents must have power over "the determinations of their own wills" (1991: 55).

I think this correctly captures the motivations of agent-cause theories. A persistent libertarian intuition down through the ages has been that, although free actions are not determined by antecedent circumstances (i.e., occurrences), they are nonetheless determined by a self or agent; they are *self-determined*, though not event-determined. I think the continuing appeal of agent-cause theories is that they try to capture this intuition. I do not fault them on this score, because the intuition is central. My problem is that I cannot see what is added to what can otherwise be said about self-determination by invoking a special relation of nonoccurrent causation between an agent and an action. I agree, in other words, with the criticism of Gary Watson, John Bishop, and Bernard Berofsky, among others, that agent-causation merely "labels" what libertarians want rather than "illuminating" it.[19] If we are to illuminate what libertarians want on this matter, I think we have to do what I have at least tried to do in theses 1 through 90—that is, put some filling in the pie. On my account, as indicated in T87 through 89, the filling would look something like this:

> T91 (*on* FW) ("Self-determination or Agent Causation"): To say that persons (*self*) *determine* or (*agent*) *cause* their undetermined free willings or acts of will (SFWs) is to say that they perform the acts *and* that they *have plural voluntary control* over their doing so and doing otherwise.[20] Agents have plural voluntary control when they are able to do what they will to do, when they will to do it, on purpose rather than by accident or mistake, without being coerced or compelled in doing, or willing to do, it, or otherwise controlled by other agents or mechanisms (Frankfurt controllers, etc.). It is by virtue of the satisfaction of such conditions that we say it is "up to the agents" themselves (and no one and nothing else) what they do; and when the agents actually do one thing or another it is by virtue of such conditions that we say they (and not some other agents or mechanisms) *cause* or *determine* what they do. They are "self-determining" in the sense that they do what they do *under their own voluntary control*.

Agent-causalists will argue either that this is not enough or, more plausibly, that one or more of the conditions of T91 cannot be satisfied without bringing in agent-causation of a special nonoccurrent kind. Without adding nonoccurrent causation, can one really say or assume in T91 (i) that the undetermined willings or SFWs are "actions" or "doings" of the agent rather than mere happenings; (ii) that the agent actually "controls" their occurrence; (iii) that they do not occur by accident, mistake, or merely by chance; (iv) that they are not controlled by Frankfurt or other controllers; or (v) that they really are "produced" or "brought about by" the agents? In response to these questions, I have already argued at length for claims (i) and (ii) in sections 6 to 9 of this chapter, and need not repeat those arguments.

Concerning claim (iii), it is worth recalling the arguments of T36 through 40 and section 6 of this chapter that undetermined actions need not occur by accident, mistake, or merely by chance. I argued in section 6 that Jane's accidental selection of Colorado by virtue of an undetermined occurrence in her brain is very much unlike the case of the businesswoman who chooses between helping the assault victim or going on to her meeting, even though both are undetermined. The businesswoman's case satisfies the conditions of plural voluntary control of T91, while Jane's accidental selection does not. It is a mistake, therefore, to say that the businesswoman's choice happens by accident, mistake, or merely by chance simply because, under very different circumstances, Jane's selection happens by accident, mistake, or merely by chance.

Regarding claim (iv)—about control by other agents such as Frankfurt controllers—it is worth recalling what was said about Frankfurt control and SFWs in T41 through 42. If an action is an SFW (say, a choice), then a Frankfurt controller faces a dilemma in carrying out his strategy for controlling it. The controller plans to make

Jones do A, but he waits to see if Jones is going to do A on his own and only inter-venes if Jones is about to do B instead. But if A is an SFW, the choice is preceded by an indeterminate effort and the controller cannot know whether one or the other, A or B, is going to occur unless he predetermines one of them to occur. The controller can therefore wait until he finds out whether the agent will do A or B, but then it is too late to control the choice. Or he can intervene in the brain, shutting down the indeterminacy or its effects before either one occurs, thereby determining the out-come he wants.[21] In the latter case, the choice will be determined by the controller and the controller, not the agent, will be ultimately responsible for it. It will not be an SFW. In the former case, in which the controller waits and the indeterminacy remains in place until the choice is made, the outcome *is* an SFW and the agent, not the controller, is ultimately responsible for it. But then—when the choice is an SFW—it will not be controlled by the controller.

The point to notice about this result for present purposes is that it does not re-quire the postulation of nonoccurrent causation. The fact that SFWs, *qua* SFWs, cannot be Frankfurt controlled follows from the assumption of *indeterminism* of SFWs alone. The pivotal fact is that, if the controller does not intervene, the choice remains undetermined up to the moment that it occurs.

12. Agency

This brings us to the agent-causalists' final challenge—to claim (v). Can we really say that undetermined actions are "produced" or "brought about" "by" the agents at all without invoking agent-causation of a special nonoccurrent kind? O'Connor says revealingly that, while the notion of agent-causation is difficult to spell out and is regarded as mysterious by most philosophers, it is nonetheless meant to account for something important, namely "how a particular piece of behavior is connected to, or [is] an 'outflowing of' the agent'" (1993: 500). I agree that this idea of outflowing is important. (It was a metaphor first used by Locke.) But what does the statement that agents nonoccurrently cause their free actions do to illuminate this idea?

What light does the postulation of *nonoccurrent* causation throw on "how a par-ticular piece of behavior" outflows from, or is produced by, an agent? At best, nonoccurrent causation seems to be a "label" for what is wanted here, as Watson, Bishop, and Berofsky say, and not an explanation; it does not supply the filling to the pie. Moreover, it is difficult to see how nonoccurrent causation could supply the fill-ing to this pie, because "outflowing" suggests that something is *going on* involving the agent such that the action *comes from*, or is *produced by*, the agent. But whatever may be specifically added by postulating nonoccurrent causation cannot by hypoth-esis be spelled out in terms of occurrences or goings on of any kinds involving the agent, physical and/or psychological.

Agent-causalists will have to say that "outflowing" is then only a metaphor that should not be taken too literally. For the whole point of introducing agent-causation is precisely to say that the agent is able to *just do* one thing or the other then and there, not *by* doing something else, or by virtue of some other goings on (such as outflowing) that *constitute* the agents' causings of their action. Now, the first half of this twofold claim is something I can, and do, say as well. On my theory also, at some point the agent *just does* one thing or the other then and there (e.g., makes one choice or another), and does not have to do so by doing anything else. But you don't have to postulate a special relation of nonoccurrent causation to say *that*. If we libertarians are going to say that the free agent has the ability to *just do it* then and there—to settle indecision one way or the other—in a manner that is undetermined, then we ought to come right out and *say this*. Let's not beat around the bush and postulate special ontological relations to obscure what we must say anyway and can say more simply. At crunch time, the agents just do it; they settle indecision, respond to indeterminacy, and take responsibility then and there for setting their lives on one or another future branching pathway.

But libertarians who say this do not have to agree with the second half of the agent-causalist's claim cited at the beginning of the preceding paragraph—that when agents do make free choices, there are no other events or "goings on (like outflowing) that *constitute* the agents' causing of their actions." On the contrary, I think it is incumbent on libertarians (if they ever hope to dispel charges of obscurantism against their view) to say something about this "outflowing" of the action from the agent that constitutes the agent's causing or producing the action. But I also do not think that postulating nonoccurrent causation says anything illuminating about this. If something illuminating is going to be said about "*how* a particular piece of behavior . . . is the outflowing of," or is produced by, the agent, it will have to be in terms of what is *going on* with respect to the agent when action takes place, including what is going on in the agent's brain (which is the kind of information that nonoccurrent causation does not supply). To be sure, there is much left to be learned about what is going on with respect to the agent when action takes place. But I made some suggestions that are relevant to this question in chapters 8 and 9 in terms of the notion of a self-network and these suggestions are worth reconsidering here.

The self-network, in Owen Flanagan's words, is the "recurrent brain network" that sets out the "plans, aspirations and ideals" of the agent and embodies the broader motivational structures of the brain that influence and guide the agent's practical reasonings.[22] To suppose there is such a thing, one does not have to suppose, as Flanagan notes, that the self-network controls everything in the brain, or that it has a specific location rather than being a complex network distributed widely throughout the brain. Its unity would lie in the dynamical properties of neural circuits and connections that make possible synchronized and causally interacting oscillations or patterns of firings throughout the entire network, like those described by Crick, Koch, Llinas and others, for conscious awareness and wakefulness.[23]

The suggestion of T37 was this: the feeling that certain events in the brain—for example, those corresponding to our efforts and choices—are things we are doing rather than things that are merely happening to us would result from the superposition of the synchronized wave patterns of the self-network upon those neural events. The idea, in other words, is that the neural events corresponding to our efforts, choices, and other mental actions would be overlaid by the patterns of oscillations unifying the self-network, so that these patterns and the effort or choice events are coupled, causally influencing and interacting with each other. The effort and choice events would occur, so to speak, "within" the self-network whose distinctive patterns of oscillations were superimposed upon them, and the patterns of the self-network would

[handwritten margin note: Here's the answer, but I don't understand it.]

be contributing causes to choice, pushing one competing reason-network over the top and thus supporting the belief that the choices are *our* doings, the products of our selves.

I argued that something along these lines is needed to account for mental action and agency in general, whether deterministic or nondeterministic, compatibilist or incompatibilist. For there are further issues involved in accounting for agency even if actions are determined by reasons, as argued in T38—issues about what makes the reasons reasons *of* the agent (the reason-networks must also be inside the self-network) and about the "deviant" or "wayward" causation of actions by reasons (circumventing the self-network), such that the action is not brought about by the agent *for* the reasons. So even when choice is determined (as in Luther's case, on Dennett's account of it), the fact that the choice is the *agent's* doing rather than a mere happening means that something playing the role of a self-network must be involved (for compatibilists as well as incompatibilists). This is also important if one wants to hold, as I do, that some actions, such as Luther's, may be done of our own free wills and may be ultimately responsible even though they are determined. We want to say that these also are produced by the agents.

The crucial difference for undetermined free willings (or SFWs) would then be that (a) the contributing wave patterns of the self-network would involve chaotic indeterminacies as described in T25 through 26, so that the willed outcome would not be determined (though it would be causally influenced) by the self-network, and (b) there would be more than one feasible option (A for reasons R or B for R') that the wave patterns of the self-network might push over the top, thus triggering the choice outcome. Whichever outcome is pushed over the top, however, the impetus for it would be recognized as coming from within the self-(network) either way. For this impetus would be, in the one case, the reasons R for choosing A (say, moral reasons) and in the other case, the reasons R' for choosing B (self-interested reasons); and the reason-networks corresponding to both R and R' would be part of the self-network and potential motivators for it.[24]

Finally, can the self-network be said to produce the outcome if its distinctive wave patterns only causally influence the outcome without determining it? Yes, for reasons explained by Anscombe.[25] Our understanding of what it means to produce something allows for nondeterministic production. It is undetermined whether a radioactive nucleus will now emit an alpha particle in direction x or direction y. Yet, if an emission event does take place in direction x (or direction y), it will have been *produced* by the forces inside the nucleus either way. The difference for human agents is that the forces within their nucleus (the self-network) represent different expressions of their own wills.

I am sure that this is far from the whole story of "how a particular willing or mental action . . . is the *outflowing* of the agent." What I am arguing, however, is that whatever is missing and yet to be learned on this subject is *not* supplied by saying that agents nonoccurrently cause their actions. For further illumination about how actions outflow from agents will only come from better understanding of what is going on involving the agents when the actions occur. And nonoccurrent causation by its nature does not supply any further information of *that* kind. I think this is what is right about Hobbes's comment that agent-causation is "empty" of explanatory content and what is right about the charges of Watson, Bishop, and Berofsky that it merely "labels" a problem without solving it. Agent-causalists may try to provide substance to their theories by postulating noumenal selves, transempirical power centers, nonmaterial egos, the Will as an inner homunculus, or other traditional strategems as agent-causes. But the problem is the same, whether they do this or postulate ordinary agents in space and time having physical and psychological properties. In order to provide illumination about the outflowing or production of actions by these entities, they have to say something about the conditions of the agents and what is going on involving the agents when the actions occur. And this is the sort of information that, by its nature, nonoccurrent causation does not supply.

I said that my theory would not eliminate all mystery from free will, and in chapter 8 I mentioned two unsolved cosmological enigmas deeply implicated with free will, the problems of consciousness (T51) and of indeterminacy in nature (T53). I think that a full understanding of how actions outflow from agents would require a better understanding of both these problems, and it may be (as indicated earlier) that both the unity of conscious experience and the unity of the self-network are somehow related to the quantum character of reality, as various scientists and philosophers have suggested.[26] This may be one direction in which to look for greater insight into the relation between consciousness, on the one hand, and human agency, on the other. But if we look in this direction, trying to unravel the mysteries of quantum reality, I cannot see that nonoccurrent causation will provide much help there either.

Two major defenders of agent-cause theories when I began thinking about free will, Roderick Chisholm and Richard Taylor, have since abandoned agent-causation, suggesting that it isn't needed.[27] Another prominent libertarian, Carl Ginet, thinks, as I do, that agent-causation of a nonoccurrent kind isn't needed by libertarians.[28] David Wiggins and Robert Nozick have suggested that libertarians may, and perhaps should, do without it.[29] Yet another prominent libertarian, Peter van Inwagen, remains noncommittal about agent-causation, but has said, "I find the concept of immanent or agent causation puzzling, as I suspect most of my readers do (those who don't find it downright incoherent). In fact, I find it more puzzling than the problem it is supposed to be a solution to" (1983: 51). In addition to these libertarians, there are phalanxes of compatibilists, determinists, skeptics, and fence-sitters on free will who agree with Hobbes that agent-causation is either confused or empty. Nonetheless, agent-cause theories have able new defenders in Rowe, O'Connor, Clarke, John Thorp, and others.[30] And many libertarians continue to believe that agent-causation must somehow be part of the libertarian view.[31] So maybe theories of agent-causation can be resuscitated. But the burden of proof must be on anyone who would do so.

11

Conclusion

1. Looking Back

The aim of this concluding chapter is to situate the debates about free will discussed in previous chapters within broader intellectual currents of the late twentieth century and of the modern era in philosophy generally. I turn to this task in section 2, after a brief review in this opening section.

Free will was defined in chapter 1 as "the power of agents to be the ultimate creators (or originators) and sustainers of their own ends or purposes." In subsequent chapters, explanations have been offered of central notions of this definition. *Purposes* or *ends* are the contents of intentions that guide and coordinate present and future actions and reasonings (chapter 2). We *create* or *originate* purposes by way of choices, decisions, and changes of intention in action (chapters 8 and 9). We *sustain* purposes by various efforts of will in action and practical reasoning (chapter 9). We are *ultimate* creators and sustainers of our own purposes or ends in the sense defined by the condition of Ultimate Responsibility or UR (chapters 3 and 5). It is by virtue of being such ultimate creators and sustainers that we shape and reshape our characters and dispositions (as well as our destinies) gradually over time, and in that sense are self-creating or self-determining beings (chapter 10).

The notion of *power* in this definition of free will is distinguished by the fact that it is the power to make ultimate choices and other acts in the sense of UR. We exercise this power when we act "of our own free will," either by directly engaging in undetermined self-forming willings (SFWs) or by acting from a will formed by earlier self-forming willings—that is to say, from a will of our own making, and in that sense our own free will (chapter 5). This is what it means to say, as Bramhall did, that the "freedom of the agent is from the freedom of the will" (chapter 2). Finally, the power we have over self-forming willings that are not determined by the past and laws of nature is the power to make them "with plural voluntary control" (as spelled out in chapters 8, 9, and 10[1]).

I have argued that free will so defined is the notion that has been the traditional subject of centuries-old debates about the "problem of free will." Such a free will is not, by any means, the only significant freedom we may have or desire. I argued in chapter 1 that incompatibilists can and should concede that many everyday freedoms—e.g., from coercion, compulsion, or political oppression—are compatible with

196

determinism. Even in a determined world, we would prefer to have these freedoms than to lack them. But that is not what the free will debate is about. Rather, it is about a special kind of freedom to be the ultimate creator and sustainer of one's own ends or purposes that goes beyond everyday compatibilist freedoms.

Concerns about this special kind of freedom arise at a certain advanced stage of human self-consciousness, when we realize how profoundly the world influences us in ways of which we are unaware (chapter 6). The advent of doctrines of determinism in the history of human thought is an indication that this stage of self-consciousness has been reached. Thus, the problem of free will arises historically in response to threats of determinism, as explained in chapter 1. But, once having arisen, concerns about free will take on a life of their own. For when we realize that there is a kind of freedom that might be threatened by determinism, we begin to wonder what such a freedom could be or if it could be at all (whether determinism is true or not); and, as we know, philosophy begins in such wonder.

I further argued that this traditional idea of free will, which has been the subject of centuries-old debates, has been increasingly under attack in the modern era (beginning in the seventeenth century) for being obscure and unintelligible, and for its supposed lack of fit with present images of human beings in the natural and human sciences. This book has been directed against these modern attacks on free will. I have tried to show that the ancient conflict between free will and determinism is real; that the traditional idea of free will is not necessarily obscure, as is often claimed; and that the question of whether or not it can be fitted into the emerging picture of human beings in the natural and human sciences is one that deserves to be looked at anew.

On the four central questions of the book, I have argued that new ways of thinking about them are needed and are possible. Regarding the Compatibility Question, we have to look beyond the usual debates about alternative possibilities, or AP, to issues about UR. Regarding the Significance Question, we have to look beyond the usual debates about creativity, moral responsibility, and the reactive attitudes to fundamental intuitions about selfhood and worth that lie behind these debates. Regarding the Intelligibility Question, we have to look beyond the usual libertarian appeals to mysterious forms of agency or causation in the attempt to reconcile traditional free will with twentieth-century developments in the sciences and in social and humanistic studies. Regarding the Existence Question (whether and where free will might exist in the natural order), we must be willing to engage, however tentatively, in thinking about how free will is related to such topics as evolution, neural network theory, nonlinear thermodynamics, chaos theory, and quantum physics. These speculations by no means settle the question of whether we have free will, but they deal with issues that I think have to be explored if the ancient problem of free will is to be dragged wholly into the modern world.[2] What has been said here on these issues is far from the last word, but I hope it will stimulate others to do better.

2. Indifference and Incommensurability

I now turn to the task of relating discussions of previous chapters to broader intellectual currents of the late twentieth century and of the modern era generally. The story

I want to tell begins with a medieval notion whose relevance to the modern era is not immediately evident, though it will become evident in due time. Modern critics of a traditional nondeterminist free will such as Hobbes, Hume, and Schopenhauer took delight in referring to this kind of freedom as a "liberty of indifference" and comparing it to the laughable medieval image of Buridan's ass starving between two equidistant bales of hay.[3] These same authors then unflatteringly contrasted the liberty of indifference with a "liberty of spontaneity"—which was their designation for the Hobbesian, or compatibilist, freedom to do what you will. Neither of the expressions "liberty of indifference" nor "liberty of spontaneity" was very accurate for the kinds of freedom they were supposed to describe, but both expressions served well the purposes of modern critics of free will and both are still employed in twentieth-century debates.[4] One reason for the persistence of these expressions is that there is a kernel of truth in the association of nondeterminist free will with the medieval notion of a liberty of indifference. But the whole truth is more complicated than this kernel—and more interesting.

On my theory, the role of "indifference" (to alternatives) in free will is taken over by the notion of "incommensurability" (of alternatives and points of view)—a seminal notion having significance for twentieth-century philosophy beyond free will debates.[5] In T74, the claim was made that exercises of free will in self-forming willings typically involve incommensurable alternatives and points of view in the following sense: A and B are incommensurable alternatives (possible actions, purposes, or plans) for an agent at a time just in case the agent has reasons (or motives), $a_1 \ldots a_n$, for preferring A to B and to all other alternatives (C, D . . .) at the time, and reasons, $b_1 \ldots b_n$, for preferring B to A and to all other alternatives, but no reasons for preferring either of the sets of reasons, $a_1 \ldots a_n$ and $b_1 \ldots b_n$, over the other at the time—and hence no all-things-considered preference for either alternative. The competing subsets ($a_1 \ldots a_n$ and $b_1 \ldots b_n$) of an agent's total reason set represent incommensurable points of view within the agent (T62). In self-forming willing, agents are moved by such competing internal points of view (e.g., motives of duty versus self-interest, reasons favoring Hawaii or Colorado as vacation spots, etc.) and have *as yet* no all-things-considered preference between them—until choice or action makes one set prevail over the other (T27 through 29).

One way of understanding such incommensurable alternatives and points of view is to see them as combining two notions that have been at the center of free will debates for centuries—the "Leibniz thesis" that "reasons may incline without necessitating" and the medieval notion of a liberty of indifference.[6] Each set of incommensurable reasons, $a_1 \ldots a_n$ and $b_1 \ldots b_n$, inclines the agent to one alternative over all others, while no one of the sets represents an all-things-considered preference of the agent prior to choice. But the problem is that "indifference" is a misleading way of describing this lack of a prior all-things-considered preference. Indifference suggests that the agents do not care which outcome is chosen and might just as well flip a coin to decide between them. But this is not the way it is for free willings of the kinds we have described.

In cases of efforts sustaining purposes or in moral and prudential choice, agents are anything but indifferent to the outcomes. The problem in free willings is not that the agents *couldn't care less* what happens; the problem is that *they care too much*

But on Kane's θ, is it fair that the agent could flip coin and be happy w/ whatever came up?

about what happens. They are afflicted with an excess of powerful motives pulling in different directions (e.g., to drink or to save a marriage) — a state that is inadequately described as "indifference" to outcomes. They may even be trying to make one set of motives prevail over others (not because they don't *care* about the other motives, but because they don't think they *should* care about the other motives as much as they in fact *do* care); and so it is also with other self-forming willings we have considered.

One can see from this description how misleading and tendentious it is to describe free will as a liberty of indifference and to compare all examples of it to cases like Buridan's ass. It turns out that Buridan's cases are atypical, limiting cases in which the alternatives are desirable for exactly the same reasons (e.g., wanting food). Thus, Buridan's cases satisfy *one* condition of incommensurable alternatives — that the agent have no overall preference for one alternative over the other — but they satisfy this condition because the agent has the same reasons for desiring both. By contrast, Buridan's cases fail to satisfy the further important requirement of incommensurable alternatives that the reason sets, $a_1 \ldots a_n$ and $b_1 \ldots b_n$, provide reasons for the agent to favor one of the incommensurable alternatives *over the other*, as well as over all other alternatives. Thus, Jane's reasons ($a_1 \ldots a_n$) for preferring Hawaii over all other alternatives (including Europe or Timbuktu) include desires to see a friend and to eat at her favorite Polynesian restaurant, which are reasons for *also* favoring Hawaii *over Colorado* — even though she may as yet lack an all-things-considered preference for Hawaii over Colorado, or vice versa. This, of course, is because the reasons for favoring these two options are different and represent *different aspects of herself and her personality* (T29, 62, 74). By contrast, if the alternatives, as in Buridan cases, are (A) walking-to-food-left and (B) walking-to-food-(of-the-same-kind)-right, the reasons a man or an ass may have (e.g., desiring food) for favoring A over other alternatives, such as standing still (C), are not also reasons for favoring A *over* B or B over A. This is true liberty of indifference.[7]

I allow that Buridan's cases may occur in everyday life. But I think they are comparatively rare, if they ever occur at all, and their role has been overplayed in free-will debates. What is clear is that Buridan's cases are *not* paradigmatic exercises of incompatibilist free will.[8] In reality, the typical cases of free will, as T74 asserts, are cases such as those of moral or prudential choice, or Jane's choice between Hawaii and Colorado, or efforts sustaining purposes, in all of which agents are torn between conflicting internal points of view that represent *different and incommensurable visions of what they want in life* or what they want to become. In such situations agents care too much, not too little, about which alternative occurs for different and competing reasons.

3. Pluralism, Values, and Morality: Berlin

These notions of incommensurable alternatives and points of view have significant implications for the relation of free will to numerous other topics of philosophical interest in the modern era, such as values, morality, and social and political ideals and freedoms. To see this, we may begin by considering two essays by Isaiah Berlin (1969) that have had a major influence on discussions of liberty in the English-speaking world of the past half century. In the first of these essays, "Historical Inevi-

tability," based on a 1953 Comte lecture, Berlin defends a nondeterminist or libertarian conception of free will against the tendencies of modern historians, political
thinkers, and other students of the psychological and social sciences to interpret
human affairs deterministically. In the second essay, "Two Concepts of Liberty," a
1958 inaugural lecture at Oxford, Berlin defends a second theme of "value pluralism" in opposition to utopian and totalitarian political ideals. "Pluralism," he says,
"seems to me a truer and more humane ideal . . . because it does at least recognize
that human goals are many, not all of them commensurable and in perpetual rivalry
with one another" (p. 171). He further invokes this pluralist ideal against authoritarian and utopian thinkers who believe they have found the ideal scheme of values
and have the right to impose it on others. These thinkers, Berlin argues, systematically ignore the fact that the legitimate "ends of men are many, and not all of them
are compatible with one another" (p. 169).[9]

Berlin does not tell us exactly how, if at all, the two leading ideas of his separate
essays — *libertarian free will* and *value pluralism* — are related. The issue is muddied
by the fact that he relates value pluralism to "negative liberty" (noninterference by
others), which could be interpreted in compatibilist terms, while his account of libertarian free will seems to associate it with "positive liberty" (or self-mastery) (1962:
122–34). Moreover, Berlin notably holds that desires for negative and positive liberty spring from different roots and that conflicts between these two conceptions of
liberty lie behind many modern disputes between competing political ideologies.
Yet, it is also true that Berlin staunchly defends *both* libertarian free will and value
pluralism — albeit in separate essays — and seems to be assuming some connection
between them.[10] What I do not think he recognizes is just *how* closely related these
two ideas are. It is an implication of my account of free will that *value pluralism*, in
Berlin's sense — the possibility of "incommensurable" human ends and ways of life
"in perpetual rivalry with one another" — *is an idea that is essential to the intelligibility of libertarian free will.* Without it, we could not make sense of *plural* rationality
and the other plurality conditions for free will, and failing that, we could not make
sense of a free will that is incompatible with determinism.

The value pluralism in question, envisaged by Berlin and required, I think, for
free will, is not the same as value relativism. It does not imply that any end or way of
life is just as good as any other — for all persons, or for a particular person at a particular time. When Jane gets out of law school, it may be rational for her to join a
large law firm in Dallas or a small firm in Austin, but not rational (given her total
reason set at the time) to become a topless dancer in Seattle. Free will often involves
conflicts between disparate ideals that could be good in different ways for the same
person or for different persons, but not anything can count as such an ideal for anyone.

Nor does the value pluralism of the kind envisaged by Berlin and required for
free will necessarily rule out a "moral" point of view that might override all other
points of view. Indeed, the moral point of view is itself a reaction to the realization
that "the ends of human beings are many and not all of them are compatible with
one another." Morality is one way of coping with value pluralism by respecting to
the degree possible the disparate ideals and ways of life of others when they come in
conflict with one another. It counsels against domination or exploitation of some
persons or groups by others in such conflicts. But the irony is that taking such a moral

point of view does not normally end *either* value pluralism *or* free will for the individual—and this for two reasons. First, respecting other points of view when they come in conflict with one's own or others is not a denial of value pluralism, but an affirmation of it. Second, and more significantly, taking the moral point of view does not eliminate the point of view of self-interest within us, which is not easily eradicated in beings who want to be independent sources of activity in the world, that is to say, beings who want to have free will. Thus, by internalizing a moral point of view to cope with conflicts of values in the world outside of ourselves, we create *within* ourselves two disparate points of view, the moral and the self-interested, "in perpetual rivalry with one another"—*thereby providing further occasions for the exercise of free will.*

The fact that such additional inner conflicts are created by taking the moral point of view is no argument against morality—which consists, I think, precisely in taking upon ourselves some of the burden of the world's conflicts. Nor is it an argument against free will, which consists in taking ultimate responsibility for our own inner conflicts and any consequences they may have upon the outer world. The psychopath or sociopath, having no effective moral conscience and hence no moral point of view that could conflict with self-interest, is not capable of incompatibilist free choices of a *moral* kind and so lacks a kind of free will that those with moral consciences possess. Psychopaths may still have conflicts of prudential and practical kinds, so they are not beyond free will altogether (and they may also have been ultimately responsible for becoming what they now are). Yet someone may want to claim that the psychopath is better off than those who have moral consciences, being immune to the inner conflicts and consequent discomforts those with moral consciences suffer. But my argument in this book has been that the inner conflict, struggle, and effort that accompany free will are the price we pay for being ultimately responsible for our destinies. (Compare Augustine's answer in *De Libero Arbitrio Voluntatis* to Evodius's question of why God gave us free will, since it is the cause of so much struggle and suffering.) Whether free will and ultimate responsibility *are* worth the price is something no person can answer for another, as I argued in chapter 6, though one can try one's best to spell out what must be considered in answering it.

4. Free Will, Utopia, and Totalitarianism

But now let us return to Berlin's chief interest in value pluralism—its relation to social and political ideals and freedoms. In his second essay, mentioned in the preceding section, Berlin invokes the idea that "human goals are many, and not all of them are commensurable with one another" to argue against utopian, totalitarian, and authoritarian political views that would impose one set of ends or one way of life on everyone. If I am right about the connection of Berlin's value pluralism and libertarian free will, then libertarian free will should have implications concerning utopian and totalitarian views as well. The best way to see that it does is to return to a topic briefly discussed in chapter 5—B. F. Skinner's utopian society Walden Two (1962).

I argued in chapter 5 that, in Walden Two, *compatibilist* freedoms (being able to do what you will and to will what you will in Frankfurt's hierarchical sense) are maximized by minimizing *incompatibilist* free will. The citizens of Walden Two can have and do whatever they want because they have been conditioned by their behavioral engineers to want and choose only what they can have and do. Their freedom of action and even their freedom of will, in Frankfurt's sense of "wholeheartedness," is purchased at the expense of freedom to be ultimate creators of their own ends. To be sure, totalitarian and authoritarian societies of the past and present have usually employed harsher and more coercive measures than Skinner's to make people conform to their visions of the good life. But they have also often used subtle forms of propaganda and manipulation, not unlike Skinner's, to work their way. Moreover, totalitarian and authoritarian societies could use more of this "covert nonconstraining" (CNC) control in the future as knowledge of human nature and the techniques of manipulation progress (since, as Skinner notes, such control is often far more effective and efficient than coercive measures). Nor should we forget the widespread use of covert manipulation in existing democratic societies by hordes of media consultants, public relations experts, advertisers, and other modern incarnations of the ancient sophists—with the threat this poses to social and political freedoms.

In summary, the argument of chapter 5 focused on how libertarian free will is undermined by covert conditioning and control in Walden Two. But nothing was said there about *value pluralism*. What does Berlin's value pluralism have to do with the Walden Two story? The answer becomes evident when we consider a central theme of Skinner's work enunciated by Frazier, the fictional founder of Walden Two: if we had an effective science of human behavior, Frazier argues, and knew what the good life was, it would be foolish not to use our scientific knowledge to make people happy, to bring about the good life for all.[11] Perhaps it would be foolish not to use such knowledge, if we had it. But what *is* the good life, and who will decide what the good life is for human beings? This is the question immediately asked of Frazier by the philosopher Castle, one of the skeptical visitors to Walden Two (p. 158); and it is this question that takes us from issues about control of human beings discussed in chapter 5 to issues about value pluralism.

Frazier responds to Castle's question by summarizing the vision of the good life that Skinner's utopian society is designed to realize. The good life, he says, consists first in physical and psychological health, second in a minimum of unpleasant labor, third in opportunities to exercise talents and abilities, fourth in intimate and satisfying personal relations, and fifth in relaxation and rest. Frazier then adds: "And that's it, Mr. Castle—absolutely all. I can't give you a rational justification of any of it, I can't reduce it to any principle of 'the greatest good.' This is the Good Life. We know it. It's a fact, not a theory. It has an experimental justification, not a rational one" (p. 158). The experimental justification Frazier has in mind is the community of Walden Two itself, in which, as he continually reminds his visitors, people are happy and wholeheartedly committed to their way of life. As for Skinner, he has defended a similar account of the good life in other writings (e.g., 1971), in which he stresses the evolutionary values of health and survival for the design of cultures and sees the other values mentioned by Frazier as contributing to health and survival.

This response by Frazier temporarily silences poor Castle, because few persons would deny the importance of the five values Frazier lists for a happy life. But, for all that, Frazier has not defined "the good life" for his visitors. Nor has he adequately answered Castle's question about who will decide what the good life is. The reason is that the five values described by Frazier do not define any *particular* life at all. They are both too general and incomplete. Walden Two might satisfy these values, but they might in principle be satisfied by an indefinite number of other ways of life or cultural arrangements—which might compete with and conflict with one another if they came in contact.

This is where Berlin's value pluralism comes into the picture. If there are alternative realizations of the good life as envisaged by Frazier, someone might say, "I can think of other ways of life besides Walden Two in which these general values could be realized, some of which suit my temperament, interests, and abilities better. And I would like to decide for myself which of these ways to follow." Suppose some imaginative and creative young people in Walden Two took this attitude. Let us say they had done a lot of reading in the Walden Two library (there is no censorship in Walden Two) and are intrigued by other human possibilities. Some want to found communities of their own based on different principles; others want to climb mountains, or found businesses; still others may want to follow the eightfold way or some other religious path to enlightenment or salvation; and so on.

The Walden Two elders might feel their behavioral techniques had gone awry in the case of these young people, but what could the elders say to dissuade their young rebels from leaving? Could they claim to have shown that Walden Two is not just *a* good life, but *the* good life? These bright young people would surely ask, "How do you know that? Have you experimented with all other ways of life we have read about, or others not yet invented that we want to try out, so that you can say for sure they will not make us happy or have not made other people happy? And how do you know that what may make you happy will make us happy? You yourselves have taught us that justifications of the good life are 'experimental.' They cannot be established on rational or a priori grounds, as traditional philosophers believed. But doesn't that imply that you cannot show that Walden Two is the one and only good life by merely showing that it is *a* good life? And if this is so, then we want to do for our own lives what Frazier did for Walden Two—to be the designers of those lives and of our own ends or purposes. Perhaps we shall fail. But then again, perhaps we shall succeed in finding, or creating, something worthwhile of our own, as Frazier did. In any case, we want to try."

The Walden Two elders may decide to go back to the drawing board at this point. They cannot dissuade these young people from rejecting their way of life *on their own* (experimental) *principles* concerning values. The safer course would be to ensure instead that other young people do not get similar ideas in the future. But doing that means either carefully censoring what young people read and study in Walden Two or behaviorally engineering them so that they lack the curiosity and creativity characteristic of the young that might lead them to be intrigued by alternative ways of life. Only by one of these methods, or by a combination of them, can the elders ensure that their young people will "wholeheartedly" follow the life designed for them and will not desire to try some other for themselves. But, of course, it is by the very same methods, especially the covert control, that the creators of Walden Two have taken away the *libertarian free will* of its residents in the first place. When such methods succeed, there is no more ambivalence about ways of life in the citizens, but only wholeheartedness; and there is no more plural rationality about ways of life because the reason sets of people have been so designed that only one way of life appears rational to them.

5. Social and Political Freedoms

Here we have arrived at the connection between value pluralism and libertarian free will in the social and political spheres. Libertarian free will is undermined (as in Walden Two) by creating an inner environment in the minds of agents that has no room for the recognition that the legitimate "ends of human beings are many, and not all of them are commensurable or compatible with one another"—an inner world that eliminates ambivalence about ends, conflicting internal points of view, and, with them, plural rationality and motivation. To create such a restricted inner environment, however, *in normally curious and creative human beings*, one must create a social and political order with sufficient censorship and covert noncoercive control or manipulation to eliminate interest in, and access to information about, alternative plans of action and ways of life. Such a social or political order would then be utopian and totalitarian, and most likely also authoritarian, in the sense that it would impose one set of ends or one way of life on everyone and would do so in a most sinister manner—by controlling the inner life of thought, conscience, and imagination of its citizens.

By contrast, a social and political order hospitable to free will in all its citizens would allow for a plurality of ends and would leave it to individuals to make ultimate choices among those ends. Power in such a social and political order would flow upward from individual decision makers, who would be *ultimately responsible* for their decisions and actions (and who would highly value this ultimate responsibility), rather than flowing downward from authorities who would decide on the ultimate ends worth pursuing for everyone. Such a social order would, as a consequence, tend to favor democratic political institutions, as well as social and political conditions that protected the inner life of thought and conscience of those in whom ultimate responsibility was vested—especially against covert manipulation by other groups or authorities. One would therefore expect such an order to place a high premium on freedoms of speech and expression, of the press and of religion, and on education of all citizens—in other words, on all those conditions that would (i) enhance rather than restrict the life of thought and imagination required to deal with incommensurable alternatives and would (ii) protect against manipulation and control of the processes of decision-making of some individuals by others. In sum, societies of the kind that would be hospitable to free will in all their citizens (rather than settling for wholeheartedness at any cost) would look very much like modern free democratic societies that allow for a plurality of ends and ways of life and, at least in principle, leave it to individuals to make ultimate choices among these ends and ways of life.

But this is not the whole story about a social and political order that would be hospitable to free will in all its citizens. On my account of free will, value pluralism is essential to such an order, but it is not enough. To have free will, there must be a plurality of incommensurable goals to which individuals can be attracted. But a further feature of free will on my account of it (a feature that may at first appear surprising and in conflict with incommensurability) is that individuals having free will must also *believe* that some of the goals to which they are attracted are *more worthy of being pursued* than others. This is evident in all SFWs. Moral and prudential agents believe their moral or prudential principles ought to override self-interest and present satisfaction, respectively, even though they are strongly attracted to both. If they did not believe this, as I said, *there would be no* moral or prudential conflicts (T28); the businesswoman would go on to her meeting and the engineer would drink without qualms. Agents sustaining purposes similarly believe at the time that their purposes are more worthy of pursuit than not, whether the purposes are playing in tune, completing a loathsome task, performing a heroic act, attending to the image of a dying father, or killing a beloved horse—though there is also resistance in their wills to these purposes.

This pattern holds even in cases of practical deliberation and choice that seem to involve a plurality of incommensurable ends, pure and simple—vacationing in Hawaii or Colorado, joining a law firm in Dallas or one in Austin, being a teacher or a lawyer, and so on. The pattern holds because we saw that indeterminism enters into practical deliberation by virtue of various efforts of will (T70, T75) through which practical deliberation is advanced and guided by the deliberating agent—efforts aimed at keeping one's mind open to new alternatives, at not making hasty decisions, at seeking further relevant information, at avoiding self-deception and rationalization, and so forth—all in the interest of making the most prudent, wise, and informed decisions. If these goals were not thought to be worthy of being pursued by the agent, then little effort would go into deliberation and poor decisions would be more likely to result (or good decisions would be more matters of luck than the agent's doing).

Thus, there is a curious duality about free will—one of many features that make it appear paradoxical to many persons. To have free will, individuals must be attracted to a plurality of incommensurable goals. But they must also believe that some of the goals to which they are attracted are more worthy of being pursued than others. How can these two apparently conflicting requirements coexist? It is possible because the belief (a_i) that one goal, A, is more worthy of being pursued than others is *from a particular point of view* $(a_1 \ldots a_n)$ within the agent (e.g., the moral or prudential point of view) which is not the only point of view capable of motivating the agent at a given time (T28, T61 through 62).

Return now to the issue of a social or political order that would be hospitable to libertarian free will in all its citizens. We saw earlier that such an order would allow for a plurality of ends and would leave it to individuals to make ultimate choices among those ends. But we have now seen that persons with free will must also believe some ends are more worthy of pursuit than others, despite the fact that pursuing those ends requires effort and struggle. A society of wantons who made no efforts to control their whims would not be hospitable to free will, even if such a society liberally provided a plurality of ends to pursue. Nor could a society, if it was to continue to be hospitable to free will in all its citizens, be completely indifferent to the *kinds* of ends pursued. A society of psychopaths or ruthless egoists would be no better for this purpose than a society of wantons. In either case, the free will of all would be endangered by the free actions of some.

In other words, of special importance to a society hospitable to free will (in addition to the freedoms of thought and conscience, speech and expression, mentioned earlier) would be the cultivation of moral motives curbing self-interest when self-interest comes into conflict with the interests of others. Such motives curbing self-interest—the very ones necessary for exercises of free will of a *moral* kind—are just the ones required for the maintenance of a political order that would be hospitable to the exercise of free will of *all* other kinds (prudential and practical as well) in all its citizens. But at the same time, if free will was to be retained, the citizens could not be programmed, as in Walden Two, always to act in the right or prescribed way—so they were never tempted by self-interest to do otherwise. The maintenance of the moral order in society would be ultimately "up to" its citizens, and not up to their behavioral engineers.

6. Free Will and the Moral Law: Kant

The argument of the preceding section does not imply that one can *derive* a moral code curbing self-interest from a belief in the importance of libertarian free will for individuals alone. Kant made a profound, but nonetheless grievous, mistake in arguing that the very exercise of libertarian free will required a commitment to a moral law demanding respect for the free will or autonomy of all other persons.[12] There are serious deficiencies in any such direct derivation of morality. It is too great a leap from valuing free will or autonomy for oneself (being an independent source of activity in the world) to valuing it for all other creatures. To make that leap may be a good and noble act, but it is too easy to suppose that one can rationally prove it is the right thing to do from incontestable premises.

To provide such a proof—that is, to show, in one way or another, that immorality is *irrational* and that being moral is the only rational thing to do—has always been the dream of rationalist moralities such as Kant's. The egoist would then not only be selfish, but logically muddled or guilty of some conceptual error or factual oversight. As attractive as this rationalist line has been to philosophers, I think it is not only doomed to failure, but it diminishes the significance of the moral life—as Kierkegaard argued against Kant—because, among other things, it turns morality into a matter of calculation rather than commitment.[13] But more important for our purposes, rational proof in morality would also change the dynamics of moral free will of the kind Kant was anxious to defend, turning it into an extension of self-interested, or prudential, choice. Self-interested reason would always come down on the side of morality, never against it; and morality and self-interest would not appear as incommensurable alternatives to each other. By contrast, a distinctively *moral* free will, as I see it, requires that, while there are good reasons to be moral, they are not absolutely compelling reasons, because self-interest is at times irreducibly incompatible with morality, and yet self-interest is also rational *in its own way*.[14]

Paradoxically, Kant's attempt to forge too direct a logical link between belief in the moral law and belief in (libertarian) free will altered the dynamics of the moral freedom he so valued and caused problems for both his accounts of morality and of free will. By attributing moral choice to reason alone, Kant left immoral choice to be motivated by desire alone; and then, since desires were in the phenomenal realm, on his view, and therefore determined, he had to contend with the consequence that immoral choices were always determined by the agent's desires—a result that troubled

Kant into his latest works.[15] The answer to this enigma, I think, must come from recognizing that free will has to be analyzed in a manner that is more complicated than pure reason versus pure desire. It involves reason-*plus*-desires on one side versus reason-*plus*-desires (of different kinds) on the other side. You don't get moral action merely from the belief that something ought to be done, as Aristotle noted, without also having the desire to do what you think ought to be done, and this holds for the Kantian moral law as well (as Sidgwick, Ross, and other critics of Kant argued).[16] Reason may tell you that something is your duty, but you will not do it unless you also desire to do your duty.[17]

For all that, I think there *is* a connection between the moral law in Kant's sense and libertarian free will, but it is less direct than Kant believed. The argument for such a connection, suggested in the previous section, concerns a *society* or political order that would be hospitable to free will in *all* its citizens—a society that, in contrast to Walden Two, would place a high value on the cultivation of libertarian free will rather than sacrificing it to maximize other (compatibilist) freedoms. A society valuing free will in this way would not devalue compatibilist freedoms (from constraint, coercion, and oppression) because, as argued in chapter 6, the desire to be an independent source of activity in the world is the desire to make some impact *upon* the world through one's will—a desire that would be thwarted if free willings could never be expressed in other free actions, including overt actions. But a society hospitable to free will would also emphasize that freedom of action for which agents are ultimately responsible is "from the freedom of the will," and it would regard the minimizing of free will to maximize compatibilist freedoms (as in Walden Two) as a case of throwing the baby out with the bathwater.

Both this hypothetical free willist society and Walden Two would need a moral code to hold them together. In fact, Walden Two had a very explicit moral code, like all totalitarian societies. But the desire to follow the Walden Two code was conditioned into everyone so that no one ever wanted to disobey it. By contrast, the moral code of our hypothetical free willist society would have to be different. First of all, as mentioned earlier, the citizens cannot be so conditioned that the moral option is all they are ever tempted to choose, if free will is to survive. They cannot be turned into moral robots, but must remain independent sources of activity in the world whose self-interested pursuits amid a plurality of ends may come in conflict with the pursuits of others. But, in addition, if free will is to survive in all citizens, they must respect each other as independent sources of activity in the world having ultimate responsibility for their own behavior. In other words, using Kant's own language, they must treat each other as "ends in themselves rather than as mere means to one's own ends" because they are valued as ultimate originators of their own ends.[18] In sum, the moral code of such a society that would be hospitable to libertarian free will in all its citizens would take a form very much like one of Kant's best known versions of his Categorical Imperative.

But this moral imperative in the present case is not derived in Kant's manner as a precondition for the exercise of free will generally, nor is it directly derived from the value of libertarian free will or autonomy *to the individual*. Rather, the argument is that this is the kind of moral principle one would get, *if* one wanted a society that placed the highest possible value on *each citizen's* having ultimate responsibility for his or her own life. One would get (as the ideal) something like a Kantian Kingdom of Ends rather than a Walden Two, a Brave New World, or some other such totalitarian or utopian scheme.[19] If this is correct, then Kant was right after all in thinking there was some sort of connection between free will and the moral law—as he understood both—though not a connection exactly of the kind he envisaged.

7. Value Experiments: Pragmatists

Another feature of free will as described in this book with wide-ranging implications also emerges from the tale of the young people of Walden Two. Not only is free will essentially value pluralistic, as argued above, it is essentially *value experimental* as well. Recognizing that there was no one version of the good life, the young people of Walden Two wanted to do for their own lives what Frazier had done for Walden Two—be the ultimate designers of their own ends or purposes. Though admitting the possibility of failure, they nonetheless wanted to find or create something worthwhile on their own, as Frazier had done—much like the child learning to walk in chapter 6 who pushes the parent aside and says, in effect, "Unhand me. I want to do this on my *own*."

In T43, I said that every self-forming willing is "the initiation of a value experiment whose justification lies in the future and is not fully explained by the past." The chosen path may turn out well or poorly, but the free willer is ready to take responsibility for it one way or the other. This is of the essence of free will, as I understand it. Every undetermined free willing is a probe into the future, whose rightness or wrongness cannot be demonstrated by *past* reasons or motives alone (i.e., by what we already know) but only by what we already know *and* what we shall *learn* in the future *by choosing*. To exercise free will is to take a risk, as in any experiment in which the result is not foreknown; and we must be willing to take the risk if we want to explore new possibilities and be ultimate creators of our own ends or purposes. The young people of Walden Two must leave the secure womb of their conditioning if they are to become self-determining beings.

It is often said, or assumed, that one can perform experiments about matters of fact but not about values. But this is utter nonsense. We experiment with values all the time. Any plan of action or way of life is a value experiment whose results can be tested against the prior expectations, preferences, and ideals of the person (or persons) undertaking it. We initiate such experiments by making choices. A career is a value experiment, as is a marriage, a vacation, a party, a date, a research project, a utopian community (like Walden Two), an economic policy, a political theory, and so on. And heaven knows, each of these undertakings can *fail* in various ways, producing much misery. Karl Popper is well known for emphasizing that genuine scientific experiments are those that can fail to support the hypothesis or conjecture they are testing, as well as support it (this is his well-known "criterion of falsifiability").[20] By this standard, value experiments can also be genuine insofar as they can fail to support the plan of action or way of life they are testing as well as support it.

The ultimate test for *value* experiments is happiness, but happiness broadly construed, so that what constitutes happiness (as a specific activity or way of life for individuals) is itself a contestable matter and may differ for different people. Thus, in the exercise of free will, persons take ultimate responsibility not only for choosing the means to attain happiness, but also for choosing the ends that define happiness for themselves. Such a consequence is built into the very definition of free will as the creation or origination of ends. But it implies something of great significance: the value experimentation involved in the exercise of free will is radical in the sense that it is not merely about how one attains happiness, but also about *what happiness is.* One might even say that the experimentation of free will is "philosophical," in accordance with the Socratic dictum that "the unexamined life is not worth living."

But, above all, the value experimental nature of free will means that the rightness or wrongness of free choices cannot be known with certainty in advance, that is, a priori. If one had such certainty, there would be no incommensurability and plural rationality prior to self-forming choice. What can be established prior to self-forming willings is that a plan of action or way of life is *worth trying* as a value experiment (that, indeed, is the goal of deliberation), but not that it is the right choice with certainty in advance—not if we are engaged in *ultimate* self-formation, that is. With certainty, there would be no risk of failure, such as we expect in genuine experiments, and such risk is of the essence of self-formation for which we take ultimate responsibility.

If the value experimental nature of free will is therefore philosophical, the philosophizing involves some living and cannot be a matter of armchair speculation alone. Speculation is necessarily involved in the form of deliberation about means and ends, but in value experimentation there is always the additional element of acting, with risk of failure. On these points, the American pragmatists Charles Peirce, William James, and John Dewey had the right idea. Indeed, their emphasis on the ineliminable experimental nature of knowledge (of fact in science) and of value (through choice and experiments in living) is to my mind the most important contribution of classical American pragmatism to modern philosophy.[21] It is, in any case, a contribution of singular importance for understanding free will, as I have argued.[22]

Free will thus presupposes an anti-a priori, anti-rationalistic approach to choices concerning ultimate ends and values—a kind of "value empiricism," as I have elsewhere called it, as opposed to value rationalism. The value empiricist view does not imply that there are no right and wrong choices about ends and values, or that no way of life is more worthy of pursuit than any other. It does not imply a value relativism, as indicated earlier, such as some latter-day pragmatists have espoused. Rather, it is a view about how we come to know what ends are worth pursuing and what values are worth caring about. Value empiricism says that we address ultimate questions of this kind through freely chosen experiments in living and cannot settle them by a priori reasoning from certain or necessary premises that no rational person could deny. This holds also for moral choice, as we found in the previous section; and it holds even for the ultimate value *of free will itself*, as we saw in chapter 6. The value experimentation takes place not only in living, but also by way of thought experimentation "in the mind"—that is, practical reasoning—through which (to the extent that we are wise) we eliminate ends and ways of life that are not worth pursuing before undertaking them in reality (T67).

8. On Liberty and Happiness: Mill

John Stuart Mill is another philosopher—quite different in orientation from the American pragmatists—who also emphasized value experiments in his account of freedom (Mill called them "experiments in living"). Much has been written about the underlying principles of Mill's classic essay *On Liberty* (1947) concerning whether or not the principles of that influential work stem from his utilitarianism, as Mill suggested, or from other roots. My own view is that the basic themes of *On Liberty* derive not from Mill's utilitarianism, but from Mill's commitment to a view that I described in the previous section as value empiricism. Value empiricism is the view that we must address questions about values and ultimate ends through freely chosen experiments in living and cannot settle these questions by a priori reasoning from certain or necessary premises that no rational person could deny. Such a value empiricist view is consistent with Mill's empiricism generally. It is, indeed, a plausible extension of empiricism to the domain of values, and I suggest that *On Liberty* is more a reflection of Mill's value empiricism than of his utilitarianism.

If this suggestion is correct, it brings with it a supreme irony. For the value empiricism that would thus lie behind the arguments of *On Liberty* is the very view that, according to the preceding section, is required by a libertarian free will—the kind of freedom that Mill, as a compatibilist, rejects. There is no logical inconsistency here for Mill because libertarian free will entails value empiricism, but is not entailed by value empiricism. Yet Mill's rejection of libertarian free will (on grounds that are independent of, and not discussed in, *On Liberty*) blinded him, I think, to some of the real roots of the arguments in his justly admired essay. Consider how many of the things Mill says or defends in *On Liberty* can be seen to follow from the idea that the aim of society is to respect and promote the ultimate responsibility of individuals to be creators and originators of their own ends or purposes rather than to have those ends imposed upon them by other individuals, by social conditioning, or by governments. From this idea flow many of the characteristic themes of *On Liberty*: "the individual is not accountable to society for his actions insofar as these concern the interests of no person but himself" (p. 115); "the only reason for which power can be rightfully exercised over any member of a civilised community against his will is to prevent harm to others. His own good, either physical or moral, is not sufficient warrant. He cannot rightfully be compelled to do or to forbear . . . because in the opinion of others, to do so would be wise or even right" (p. 15).

It is no accident that the society described in previous sections of this chapter that would be hospitable to libertarian free will in all its citizens (a society emphasizing freedom of speech, expression, pursuits, etc.) looks very much like a society conforming to the vision of *On Liberty*. The connecting principles that account for this resemblance, I believe, are (1) *value pluralism*, in Berlin's sense; (2) *value empiricism*, in the sense of the previous section; and (3) *fallibilism* in the pursuit of correct values and ends (which follows from [2]). All three of these themes, I am suggesting, play a fundamental role in *On Liberty*. But, more important for our purposes, all three of them are *entailed by libertarian free will* for values that are the subjects of self-forming willings. I am in agreement, therefore, with Berlin's assertion that

At the centre of Mill's thought and feeling [in *On Liberty*] lies, not his utilitarianism, nor the concern about enlightenment, nor about dividing the private from the public domain—for [Mill] himself at times concedes that the State may invade the private domain in order to promote education, hygiene or social security or justice—but his passionate belief that men are made human by their capacity for choice—choice of evil and good equally. Fallibility, or the right to err as a corollary of the capacity for self-improvement; distrust of symmetry and finality as enemies of freedom—these are the principles which Mill never abandons. . . . because he believes . . . there are no final truths not corrigible by experience, at any rate in what is now called the ideological sphere—that of value judgments and of general outlook and attitude to life. (pp. 190, 192)

It goes without saying that the capacity for choice "of good *or* evil equally" may or may not lead to personal happiness or even to the greatest good of the greatest number. When the young rebels of Walden Two make their case for leaving, they may concede that their chances of failure and misery may be greater if they strike out on their own, given the risks of value experimenting, than if they stayed in the womb of Walden Two. But what these young people are saying is that the exercise of the capacity to design their own lives and create their own ends is part of their conception of happiness, even if that involves the risk of failing to satisfy many of their other desires. The choice to leave ought therefore to be ultimately theirs alone to make, so long as it does not harm others. Can anyone doubt that the author of *On Liberty* would have agreed with them?

What, then, would Mill say if the preponderance of empirical evidence were to indicate that a society with as much behavioral engineering as Walden Two should satisfy a greater number of desires of a greater number of people than a liberal society of the kind envisaged in *On Liberty*? If Mill would say that we should then go with the Walden Two society on utilitarian grounds, then the reading of *On Liberty* being suggested here (which also seems to be Berlin's reading) is surely wrong. But, as Robert Young has persuasively argued (1982: 43), it is difficult to imagine the author of *On Liberty* responding in that way. For him to do so would be like announcing to us after we had just finished reading *On Liberty* that the society that best realized the principles of *this* book *might* turn out to be Walden Two! Even if the probability of this being the case were low, the mere possibility of it makes a mockery of Mill's essay and everything it stands for.

But if I am wrong about this, we could nonetheless opt in political philosophy for a substitute version of *On Liberty* that would leave no doubt about the fact that (1) value pluralism, (2) value empiricism, and (3) fallibilism, rather than utilitarianism, are the guiding principles of the work. My guess is that there would be very few changes in Mill's original essay if we made this revision—either in his arguments or in his prescriptions about the extent of individual freedoms. But the extent of the changes that would result is less important than the fact that this substitute version of *On Liberty* would be the one that I think should be favored by believers in libertarian free will. For libertarian free will entails (1) through (3), which would take the place of utilitarianism as the guiding principles of this revised version of *On Liberty*; and, in the light of (1) through (3), I think libertarian free will provides a more coherent rationale for the kinds of free societies prescribed in On Liberty (namely, the goal of promoting the ultimate responsibility of all citizens for the design and pursuit of their own ends or purposes) than Mill himself provides.

9. Modernity and Irony

These remarks about On Liberty illustrate an important general theme concerning free will to which our attention should be drawn in this concluding chapter. While the traditional libertarian conception of free will has been increasingly under attack in the modern era since the seventeenth century, as I have often noted in this work, it is ironic that this same traditional conception of free will should be intimately related to many things that the modern era (the era of "modernity" so-called) has come to regard as supremely important—value pluralism; value empiricism; fallibilism; suspicion of a priori certainties and authoritarianism in all matters, but especially in matters of value; individual autonomy (being an independent source of activity in the world); individual dignity or worth; freedoms of speech, expression, and conscience; rights to life, liberty, and the pursuit of happiness (being treated as an end in oneself because one is an ultimate originator of one's own ends); individual creativity, novelty, and self-creation; abhorrence of totalitarianism and governmental paternalism; and so on. (It was Kant, the libertarian on free will, not Mill, who said, "Paternalism is the greatest despotism imaginable."[23]) It is true that the modern era has often tried to make sense of such values as these or to ground them without reference to libertarian free will. But it is not so often mentioned that these very modern values are just those one would promote if one believed in the significance of libertarian free will, that is, if one believed that persons are most fully human and have greatest worth when they are ultimately responsible for their own destinies.

This is one of the many ironies of the modern history of debates about free will: libertarian free will has been under attack in the modern era as a premodern and outdated conception, while the values associated with libertarian free will have become the defining values of post-Enlightenment modernity. Why has this happened? The answer is that many moderns have come to believe that a traditional incompatibilist free will is unintelligible and cannot be reconciled with modern science. Here we encounter another, equally relevant characteristic of modernity—the fact that in the modern era, science has gradually come to replace religion as the last court of appeal on matters of philosophical import. "Libertarian free will," so the modernist argument goes, "cannot be fitted to the scientific picture of the world, so it must be abandoned. Such a free will is obscure and mysterious, better suited (like ghosts and witches) to premodern, religious worldviews. (As Hobbes said of libertarian views, like Bramhall's, they 'hang together like a sick man's dream.') If it should turn out that this outdated and obscure conception of free will is related to many things that have come to be the values of post-Enlightenment modernity, then this must be a coincidence, or if it is not a coincidence, it is no longer anything we moderns can afford to be concerned about."

It should be evident from these remarks why anyone who would defend libertarian freedom in the modern age must pay more attention to the Intelligibility and Existence questions (the "descent problem"), as I have done in this book, and make greater efforts to show how an incompatibilist free will can have a place in the scientific picture of the world. I think those who continue to defend libertarian free will by appealing to obcure or mysterious forms of agency or causation (in violation of the Free Agency Principle of chapter 7) are doing a disservice to their cause by perpetuating the conviction that this kind of freedom has significance only for a premodern worldview, but not for the modern one—a conviction that leads to another conviction that is also prevalent in the modern age, namely that the free will issue is a dead issue.

Another kind of disservice is done by continuing to appeal to mysterious forms of agency to account for free will. Appeals to noumenal selves, transempirical power centers, and the like may leave the impression that exercises of free will are entirely above and beyond the influences of natural causes and conditioning. This can easily lead one to think in turn that the abused child or ghetto dweller has as much free will and ultimate responsibility for what he or she does as one who lives in more advantaged circumstances. For if each has free will and if free will is a mysterious power to rise above one's circumstances, whatever they may be, then each is responsible to the same degree, no matter what the past circumstances. The theory of this book implies no such consequence. Precisely because that theory recognizes the embeddedness of free will in the natural order, it recognizes that free will and ultimate responsibility are matters of degree, and our possession of them can be very much infuenced by circumstances. That is why, if one believes in the value of free will and ultimate responsibility, it is important to cultivate a social order in which they can flourish, rather than one like Walden Two, or some totalitarian regime, in which they cannot.

The fact that free will and ultimate responsibility are matters of degree is also why it is the case that, if we should learn, say, of the young rapist of chapter 6 that his childhood was one of horrendous abuse and mistreatment, our resentment, indignation, and other negative reactive attitudes would tend to change. We tend to think, as Nicholas Nathan puts it, that his guilt and (ultimate) responsibility are lessened. We may not conclude he has no responsibility whatever for what he has done. But that will depend, as I argued, on whether we think there is anything the young man *could have voluntarily done* in the past despite his unfortunate circumstances *to make himself different than he was*. In other words, we invoke UR. Since this example of the young rapist was introduced specifically to support UR, and hence an incompatibilist interpretation of responsibility and the reactive actitudes, it would be contradictory to conclude that incompatibilist free will and ultimate responsibility cannot be matters of degree or cannot be lessened by circumstances.

Thus, libertarians go wrong, I think, when they make free will an all-or-nothing affair, or suppose that exercises of free will are transcendent interventions into the natural order not limited by the influences of natural circumstances. Bernard Williams (1985) notes that the traditional conception of free will, about which he is skeptical, was supposed to be an all-or-nothing affair of this sort, and Rogers Albritton (1985), who has more sympathy for the traditional view, has nonetheless noted that the supposed logic of the libertarian freedom seems to have forced many libertarians, from Descartes to Sartre, to the conclusion that we must enjoy a perfect freedom of will unlimited by circumstances. Gary Watson comments that "this breathtaking opinion is widespread among defenders of free will, even though it is hard to understand (as Albritton himself emphasizes) how a real power in the world can be unlimited" (1987: 163–4). I think that once we try to make sense of what free will might be as a "real power" in the world, as I have tried to do in this work, we see how it is limited by circumstances, yet need not be completely limited.

Such all-or-nothing views of free will also tend to lead in some thinkers to harsh retributive theories of punishment that recognize few circumstances mitigating guilt or responsibility. Libertarians are often accused of holding such unyielding retributive views as a consequence of their accounts of free will; and some libertarians, like Kant, may have done so. But if free will is embedded in the natural order, as in the theory of this book, libertarians can avail themselves of the same everyday intuitions for excusing or mitigating guilt and moral responsibility (childhood abuse, etc.) as any compatibilists or hard determinists would recognize. Where libertarians might differ (especially from hard determinists) is in being reluctant to jump too hastily to conclusions that persons in disadvantaged circumstances, whose responsibility is thereby diminished, lack any ultimate responsibility for their actions at all (though this might have to be admitted in some cases).

What is needed for a mature libertarianism in the modern age is a recognition of the many ways in which circumstances of birth and upbringing can limit free will and responsibility (for this is one of the prevailing themes of modernity) without yielding to the temptation to think that we are all always helpless victims of circumstances. Such recognition would provide a middle way between political extremes as well. It would mean resisting the debilitating assumption that we are all always victims of circumstances and never have ultimate responsibility for what we do or are. But it would also mean rejecting the harsh political judgment that the disadvantaged of society are wholly responsible for their disadvantaged condition because they retain their free will undiminished and are therefore undeserving of government or societal support or assistance. While a political order hospitable to libertarian free will would be a free society of the Millian sort, it would not necessarily be unrestrictedly "libertarian" in the political sense of that term, if that meant abdicating all governmental efforts of social assistance. Yet governmental assistance in a political order hospitable to free will would also be judged by particular standard—namely, the extent to which it empowered recipients to be self-determining and ultimately responsible citizens rather than merely reducing them to dependence. If such self-determination and the dignity usually associated with it are generally what the disadvantaged (like other human beings) want anyway, that is only further evidence for the significance of free will. Humans do not live by bread alone.

Hans Blumenberg, author of *The Legitimacy of the Modern Age* (1983), has said that the idea that we might attain complete autonomy or perfect freedom is the "final myth" of modernity. The quest for autonomy is integral to the modern age, Blumenberg argues, but complete autonomy is an impossible ideal. If we seek an end to dependency and determination from without, he says, we must accept an "eliminable contingency within" ourselves.[24] I think this is profoundly correct. If we want to be independent sources of activity in the world, we must accept ambivalence, uncertainty, struggle, and conflict within ourselves—all of which are connected to the indeterminacy that is required for free will. The ambivalence, uncertainty, and risk are in turn related to competing images of the good that must inevitably confront those who would be ultimate creators of their own ends.

But, as I argued, while those who have free will must confront competing images of the good, they must also believe that some of the competing ends are more worthy of pursuit than others. In self-forming willings, there are perceived better or higher goals to which agents aspire and worse or lower ones to which they remain attracted. We might say that free willers are always trying to be better than they are by their own lights. This questing or striving for worthy ends is the goal of free will — and, indeed, the goal of life itself, if we are to believe the great myths of humankind. Without this questing, life would become, in the words of Herman Melville in *Moby Dick*, "an ice palace made out of frozen sighs."[25]

Notes

Chapter 1

1. Wolf, 1990: vii; Matson, 1987, vol. 1: 158.

2. See Kane, 1985, 1988a, 1988b, 1989, 1991,1994, 1995a, 1995b. Those familiar with my *Free Will and Values* (FWV) (1985), now out of print, may want to know how the present volume relates to it. The general free willist or incompatibilist view defended is the same in both volumes but, beyond that, the differences are great. Three years ago, when FWV went out of print, I set out to write a new, updated edition of it for republication, but found that my views had evolved so much in the intervening period that I was writing an entirely new work that has (in its present form) 85 to 90 percent new material not contained in FWV. (About 10 percent of the new material is from intervening articles cited in the bibliography.) Thus, chapters 3, 4, 5, 10, 11, and much of 6 and 9 contain largely new material and often deal with topics I have not previously discussed elsewhere in print. Even in chapters such as 7 and 8, and portions of others in which I cover topics also discussed in FWV, the substance of my view has changed in significant ways (as readers of FWV will be able to verify). For example, in chapter 7, the discussion of the plurality conditions and of the Free Agency Principle are new to this work, and in chapter 8, all but four or five of the thirty-six theses contain substantial new additions to my view. Finally, the introductory chapters, 1 and 2, have been revised to make them more user-friendly introductions to the history of debates about free will and the will respectively.

3. Weatherford makes this point (1991: 12).

4. For an interesting account of the origins of the free will issue in ancient thought, see, Huby, 1967; on the ancient origins of the concept of the will, see Irwin, 1992, and on the history of ideas about the will, Bourke, 1964.

5. Frankfurt, 1971; McCann, 1974; Kenny, 1976; Davis, 1979; O'Shaughnessy, 1980.

6. E.g., Schlick, 1966.

7. E.g., Grünbaum, 1971, P. Strawson, 1962, R. Rorty, 1979.

8. Wilbur, 1979: 163.

9. See Shapiro, 1993, on Herodotus.

10. See Bailey, 1964: 115–21; Sorabji, 1980: 60–66; White, 1985: ch. 4.

11. On the Epicurean doctrine and pertinent quotes from Epicurus, see Bailey, 1964: 477.

12. See Plato's *Protagoras* (Plato, 1937, vol. 1).

13. Notable exceptions to this claim include Watson, 1977, and Mele, 1995.

14. See, e.g., Hospers, 1958.

15. See Rauf, 1970: 289 ff.

16. Milton, 1955: prologue.

17. Erasmus-Luther, 1961; Edwards, 1969; Augustine, 1964. Two excellent recent works on traditional and modern theological controversies about divine foreknowledge and human freedom are Hasker, 1989, and Zagzebski, 1991. Both have comprehensive references to traditional and contemporary writings on these controversies.

18. Smart, 1967, vol. 4: 325–6.

19. Prabhavananda et al., 1956: 64.

20. Tobias, 1991: 73.

21. Ibid., 326. In Buddhist terms, right effort follows upon right belief (two stages of the Buddhist eight-fold way), and fatalistic beliefs could undermine right effort.

22. For penetrating discussion of ancient debates on logical determinism, see White, 1985.

23. A recent, excellent treatment of this argument and related issues of fatalism and logical determinism (including comprehensive references to earlier work) is Mark Bernstein, 1992.

24. The "must" here expresses what Alvin Plantinga (1974) has called "necessity in the broadly logical sense," which can be represented logically by the standard system of modal logic S5.

25. Cf. Suppes, 1984; Dupré, 1993; Lucas, 1993; McCall, 1994; Penrose, 1994; Compton, 1935; Fine, 1971; Hobbs, 1991; Popper, 1972; Salmon, 1984; Stapp, 1993; and F. A. Wolf, 1984, among many others.

26. See Honderich, 1988; Weatherford, 1991; Dennett, 1984; Berofsky, 1971; Churchland, P. S., 1986; Churchland, P. M., 1988; Lycan, 1987; Calvin, 1990; Double, 1991; Smilansky, 1994; Skinner, 1971; Flanagan, 1992; Waller, 1990; Hospers, 1958.

27. Another sophisticated defender of what is called "hard determinism" in recent philosophy is Pereboom, 1995. Hard determinism is the view that determinism is true and is incompatible with free will, so that free will does not exist. For other perceptive recent articles on hard determinism, see Smilansky, 1993, 1994.

28. E.g., Strawson, G., 1986; Dennett, 1984; Berofsky, 1987; Waller, 1990; Double, 1991; Klein, 1990; Broad, 1966; S. Wolf, 1990.

29. Two influential twentieth-century articles that mirror this line of argument are Broad, 1962, and Watson, 1987.

30. These and other traditional libertarian strategems are critically discussed in chapter 7.

31. Many contemporary philosophers share Strawson's skepticism about whether compatibilist accounts of freedom capture all of our important intuitions about freedom and responsibility while also remaining skeptical about whether incompatibilist theories can be made intelligible: e.g., Nagel, 1986; Klein, 1990; Nathan, 1992; Honderich, 1988; Smilansky, 1994; and Pereboom, 1995, among many others. These philosophers differ from Strawson, however, in various ways. Nagel and Nathan seem less willing than Strawson to close the case against the intelligibility of libertarian freedom. Honderich and Pereboom are hard determinists, arguing that even if you could make sense of incompatibilist freedom (which they doubt), it would not exist because determinism is true. Smilansky calls himself a "dualist" on the Compatibility Question, seeing some truth in hard determinism and some truth in compatibilism. (For the differences between Strawson and Honderich, see Strawson, 1989.)

32. For interesting recent discussion of the varied meanings of *freedom* (and *responsibility*) see M. Zimmerman, 1984, 1989; Swanton, 1992; Nathan, 1992; Shatz, 1985, 1988; Honderich, 1988; Benn, 1988; Double, 1991; Schlossberger, 1986; Taurek, 1972; Mellema, 1984; Fischer, ed., 1986; and Fischer and Ravizza, eds., 1993.

33. But compare Christine Swanton, 1992, for an insightful account of the different

strands of meaning of *freedom* in ordinary discourse and an attempt to find a core meaning to them.

34. John Thorp's statement (1980: 3) is apt in this connection: "Perhaps the fact that libertarianism offers *more* freedom . . . than does compatibilism would be something to be weighed in the balance"—but only, of course, if one could make sense of this additional freedom.

35. Dennett, 1984; Nagel, 1986; Honderich, 1988; Wiggins, 1973; Double, 1991; G. Strawson, 1986; S. Wolf, 1990; B. Williams, 1986; P. Strawson, 1962; Frankfurt, 1988; Kenny, 1976; Fischer, 1994; Nathan, 1992; Nozick, 1981; Slote, 1980; Klein, 1990; Anglin, 1990; Waller, 1990; Benson, 1987; Kapitan, 1989; Warner, 1987; Smilansky, 1994; Pereboom, 1995; Magill, 1995; and others. Of special interest in this connection is Nicholas Nathan's view (1992) that metaphysical disputes generally involve "want-belief" conflicts—conflicts between what we want to believe about some important subject matter and what we think we can believe, given the evidence. Nathan uses the free will dispute as his primary example of a metaphysical dispute fitting his pattern. In a review of Nathan's book (Kane, forthcoming in *Philosophia*) I argue that Nathan is largely right in his characterization of the free will dispute as fitting his want-belief pattern, while disputing some aspects of his treatment of the issue.

36. A good sampling of this work is contained in three excellent anthologies: Watson, 1982; Fischer, 1986; and Christman, 1989.

Chapter 2

1. This chapter has been improved by the critical input of many philosophers, especially of Hugh McCann, Michael Bratman, Alfred Mele, and Robert Audi.

2. The distinction between *intellectus* and *voluntas* is ubiquitous in the medieval period (cf. Aquinas, 1945: 792), though it is characterized somewhat differently by different authors, and not always in just the way I characterize it here. Aquinas, for example, makes practical reasoning a function of the intellect (p. 763), yet he designates choices and other practical judgments that terminate practical reasonings as functions of the will (pp. 787, 792). Reasoning powers thus belong to the intellect, but the exercise of will depends upon the intellect in its practical functioning (p. 792).

3. Aquinas, 1945: 196.

4. Aquinas, 1945: 787. "Choice is a kind of judgment," but of the will, not the intellect (p. 790). Aquinas, unlike some other thinkers, places practical or normative judgments on the intellectual side. But I think it is ultimately more enlightening for understanding free will to place normative judgments on the side of will, because they are intellectual judgments of special kinds oriented toward action.

5. The result of an action, in this sense, is to be distinguished from its "consequences." The arm-raising may knock over the lamp and the prince's killing may start a revolution, but, unlike the result, these consequences are not part of the definition of the action.

6. For useful discussion of the uses of *choice* and *decision*, see Oldenquist, 1967, and Donagan, 1987.

7. Ginet, 1990; McCann, 1974; Davis, 1979.

8. As I said at the beginning of the section, choices or decisions that have these properties are always choices or decisions "to do something or other," and this is the sense that will concern us throughout the book. *Choose* and *decide* have other uses (e.g., choosing an object, say, from a tray of fruit, which is itself an overt action and not the formation of an intention "to do something" further; or deciding *that* something or other ought to be done, which is a case of practical judgment). Both *choice* and *decision* may also refer to the act of

deciding or its content—what is decided. Uses of the terms hereafter will refer to the former, unless otherwise indicated.

9. Searle, 1983; Brand, 1984; Harman, 1986; Bratman, 1987; Mele, 1987, 1992; Wilson, 1989; Ginet, 1990.

10. Cf. Harman, 1986, and Brand, 1984, who says "the cognitive component of a prospective intention is a plan" (p. 153).

11. Volitions as initiators of action do play a role at one point in the theory (chapter 9, section 10) but only when their is resistance to the initiation of action. They are not required as initiators of all actions.

12. There will be more discussion of this distinction in chapter 8. For recent works dealing with it, see Audi, 1986; Bishop, 1989; Mele, 1992.

13. Peters, 1958: 28; Grice, 1967: chap. 1.

14. See Sorabji, 1980: 143–87. For excellent recent accounts of Aristotle on the voluntary with references to much of the recent literature, see Broadie, 1992, chap. 3, and also Irwin, 1980, Fine, 1981, and the essays in A. Rorty, ed., 1980b.

15. In chapter 4, section 6, in which I reject this doctrine. I want to thank Timothy O'Connor for alerting me to the possibility that some readers might mistakenly think that W begged certain questions about acting on the strongest motive.

16. For discussion and references to the large literature on coercion, see Carr, 1985, and also Nozick, 1981, and Stampe and Gibson, 1992. On compulsion see Audi, 1974; Russell, 1988; Dworkin, 1988; Berofsky, 1995; Mele, 1995; and the essays and references in Fischer, 1986; Christman, 1989; and Fischer and Ravizza, 1993.

Chapter 3

1. Plotinus, 1950: *Ennead* 6.8.4: 4–7. For a good discussion of Plotinus's views on freedom, see Michael White, 1985: chapter 6.

2. Sorabji also holds that the two conditions Aristotle cites lead Aristotle to an indeterminist and incompatibilist position on free will, a contention that is challenged by other Aristotelian scholars. Cf. Terence Irwin, 1980; Gail Fine, 1981; Sarah Broadie, 1991.

3. Cf. 1915: 256a6–8 (*Physics* VIII): "The stick moves the stone and is moved by the hand, which is again moved by the man; in the man, however, we have reached a mover that is not so in virtue of being moved by something else."

4. 1915: 1114a13–22; also 255a8, 110a17, 1113b21, 1114a18–19; and Sorabji, 1980: 234–8.

5. 1950: *Ennead* 3.1.4.16–27.

6. Bramhall, 1844: 30, 151; Reid, 1983: 599.

7. E.g., Kane, 1989. The first author to my knowledge in recent times to use the expression "ultimate responsibility" was Paul Gomberg, 1975. Gomberg argues that ultimate responsibility, as he understands it, would require an actual infinite regress of responsible acts. But rather than reject it for that reason, as do many others (see note 8), Gomberg argues that liberarians ought to accept such a regress and try to make sense of it. I argue later that an infinite regress is not in fact inevitable.

8. For example (in addition to G. Strawson, 1986, and Klein, 1990), Nagel, 1986, Watson, 1987, Honderich, 1988, S. Wolf, 1990, and Double, 1991, all of whom are skeptical about whether such a condition can be fulfilled. A less skeptical author is Gomberg, 1975 (see preceding note). A very important recent paper by James Lamb (1993) introduces a principle like UR into debates initiated by Frankfurt about alternative possibilities. Lamb's way of responding to Frankfurt is, I think, the direction incompatibilists should go (as indicated by the arguments later in this chapter). Also, David Widerker has written a number of

insightful articles on the debate about alternative possibilities (1987, 1991) in which he emphasizes the importance of a principle that points in the direction of UR. I single out Klein and Strawson in the text because they give the condition more attention than any other recent authors.

9. It is not assumed here that the something the agent voluntarily did or omitted that contributed to E's occurrence had to take place at the same time as E itself, unless of course the something the agent voluntarily did was E itself.

10. The expression "could have voluntarily done otherwise" of this condition R may be given a compatibilist reading, e.g., it might mean only that the agent would have voluntarily done otherwise, if something in the past had been different. Thus, R alone of UR does not beg questions about incompatibilism, as indicated. We shall also see later that "could have voluntarily done otherwise" in R could be omitted because it is implied by U + R.

11. The voluntary doing or omission "made a difference to whether or not E occurred" means that it played an essential role in the actual causal sequence leading to E—had this causal sequence not included it, the sequence would not have led to E or would have been less likely to have led to E. If E were produced anyway by some other causal sequence, but no voluntary act or omission of the agent would have made a difference in whether that alternative sequence issued in E, then the agent would not in that case be personally responsible for E.

12. This notion of an *arche* or sufficient ground is explained in a preliminary way in the next section and in greater detail in subsequent chapters, most notably chapter 5, section 10 and chapter 7, section 6.

13. For completeness, the following qualification must be appended to U: "or if there is more than one sufficient ground for X, the agent must be personally responsible for at least one of those grounds." This qualification applies in special circumstances of "overdetermination" when there is more than one *arche* or sufficient ground for an event. Consider an example suggested by Mark Ravizza in another context (1994: 77). Two assassins, A and B, simultaneously fire bullets into the head of a victim, and each shot on its own would have been sufficient to kill the victim. Let us say that the fatal shots fired by A and B can be explained respectively by their characters and motives (plus background conditions) at the time they fired. There are then two *archai* or sufficient grounds for the victim's death, A's character plus motives plus background conditions (G_A) and B's character plus motives plus background conditions (G_B). To be ultimately responsible for the victim's death in the sense of UR, agent A must be responsible (to some extent) for G_A (i.e., for his own character and motives being what they were), but A does not also have to be responsible for G_B (for B's character and motives being what they were), even though G_B is also a sufficient ground for the victim's death. This explains the appended qualification "if there is more than one sufficient ground for X, the agent must be personally responsible for *at least one* of these grounds." If two causal chains converge on a single event, then, for ultimate responsibility, the backtracking responsibility need only go back through one of the chains. But it must go back through *some* chain, so the problem of a regress is not averted.

14. Plotinus, 1983: *Ennead* 3.1.4: 16–27.

15. On collective responsibility, see the fine collection of essays in Peter French, ed., 1972; also May, 1992, and French, 1992.

16. Nagel, 1986; Watson, 1987; Honderich, 1988; Wolf, 1990; Double, 1991; and Waller, 1990.

17. See note 13 of this chapter, however, for a qualification to the "any X and Y": "if there is more than one sufficient ground for X, the agent must be personally responsible for *at least one* of those grounds." But as explained in note 13, this qualification does not eliminate the potentiality for a vicious regress.

18. See especially chapter 5, section 10, and chapter 7, section 6.

19. The conditions in question may be reasons or causes and the explanations may be explanations in terms of reasons as well as explanations in terms of causes. The *archai*, in other words, may be sufficient motives as well as sufficient causes. For more on sufficient motives, see chapter 7, section 6, in which it is argued, among other things, that an event E can have sufficient motive even when it is not determined (does not have a sufficient cause). UR would require backtracking in that case too, so *mere* indeterminism will not stop a U-generated regress. What is to be said about an event E that happens by chance and has no sufficient explanation of either kind, cause or motive? Can an agent be ultimately responsible for such an event? Yes, under certain circumstances. If the E in question has no sufficient ground, then U is trivially satisfied. That means UR is satisfied for E *if* R is, and R is satisfied if there is something the agent voluntarily did or omitted, such that the agent could have voluntarily done otherwise that contributed to E's occurring. Suppose E is a chance spark that sets fire to a pile of oily rags burning down a building. Though the event was not determined, it would not have occurred if a worker had not willingly left the rags there against company policy. So something the worker voluntarily did would have made a difference. Of course, true negligence would also have to be shown in the worker's case, since R is a necessary, not a sufficient, condition for personal responsibility.

20. This possibility was also mentioned by Frankfurt, 1969: note 4.

21. A pertinent collection of essays with an excellent introduction to this and other recent controversies about alternative possibilities is John Martin Fischer, 1986. Also see Fischer, 1994, and Fischer and Ravizza, eds., 1993, and *Responsibility and Control: A Theory of Moral Responsibility* (forthcoming). Other notable recent contributions to this literature include van Inwagen, 1983; Naylor, 1984; Heinaman, 1986; Widerker, 1991; and Lamb, 1993.

22. Fischer's new book (1994), which I only saw in manuscript when the writing of this book was nearly completed, contains to my mind the best general account of the issues surrounding Frankfurt examples (chapter 7).

23. I should add that this is not Fischer's own response to the problem he diagnoses. What I am suggesting is rather that it is a natural response for incompatibilists to make if they believe, as I do, that UR as well as AP is a necessary condition for free will. Fischer himself (1994) ultimately accepts Frankfurt's view that moral responsibility does not require "could have done otherwise," and so moral responsibility is compatible with determinism — though he denies that "could have done otherwise" is compatible with determinism. This unusual view he calls "semi-compatibilism." Cf. Ravizza, 1994, which defends a similar view, as well as Fischer and Ravizza, *Responsibility and Control: A Theory of Moral Responsibility* (forthcoming).

24. I want to reemphasize that this is an *incompatibilist* strategy that I am using against Frankfurt in this chapter. Compatibilists may not like it, but, if so, they will have to work out their own strategies or concede Frankfurt's point. A similar strategy against Frankfurt examples has been proposed by James Lamb in an important recent article (1993) that I think correctly captures what a proper libertarian strategy against Frankfurt examples ought to be when juxtaposed with some further moves that are made against Frankfurt examples in chap. 8, sec. 9.

25. I am indebted to Timothy O'Connor, Alfred Mele, and to some remarks made by John Martin Fischer for bringing to my attention this problem of an ever-present, non-intervening controller.

26. These claims are promissory notes at this stage. Fulfilling them requires showing, first, that if UR is satisfied, some actions in the agent's life history must be undetermined (the task of chapter 5; see especially section 10) and then showing that if the actions are

undetermined and a controller, though present, does not intervene in them, the agent could have done otherwise (one of the tasks of chapter 8; see especially section 9).

27. We can thus also salvage the intuition that if the the controller does not intervene, but allows the agent to act on his own, the mere presence of the controller would not undermine the agent's responsibility for acting on his own. We can acknowledge this plausible intuition without denying that (with respect to some actions at least) the responsible agent could have done otherwise.

Chapter 4

1. See Kenny, 1976, for a penetrating discussion of Scotus and other medieval thinkers on this topic.

2. In addition to the classic statements of the argument mentioned above by Ginet, Wiggins, van Inwagen, Lamb, and Pike, other noteworthy recent attempts to improve on the argument include those of Widerker, 1987; Ginet, 1990; and O'Connor, 1993a. Another insightful recent article on it is Blum, 1990. Excellent recent critical discussions include Fischer, 1986, 1994, and Bernard Berofsky, 1987.

3. One can also define an equivalent "Transfer of Powerlessness" principle that has also appeared in debates about the Consequence Argument: (T-P-) "For every agent a and time t, if a cannot at t render Q false and Q entails R, then a cannot at t render R false." Still other versions of the argument replace "Q entails R" in T-P- with "a at t cannot render it false that Q entails R" on the plausible assumption that no agent can render false a true logical entailment.

4. We shall see later that not all critics of the Consequence Argument accept this result. Some think premise 3 is acceptable, but only if other premises are rejected.

5. Gallois, 1977; Narveson, 1977; Foley, 1978, 1979.

6. Slote, 1982, Fischer, 1983, Watson, 1987, Lewis, 1986, Berofsky, 1987, Horgan, 1985, Flint, 1987, C. Hill, 1992, Foley, 1978, Gallois, 1977, Narveson, 1977, Vihvelin, 1988, 1991.

7. E.g. Saunders, 1968, Narveson, 1977, Gallois, 1977, Foley, 1979, Lehrer, 1980, Davies, 1983.

8. The introduction to Fischer, 1986, is an excellent overview of these discussions, as are the first six chapters of Fischer, 1994.

9. The in-house debate between compatibilists about whether to reject 4 or 5, or both, depends in part on how counterfactual conditionals are interpreted. For a useful overview of the relevant debates about counterfactuals in relation to free will, see Nathan, 1992, chapter 5. The main point being made here, however, is independent of the outcome of these debates, since whatever account of counterfactuals one accepts, it must be conceded that the Consequence Argument is in trouble if "can render false" is interpreted in Lewis's weak sense. Either 4 or 5 will be false.

10. Van Inwagen, 1990; Ginet, 1990: chap. 5.

11. In the papers just cited, Lewis, 1981, Fischer, 1983. For a more thorough discussion see Fischer, 1994.

12. We might easily overlook this fact because the argument assumes Lewis's strong sense of "can do otherwise," which is not so obviously a compatibilist notion as is his weak sense. But, as Lewis is well aware, his strong (or causal) sense of "can do otherwise" is not necessarily incompatibilist. It can also be given a compatibilist analysis.

13. Fischer, who has been a persistent critic of previous versions of the Consequence Argument by van Inwagen and others, nonetheless argues in his most recent work (1994) that a revised version of the Consequence Argument which he formulates "probably" does work.

14. E.g., Berofsky, 1987.

15. Austin, 1966. The paper was originally delivered to the British Academy in 1956 and published in Austin's *Philosophical Papers* (1961: 153–80). For an insightful discussion of Austin's arguments and their limits, see Sanford, 1991; also Falk, 1981. Michael Ayers's 1968 book discusses the issues surrounding Austin's arguments at great length, clarifying many of their implications. A recent work devoted to these debates is Morton White, 1993.

16. Soft determinists are those who believe that freedom is compatible with determinism and that determinism is true.

17. Cf. Berofsky, 1987, on this point.

18. E.g., Berofsky, 1987.

Chapter 5

1. Frankfurt, 1971; Dworkin, 1970a; Neely, 1974. According to Thalberg (1989), Dworkin, 1970a, was the first published account of a hierarchical view. Frankfurt, 1971, made a number of refinements in the theory that Dworkin subsequently accepted. The Thalberg article is a critique of hierarchical views. Other critiques are mentioned later. David Shatz, 1985, identifies other authors besides Frankfurt, Dworkin, and Neely who advocate hierarchical views, or at least significant aspects of such views, including William Alston, 1977, Lawrence Davis, 1979, Richard Jeffrey, 1974, Stephen Körner, 1973, Michael Levin, 1979 (chap. 7), Robert Young, 1979, 1986, Stephen Shiffer, 1976, Keith Lehrer, 1980, David Zimmerman, 1981, and Charles Taylor, 1982. Lehrer, Davis, Levin, Dworkin, Neely, Young, and D. Zimmerman explicitly link hierarchical accounts with compatibilism.

2. Watson, 1975; Benson, 1987; S. Wolf, 1990; Double, 1991; Mele, 1992, 1995; Kapitan, 1989.

3. This point is made in Watson, 1987, which is a superb review of recent work on free will generally and is especially good on hierarchical theories.

4. As David Shatz has said (1985: 451): "For the most part, advocates of hierarchical accounts see themselves as continuators or rehabilitators of classical compatibilism." This article by Shatz is one of the best critical studies of hierarchical theories in the recent literature.

5. Important critiques besides Watson, 1975, Shatz, 1985, and Thalberg, 1989, include Marilyn Friedman, 1986, Fischer, 1986, and Double, 1991. Fischer, 1986, Shatz, 1985, and Watson, 1987, provide excellent overviews of the debates.

6. This point is developed by David Shatz, 1985, and Marilyn Friedman, 1986, as well as by Watson and Fischer.

7. Kane, 1985, chapter 3.

8. This notion of CNC control defined in my 1985, pp. 34–5, has made its way into subsequent discussion of free will issues, e.g., in Waller, 1990, Double, 1991, and Mele, 1995.

9. Huxley, 1989, Skinner, 1962. Huxley's work originally appeared in 1932 and Skinner's in 1948. With examples of such utopias in mind, Watson, 1987, refers to global cases of CNC control as "Brave New World scenarios." CNC control itself is a more general notion than global scenarios suggest, however, since it can take place to various degrees in everyday life as well as globally in utopian scenarios like Huxley's or Skinner's.

10. Paul Benson, 1987, also effectively makes the case for this point, as do Duggan and Gert, 1979; Davis, 1979; Young, 1979; D. Zimmerman, 1981; C. Taylor; 1982; Dworkin, 1988; Velleman, 1989; M. Zimmerman, 1989; Kapitan, 1989; and others.

11. Mele (1995, 179, 187ff.) offers an insightful discussion of my notion of CNC control, attempting to reconcile it with a compatibilist account of autonomy.

12. Kane, 1985: chap. 3.

13. In correspondence, Frankfurt has indicated that he is also inclined to take this hard compatibilist line in response to criticisms of his view such as those we have been discussing. He admits that many philosophers find this hard line difficult to swallow, but it is in fact consistent with his general views about identification and wholeheartedness. Other philosophers who offer a sophisticated case for taking the hard compatibilist line are David Blumenfeld, 1988, and Bruce Waller, 1990.

14.. It is interesting that Hobbes seems oblivious to this further freedom in politics as well as in religion. He is prepared to give the political sovereign almost as much power over us as he thinks the divine sovereign already has.

15. One indication that it is more difficult lies in the phenomena of socialization and enculturation (the processes by which persons come to accept and internalize the norms and values, purposes and practices, of their societies or cultures). As David Shatz points out (1988: 162–3), socialization and enculturation present special problems for compatibilists because they lie midway between behavioral control of the Skinnerian type and mere determination by natural causes. Should compatibilists say that complete determination by socialization or enculturation is objectionable, like CNC control, or should they say it is unobjectionable, like mere determination by natural causes? Socialization and enculturation are the result of human purposes and intentions, not mere natural causes, but the persons involved are less aware of what they are doing than are behavioral controllers. Yet, as Shatz notes, the results of socialization and enculturation might in principle be exactly the same as the results of conscious behavioral control. What then would be the difference for the controlled agents, if both methods were completely determining and reached the same results? If, on the one hand, there is no relevant difference and CNC control is objectionable, then socialization and enculturation that are completely determining would be objectionable too. If, on the other hand, there *is* a relevant difference, and socialization and enculturation are unobjectionable, like mere determination, then what counts as unobjectionable "mere" determination turns out to be something more problematic regarding issues of individual freedom and autonomy than mere determination by natural causes. These questions are all the more important because of the pervasiveness of socialization and enculturation in human development. For further discussion of these issues, see Greenspan, 1978; Young, 1979; Bernstein, 1983; and Benson, 1987.

16. This example and the one used in the next paragraph were used in my 1985: 41–43. Watson, 1987: 151, makes the same point, citing my 1985.

17. I do not mean to suggest that Dennett's discussion is superficial in this way. His discussion of "intuition pumps" that support incompatibilist arguments is more sophisticated than ordinary-language arguments of the past against incompatibilist intuitions. Still, the issues call for a deeper understanding of what lies behind these intuition pumps, as I suggest in the remainder of this section.

18. Schopenhauer, 1889. The three meanings I give correspond to three of Schopenhauer's "four roots" of the principle of sufficient reason, except that Schopenhauer tendentiously interprets sufficient motive as a special kind of sufficient cause. His fourth root is based on Kant's theory of space and lacks general significance beyond his particular interpretation of Kant. For further discussion of the principle of sufficient reason in relation to other principles of reason, see my 1976 and 1986.

19. "Making a difference," as I noted in note 11 of chapter 3, means being an essential part of a causal chain leading to the circumstances. The circumstances may have been produced by another causal chain not essentially involving the voluntary contributions of the agent, but in that case the agent would not be personally responsible for the resulting circumstances.

20. The reason that U requires sufficiency in the ground or *arche* is the following. As

finite agents, we know that the conditions of our existence (heredity, environment, etc.) are going to limit our choices and actions to a great degree. The question of our freedom is whether *anything* is *left over* by these surrounding conditions that is wholly and finally "up to us." Though the conditions of my existence limit my choices here and now to, say, doing A or doing B, something should be left over by these conditions that is wholly and finally up to me, namely, whether I (willingly) do A rather than B or B rather than A here and now. A sufficient ground would leave nothing over to me since it would entail A (or B), or my willing to do one or the other—unless, of course, as U insists, I am responsible for the sufficient ground's being the case.

21. Paul Gomberg (1975) suggests that such a regress might be the only way to salvage incompatibilist intuitions; Peter Forrest (1985) has a somewhat different vision of actual infinite backward change of the past, had we done otherwise.

22. T6 and T7 show how UR is involved in another familiar dispute in the history of free will debates. Some compatibilists have claimed that the problem of free will and determinism is generated by a mistaken view of laws of nature. If laws describe "necessary connections" between phenomena, we may come to think that laws "force" or "constrain" us to act as we do. By contrast, if we accept a Humean or regularity view of laws—according to which laws do not necessitate but merely describe unbroken regularities in nature—then, on this view, incompatibilist worries about causal determinism should dissolve. This compatibilist view was initiated by Hume, continued by J. S. Mill, and has been defended by some twentieth-century compatibilists, such as Ayer, Schlick, and Hobart. (An interesting critique of it is made by Paul Russell, 1988.) Its most recent defender is Bernard Berofsky, whose 1971 and 1987 books are the best, and I think, definitive statements of such a view. Now, it turns out that UR gives us a new perspective on such a view in free-will debates. If a Humean regularity—say, "if A then B"—obtains, and if it is also true that "A," then it follows logically that "B." So, the conjunction of "if A then B" and "A" constitutes a logically sufficient condition, or sufficient reason, for its being the case that B. Thus, UR is brought into play—*even if* the law is not necessary but only a universal regularity. This, I think, is the reason that incompatibilists have always held that determinism poses a threat to free will, whether laws are interpreted in a necessitarian or Humean way—and why they believe Hume's compatibilism is no less a threat to their view than Hobbes's view, though Hume holds a regularity view of laws and Hobbes a necessitarian view.

23. Klein, 1990: 50–1. Klein's work has influenced me in the formulation of this thesis.

24. David Widerker's insightful discussion of the Consequence Argument (1987) provides some indirect support for this thesis. Widerker believes that the Consequence Argument has to be strengthened by the replacement of the usual Transfer of Power principle by a principle that points in the direction of UR. Cf. also O'Connor, 1993b.

25. Of special note are the efforts of Michael Slote, 1980, Paul Benson, 1987, Tomis Kapitan, 1989, and Dennis Stampe and Martha Gibson, 1992.

26. The requirement that the actions in question must be "willed" (in the sense of V of chapter 2)—as Luther's action certainly is—is meant to rule out actions that are performed accidentally or happen by mistake or by chance and are not under the control of the agent.

Chapter 6

1. Italics under the word "whole" have been removed.

2. The expression "sole authorship" is one I borrow from Nicholas Nathan, who uses it in Nathan, 1992, to characterize my conception of free will. I don't recall previously using the expression myself, but it seems an apt one.

3. Cf. Anglin, 1990: 16, from whom I borrow the expression "moral destiny."

4. Cf. Saul Smilansky, 1990a, 1994, who argues that "desert for punishment," and indeed "desert for suffering," generally are among the strongest motivators for UR. If we lack ultimate responsibility, he says (in correspondence), then "people are being punished for what was ultimately beyond their control. . . . Without UR . . . people are often *victims.*" I am indebted to Smilansky for many helpful comments on this chapter.

5. E.g., Dennett's view, 1984, is similar. Cf. also Glover, 1970; an excellent recent work on the reactive attitudes, freedom, and responsibility is R. Jay Wallace, 1994.

6. Two other non-libertarians who have nonetheless recently written perceptive papers defending incompatibilist intuitions with a different focus than Honderich's, are Saul Smilansky, 1990a, 1993, 1994, and Derk Pereboom, 1995.

7. Similar sentiments are also powerfully expressed by Nagel, 1986, chapter 7.

8. The idea of a "book of life" with all this written down is of course a biblical idea. Interesting philosophical use is made of it by Alvin Goldman (1970) to discuss issues of freedom and determinism. Another well-known literary use of the book of life theme is Gabriel García-Márquez's novel *One Hundred Years of Solitude.*

9. To say this is not to endorse Kant's stronger claim that the possession of (an ultimate incompatibilist) free will *entails* that one is deserving of respect as a person by others. If this were true, one could derive strong ethical conclusions (namely, a version of Kant's Categorical Imperative) merely from the possession of incompatibilist free will. The distinguished Kant scholar Henry Allison (1990: 201–13) relates this claim to what he calls Kant's "reciprocity thesis": free will entails the moral law and vice versa. It would be nice for us incompatibilists if something like this were true, but wishing cannot make it so. What *is* true, I think, is a weaker, but nonetheless important, reciprocity: if we are to be held ultimately responsible for our purposes and actions by others (including God) because it is believed that we are their ultimate sources, then we feel that justice (reciprocity) requires that our purposes and actions also be respected by others because we are their ultimate sources (and not merely because our purposes and actions are useful for others). In sum, we believe that free will is a precondition for *claiming* a kind of dignity worth wanting. (I return to the issue of free will and ethics, discussing Kant's view further, in chapter 11, section 4 forward.) Another illuminating discussion of Kant on freedom and morality is Allen Wood, 1984. I owe a debt in this work to Jeffrey Tlumak for enlightening discussions of Kant's view of freedom and related issues.

10. Even a determinist like Honderich admits that some important things would be lost regarding our life-hopes if determinism were true. However, he also argues that enough could be retained of importance if determinism were true to give life meaning (1988: vol. 2, and 1993).

11. I am indebted to Saul Smilansky for reminding me of Strawson's insightful comments on this topic.

12. Anglin expresses this libertarian desire for "a more exalted kind" of creativity in 1990: 18.

13. See, e.g., Glover, 1970; Audi, 1974; Kenny, 1978; Slote, 1980; Bennett, 1980; Kapitan, 1986; Berofsky, 1987, 1995; Frankfurt, 1988; Klein, 1990; S. Wolf, 1990; and the papers in Fischer, 1986; Schoeman, 1987; Christman, 1989; and Fischer and Ravizza, 1993. (Also see note 14 for further references.)

14. Recent works of interest on the diverse conditions that go into everyday judgments about moral responsibility, in addition to the works cited in the previous footnote, include M. Zimmerman, 1989, Peter French, 1992, and R. Jay Wallace, 1994. Other noteworthy recent discussions of moral responsibility include Mellema, 1984; Schlossberger, 1986; Swinburne, 1989; Klein, 1990; Lucas, 1993; Fischer and Ravizza, forthcoming.

15. Gerald Dworkin, 1988, Bernard Berofsky, 1995, and Alfred Mele, 1995. Other

excellent recent works on autonomy (a topic that has received an enormous amount of critical attention in the past decade) include Laurence Haworth, 1986; Richard Lindley, 1986; Robert Young, 1986; and Thomas Hill, 1991. Some of these authors (e.g., Mele) do not take sides on the compatibility question, but their analyses show how autonomy might be defined without presupposing incompatibility. By contrast, Dworkin and Berofsky are explicit about the compatibilist nature of their theories. A very good overview of recent work on autonomy is Christman, 1988. Also see Christman's collection of essays on individual autonomy, 1989.

16. Some Eastern philosophies, such as early Buddhism, have a view of the self much like Hume's. Moreover, these Buddhists were well aware of the connection between individual selfhood, on the one hand, and will and action, on the other. Following the second and third of the Buddha's four noble truths, they held that the way to extinguish selfhood was to extinguish the will (i.e., *tanha*, or personal desires) so that the desire for action would give way and one would no longer be trapped by the illusion of personal or finite selfhood. I discuss this Buddhist view later in the chapter. (For an interesting defense of a Buddhist approach to freedom and determinism, see Mark Siderits, 1987.)

17. Nagel (1986: chap. 7) aptly describes this crisis as a conflict between the subjective point of view, in which we are independent agents, and the objective point of view, in which we are physical beings in the world and influenced by it.

18. "Inner citadel" is an expression used by Isaiah Berlin and taken over by John Christman to describe the autonomous self in the title of Christman's collection of essays on autonomy (1989: 3).

19. See note 9 and also Siderits, 1987.

20. See chapter 11, sections 3 to 7, for further discussion of the relation of free will to ethics.

21. Kane, 1994b and 1993, in which this notion is discussed in connection with ideas of value, ethics, and metaphysics.

22. Philosophers will recognize a connection between this example and Robert Nozick's well-known example of the "experience machine" in his 1974, p. 18. This is not accidental, because Nozick's experience machine is another way of getting at the idea of objective worth. But I use the example of Alan—and other examples in Kane, 1994b—to bring out features of this complex notion that Nozick does not discuss.

23. Kane 1993 and 1994b.

24. This is the case because the worth in question is not just the worth of the life or the goals, but of the *self* that is the source of that life. I am indebted to an anonymous reader for alerting me to this distinction.

25. Laurence Haworth (1986: 187–8) expresses this connection nicely when he says, speaking of autonomy, "one simply wants to *be* as an individual . . . [and] to make a mark on the world that is distinctively one's own." He adds: "This interest in existing as an individual is probably more fundamental than any other interest we have."

26. There are other issues that might be addressed here about the value of these desires. For example, one might ask whether the extension of the desire to be independent selves that leads to desiring ultimate responsibility is misguided or pathological in some way, as agoraphobia is a pathological extension of the desire to live in a safe and predictable world or megalomania is the extension of the need for self-esteem. These are legitimate questions, but there are also significant differences between the desire for ultimate responsibility and these pathological conditions. Insofar as it is pathological, the agoraphobic's condition is destructive and disabling in ways that make her less happy than she might otherwise have been. But there is no reason to believe that the desire for ultimate responsibility in and of itself is destructive and disabling in similar ways. Megalomania is another matter. It may be

considered pathological because it leads to counterproductive or self-destructive behavior or to harmful or destructive relations with others (or for both reasons). The question to ask would be whether the desire to be ultimately responsible for one's actions necessarily has similar consequences. I do not see that it does because desiring to be (or being) ultimately responsible for one's actions is compatible with being a good person who does not harm others and does not of itself seem to imply self-destructive behavior. This is not to say that some of those who desire ultimate responsibility may not be self-destructive, phobic, obsessive, megalomaniacal, immoral, or whatever, just as some might also be self-realizing, well adjusted, or morally good. The point is simply that desiring ultimate responsibility does not in and of itself make them one or the other. (I am indebted to an anonymous reader for insightful comments in which these questions were raised.)

27. Kane, 1994b.

Chapter 7

1. These charges are common, e.g., in Hobbes, 1962; J. Edwards, 1969; Hume, 1960; Schopenhauer, 1960; Mill, 1962; Bradley, 1927; Ayer, 1954; Schlick, 1966; and Broad, 1962, among many others.

2. Leibniz, 1951: 435; Bramhall, 1844: 150–1; Reid, 1970: 88; and Chisholm, 1966: 25.

3. Double, 1988a, 1991; Waller, 1988; Clarke, 1992; O'Connor, 1993a; G. Strawson, 1994; and essays in O'Connor, ed., 1995.

4. Bramhall discusses the medieval notion of liberty of indifference in 1844: 414–15. J. Edwards (1969: 71, 160) and Schopenhauer (1960: 60) also discuss and criticize it. For other medieval references, see Bourke, 1964: chap. 4.

5. Hobbes 1962: 42ff.; Schopenhauer, 1960: 47; Hume, 1955: chap. 8.

6. We shall see in the next chapter, in which plural voluntary control is discussed in more detail, that it subsumes the other two plurality conditions, rationality and voluntariness. In particular, the plurality conditions are nested. Plural voluntary control entails plural voluntariness, which in turn entails plural rationality or motivation. I nonetheless label the three conditions separately because each of them brings into play distinctive plurality requirements that often have to be distinguished and separately discussed. It may seem, for example, that plural voluntary control adds nothing to plural voluntariness except the emphasis on ability to go both ways voluntarily. But we shall see in the next chapter that plural voluntary control makes additional requirements.

7. Kane, 1976, 1986, discuss the principle of sufficient reason and its relation to other historically important principles of reason and to determinism.

8. Indeed, if the principle of sufficient reason were true, there would be no free will of the kind requiring UR. Much of the philosophical discussion of the relation of the principle of sufficient reason to free will has concerned Leibniz's complex views about both. Despite Leibniz's subtle efforts to make room for free will in his metaphysics, many Leibniz scholars assume he does not capture an incompatibilist free will because of his commitment to the principle of sufficient reason . (Cf. Sleigh, 1990: 29, Adams, 1982: 245, Burms and DeDijn, 1979: 124.) This common assumption is questioned in some insightful recent papers on Leibniz view of freedom by R. Cranston Paull, 1992, and Michael Murray, 1995, who argue that Leibniz's commitment to the principle of sufficient reason is consistent with his acceptance of causal or physical indeterminism in the natural order. Such a position remains a controversial one among Leibniz scholars. (For an excellent critical discussion of it and other related issues, see Sleigh, 1994.) What is worth noting, however, is that even if true, the view that the Leibnizian principle of sufficient reason is compatible with causal indeterminism

would not show that the principle of sufficient reason is compatible with free will in a sense requiring UR. For sufficient reasons include sufficient conditions and sufficient motives as well as sufficient causes; and even if Leibnizian free choices were to lack sufficient natural causes, they would have sufficient conditions and motives in the created essences or "natures" of the individuals who make them—from which, according to Leibniz, all of the individuals' perceptions and actions inevitably flow. As Paull notes (1992: 228), "even though a [Leibnizian] choice" may be causally undetermined, "the fact that the chooser has the specific nature that he does [created by God] provides a sufficient reason for the . . . [free] choice." An important consequence following from this is often underappreciated by writers on free will. Consider a world in which some events, including some human actions, were causally undetermined but in which all of the *motives* and *purposes* of agents were nonetheless predetermined by God. In such a world, agents would sometimes fail to realize their predetermined purposes in action by chance or accident in a manner that is undetermined (like Austin or the sniper, they might sometimes miss their targets by chance), but they would not be the ultimate creators of any of their own purposes. Those purposes would have been created by God. Such agents would live in an undetermined world and some of their own actions would be undetermined, but they would not have free will. The point is that causal determinism is not the only problem for free will and causal indeterminism not the only solution.

9. Cf. Greenspan, 1978, on this point.

10. Cf. Martha Klein, 1990, chap. 4, which makes an excellent case for the role that motives, intentions, and ultimacy play in ordinary judgments about blameworthiness. Also see Smilansky, 1990a.

11. Chap. 8, sec. 9. Interestingly, we also learn in the next chapter that plural voluntariness for SFAs follows as well from U of UR, if SFAs are plural motivated, as just argued, since the further conditions of absence of coercion and compulsion can be shown to follow for undetermined SFAs. This means that the clause "the agent could have voluntarily done otherwise" is not needed in R of UR, since the regress stopping SFAs required by R will satisfy this clause if U is also satisfied. Nonetheless, I included this clause in the original statement of UR because we thus far lack the resources to show why it is not needed.

12. What we learn from this additional Thesis 15 is that, for self-forming actions, the agents must not only be able to do otherwise, they must be able to do otherwise rationally, voluntarily, and under their voluntary control. The fact that SFAs satisfy AP (T3) therefore turns out to be a consequence of a stronger requirement that they satisfy the plurality conditions.

13. If the plurality conditions and UR are related as I have suggested, this would account for the importance of plurality for incompatibilists. The question of why many compatibilists are also committed to plurality conditions or have strong intuitions about plurality seems to me a question worth pursuing. If compatibilists do have other reasons for supporting plurality conditions than UR, this would only strengthen the argument of this chapter. For the argument has been that the plurality conditions are deeply involved in standard charges (of arbitrariness, irrationality, etc.) made against indeterminist theories of freedom and that these conditions must be satisfied (at least for some actions) by any adequate account of free agency.

14. Among those who voiced skepticism about such a project in its early stages were Robert Audi, Daniel Dennett, Robert Causey, Edwin Allaire, Bernard Katz, Bernard Gendron, and my long-time mentor, Wilfrid Sellars. Sellars was a staunch compatibilist who had me convinced for a time. But I could not entirely still my incompatibilist intuitions.

15. See Eccles, 1970; and Popper and Eccles, 1977.

16. For an excellent compatibilist critique of libertarian theories that postulate such

sui generis acts or other similar strategems, see Berofsky, 1992. Berofsky effectively criticizes all views which argue that the will is (as Descartes put it [1955: 350]) "by its nature free in such a way that it can never be constrained."

17. Descartes, 1955: 234–5; Mansel, 1851. The best known modern defenders of a dualist approach specifically to free will are Popper and Eccles, 1970. Another well-known defender is Swinburne (1986: 231ff.)

18. The most well-known defense of E is Norman Malcolm, 1968.

19. See, e.g., Davidson, 1966; Goldman, 1970; Berofsky, 1971; Dennett, 1973; Aune, 1977; Kim, 1984; Audi, 1986; Dretske, 1988; Lennon, 1990; Mele, 1992; and Baker, 1993, among many others.

20. Ironically, Chisholm has abandoned agent-causation in recent years (see Chisholm, 1982 and 1995), no longer believing it necessary to account for libertarian freedom. Richard Taylor, the other prominent agent-cause theorist cited in this paragraph, has also abandoned the theory (see Taylor, 1982).

21. For thoughtful recent attempts to answer this and other standard objections to agent-causation, see Rowe, 1991, Clarke, 1993, and O'Connor, 1992.

22. Hobbes, 1962: 35, 77, 113; Watson 1982: 10; J. Bishop 1989: 69; Berofsky, 1987.

23. Kane, 1985, 1988a, 1989; also see Broad, 1962; Kenny, 1976; Bonjour, 1976; Aune, 1977; Dennett, 1984; G. Strawson, 1986, 1994; B. Williams, 1986; C., Williams, 1986; Berofsky, 1987; Watson, 1987; Honderich, 1988; Goetz, 1988; S. Wolf, 1990; Waller, 1990; Ginet, 1990; Klein, 1990; Double, 1991; Nathan, 1992.

Chapter 8

1. Some of the six categories may also overlap and some are special cases of others, but they are special cases worthy of separate treatment because of the roles they play in self-formation.

2. C. A. Campbell, 1967; Kant, 1959; for a different view of Kant's theory, see Allison, 1990.

3. Adapted from the closing line of Joyce, 1960. It is interesting in connection with T22 that "ambivalence," in Frankfurt's sense, rather than its opposite, wholeheartedness, is the key to the exercise of incompatibilist free will by way of SFWs. Wholeheartedness may be a good from the point of view of a will already formed, but ambivalence is a condition for the self-forming of the will in an ultimate way. Cf. Galen Strawson's apt remark (1986: 70) that difficult or painful choices are "the central fact of the phenomenology of freedom."

4. Glass and Mackey, 1988; Scott and McMillan, eds., 1980; Babloyantz and Destexhe, 1985; Skarda and Freeman, 1987.

5. See Hunt, 1981, Stone, 1989, Ford, 1989. For arguments that unpredicability is not a sufficient condition for chaos, see Batterman, 1993.

6. Also see Robert Bishop (1995 and forthcoming) for careful discussions of the relation of quantum mechanics to classical chaos.

7. Scott, 1991a: 265. Also see in this connection Showalter, Noyes, and Turner, 1979. Pete Gunter (1991) relates nonequilibrium thermodynamics and Prigogine's views in interesting ways to the views about indeterminacy and free will of Henri Bergson, 1960. Other interesting recent defenses of Bergson's views (which have some affinities to [but also some significant differences from] the view of this book) are James Felt's insightful introductory work, 1994, and Ran Lahav, 1991.

8. See, e.g., Huberman and Hogg (1987), which shows that chaos exists in neural net models designed to model human mental abilities. I owe this reference to James Garson.

9. It may be, as some of the above writers suggest, that such sensitivity to indetermina-

cies is always present to some degree in the normal functioning brain, lending flexibility to its responses to the environment. In that case, the point of Thesis 25 would be that conflicts within the wills of agents create tensions in the brain that heighten these sensitivities.

10. Stapp, 1990, 1993; Scott, 1991a.

11. For essays on the history of the problem of *akrasia*, or weakness of will, see Mortimore, ed., 1971. For more recent discussions, see Jackson, 1984; Pears, 1985; Mele, 1987; Dunn, 1987; Charlton, 1988; Gosling, 1990; Bigelow, Dodds and Pargetter, 1990; Robinson, 1991; and Hurley, 1993. Charlton and Gosling provide valuable historical overviews as well as presenting challenging views of their own. An excellent review of recent work on the subject is Walker, 1989.

12. Those who are familiar with the much discussed experiments of Benjamin Libet (1985) on willing and consciousness might wonder how they are related to the theory of this book. Building on the work of H. H. Kornhuber and his associates (see Deeke et al., 1976), Libet did experiments on human volunteers who were asked to flex their index fingers whenever they felt like doing so and to pay close attention to the instant of onset of the urge, desire, or act of will to do so. The subjects were told to let the acts of will arise spontaneously without prior deliberation or paying attention to the prospect of so acting. By measuring brain activity while this was occurring, Libet found that the recorded electrical potential (the readiness potential) for initiating the finger movement occurred before (usually a fraction of second, e.g., 350 milliseconds, or up to a second or more before) the agent is consciously aware of the urge or decision to flex. Conflicting claims have been made about what the Libet experiments imply. Some have claimed they show that consciousness is merely an epiphenomenon which makes the agent aware of what has already happened but does not play a significant causal role in volition. But this was not Libet's own conclusion. He asks "if the brain can initiate a voluntary act before the appearance of conscious intention, . . . is there any role for the conscious function?" and answers, "Conscious control can be exerted before the final motor outflow to select or control volitional outcome. The volitional process, initiated unconsciously, can either be consciously permitted to proceed to consummation in the motor act or be consciously 'vetoed' " (1985: 536–37). These remarks suggest that the role of consciousness in voluntary activity and other mental activity is that of "oversight" with possible "veto" power over final outcomes after the initial onset of readiness, but before consummation. Several writers, including Penrose (1994: 386–8) and Flanagan (1992: 136–7), suggest on the basis of Libet's experiments (and in agreement with the above statements of Libet) that this might be the role that consciousness plays. (See also van Gulick, 1990, who has written perceptively on these matters; and for a contrary view well defended, see Dennett, 1991.) This oversight-plus-veto role for consciousness fits nicely the theory of this work. Specifically, in the conflict situations within the will described in T22 through T30, the urges, desires, and attendant readiness potentials to act from self-interest or for present satisfaction might at times be present before agents are conscious of the inner tension in their wills. The role of consciousness in these inner struggles would be *either* to exercise veto power, preventing these urges and desires from being fulfilled, *or* to *allow* them to go through to completion (cf. T27). The uncertainty about which of these options is to be taken would be experienced as inner tension in the will, as described in preceding theses. In the next chapter, we shall see that this role (of vetoing or allowing to fruition) can also function with regard not only to urges, desires, and other motives, but with regard also to intentions already formed and presently being carried out. These cases of conscious oversight would represent other instances of SFWs discussed in the next chapter, which I call "efforts sustaining purposes."

13. T33 involves some refinements in my earlier statements of plural rationality (called "dual rationality" in earlier works, such as Kane, 1985). The changes result from criticisms

of a number of philosophers, including Timothy O'Connor, 1992, 1993a. Randolph Clarke, 1992, Matthew Posth, 1990, Richard Double, 1988a, 1991, Bruce Waller, 1988, Alfred Mele, 1995, and several in conversation and correspondence with the above and David Blumenfeld, John Post, Jeffrey Tlumak, John Compton, Clement Dore, and Crispin Sartwell. One change is of particular importance. In an earlier work (Kane, 1989) I suggested that when the agents choose for reasons one way or the other they "come to believe" that the reasons from which they choose are the best ones to act upon. Criticisms specifically of O'Connor, Clarke, and Mele convinced me that, while this "coming to believe" the reasons are the best may sometimes be the case, it does not always have to be so. Discussions with the philosophers mentioned in this note also provoked improvements in formulations of other plurality conditions.

14. For a contrary view, see Stewart Goetz, 1988, George Wilson, 1989, and Carl Ginet, 1990. The books by Wilson and Ginet are the most elaborate and most challenging attempts to give noncausal, teleological accounts of action in recent literature. For a critical discussion of both, see Mele, 1992, chap. 13. A valuable collection of original essays, many of which defend causal accounts of action, is Heil and Mele, eds., 1993.

15 Another libertarian who has effectively argued for this point in several papers is Randolph Clarke, 1992, 1993.

16. For discussion of the relevant research referred to in the remainder of this section, see P. S. Churchland, 1986, 1994; Edelman, 1987; P. M. Churchland, 1988; Calvin, 1990; Crick and Koch, 1990; Dennett, 1991; Llinas and Pare, 1991; Llinas and Ribary, 1993; Flanagan, 1992; Crick, 1994.

17. Eckhorn et al., 1988; Gray and Singer, 1989.

18. For further discussion of this research, see P. S. Churchland, 1994, Flanagan, 1992, and Crick, 1994. Such waves were discovered by Wolf Singer and his colleagues at the Max Planck Institute for Brain Research in Germany.

19. Roger Penrose (1994 : chap. 7) suggests that one might even look more deeply into the quantum coherence involved in the activity of the tubules of the neural cell membranes.

20. This point was also made to me by Timothy O'Connor in correspondence.

21. For determined choices, by contrast, chaotic indeterminacies in the wave patterns of self-network would become negligible and the feasible options would be reduced to one.

22. After this book was in production, I came upon two excellent articles by David Widerker (1995a and 1995b) in which he makes arguments for libertarianism and against Frankfurt control similar to those made here in T41. I think Widerker is correct in the conclusions he draws in both these articles that if an action is undetermined, the agent could have done otherwise, even if a Frankfurt controller was present. But to complete the case for libertarian free choice in relation to Frankfurt control, I think one also has to add the arguments in the remainder of this section, including T42, along with the arguments on Frankfurt control made in chap. 3, secs. 6 and 7. One only has to deny the possibility of Frankfurt control for some ultimately responsible choices or actions done "of one's own free will," namely SFWs. With regard to other, determined, choices or actions done of our own free wills, we can still be ultimately responsible for them, though we could not have done otherwise then and there, *if we nonetheless do them on our own* and the controller does not in fact intervene, though he could have intervened. John Martin Fischer attempts to respond to Widerker's 1995b by, among other things, invoking a version of libertarian choice suggested in Dennett, 1978. Fischer's response is clever, but ultimately, I think, unsuccessful. Dennett's version of libertarian free choice would indeed escape Widerker's argument, but, as I argue later in chap. 9, secs. 6 and 7, Dennett's suggestions give us only a partial, not a completely adequate, account of libertarian free choice. Another perceptive, but earlier, article on Frankfurt scenarios by Robert Heinaman (1986: 266–76) also argues, rightly I believe, that if an

action is undetermined, there is a sense in which the agent could have done otherwise, even if a Frankfurt controller was present. Heinaman adds, however, that it might have been the case that the controller could have brought the action about anyway if the agent had not done it (indeterministically) on his own, so that "all the alternative routes" the agent might have taken would have ended in that same action's being performed. In that case, Heinaman says, the agent could not have done otherwise in "Frankfurt's sense," though the agent could still have done otherwise in an indeterminist sense with respect to the route chosen. But while this is possible for some actions, in the case of SFWs the distinction between action and route chosen collapses. When the action A is an SFW it is the immediate resolution of uncertainty and indeterminacy in the mind, and the agent could have done otherwise with respect to A itself, not merely with respect to the route to it as T41 argues.

23. In an interesting recent book on Thomas Reid, William Rowe (1991: 51ff.) has suggested that postulating agent-causation (of a nonoccurrent kind) might help libertarians answer Frankfurt's claim that responsibility does not entail "could have done otherwise." According to Rowe, agent-causalists such as Thomas Reid could say that if Jones does A on his own, then he (nonoccurrently) causes his doing of A; but if Black makes Jones do A, then while Jones *does* A, he does not (nonoccurrenty) *cause* his own doing of A. Rather, he is caused to do A by Black. Then libertarians could say that if Jones acts on his own, while Jones could not do other-than-A, he nevertheless could have done otherwise in an important sense. He could have done other than agent-cause his doing of A. Rowe's suggestion is ingenious (though also see Fischer, 1994: chap. 7, for perceptive criticisms of it.) But I would argue that Frankfurt's challenge can be answered more directly by libertarians *without* postulating agent-causation or nonoccurrent causation of the Reidian or any other kind. As shown by T41, the simple fact of indeterminacy right up to the moment of choice does the job quite well on its own. Notice also that T41 concedes less to Frankfurt than Rowe's Reidian proposal. Rowe concedes to Frankfurt that if Jones acts on his own and Black does not intervene, then Jones cannot in fact do *other than* A (even if Jones can do other than agent-cause his doing of A). By contrast, on the account given in T41, no such concession has to be made to Frankfurt. If Black does not intervene and Jones does A on his own, and A is an undetermined SFW, then Jones can do other *than A itself*. Jones might have made choice B rather than A in an incompatibilist sense.

24. Note that plural voluntary control as defined by this thesis subsumes the other two plurality conditions, plural rationality and voluntariness. Indeed, the three plurality conditions are nested. Plural voluntary control includes plural voluntariness and plural voluntariness in turn includes plural rationality. I nonetheless treat the three conditions separately, because each adds distinctive requirements that are usefully distinguished.

25. This price paid for free will can seem frightening because of the value we place on antecedent determining control for biological survival, security, and flourishing. Sartre (1962) was not altogether wrong in saying that self-conscious beings might well fear indeterminist freedom and want to "escape from" it, realizing the risks and insecurity it involves. The cosmic irony is that, in the dialectic of selfhood described in chapter 6 when free will enters the picture, persons reach a stage of self-consciousness at which they realize (or should realize) that in order for their contributions to the world and their own self-making to be ultimately theirs, they have to relinquish a kind of control over events that would guarantee in advance how they will turn out.

26. The designation "TI" or "teleological intelligibility" theory was used in Kane, 1989. Watson uses the expression in 1982: 11 and 1987: 165.

27. Also see Flanagan, 1992, on this theme.

28. I use the expression "extreme" eliminative materialism for any view like the one described in this thesis that would eliminate folk psychological language altogether, leaving

only physical descriptions that do not capture the normative and intentional contents of folk psychological language. In her recent presidential address to the Pacific Division of the American Philosophical Association (1994: 26), a noted eliminativist, Patricia Churchland, seemed to distance herself from this extreme position by talking about "reconfiguring" folk psychology in a future neuroscience rather than eliminating its categories and distinctions altogether. One would have to know how far such a reconfiguration would go in order to pass judgment on whether such a view would be ruled out by T49. Churchland is mentioned in the next thesis, T50.

29. The case for saying that folk psychology cannot be dispensed with even for a scientific psychology is made by Terence Horgan and James Woodward, 1985, by Horgan and George Graham, 1991, and by Graham, 1993. For a forceful statement of the opposing view, see Paul Churchland, 1988.

30. These explanatory roles are more than merely causal. They include, for example, intentionality and propositional content (consider, e.g., that a purpose is the content of an intention), and much depends upon how these features of folk psychological states would be "reconfigured" in a future psychology. Similarly, regarding the action/happening distinction, from a *merely* physical point of view every process in the brain is simply a happening; yet some of those physical happenings are mental actions the agents are performing (such as concentrating, attending, or choosing) while others are experiences they are undergoing.

31. Other views of willing with some affinities, include Hugh McCann, 1974, 1986; Carl Ginet, 1990; and Lawrence Davis, 1979. But note that, unlike volitions, as generally conceived by these authors, including O'Shaughnessy, efforts or tryings specifically involved in SFWs are always made against resistance within the will.

32. I owe this way of formulating the matter to discussions with Nathan Kane about neuroscience, the mind/body problem, and determinism.

33 Scott, 1991a; Stapp, 1990; Huberman and Hogg, 1987.

34. Wittgenstein 1980: 75. I am indebted to Hilary Putnam for pointing me to this wonderful quote.

35. A possible physical representation for this fusion might be a quantum wave function for the entire neural network that would be a superposition of the wave functions of its parts. (Cf. suggestions of F. Wolf, 1986; Zohar, 1990; Goswami, 1990; Stapp, 1993; and Zohar and Marshall, 1994). Another possible mechanism for conscious fusion is a further holistic quantum phenomenon, namely, boson (or Bose-Einstein) condensation (see references in note 36).

36. This possible connection is a much discussed topic of late and is a subject of more than a few interesting recent works, notably, Penrose, 1989 and 1994; Lockwood, 1989; Hodgson, 1991; Bohm, 1986; F. Wolf, 1984, 1986; Goswami, 1990; Stapp, 1990, 1993; Zohar, 1990; and Zohar and Marshall, 1994. On Bose-Einstein condensation, which some of these authors mention as a possible mechanism for fusion, see the pioneering work of Frohlich, 1986, as well as Vitiello and del Giudice, 1984, and Marshall, 1989; for further discussion of it, see Lockwood, 1989; Penrose, 1994; Zohar, 1990; and Zohar and Marshall, 1994. Stapp (1993: 29) says that he shares Penrose's view that the "main reasons for believing that the quantum character of reality is essential to the occurrence of consciousness is the shared 'global' character of conscious thought and quantum reality."

Chapter 9

1. This quoted example is from correspondence carried on with Rockwell. His arguments, as well as those of Claudette Kane, and of several other readers of my earlier work, including George Graham, John Post, David Blumenfeld, and Noah Lemos, led me to think about expanding the scope of free willings in this chapter by comparison with earlier work.

2. How these efforts sustaining purposes might be reconciled with the well-known experiments of Libet (1985) concerning unconscious initiation of voluntary action is indicated in note 12 of chapter 8. There may be dispositions to act contrary to avowed purposes—and correlative readiness potentials in the brain—before the agent is conscious of them. In such cases, consciousness would then come on the scene milliseconds later, with accompanying tension or tautness, playing an oversight role (as indicated in note 12, chapter 8), with veto power over whether or not these readiness potentials would be consummated in action.

3. Some of the examples and much of my understanding of cases in this category comes from lengthy discussions with Claudette Kane, whose influence on this as well as many other topics in this book is greater than I can recount. I've also benefited from correspondence on self-control with Alfred Mele and Howard Rachlin.

4. For discussion and further references see Mele, 1987, and Rachlin, 1994.

5. See Dennett, 1978, chap. 15.

6. This point is nicely made in Mele, 1995, chap. 13.

7. Kane, 1985: 102.

8. Nozick (1981: 294–5) expresses a similar idea in a different way when he talks about "assigning" or 'bestowing" more or less "weight" upon reasons one already has. Timothy O'Connor (1993a) effectively criticizes some ideas that Nozick adds to this basic one, but the themes O'Connor criticizes in Nozick's view do not affect the notion of "endorsement" of reasons introduced here .

9. The view of practical choice so far put forward has been called a "Valerian" theory, after Dennett's citation from the poet Valery. The expression "Valerian theory" was first introduced by Mark Bernstein (1989) and subsequently used by others (e.g., Double, 1991, and Hasker [unpublished paper]) to describe models of undetermined choices such as mine and Dennett's (1978). While I think the designation "Valerian theory" is useful, I have resisted it as an adequate designation of my own view (cf. Kane, 1988) because the Valerian theme is only a part of my theory, not adequate in itself even for an account of free practical choice—for the reasons just considered. It is one piece of the overall puzzle of free will, but it is misleading, I think, to make it the defining theme.

10. For this theme in Taoism, see Blakney, ed., 1955: 39–40, 54, 100; in Zen Buddhism, see Suzuki, 1956: chaps. 1, 6.

11. Blakney, ibid.

12. Specifically, A and B are incommensurable alternatives (possible actions, purposes, or plans) for an agent at a time just in case the agent has reasons (or motives), $a_1 \ldots a_n$, for preferring A to B and to all other alternatives (C, D . . .) at the time, and reasons, $b_1 \ldots b_n$, for preferring B to A and to all other alternatives, but no reasons for preferring either of the sets of reasons, $a_1 \ldots a_n$ and $b_1 \ldots b_n$, over the other at the time—and hence no all-things-considered preference for either alternative. The alternatives are incommensurable in the sense that the agent's overall view at the time allows no definitive ordering (or measure) of them as better or worse relative to one another.

13. Kane, 1985, chaps. 5, 10.

14. For other discussions, some of them more skeptical about the phenomenon, see Mortimore, ed., 1971; Jackson, 1984; Charlton, 1988; Gosling, 1990; Bigelow, Dodds and Pargetter, 1990; Robinson, 1991; Hurley, 1993; and Walker, 1989.

Chapter 10

1. By Talbott and Double in correspondence; by Bernstein and Blumenfeld in discussion. Galen Strawson puts it this way (1994: 19): "If my efforts of will shape my charac-

ter in an admirable way, and in so doing are partly indeterministic in nature, while also being influenced (as Kane grants) by my already existing character, why am I not merely lucky?"

2. A natural objection here would be that the quantum-wave functions of the brains of the two persons would be exactly the same (albeit very complex) combinations of the wave functions of their component particles. But these wave functions are abstract descriptions of the real brains that do not tell us what the exact positions and momenta of the component particles are. Rather they yield various probabilities that the particles will have such-and-such positions and momenta. And if the particles of the two brains cannot be described as having exact positions and momenta, then the two brains cannot be said to be in exactly the same states despite the sameness of their abstract descriptions. (Neither, of course, can they be said to be in exactly different states.) Of course, it is precisely this sort of situation that leads people to think that quantum theory must not be telling the whole story and that there must be more to say about the physical reality in the form of hidden variables or some new theory. Or, it leads others to instrumentalist or nonrealist interpretations of the theory, in which the wave or other representations of quantum states do not represent or picture states of reality, but are merely instruments for prediction. The latter position would seem to support the claim that exact sameness is not defined, while the former (some new theory) is at this stage only a wish. I should add that I am fully aware that the claims of this thesis are controversial and raise all sorts of questions about the interpretation of quantum reality to which there are no generally agreed-upon answers. But I put the thesis forward speculatively in the hope of stimulating further thought and discussion about these matters.

3. John Earman (1986) has offered imaginative and powerful arguments to show that classical Newtonian worlds (excluding global conservation laws) do allow for the possibility of such different futures given the same determinate past, contrary to the usual assumptions about their deterministic nature.

4. John Earman, 1986: 150, Arthur Fine, 1971, and Paul Teller, 1979, have shown how to imagine worlds of the latter kind in terms of set- or interval-valued properties. Systems would evolve uniquely from ranges or sets of magnitudes, say, positions or momenta, to other ranges or sets of magnitudes. Also see Kellert on these possibilities, 1993: 60–61; 69.

5. On the objection that the quantum-wave functions themselves are exact descriptions, see note 2 of this chapter.

6. As suggested, e.g., by Penrose, 1989, 1994; Bohm, 1986; Lockwood, 1989; Goswami, 1990; Stapp, 1990, 1993.

7. Earman (1986) suggests defining determinism in terms of uniform evolution alone, thus allowing one to say that quantum mechanics is deterministic, though in a way that is consistent with indeterminacy and probabilistic law (as described in note 4). This suggestion has merit in showing that quantum indeterminism is not mere chance or randomness and is consistent with uniform laws, but it does not alter the stakes in free-will debates in which determination of a unique future is at issue.

8. Cf. Kane, 1988a, 1989 .

9. An excellent collection of essays on explanation is Ruben, 1993, which contains selections from Salmon 1984 (pp. 78–112) and Lewis 1986 (pp. 182–206) dealing with this point. Also see Railton, 1978.

10. See Kane, 1988a, and Clarke, 1992.

11. Kane, 1988a, which was a response to Double, 1988. Double responded in turn in Double, 1991, and (to both Clarke and Kane) in Double, 1993. My response to Double 1991 and 1993 is contained in these sections.

12. This point is nicely made by Audi in an article on inductive generalization and psychological laws (1981).

13. This, I believe, is the important connection between free will and what is sometimes called "virtue ethics."

14. See chap. 8, note 33.

15. To put this another way, a "hard determinist" position like that advocated by Honderich, 1988, Weatherford, 1991, and also Waller, 1992, and Pereboom, 1995, is one that libertarians cannot dismiss out of hand, inasmuch as it could turn out to be true. (Waller's position is unusual in that he is a hard determinist about moral responsibility, but not about freedom to do otherwise.)

16. See the references on these matters in notes to section 4 of chapter 8.

17 As most agent-causalists themselves would admit. For, most of them hold that nonoccurrent causation is only needed to account for undetermined actions, not for actions in general, whether determined or not. See the discussion in chapter 7, section 10.

18. See the last two sections of chapter 7 for citations in support of this claim.

19. See chapter 7, section 10.

20. I mean to include omissions here as well, but leave them out of this and following descriptions to avoid complicating the discussion further.

21. And the same is true for other controllers, e.g., CNC controllers, or mechanisms.

22. Flanagan, 1992. See chapter 8, section 8 for further details.

23. See chapter 8, section 8.

24. For determined choices, by contrast, chaotic indeterminacies in the wave patterns of the self-network become negligible and the feasible options are reduced to one.

25. Anscombe, 1971. See chapter 7, section 6, for further discussion.

26. See references in chapter 8, notes 35 and 36.

27. Taylor repudiates agent-causation in Taylor, 1982. Chisholm (in his "Self-Profile" and "Replies to Critics" in Chisholm, 1982: 61–4, 213–15) reconstructs his theory without appealing to agent- or "immanent" causation, as he has sometimes called it. He now thinks that causal contribution by psychological events without sufficient causal conditions will do the job and agent-causation isn't needed (1995: 95). Stewart Goetz (1988) is another libertarian who thinks that libertarians can, and should, try to do without agent-causation. He argues, however, against both Chisholm and Taylor, and in contrast to my view, for a "noncausal" theory of agency—one that does not appeal essentially to causal contribution, or causation (even nondeterministic causation) by psychological events. (See note 28 for a general categorization of this sort of view.)

28. Ginet, 1992: 12–14. Among contemporary libertarians, Ginet's view is as close to mine as any, especially in its repudiation of agent-causation. Still, there are major differences, as pointed out by O'Connor, 1993a, 1995, and Clarke, 1995, who distinguish three categories of contemporary libertarian theories: (1) simple indeterminists, (2) causal indeterminists, and (3) agent-cause theorists. O'Connor and Clarke place Ginet's view in category 1 and mine in category 2. Simple indeterminists and causal indeterminists both reject agent-causation; the difference between them is that simple indeterminists do not appeal to event-causation (even of a nondeterministic kind) to account for undetermined free actions (they appeal to reasons explanations alone), while causal indeterminists believe that reasons explanations are compatible with causal explanations and that nondeterministic event causation has an essential role to play, along with reasons explanations, in accounts of libertarian free action. It is fair to say that most libertarians continue to be agent-causalists of one kind or another (category 3), but in the past two decades a few libertarians have moved to positions 1 or 2. O'Connor and Clarke list only Ginet as a simple indeterminist, though another libertarian who seems to fit the mold is Goetz, 1988 (see note 27). As causal indeterminists, O'Connor (1995: 7–8) lists, Nozick, Kane,

and Chisholm (i.e., Chisholm after his repudiation of agent-causation). Nozick's position is not entirely clear since, in 1981, he puts forward several accounts of free action without clearly endorsing any one of them , though one of the views he puts forward is causal indeterminist. Another philosopher who may fall into the causal indeterminist camp is David Wiggins (see the next note).

29. Nozick, 1981; Wiggins, 1973: 52. Wiggins has not attempted to develop a libertarian alternative to agent-causation in any detail, but his occasional comments on the matter (some of them quoted in earlier chapters) are insightful and point, it seems to me, in a causal indeterminist direction. John Thorp is another interesting case. Thorp defends libertarianism in Thorp, 1980, by invoking agent-causation. But he admits with characteristic frankness that his discussion of agent-causation is "at times distressingly abstract and obscure" (p. 96). In fact, much of what Thorp says about agents causing their decisions (cf. p. 102), as well as some of his interesting discussions of "hegemony" and the "correlation thesis" between mental and physical events, suggests that he is closer to the causal indeterminist view favored in this book than to the agent-causal view.

30. On Thorp, see note 29.

31. E.g., Alan Donagan, 1987, and, with some reservations, Peter van Inwagen, 1983. Van Inwagen has recently said in correspondence that his view on this topic remains the same as that expressed in his *An Essay on Free Will* in 1983, in which he said, "I find the concept of immanent or agent causation puzzling, as I suspect most of my readers do (those who don't find it downright incoherent). In fact, I find it more puzzling than the problem it is supposed to be a solution to" (p. 151). Yet, van Inwagen goes on to suggest (p. 152) that if libertarians wish to answer all familiar objections against their view, they must strive to make the notion of immanent causation less puzzling than it is.

Chapter 11

1. Chap. 8, sec. 9 (T40) and 12 (T49); chap. 9, sec. 2 (T55); chap. 10, sec. 11 (T86).

2. George Graham in correspondence has rightly noted that I could have added a fifth question about free will to the four major ones considered in this book—namely, an "Epistemological Question": "If free will actually exists in the natural order, do we, or can we, know that we possess such a freedom?" As a sub-question, Graham adds, "Is the knowledge we might possess of such a freedom direct, immediate or privileged?" The answer to the second question is clearly no, on my account. As indicated in the first chapter, I agree with the arguments of Mill and many others that we cannot know we have incompatibilist free will by introspection alone. Empirical evidence is needed about the hidden causes of our behavior, including physical ones, and this must come about by indirect, empirical inquiry. So the answer to Graham's Epistemological Question is that we can have good empirical evidence for (or against) the existence of free will in the natural order, but not direct, immediate or certain knowledge. We cannot know we have free will by introspection alone, or indeed on a priori grounds. It follows from these remarks, as Graham also notes, that the view presented here is "realist" about incompatibilist free will. That is to say, there is a "fact of the matter" about whether we do or do not have such a freedom (however it may be known). Thus, the view defended here is also opposed to a non-realist view like Richard Double's (1991), according to which "free will" is a value-laden term whose ascription to acts or agents tells us about the attitudes of the ascribers toward the acts or agents, rather than describing facts about the acts or agents themselves. My response to Double on this point is as follows: I agree with him (and with many others cited in the first chapter (section 7)) that the positions we take on free will depend to some extent on our attitudes and values, via the Signifi-

cance Question (i.e., whether or not we think a freedom requiring ultimate responsibility is worth wanting). But, unlike Double, I do not believe that questions about value and worth (as difficult as they may be to answer) lack objective answers. (Double is a nonrealist about values as well as about free will, believing statements about values are neither objectively true nor false.) Second, if, as I have argued, the traditional debate about free will has historically been about a kind of freedom that requires ultimate responsibility, then there are "facts of the matter" about whether a freedom of _such_ a kind can exist or does in fact exist. In other words, if one means by "free will" the kind of freedom that I believe has been the subject of continuing philosophical and theological controversy down through the ages, then there are facts of the matter about whether such a freedom exists.

3. For the appropriate references here to the liberty of indifference, see chapter 7, section 3.

4. E.g., Kenny, 1976, Nathan, 1992.

5. Cf. Berlin, 1969; Rorty, 1979; Blumenberg, 1983; and Lyotard, 1987.

6. See chapter 7, section 3.

7. If the options were filet mignon left and vegetarian salad right, it would be another matter.

8. Which is why the Incommensurability Thesis says that "typical" exercises of free will involve incommensurable alternatives.

9. In a new book on Berlin, which I have not seen, but only read about while putting the finishing touches on this work, John Gray (1995) argues that this notion of "value pluralism" is the central, unifying theme of all of Berlin's work.

10. Cf. Berlin, 1969, p. 171, in which he relates the denial of incommensurable values to the giving of complete (presumably, deterministic) explanations of human behavior.

11. Skinner, 1969: chap. 29.

12. Kant, 1956, 1959.

13. Kierkegaard, 1959, vol. 2.

14. That is to say, self-interest has its own rationality, amply studied by rational decision theorists and others. Some latter-day Hobbesians on ethical and political matters, such as David Gauthier (1986), argue that one can get from self-interested rationality to morality by way of a social contract theory that employs reasoning in the manner of a "prisoner's dilemma." Subtle as these modern theories are, I think they, too, fall short of morality. But that is another complex topic, not to be pursued in this work. (I have pursued it and other ethical issues discussed in this chapter and in chapter 6 in Kane, 1994b.)

15. Especially in Kant, 1960. Various ingenious suggestions have been made about how Kant might have resolved the problems created by this consequence, e.g., by John Silber in the introduction to Kant, 1960; by Allen Wood, 1984; and by Henry Allison, 1990. For further discussion of the issues, see Shatz, 1988.

16. See Sidgwick, 1907: book 1, chap. 5, sec. 1; Ross, 1939: 226–7. Also see Nagel, 1986: 137.

17. If someone were to respond to this by saying that what they mean by reason when they oppose reason to desire is something richer than merely theoretical or pure reason—something that (like Plato's conception of eros) involves a love or striving for higher purposes that transcend merely _sensuous_ desires—I would take that not to be a refutation of the above argument, but a confirmation of it. For it would be conceding the key point that free will involves a conflict between different kinds of desires, conceived though they may be as higher and lower desires by the agents.

18. Kant, 1959: 47.

19. I offer a fuller defense of such an ethical view on other grounds in Kane, 1994b.

20. Popper, 1965: chap. 1.
21. The clearest expression of these pragmatist themes are the essays in James, 1956.
22. I make a more detailed case for the claims of this paragraph in Kane, 1995c.
23. Quoted by Berlin 1969, p. 137.
24. While this theme is implicit in Blumenberg's 1983, it is explicitly stated in his 1985.
25. Melville, 1987, p. 15 (end of chap. 2).

References

Abelson, Raziel. 1988. *Lawless Mind*. Philadelphia: Temple University Press.
Adams, Robert M. 1985. "Involuntary Sins." *Philosophical Review* 94: 3–31.
——. 1982. "Leibniz's Theories of Contingency." In M. Hooker, ed., *Leibniz: Critical and Interpretive Essays*. Minneapolis: University of Minnesota Press, 243–83.
Adler, Mortimer, ed. 1958. *The Idea of Freedom*. 2 Vols. New York: Doubleday and Company.
Albritton, Rogers. 1985. "Freedom of the Will and the Freedom of Action." *Proceedings of the Americal Philosophical Association* 59: 239–51.
Allison, Henry. 1990. *Kant's Theory of Freedom*. Cambridge: Cambridge University Press.
Alston, William. 1977. "Self-intervention and the Structure of Motivation." In T. Mischel, ed., *The Self: Philosophical and Psychological Issues*. Oxford: Oxford University Press, 65–102.
Anglin, W. S. 1990. *Free Will and the Christian Faith*. Oxford: Oxford University Press.
Anscombe, G. E. M. 1971. *Causality and Determinism*. Cambridge: Cambridge University Press.
Aquinas, Saint Thomas. 1945. *Basic Writings of St. Thomas Aquinas*. Vol. 1. Ed. by A. Pegis. New York: Random House.
Aristotle. 1915. *Nichomachean Ethics*. Vol. 9 of *The Works of Aristotle*. Ed. by W. D. Ross. London: Oxford University Press.
Audi, Robert. 1993. *Action, Intention, and Reason*. Ithaca: Cornell University Press.
——. 1989. *Practical Reasoning*. London: Routledge & Kegan Paul.
——. 1986. "Acting for Reasons." *Philosophical Review* 95: 511–46.
——. 1981. "Inductive Nomological Generalizations and Psychological Laws." *Theory and Decision* 13: 229–49.
——. 1974. "Moral Responsibility, Freedom, and Compulsion." *American Philosophical Quarterly* 19: 25–39.
——. 1973. "Intending." *Journal of Philosophy* 70: 387–403.
Augustine. 1964. *On the Free Choice of the Will*. Indianapolis: Bobbs-Merrill.
Aune, Bruce. 1977. *Reason and Action*. Dordrecht: Reidel.
Austin, J. L. 1966. "Ifs and Cans." In Berofsky, ed., 1966: 295–321.
——. 1961. *Philosophical Papers*. Oxford: Oxford University Press.
Ayer, A. J. 1954. "Freedom and Necessity." in A. J. Ayer, *Philosophical Essays*. New York: St. Martin's Press, 3–20.
Ayers, M. R. 1968. *The Refutation of Determinism*. London: Methuen.
Babloyantz, A. and A. Destexhe. 1985. "Strange Attractors in the Human Cortex." In Ludger Rensing, ed., *Temporal Disorder in Human Oscillatory Systems*. New York: Springer-Verlag, 132–43.

Bailey, Cyril. 1964. *The Greek Atomists and Epicurus*. New York: Russell and Russell.

Baker, Lynne Rudder. 1993. "Metaphysics and Mental Causation." In Heil and Mele, eds., 1993: 75–96.

Barrett, William. 1958. "Determinism and Novelty." In Hook, ed., 1958: 46–54.

Batterman, Robert. 1993. "Defining Chaos." *Philosophy of Science* 60: 43–66.

Benn, Stanley. 1988. *A Theory of Freedom*. Cambridge: Cambridge University Press.

Bennett, Jonathan. 1980. "Accountability." In Z. van Straaten, ed., *Philosophical Subjects*. Oxford: Clarendon Press, 74–91.

Benson, Paul. 1987. "Freedom and Value." *Journal of Philosophy* 84: 465–87.

Bergmann, Fritjoh. 1977. *On Being Free*. Notre Dame: Notre Dame University Press.

Bergson, Henri. 1960. *Time and Free Will*. New York: Harper & Row.

Bernstein, Mark. 1995. "Kanean Libertarianism." *Southwest Philosophy Review* 11: 151–7.

——. 1992. *Fatalism*. Lincoln: University of Nebraska Press.

——. 1989. Review of R. Kane, *Free Will and Values*. *Noûs* 23: 557–9.

——. 1983. "Socialization and Autonomy." *Mind* 93: 120–3.

Berlin, Isaiah. 1969. *Four Essays on Liberty*. Oxford: Oxford University Press.

Berofsky, Bernard. 1995. *Liberation from Self*. Cambridge: Cambridge University Press.

——. 1992. "On the Absolute Freedom of the Will." *American Philosophical Quarterly* 29: 279–89.

——. 1987. *Freedom from Necessity*. London: Routledge & Kegan Paul.

——. 1971. *Determinism*. Princeton: Princeton University Press.

——. ed. 1966. *Free Will and Determinism*. New York: Harper & Row.

Bigelow, John, S. Dodds, and R. Pargetter. 1990. "Temptation and the Will." *American Philosophical Quarterly* 27: 39–49.

Bishop, John. 1989. *Natural Agency*. Cambridge: Cambridge University Press.

Bishop, Robert. 1995. "Is Classical Chaos Indeterministic?" Paper delivered at the Tenth International Congress on Logic, Methodology, and Philosophy of Science, Florence, Italy.

——. Forthcoming. "Chaotic Dynamics, Quantum Mechanics, and Free Will." Ph.D. diss. in progress, University of Texas at Austin.

Blakney, R. B., ed. 1955. *The Way of Life of Lao-Tzu: Translation of the Tao-Te-Ching*. New York: New American Library.

Blum, Alex. 1990. "On a Mainstay of Incompatibilism." *Iyyum* 39: 267–79.

Blumenberg, Hans. 1985. *Work on Myth*. Cambridge, Mass.: MIT Press.

——. 1983. *The Legitimacy of the Modern Age*. Cambridge, Mass.: MIT Press.

Blumenfeld, David. 1988. "Freedom and Mind Control." *American Philosophical Quarterly* 25: 215–27.

——. 1971. "The Principle of Alternative Possibilities." *Journal of Philosophy* 68: 339–45.

Bohm, David. 1986. "The Implicate Order." In D. Schindler, ed., *Beyond Mechanism*. New York: The University Press of America.

Bonjour, Laurence. 1976. "Determinism, Libertarianism, and Agent Causation." *Southern Journal of Philosophy* 14: 145–56.

Bourke, Vernon. 1964. *Will in Western Thought*. New York: Sheed and Ward.

Bradley, F. H. 1927. *Ethical Studies*. Oxford: Oxford University Press.

Bramhall, John. 1844. *The Works of John Bramhall*. Oxford: John Henry Parker.

Brand, Myles. 1984. *Intending and Acting*. Cambridge, Mass.: MIT Press.

Bratman, Michael. 1987. *Intentions, Plans, and Practical Reason*. Cambridge, Mass.: Harvard University Press.

Broad, C. D. 1962. "Determinism, Indeterminism, and Libertarianism." In Morgenbesser and Walsh, eds., 115–32.

Broadie, Sarah. 1991. *Ethics with Aristotle.* Oxford: Oxford University Press.

Bruner, Jerome. 1986. *Actual Minds, Possible Worlds.* Cambridge: Harvard University Press.

Burms, A., and H. DeDijn. 1979. "Freedom and Logical Contingency in Leibniz." *Studia Leibnitiana* 11: 124–33.

Calvin, William H. 1990. *The Cerebral Symphony: Seashore Reflections on the Structure of Consciousness.* New York: Bantam Books.

Campbell, C. A. 1967. *In Defense of Free Will.* London: Allen & Unwin.

Campbell, Donald. 1960. "Blind Variation and Selective Retention in Creative Thought." *Psychological Review* 67: 380–400.

Carr, Craig. 1985. "Coercion and Freedom." *American Philosophical Quarterly* 25: 59–67.

Charlton, William. 1988. *Weakness of Will.* Oxford: Basil Blackwell.

Chisholm, R. M. 1995. "Agents, Causes and Events." In O'Connor, ed., 1995: 95–100.

———. 1982. "Self-Profile" and "Replies." In R. J. Bogdan, ed., *Roderick M. Chisholm.* Dordrecht: Reidel, 1–16, 141–165.

———. 1982. "Human Thought and the Self." In Watson, ed., 1982: 24–35.

———. 1976. *Person and Object.* Lasalle, Ill.: Open Court.

———. 1966. "J. L. Austin's Philosophical Papers." In Berofsky, ed., 1966: 339–45.

Christman, John, ed., 1989. *The Inner Citadel: Essays on Individual Autonomy.* Oxford: Oxford University Press.

———. 1988. "Constructing the Inner Citadel: Recent Work on Autonomy." *Ethics* 99: 109–24.

Churchland, Patricia S. 1994. "Can Neurobiology Teach Us Anything about Consciousness?" *Proceedings of the American Philosophical Association* 67: 23–40.

———. 1986. *Neurophilosophy.* Cambridge, Mass.: MIT Press.

Churchland, Paul M. 1988. *Matter and Consciousness.* Cambridge, Mass.: MIT Press.

Cicero. 1960. *De Oratore, De Fato.* Trans. by H. Rackham. London: Heinemann.

Clarke, Randolph. 1995. "Freedom and Determinism: Recent Work." *Philosophical Books* 36: 9–18.

———. 1993. "Towards a Credible Agent-Causal Account of Free Will." *Noûs* 27: 191–203. Reprinted in O'Connor, ed., 1995: 201–15.

———. 1992. "A Principle of Rational Explanation." *The Southern Journal of Philosophy* 30: 1–12.

Compton, A. H. 1935. *The Freedom of Man.* New Haven: Yale University Press.

Crick, Francis. 1994. *The Astonishing Hypothesis.* New York: Scribner's Sons.

Crick, Francis, and Christof Koch. 1990. "Towards a Neurobiological Theory of Consciousness." *Seminars in the Neurosciences* 4: 263–76.

Dante Alighieri. 1932. *Paradiso.* Trans. by G. Bickersteth. Cambridge: Cambridge University Press.

Davidson, Donald. 1980. *Essays on Actions and Events.* Oxford: Clarendon Press.

———. 1973. "Freedom to Act." In Honderich, 1973: 67–86.

———. 1966. "Actions, Reasons, and Causes." In Berofsky, ed., 1966: 221–39.

Davies, Martin. 1983. "Boethius and Others on Divine Foreknowledge." *Pacific Philosophical Quarterly* 8: 313–29.

Davis, Lawrence. 1979. *Theory of Action.* Englewood Cliffs, N.J.: Prentice-Hall.

Deeke, L., B. Grotzinger, and H. H. Kornhuber. 1976. "Voluntary Finger Movement in Man: Cerebral Potentials and Theory." *Biological Cybernetics* 23: 99.

Dennett, Daniel. 1991. *Consciousness Explained.* Boston: Little, Brown.

———. 1988. "Why Everyone Is a Novelist?" *Times Literary Supplement* 4: 1016–22.

———. 1984. *Elbow Room.* Cambridge, Mass.: MIT Press.

——. 1978. *Brainstorms*. Cambridge, Mass.: MIT Press.

——. 1973. "Mechanism and Responsibility." In Honderich, ed., 1973: 159–84.

Descartes, René. 1955. *Philosophical Works*. Vol. 1. Ed. and trans. by J. Haldane and W. Ross. New York: Dover Publications.

Donagan, Alan. 1987. *Choice*. London: Routledge & Kegan Paul.

Double, Richard. 1993. "The Principle of Rational Explanation Defended." *The Southern Journal of Philosophy* 31: 133–42.

——. 1991. *The Non-reality of Free Will*. Oxford: Oxford University Press.

——. 1988a. "Libertarianism and Rationality." *The Southern Journal of Philosophy* 26: 431–39.

——. 1988b. Review of R. Kane, *Free Will and Values*. *Philosophical Books* 29: 96–7.

——. Forthcoming. *Metaphilosophy and Free Will*. Oxford: Oxford University Press.

Dretske, Fred. 1988. *Explaining Behavior: Reasons in a World of Causes*. Cambridge, Mass.: MIT Press.

Duggan, Timothy, and Bernard Gert. 1979. "Free Will and the Ability to Will." *Noûs* 13: 197–217.

Dunn, Robert. 1987. *The Possibility of Weakness of Will*. Indianapolis: Hackett.

Dupré, John. 1993. *The Disorder of Things*. Cambridge, Mass.: Harvard University Press.

Dworkin, Gerald. 1988. *The Theory and Practice of Autonomy*. Cambridge: Cambridge University Press.

——. 1986. Review of Dennett, *Elbow Room*. *Ethics* 96: 423–5.

——. 1970a. "Acting Freely." *Noûs* 4: 367–83.

——. ed., 1970b. *Determinism, Free Will, and Moral Responsibility*. Englewood Cliffs, N.J.: Prentice-Hall.

Earman, John. 1986. *A Primer on Determinism*. Dordrecht: Reidel.

Eccles, John. 1970. *Facing Reality*. New York: Springer-Verlag.

Eckhorn, J., R. Bauer, W. Jordan, M. Brosch, W. Kruse, M. Monk, and H. Reitbueck. 1988. "Coherent Oscillations: A Mechanism of Feature Linking in the Neural Cortex?" *Biological Cybernetics* 60: 121–30.

Edelman, G. M. 1987. *Neural Darwinism*. New York: Basic Books.

——. 1993. *Bright Air, Brilliant Fire*. New York: Basic Books.

Edwards, Jonathan. 1969. *The Freedom of the Will*. Indianapolis: Bobbs-Merrill.

Eells, Ellery. 1991. *Probabilistic Causality*. Cambridge: Cambridge University Press.

Erasmus-Luther. 1961. *Discourse on Free Will*. New York: Frederick Unger.

Falk, Arthur. 1981. "Some Modal Confusions in Compatibilism." *American Philosophical Quarterly* 18: 141–8.

Felt, James, S.J. 1994. *Making Sense of Your Freedom*. Ithaca, N.Y.: Cornell University Press.

Fine, Arthur. 1971. "Probability in Quantum Mechanics and Other Statistical Theories." In M. Bunge, ed., *Problems in the Foundations of Physics*. New York: Springer-Verlag, 79–92.

Fine, Gail. 1981. "Aristotle on Determinism." *The Philosophical Review* 90: 561–79.

Fischer, John Martin. 1995. "Libertarianism and Avoidability: A Reply to Widerker." *Faith and Philosophy* 12: 119–25.

——. 1994. *The Metaphysics of Free Will: A Study of Control*. Oxford: Basil Blackwell.

——. ed. 1986. *Moral Responsibility*. Ithaca, N.Y.: Cornell University Press.

——. 1983. "Incompatibilism." *Philosophical Studies* 43:127–37.

——. 1982. "Responsibility and Control." *Journal of Philosophy* 79: 24–40.

Fischer, John Martin, and Mark Ravizza, eds. 1993. *Perspectives on Moral Responsibility*. Ithaca, N.Y.: Cornell University Press.

———. 1992. "When the Will Is Free." In J. Tomberlin, ed., *Philosophical Perspectives*. Vol. 6. Atascadero, Calif.: Ridgeview Publishing, 423–51.

———. Forthcoming. *Responsibility and Control: A Theory of Moral Responsibility*. Cambridge: Cambridge University Press.

Flanagan, Owen. 1992. *Consciousness Reconsidered*. Cambridge, Mass.: MIT Press.

Flew, Antony, and Godfrey Vesey. 1987. *Agency and Necessity*. Oxford: Basil Blackwell.

Flint, Thomas. 1987. "Compatibilism and the Argument from Unavoidability." *Journal of Philosophy* 84: 423–40.

Foley, Richard. 1979. "Compatibilism and Control over the Past." *Analysis* 39: 70–4.

———. 1978. "Compatibilism." *Mind* 87: 421–8.

Foot, Philippa. 1966. "Free Will as Involving Determinism." In Berofsky, ed., 1966: 95–108.

Ford, Joseph. 1989. "What Is Chaos?" In P. Davies, ed., *The New Physics*. Cambridge: Cambridge University Press, 348–71.

Forrest, Peter. 1985. "Backwards Causation in Defense of Free Will." *Mind* 94: 210–17.

Frankfurt, Harry. 1992. "The Faintest Passion." *Proceedings of the American Philosophical Association* 66: 5–16.

———. 1988. *The Importance of What We Care About*. New York: Cambridge University Press.

———. 1971. "Freedom of the Will and the Concept of a Person." *Journal of Philosophy* 68: 5–20.

———. 1969. "Alternative Possibilities and Moral Responsibility." *Journal of Philosophy* 66: 829–39.

French, Peter. 1992. *Responsibility Matters*. Lawrence, Kan.: University of Kansas Press.

———. ed. 1972. *Individual and Collective Responsibility*. Cambridge, Mass.: Shenkman.

Friedman, Marilyn. 1986. "Autonomy and the Split-Level Self." *Southern Journal of Philosophy* 24: 19–35.

Frohlich, H. 1986. "Coherent Activation in Active Biological Systems." In F. Gutman and H. Keyzer, eds., *Modern Bioelectrochemistry*. New York: Plenum, 241–61.

Gallois, Andre. 1977. "Van Inwagen on Free Will and Determinism." *Philosophical Studies* 32: 99–105.

Garson, James. 1993. "Chaos and Free Will." Paper delivered to the American Philosophical Association, Pacific Division meeting, March, 1993.

Gauthier, David. 1986. *Morals by Agreement*. Oxford: Oxford University Press.

Gazzaniga, M. S. 1993. *Nature's Mind*. New York: Basic Books.

Gensler, Harry. 1989. Review of R. Kane, *Free Will and Values*. *The Modern Schoolman* 66: 160–2.

Ginet, Carl. 1990. *On Action*. Cambridge: Cambridge University Press.

———. 1966. "Might We Have No Choice?" In K. Lehrer, ed., *Freedom and Determinism*. New York: Random House, 87–104.

Glass, Leon, and Michael Mackey. 1988. *From Clocks to Chaos: The Rhythms of Life*. Princeton: Princeton Unviersity Press.

Globus, Gordon. 1995. "Kane on Incompatibilism: An Exercise in Neurophilosophy." Unpublished paper.

Glover, Jonathan. 1970. *Responsibility*. London: Routledge & Kegan Paul.

Glymour, Clark. 1971. "Determinism, Ignorance, and Quantum Mechanics." *Journal of Philosophy* 68: 744–51.

Goetz, Stewart C. 1988. "A Non-causal Theory of Agency." *Philosophy and Phenomenological Research* 49: 303–16.

———. "A Non-causal Theory of Choice." Unpublished paper.

Goldman, Alvin. 1970. *A Theory of Human Action*. Englewood Cliffs, N.J.: Prentice-Hall.

Gomberg, Paul. 1975. "Free Will as Ultimate Responsibility." *American Philosophical Quarterly* 15: 205–12.

Gosling, J. 1990. *Weakness of Will*. London: Routledge.

Goswami, Amit. 1990. "Consciousness in Quantum Physics and the Mind-Body Problem." *Journal of Mind and Behavior* 11: 75–96.

Graham, George. 1993. *The Philosophy of Mind*. Oxford: Basil Blackwell.

Gray, C., and W. Singer. 1989. "Stimulus Specific Neuronal Oscillations in Orientation Columns of the Lateral Visual Cortex." *Proceedings of the National Academy of Sciences* 86: 1689–1702.

Gray, John. 1995. *Isaiah Berlin*. London: HarperCollins.

Greenspan, P. S. 1993. "Free Will and the Genome Project." *Philosophy and Public Affairs* 22: 31–43.

———. 1978. "Behavior Control and Freedom of Action." *Philosophical Review* 87: 225–40.

Grice, Paul. 1967. *The Grounds of Moral Judgment*. Cambridge: Cambridge University Press.

Grünbaum, Adolph. 1971. "Free Will and the Laws of Human Behavior." *American Philosophical Quarterly* 8: 299–317.

Gunter, Pete A. Y. 1991. "Bergson and Non-linear, Non-equilibrium Thermodynamics." *Revue Internationale de Philosophie* 177: 108–21.

Harman, Gilbert. 1986. "Willing and Intending." In Richard Grandy and R. Warner, eds., *Philosophical Grounds of Rationality*. Oxford: Clarendon Press.

Hasker, William. 1995. "Unity of Consciousness, Free Will, and Agent Causation." Unpublished paper.

———. 1989. *God, Time, and Knowledge*. Ithaca, N.Y.: Cornell University Press.

Hawkins, David. 1967. *The Language of Nature*. Garden City: Doubleday.

Haworth, Laurence. 1986. *Autonomy*. New Haven: Yale University Press.

Heil, John. 1992. *The Nature of True Minds*. Cambridge: Cambridge University Press.

Heil, John, and Alfred Mele, eds. 1993. *Mental Causation*. Oxford: Oxford University Press.

Heinaman, Robert. 1986. "Incompatibilism without the Principle of Alternative Possibilities." *Australasian Journal of Philosophy* 64: 266–76.

Hill, Christopher. 1992. "Van Inwagen on the Consequence Argument." *Analysis* 52: 49–55.

———. 1984. "Watsonian Freedom and Freedom of the Will." *Australasian Journal of Philosophy* 62: 294–8.

Hill, Thomas. 1991. *Autonomy and Self-respect*. Cambridge: Cambridge University Press.

———. 1987. "The Importance of Autonomy." In E. Feder Kittay and D. Meyers, eds., *Women and Moral Theory*. Totowa, N.J.: Rowman and Littlefield.

Hobart, R. E. 1966. "Free Will as Involving Determinism and Inconceivable without It." In Berofsky, ed., 1966: 63–95.

Hobbes, Thomas. 1962. *The English Works of Thomas Hobbes*. Vol 5. Ed. by W. Molesworth. London: Scientia Aalen.

———. 1958. *Leviathan*. Indianapolis: Bobbs-Merrill.

Hobbs, Jesse. 1991. "Chaos and Indeterminism." *Canadian Journal of Philosophy* 21: 141–64.

Hocutt, Max. 1992. "A Review of Bruce Waller's *Freedom Without Responsibility*." *Behavior and Philosophy* 20: 71–6.

Hodgson, David. 1991. *The Mind Matters*. Oxford: Clarendon Press.

Honderich, Ted. 1993. *How Free Are You?* Oxford: Oxford University Press.

———. 1988. *A Theory of Determinism*. 2 Vols. Oxford: Clarendon Press.

———. ed. 1973. *Essays on Freedom of Action.* London: Routledge & Kegan Paul.

Hook, Sidney, ed. 1958. *Determinism and Freedom in the Age of Modern Science.* New York: Collier-Macmillan.

Horgan, Terence. 1985. "Compatibilism and the Consequence Argument." *Philosophical Studies* 47: 339–56.

Horgan, Terence, and George Graham. 1991. "In Defense of Southern Fundamentalism." *Philosophical Studies* 62: 107–34.

Horgan, Terence, and James Woodward. 1985. "Folk Psychology Is Here to Stay." *The Philosophical Review* 94: 197–226.

Hornsby, Jennifer. 1980. *Actions.* London: Routledge & Kegan Paul.

———. 1993. "Agency and Causal Explanation." In Heil and Mele, eds., 1993: 161–88.

Hospers, John. 1958. "What Means This Freedom?" In Hook, ed., 1958: 126–42.

Huberman, P., and G. Hogg. 1987. "Phase Transitions in Artificial Intelligence Systems." *Artificial Intelligence* 33: 155–72.

Huby, Pamela. 1967. "The First Discovery of the Free Will Issue." *Philosophy* 42: 333–62.

Hume, David. 1960. *A Treatise on Human Nature.* Ed. by L. A. Selby-Bigge. Oxford: Clarendon Press.

———. 1955. *An Inquiry Concerning Human Understanding.* Indianapolis: Bobbs-Merrill.

Hunt, G. M. K. 1981. "Determinism, Prediction, and Chaos." *Analysis* 49: 129–32.

Hurley, Paul. 1993. "How Weakness of Will Is Possible." *Mind* 102: 329–34.

Huxley, Aldous. 1989. *Brave New World.* San Francisco: HarperCollins.

Irwin, Terence. 1992. "Who Discovered the Will?" In J. Tomberlin, ed., *Philosophical Perspectives.* Vol. 6. Atascadero, Calif.: Ridgeview Publishing, 405–22.

———. 1980. "Reason and Responsibility in Aristotle." In A. Rorty, ed., 1980b: 72–91.

Jackson, Frank. 1985. "Internal Conflicts in Desires and Morals." *American Philosophical Quarterly* 22: 105–14.

———. 1984. "Weakness of Will." *Mind* 93: 1–18.

James, William. 1956. *The Will to Believe and Other Essays.* New York: Dover.

———. 1907. *The Principles of Psychology.* Vol. 1. New York: Henry Holt.

Jeffrey, Richard. 1974. "Preferences among Preferences." *Journal of Philosophy* 71: 377–91.

———. 1971. "Statistical Explanation and Statistical Relevance." In Salmon, Jeffrey, and Greeno, eds., 1971: 19–28.

Joyce, James. 1960. *Portrait of the Artist as a Young Man.* New York: Noonday Press.

Kane, Robert. 1995a. "Acts, Patterns, and Self-Control." *Behavioral and Brain Sciences* 18: 131–2.

———. 1995b. "Control, Responsibility, and Free Will: Response to Bernstein." *Southwest Philosophy Review* 11: 255–8.

———. 1995c. "Jamesian Reflections on Will, Freedom, and Value." In R. Burch, ed., *Frontiers in American Philosophy.* Vol. 2. College Station: Texas A & M University Press, 365–74.

———. 1994a. "Free Will: The Elusive Ideal." *Philosophical Studies* 75: 25–60.

———. 1994b. *Through the Moral Maze.* Armonk, N.Y.: M. E. Sharpe Publishers.

———. 1993. "The Ends of Metaphysics." *International Philosophical Quarterly* 33: 413–28.

———. 1991. Review of Anglin, 1991, Double, 1990, S. Wolf, 1990, and Zagzebski, 1991. *Times Literary Supplement* (September), 25.

———. 1990. Review of Klein, 1989. *Times Literary Supplement* (September), 23.

———. 1989. "Two Kinds of Incompatibilism." *Philosophy and Phenomenological Research* 50: 219–54. Reprinted in O'Connor, ed., 1995: 115–50.

———. 1988a. "Libertarianism and Rationality Revisited." *The Southern Journal of Philosophy* 26: 441–60.

——. 1988b. "Free Will and Responsibility: Comments on Waller's Review." *Behaviorism* 16: 159–65.

——. 1986. "Principles of Reason." *Erkenntnis* 24: 115–36.

——. 1985. *Free Will and Values*. Albany, N.Y.: State University of New York Press.

——. 1976. "Nature, Plenitude, and Sufficient Reason." *American Philosophical Quarterly* 13: 23–33.

——. Forthcoming. Review of Nathan, 1992. *Philosophia*.

Kant, Immanuel. 1960. *Religion within the Bounds of Reason Alone*. Trans. by T. Greene and H. Hudson. New York: Harper & Row.

——. 1959. *Foundations of the Metaphysics of Morals*. Trans. by L. W. Beck. Indianapolis: Bobbs-Merrill.

——. 1958. *Critique of Pure Reason*. Trans. by N. K. Smith. London: Macmillan.

——. 1956. *Critique of Practical Reason*. Trans. by L. W. Beck. Indianapolis: Bobbs-Merrill.

Kapitan, Tomis. 1994. "Critical Study of R. Double's *The Non-reality of Free Will*." *Noûs* 28: 90–5.

——. 1989. "Doxastic Freedom: A Compatibilist Alternative." *American Philosophical Quarterly* 26: 31–41.

——. 1986. "Responsibility and Free Choice." *Noûs* 20: 241–60.

Kellert, Stephen. 1993. *In the Wake of Chaos*. Chicago: University of Chicago Press.

Kenny, Anthony. 1978. *Free Will and Responsibility*. London: Routledge & Kegan Paul.

——. 1976. *Freedom, Will and Power*. Oxford: Basil Blackwell.

Kermode, Frank. 1967. *The Sense of an Ending*. New York: Oxford University Press.

Klein, Martha. 1990. *Determinism, Blameworthiness, and Deprivation*. Oxford: Oxford University Press.

Kierkegaard, Sören. 1959. *Either / Or*. 2 Vols. Garden City, N.Y.: Doubleday.

Kim, Jaegwon. 1984. "Epiphenomenal and Supervenient Causation." *Midwest Studies in Philosophy*. Vol. 9. Ed. by P. French, T. Vehling, and H. Wettstein. Minneapolis: University of Minnesota Press, 257–70.

Koons, Robert. 1992. *Paradoxes of Belief and Strategic Rationality*. Cambridge: Cambridge University Press.

Körner, Stephen. 1973. "Rational Choice." *Proceedings of the Aristotelian Society* 47: 1–17.

Lahav, Ran. 1991. "Between Pre-determination and Arbitrariness: A Bergsonian Approach to Free Will." *The Southern Journal of Philosophy*. 29: 487–500.

Lamb, James. 1993. "Evaluative Compatibilism and the Principle of Alternative Possibilities." *Journal of Philosophy* 90: 517–27.

——. 1977. "On a Proof of Incompatibilism." *Philosophical Review* 86: 20–35.

Landé, Alfred. 1958. "The Case for Indeterminism." In Hook, ed., 1958: 83–9.

Lehrer, Keith. 1980. "Preferences, Conditionals, and Freedom." In van Inwagen, ed., 1980: 76–96.

——. 1976. "'Can' in Theory and Practice: A Possible Worlds Analysis." In M. Brand and D. Walton, eds., *Action Theory*. Dordrecht: Reidel, 67–97.

——. 1968. "'Can's Without 'If's." *Analysis* 29: 29–32.

——. 1964. "'Could' and Determinism." *Analysis* 24: 159–60.

Leibniz, G. W. F. 1951. *Selections*. Ed. by P. Wiener. New York: Scribner's Sons.

Lennon, Kathleen. 1990. *Explaining Human Action*. Peru, Ill.: Open Court.

Levin, Michael. 1979. *Metaphysics and the Mind-Body Problem*. Oxford: Oxford University Press.

Lewis, David. 1986. *Philosophical Papers*. 2 Vols. Oxford: Oxford University Press.

——. 1981. "Are We Free to Break the Laws?" *Theoria* 47: 113–21. Reprinted in Lewis, 1986, Vol. 2: 291–8.

Libet, Benjamin. 1985. "Unconscious Cerebral Initiative and the Role of Conscious Will in Voluntary Action." *Behavioral and Brain Sciences* 8: 529–66.

Lindley, Richard. 1986. *Autonomy*. London: Macmillan.

Llinas, Rudolfo, and D. Pare. 1991. "Of Dreaming and Wakefulness." *Neuroscience* 44: 521–35.

Llinas, Rudolfo, and U. Ribary. 1993. "Coherent 40 Hz. Oscillation Characterizes Dream State in Humans." *Proceedings of the National Academy of Sciences* 90: 2078–81.

Locke, Don. 1974. "Reasons, Wants, and Causes." *American Philosophical Quarterly* 11: 169–79.

Lockwood, Michael. 1989. *Mind, Brain and Quantum*. Oxford: Oxford University Press.

Lovejoy, A. O. 1961. *Reflections on Human Nature*. Baltimore: Johns Hopkins University Press.

Lucas, J. R. 1993. *Responsibility*. Oxford: Oxford University Press.

Lycan, William. 1987. *Consciousness*. Cambridge, Mass.: MIT Press.

Lyotard, Jean-Francois. 1987. *The Postmodern Condition*. Minneapolis: University of Minnesota Press.

Machina, Kenton. 1994. "Challenges for Compatibilism." *American Philosophical Quarterly* 31: 213–22.

MacIntyre, Alasdair. 1981. *After Virtue*. Notre Dame, In.: Notre Dame University Press.

Magill, Kevin. *Experience and Freedom*. Unpublished manuscript.

Malcolm, Norman. 1968. "The Conceivability of Mechanism." *Philosophical Review* 77: 45–72. Reprinted in Watson, ed., 1982: 127–49.

Mansel, Henry. 1851. *Prolegomena Logica*. Oxford: William Graham.

Marshall, I. N. 1989. "Consciousness and Bose-Einstein Condensates." *New Ideas in Psychology* 7: 152–61.

Matson, Wallace. 1987. *A New History of Philosophy*. Vol. 1. New York: Harcourt, Brace, Jovanovich.

May, Larry. 1992. *Sharing Responsibility*. Chicago: University of Chicago Press.

McCall, Storrs. 1994. *A Model of the Universe*. Oxford: Clarendon Press.

McCann, Hugh. 1986. "Intrinsic Intentionality." *Theory and Decision* 20: 247–73.

———. 1974. "Volition and Basic Action." *Philosophical Review* 83: 451–73.

McCarthy, Kimberly A. Forthcoming. "Indeterminacy and Consciousness in the Creative Process." *Creativity Research Journal*.

McGinn, Colin. 1991. *The Problem of Consciousness*. Oxford: Basil Blackwell.

Mele, Alfred. 1995. *Autonomous Agents: From Self-Control to Autonomy*. New York: Oxford University Press.

———. 1992. *Springs of Action*. Oxford: Oxford University Press.

———. 1987. *Irrationality*. New York: Oxford University Press.

Mellema, Gregory. 1984. "On Being Fully Responsible." *American Philosophical Quarterly* 21: 189–93.

Melville, Herman. 1987. *Moby Dick*. New York: Modern Library.

Miles, Grahame B. 1988. Review of R. Kane, *Free Will and Values*. *Idealistic Studies* 32: 87–88.

Mill, J. S. 1962. "From an Examination of Sir William Hamilton's Philosophy." In Morgenbesser and Walsh, eds., 1962: 57–69.

———. 1947. *On Liberty*. Oxford: Basil Blackwell.

Milton, John. 1955. *Paradise Lost*. London: Methuen.

Mohanty, J. N. 1992. *Reason and Tradition in Indian Thought*. Oxford: Clarendon Press.

Morgenbesser, Sidney, and J. H. Walsh, eds. 1962. *Free Will*. Englewood Cliffs, N.J.: Prentice-Hall.

Mortimore, G. W., ed. 1971. *Weakness of Will*. London: Macmillan.

Moya, Carlos. 1991. *The Philosphy of Action*. Oxford: Basil Blackwell.

Murray, Michael. 1995. "Leibniz on Divine Foreknowledge, Future Contingents, and Human Freedom." *Philosophy and Phenomenological Research* 55: 75–108.

Nagel, Thomas. 1986. *The View from Nowhere*. New York: Oxford University Press.

Narveson, Jan. 1977. "Compatibilism Defended." *Philosophical Studies* 32: 83–8.

Nathan, Nicholas. 1992. *Will and World*. Oxford: Oxford University Press.

Naylor, Margery Bedford. 1984. "Frankfurt on the Principle of Alternative Possibilities." *Philosophical Studies* 46: 249–58.

Neely, Wright. 1974. "Freedom and Desire." *Philosophical Review* 83:32–54.

Nozick, Robert. 1981. *Philosophical Explanations*. Cambridge, Mass.: Harvard University Press.

——. 1974. *Anarchy, State, and Utopia*. New York: Basic Books.

O'Connor, Timothy, ed. 1995. *Agents, Causes and Events: Essays on Indeterminism and Free Will*. Oxford: Oxford University Press.

——. 1993a. "Indeterminism and Free Agency: Three Recent Views." *Philosophy and Phenomenological Research* 53: 499–526.

——. 1993b. "On the Transfer of Necessity." *Noûs* 27: 204–18.

——. 1992. "Some Puzzles about Free Agency." Ph.D. diss., Cornell University.

Oldenquist, Andrew. 1967. "Choosing, Deciding, and Doing." In P. Edwards, ed., *Encyclopedia of Philosophy*. vol 2. New York: Macmillan, 96–101.

O'Shaughnessy, Brian. 1980. *The Will*. 2 Vols. Cambridge: Cambridge University Press.

Paull, R. Cranston. 1992. "Leibniz and the Miracle of Freedom." *Noûs* 26: 218–35.

Peacocke, Christopher. 1979. *Holistic Explanation*. Oxford: Clarendon Press.

Pears, David. 1985. *Motivated Irrationality*. Oxford: Oxford University Press.

Penrose, Roger. 1994. *Shadows of the Mind*. Oxford: Oxford University Press.

——. 1989. *The Emperor's New Mind*. Oxford: Oxford University Press.

Pereboom, Derk. 1995. "Determinism Al Dente." *Noûs* 29: 21–45.

Peters, R. S. 1958. *The Concept of Motivation*. London: Routledge & Kegan Paul.

Pike, Nelson. 1965. "Divine Omnisicence and Voluntary Action." *Philosophical Review* 74: 27–46.

Pink, T. L. 1991. "Purposive Intending." *Mind* 103: 343–60.

Plantinga, Alvin. 1974. *The Nature of Necessity*. Oxford: Oxford University Press.

Plato. 1937. *The Dialogues of Plato*. Trans. by B. Jowett. Vols 1 and 2. New York: Random House.

Plotinus. 1950. *The Philosophy of Plotinus*. New York: Appleton, Century, Crofts.

Popper, Karl. 1972. "Of Clouds and Clocks." In Karl Popper, *Objective Knowledge*. Oxford: Oxford University Press, 206–55.

——. 1965. *Conjectures and Refutations*. New York: Harper Torchbooks.

Popper, Karl, and John Eccles. 1977. *The Self and Its Brain*. New York: Springer-Verlag.

Posth, Matthew. 1990. "Freedom and Realism." Ph.D. diss., Northwestern University.

Prabhavananda, S., and C. Isherwood, trans., 1956. *The Song of God: Bhagavad-Gita*. New York: Mentor Books.

Rachlin, Howard. 1995. "Self-Control: Beyond Commitment." *Behavioral and Brain Sciences* 18: 109–21.

Railton, Peter. 1978. "A Deductive-Nomological Model of Probabilistic Explanation." *Philosophy of Science* 45: 206–26.

Rauf, M. A. 1970. "The Qur'an and Free Will." *The Muslim World* 60: 289–99.

Ravizza, Mark. 1994. "Semi-Compatibilism and the Transfer of Non-Responsibility." *Philosophical Studies* 75: 61–94.

Raz, J. 1986. *The Morality of Freedom*. Oxford: Clarendon Press.
Reid, Thomas. 1983. *The Works of Thomas Reid*. Ed. by W. Hamilton. Hildeshein: George Ulm.
———. 1970. "Some Arguments for Free Will." In Dworkin, ed., 1970b: 85–97.
———. 1969. *Essay on the Active Powers of the Human Mind*. Cambridge, Mass.: MIT Press.
Robinson, Kirk. 1991. "Reason, Desire, and Weakness of Will." *American Philosophical Quarterly* 28: 287–98.
Rockwell, W. Teed. 1994. "Beyond Determinism and Indignity: A Reinterpretation of Operant Conditioning." *Behavior and Philosophy* 22: 53–66.
Rorty, Amelie O. 1980a. "Self-deception, Akrasia, and Irrationality." *Social Science Information* 19: 905–22.
———. ed., 1980b. *Essays on Aristotle's Ethics*. Berkeley, Calif.: University of California Press.
Rorty, Richard. 1979. *Philosophy and the Mirror of Nature*. Princeton: Princeton University Press.
Ross, W. D. 1939. *Foundations of Ethics*. Oxford: Clarendon Press.
Rowe, William. 1991. *Thomas Reid on Freedom and Morality*. Ithaca, N.Y.: Cornell University Press.
———. 1987. "Two Concepts of Freedom." *Proceedings of the American Philosophical Association* 62: 43–64.
Ruben, David-Hillel, ed. 1993. *Explanation*. Oxford: Oxford University Press.
Rumi, Jalalu'l-din. 1956. *Rumi, Poet and Mystic*. Trans. and ed. by R. A. Nicholson. London: Allen & Unwin.
Russell, Paul. 1988. "Causation, Compulsion, and Compatibilism." *American Philosophical Quarterly* 25: 313–21.
Ryle, Gilbert. 1949. *The Concept of Mind*. New York: Barnes & Noble.
Salmon, Wesley. 1984. *Scientific Explanation and the Causal Structure of the World*. Princeton: Princeton University Press.
Salmon, Wesley, R. Jeffrey, and T. Greeno, eds. 1971. *Statistical Explanation and Statistical Relevance*. Pittsburgh: University of Pittsburgh Press.
Sanford, David. 1991. "'Could's, 'Might's, 'If's and 'Can's." *Noûs* 25: 208–11.
Sankowski, Edward. 1977. "Some Problems about Determinism and Freedom." *American Philosophical Quarterly* 17: 291–9.
Sartre, Jean-Paul. 1962. "From *Being and Nothingness*." In Morgenbesser and Walsh, eds., 1962: 95–113.
Saunders, John Turk. 1968. "The Temptations of Powerlessness." *American Philosophical Quarterly* 5: 100–8.
Schlick, Moritz. 1966. "When Is a Man Responsible?" In Berofsky, ed., 1966: 54–62.
Schlossberger, Eugene. 1986. *Moral Responsibility and Persons*. Philadelphia: Temple University Press.
Schoeman, Ferdinand, ed. 1987. *Responsibility, Character, and the Emotions*. Cambridge: Cambridge University Press.
Schopenhauer, Arthur. 1960. *Essay on the Freedom of the Will*. Trans. by K. Kolenda. Indianapolis: Bobbs-Merrill.
———. 1889. "The Fourfold Root of the Principle of Sufficient Reason." In *Two Essays by A. Schopenhauer*. Trans. by K. Hillebrand. London: George Bell and Sons.
Schrödinger, Erwin. 1967. *What Is Life?* Cambridge: Cambridge University Press.
Scott, George P. 1991a. "Dissipative Structures and the Mind-Body Problem." In Scott, ed., 1991b: 259–72.
———. ed., 1991b. *Time, Rhythms, and Chaos in the New Dialogue With Nature*. Ames, Ia.: Iowa State University Press.

Scott, George P., and Michael McMillen, eds. 1980. *Dissipative Structures and Spatiotemporal Organization Studies in Biomedical Research*. Ames, Ia.: Iowa State University Press.

Searle, John. 1992. *The Rediscovery of the Mind*. Cambridge, Mass.: MIT Press.

———. 1983. *Intentionality*. Cambridge: Cambridge University Press.

Sellars, Wilfrid. 1980. "Volitions Reaffirmed." In M. Brand and D. Walton, eds., *Action Theory*. Dordrecht: Reidel, 72–96.

Senchuk, Dennis M. 1991. "Consciousness Naturalized: Supervenience without Physical Determinism." *American Philosophical Quarterly* 28: 37–47.

Sher, George. 1979. *Desert*. Princeton: Princeton University Press.

Shapiro, Susan. 1993. "Herodotus on Fate and Prophecy." Ph.D. diss. The University of Texas at Austin.

Shatz, David. 1988. "Compatibilism, Values, and 'Could Have Done Otherwise.'" *Philosophical Topics* 16: 151–200.

———. 1985. "Free Will and the Structure of Motivation." *Midwest Studies in Philosophy*. Vol. 10. Ed. by P. French, T. Vehling, and H. Wettstein. Minneapolis: University of Minnesota Press, 451–82.

Shiffer, Stephen. 1976. "A Paradox of Desire." *American Philosophical Quarterly* 13: 195–203.

Showalter, K., R. Noyes, and H. Turner. 1979. "Detailed Studies of Trigger Wave Initiation and Detection." *Journal of the American Chemical Society* 101: 746–9.

Siderits, Mark. 1987. "Beyond Compatibilism: A Buddhist Approach to Freedom and Determinism." *American Philosophical Quarterly* 24: 149–59.

Sidgwick, Henry. 1907. *The Methods of Ethics*. London: Macmillan.

Simonton, Dean K. 1988. *Scientific Genius*. Cambridge: Cambridge University Press.

Skarda, C., and W. Freeman. 1987. "How Brains Make Chaos in Order to Make Sense of the World." *Behavioral and Brain Sciences* 10: 161–95.

Skinner, B. F. 1971. *Beyond Freedom and Dignity*. New York: Vintage Books.

———. 1962. *Walden Two*. New York: Macmillan.

Sleigh, Robert. 1994. "Leibniz on Divine Foreknowledge." *Faith and Philosophy* 11: 547–71.

———. 1990. *Leibniz and Arnauld: A Commentary on Their Correspondence*. New Haven, Conn.: Yale University Press.

Slote, Michael. 1982. "Selective Necessity and the Free Will Problem." *Journal of Philosophy* 79: 5–24.

———. 1980. "Understanding Free Will." *Journal of Philosophy* 77: 136–51.

Smart, Ninian. 1967. "Karma." In P. Edwards, ed., *Encyclopedia of Philosophy*, Vol. 4. New York: Macmillan. 325–6.

Smilansky, Saul. 1994. "The Ethical Advantages of Hard Determinism." *Philosophy and Phenomenological Research* 54: 355–63.

———. 1993. "Does the Free Will Debate Rest on a Mistake?" *Philosophical Papers* 22: 173–88.

———. 1990a. "Van Inwagen on the 'Obviousness' of Libertarian Moral Responsibility." *Analysis* 50: 29–33.

———. 1990b. "Is Libertarian Free Will Worth Wanting?" *Philosophical Investigations* 13: 273–6.

Sober, Elliott. 1987. "Explanation and Causation" (review of Salmon, 1984). *British Journal for the Philosophy of Science* 38: 243–57.

Sophocles. 1962. *Antigone*. Trans. by Michael Townsend. New York: Harper & Row.

Sorabji, Richard. 1980. *Necessity, Cause, and Blame: Perspectives on Aristotle's Philosophy*. Ithaca, N.Y.: Cornell University Press.

Sperry, R. W. 1980. "Mind-Brain Interaction: Mentalism, Yes, Dualism, No." *Neuroscience* 5:195–206.

Stampe, Dennis, and Martha Gibson. 1992. "Of One's Own Free Will." *Philosophy and Phenomenological Research* 52: 529–56.

Stapp, Henry P. 1993. *Mind, Matter, and Quantum Mechanics*. New York: Springer Verlag.

———. 1990. "A Quantum Theory of the Mind-Body Interface." Unpublished presentation, Conference on Consciousness within Science, University of California at San Francisco.

Stone, Mark A. 1989. "Chaos, Prediction, and LaPlacean Determinism." *American Philosophical Quarterly* 26: 123–31.

Strawson, Galen. 1994. "The Impossibility of Moral Responsibility." *Philosophical Studies* 75: 5–24.

———. 1989. "Consciousness, Free Will, and the Unimportance of Determinism." *Inquiry* 32: 3–27.

———. 1986. *Freedom and Belief*. Oxford: Oxford University Press.

Strawson, Peter. 1962. "Freedom and Resentment." *Proceedings of the British Academy* 48: 1–25.

Suppes, Patrick. 1984. *Probabilistic Metaphysics*. Oxford: Basil Blackwell.

———. 1970. *A Probabilistic Theory of Causality*. Amsterdam: North Holland.

Suzuki, D. T. 1956. *Zen Buddhism*. New York: Doubleday.

Swanton, Christine. 1992. *Freedom: A Coherence Theory*. Indianapolis: Hackett.

Swinburne, Richard. 1989. *Responsibility and Atonement*. Oxford: Clarendon.

———. 1986. *The Evolution of the Soul*. Oxford: Clarendon Press.

Talbott, Thomas. 1986. Review of R. Kane, *Free Will and Values*. *International Philosophical Quarterly* 20: 300–2.

———. 1979. "Indeterminism and Chance Occurrences." *The Personalist* 61: 253–61.

Taurek, John. 1972. "Determinism and Moral Responsibility." Ph.D. diss., University of California Los Angeles.

Taylor, Charles. 1982. "Responsibility for Self." In Watson, ed., 1982: 111–26.

Taylor, Richard. 1982. "Agent and Patient." *Erkenntnis* 18: 223–32.

———. 1974. *Metaphysics*. Englewood Cliffs, N. J.: Prentice-Hall.

Teller, Paul. 1979. "Quantum Mechanics and the Nature of Continuous Physical Magnitudes." *Journal of Philosophy* 76: 435–61.

Thalberg, Irving. 1989. "Hierarchical Analyses of Unfree Action." In J. Christman, ed., 1989: 123–36.

Thomson, Judith. 1977. *Acts and Other Events*. Ithaca, N.Y.: Cornell University Press.

Thornton, Mark. 1990. *Do We Have Free Will?* New York: St. Martin's Press.

Thorp, John. 1980. *Free Will: A Defense against Neurophysiological Determinism*. London: Routledge & Kegan Paul.

Tobias, Michael. 1991. *Life Force: The World of Jainism*. Berkeley, Calif.: Asian Humanities Press.

Tracy, Thomas. 1990. Review of R. Kane, *Free Will and Values*. *Journal of the American Academy of Religion* 22: 389–91.

Trusted, Jennifer. 1984. *Free Will and Responsibility*. Oxford: Oxford University Press.

Tuomela, Raimo. 1977. *Human Action and Its Explanation*. Dordrecht: Reidel.

Ullmann-Margolit, Edna, and Sidney Morgenbesser. 1977. "Picking and Choosing." *Social Research* 77: 757–85.

van Gulick, R. 1990. "What Difference Does Consciousness Make?" *Philosophical Topics* 17: 211–30.

van Inwagen, Peter. 1994. "When Is the Will Not Free?" *Philosophical Studies* 75: 95–114.
——.1990. "Response to Slote." *Social Theory and Practice* 16: 385–95.
——.1989. "When Is the Will Free?" *Philosophical Perspectives*. Vol. 3. Ed. by J. Tomberlin. Atascadero, Calif.: Ridgeview Publishing, 399–422.
——.1983. *An Essay on Free Will*. Oxford: Oxford University Press.
——. ed. 1980. *Time and Cause*. Dordrecht: Reidel.
——. 1975. "The Incompatibility of Free Will and Determinism." *Philosophical Studies* 27:185–99. Reprinted in and page references to Watson, ed., 1982: 46–58.
Velleman, J. David. 1992. "What Happens when Someone Acts?" *Mind* 101: 461–81.
——. 1989. *Practical Reflection*. Princeton, N. J.: Princeton University Press.
Viney, Donald Wayne. 1986. "William James on Free Will and Determinism." *Journal of Mind and Behavior* 7: 555–66.
Vitiello, G., and E. del Giudice. 1984. "Boson Condensation in Biological Systems." In W. Aden and A. Laurence, eds., *Nonlinear Electrodynamics of Biological Systems*. New York: Plenum Books, 142–59.
Vivhelin, Kadri. 1991. "Freedom, Causation and Counterfactuals." *Philosophical Studies* 64: 161–84.
——. 1988. "The Modal Argument for Incompatibililism." *Philosophical Studies* 53: 227–44.
Walker, Arthur F. 1989. "The Problem of Weakness of Will." *Noûs* 23: 653–76.
Wallace, R. Jay. 1994. *Responsibility and the Moral Sentiments*. Cambridge, Mass.: Harvard University Press.
Waller, Bruce. 1992. "A Response to Kane and Hocutt." *Behavior and Philosophy* 20: 83–8.
——. 1990. *Freedom without Responsibility*. Philadelphia: Temple University Press.
——. 1988. "Free Will Gone Out of Control: A Critical Study of R. Kane's *Free Will and Values*." *Behaviorism* 16: 149–67.
Warner, Richard. 1987. *Freedom, Enjoyment and Happiness*. Ithaca, N.Y.: Cornell University Press.
Watson, Gary. 1987. "Free Action and Free Will." *Mind* 96: 145–72.
——. ed., 1982. *Free Will*. Oxford: Oxford University Press.
——. 1977. "Skepticism about Weakness of Will." *Philosophical Review* 86: 316–39.
——. 1975. "Free Agency." *Journal of Philosophy* 72: 205–20. Reprinted in and cited from Watson, ed., 1982: 96–110.
Weatherford, Roy. 1991. *The Implications of Determinism*. London: Routledge.
Widerker, David. 1995a. "Libertarianism and Frankfurt's Attack on the Principle of Alternative Possibilities." The *Philosophical Review* 104: 247–61.
——. 1995b. "Libertarian Freedom and the Avoidabiliity of Decisions." *Faith and Philosophy* 12: 113–18.
——. 1991. "Frankfurt on 'Ought' Implies 'Can' and Alternative Possibilities." *Analysis* 49: 222–4.
——. 1987. "On an Argument for Incompatibilism." *Analysis* 47: 37–41.
Wiggins, David. 1973. "Towards a Reasonable Libertarianism." In T. Honderich, ed., 1973: 31–61.
Wilbur, J. A. 1979. *The Worlds of the Early Greek Philosophers*. Buffalo, N. Y.: Prometheus Books.
Williams, Bernard. 1986. *How Free Does the Will Have to Be?* Lindley Lecture (1985). Lawrence, Kan.: University of Kansas Press.
Williams, Clifford. 1986. Review of R. Kane, *Free Will and Values*. *Canadian Philosophical Reviews* 6: 450–2.
——. 1980. *Free Will and Determinism*. Indianapolis: Hackett.

Wilson, George. 1989. *The Intentionality of Human Action*. Stanford, Calif.: Stanford University Press.

Wittgenstein, Ludwig. 1980. *Culture and Values*. Trans. by P. Winch. Oxford: Basil Blackwell.

White, Michael. 1985. *Agency and Integrality*. Dordrecht: Reidel.

White, Morton. 1993. *The Question of Free Will: A Holistic View*. Princeton: Princeton University Press.

Wolf, F. A. 1986. *The Body Quantum*. New York: Macmillan.

———. 1984. *Starwave*. New York: Macmillan.

Wolf, Susan. 1990. *Freedom within Reason*. Oxford: Oxford University Press.

Wood, Allen. 1984. "Kant's Compatibilism." In Allen Wood, ed., *Self and Nature in Kant's Philosophy*. Ithaca, N.Y.: Cornell University Press.

Young, Robert. 1986. *Personal Autonomy*. New York: St. Martin's Press.

———. 1982. "The Value of Autonomy." *Philosophical Quarterly* 32: 35–44.

———. 1979. "Compatibilism and Conditioning." *Noûs* 13: 361–78.

Zagzebski, Linda T. 1991. *The Dilemma of Freedom and Foreknowledge*. Oxford: Oxford University Press.

Zimmerman, David. 1994. "Acts, Omissions, and Semi-Compatibilism." *Philosophical Studies* 73: 209–23.

———. 1981. "Hierarchical Motivation and the Freedom of the Will." *Pacific Philosophical Quarterly* 62: 354–68.

Zimmerman, Michael. 1992. Review of John Bishop's *Natural Agency*. *The Philosophical Review* 101: 687–90.

———. 1989. *An Essay on Moral Responsibility*. Totowa, N.J.: Rowman and Littlefield.

———. 1984. *An Essay on Human Action*. New York: Peter Lang.

Zohar, D. 1990. *The Quantum Self*. New York: William Morrow.

Zohar, D., and I. Marshall. 1994. *The Quantum Society*. London: Bloomsbury.

Index